THE IMPOSSIBLE OFFICE?

Marking the third centenary of the office of prime minister, this book tells its extraordinary story, explaining how and why it has endured longer than any other democratic political office. Sir Anthony Seldon, historian of Number 10 Downing Street, explores the lives and careers, loves and scandals, successes and failures, of all our great prime ministers. From Robert Walpole and William Pitt the Younger, to Clement Attlee and Margaret Thatcher, Seldon discusses which of our prime ministers have been most effective and why. He reveals the changing relationship between the monarchy and the office of the prime minister in intimate detail, describing how the increasing power of the prime minister in becoming leader of Britain coincided with the steadily falling influence of the monarchy. This book celebrates the humanity and frailty, work and achievement, of these fifty-five remarkable individuals, who averted revolution and civil war, leading the country through times of peace, crisis, and war.

Sir Anthony Seldon is the acknowledged national authority on all matters to do with Number 10 and prime ministers. His first book on a prime minister, *Churchill's Indian Summer* (1981), was published forty years ago, and since then he has written or edited many books, including the definitive insider accounts of the last five prime ministers. He is the honorary historian at Number 10 Downing Street, chair of the National Archives Trust, and has interviewed virtually all senior figures who have worked in Number 10 in the last fifty years.

Jonathan Meakin was educated at Royal Holloway, University of London and at the University of St Andrews. He has had a lifelong interest in history. He has worked on many publications with Anthony Seldon, including *Cameron at 10* and *The Cabinet Office, 1916–2016*.

Illias Thoms has worked with Anthony Seldon for over ten years and this is their fourth book together, including *Cameron at 10* and *Brown at 10*. He graduated from Balliol College, Oxford with a degree in history and politics in 2014 and works as an assistant director in the UK film and television industries.

WORKS BY ANTHONY SELDON

Churchill's Indian Summer: The 1951–1955 Conservative Government (Hodder & Stoughton, 1981)

By Word of Mouth: Elite Oral History (with Joanna Pappworth) (Methuen, 1983)

Ruling Performance: Governments Since 1945 (ed. with Peter Hennessy) (Blackwell, 1987)

Political Parties Since 1945 (ed.) (Philip Allan, 1988)

The Thatcher Effect (ed. with Dennis Kavanagh) (Clarendon Press, 1989)

Politics UK (joint author), (Philip Allan, 1991)

Conservative Century: The Conservative Party Since 1900 (ed. with Stuart Ball), (Oxford University Press, 1994)

The Major Effect (ed. with Dennis Kavanagh) (Macmillan, 1994)

The Heath Government 1970–1974: A Reappraisal (ed. with Stuart Ball) (Longman, 1996)

The Contemporary History Handbook (ed. with Brian Brivati etc.) (Manchester University Press, 1996)

The Ideas that Shaped Post-War Britain (ed. with David Marquand) (Fontana, 1996)

How Tory Governments Fall (ed.), (Fontana, 1997)

Major: A Political Life (Weidenfeld & Nicolson, 1997)

10 Downing Street: The Illustrated History (HarperCollins, 1999)

The Powers Behind the Prime Minister: The Hidden Influence of Number Ten (with Dennis Kavanagh), (HarperCollins, 1999)

Britain Under Thatcher (with Daniel Collings) (Routledge, 2000)

The Foreign Office: The Illustrated History (HarperCollins, 2000)

A New Conservative Century (with Peter Snowdon) (Centre for Policy Studies, 2001)

The Blair Effect 1997–2001 (ed.), (Little, Brown, 2001)

Public and Private Education: The Divide Must End (Social Market Foundation, 2001)

Partnership Not Paternalism (Institute for Public Policy Research, 2002)

Brave New City: Brighton & Hove, Past, Present, Future (Pomegranate Press, 2002)

The Conservative Party: An Illustrated History (with Peter Snowdon) (Sutton Press, 2004)

New Labour, Old Labour: The Wilson and Callaghan Governments, 1974–1979 (ed. with Kevin Hickson) (Routledge, 2004)

Blair (Free Press, 2004)

The Blair Effect 2001–2005 (ed. with Dennis Kavanagh) (Cambridge University Press, 2005)

Recovering Power: The Conservatives in Opposition since 1867 (ed. with Stuart Ball) (Palgrave Macmillan, 2005)

Blair Unbound (with Peter Snowdon and Daniel Collings) (Simon & Schuster, 2007)

Blair's Britain 1997–2007 (ed.) (Cambridge University Press, 2007)

Trust: How We Lost It and How to Get It Back (Biteback, 2009)

An End to Factory Schools (Centre for Policy Studies, 2009)

Why Schools, Why Universities? (Cass, 2010)

Brown at 10 (with Guy Lodge) (Biteback, 2010)

Public Schools and the Great War (with David Walsh) (Pen & Sword, 2013)

Schools United (Social Market Foundation, 2014)

The Architecture of Diplomacy: The British Ambassador's Residence in Washington (with Daniel Collings) (Flammarion, 2014)

Beyond Happiness: The Trap of Happiness and How to Find Deeper Meaning and Joy (Hodder, 2015)

The Coalition Effect, 2010–2015 (ed. with Mike Finn), (Cambridge University Press, 2015)

Cameron at 10 (with Peter Snowdon) (William Collins, 2015); Cameron at 10: The Verdict (William Collins, 2016)

Teaching and Learning at British Universities (Social Market Foundation, 2016)

The Cabinet Office 1916–2016: The Birth of Modern British Government (with Jonathan Meakin) (Biteback, 2016)

The Positive and Mindful University (with Alan Martin) (Higher Education Policy Institute, 2017)

The Fourth Education Revolution: Will Artificial Intelligence Liberate or Infantilise Humanity (with Oladimeji Abidoye) (Buckingham University Press, 2018)

May at Ten (with Raymond Newell) (Biteback, 2019); *May at 10: The Verdict* (Biteback, 2020)

Public Schools and the Second World War (with David Walsh) (Pen & Sword, 2020)

Fourth Education Revolution Reconsidered: Will Artificial Intelligence Enrich or Diminish Humanity? (with Oladimeji Abidoye and Timothy Metcalf) (Buckingham University Press, 2020)

THE IMPOSSIBLE OFFICE?

The History of the British Prime Minister

Anthony Seldon

with

Jonathan Meakin and Illias Thoms

 CAMBRIDGE
UNIVERSITY PRESS

CAMBRIDGE
UNIVERSITY PRESS

University Printing House, Cambridge CB2 8BS, United Kingdom

One Liberty Plaza, 20th Floor, New York, NY 10006, USA

477 Williamstown Road, Port Melbourne, VIC 3207, Australia

314–321, 3rd Floor, Plot 3, Splendor Forum, Jasola District Centre,
New Delhi – 110025, India

79 Anson Road, #06–04/06, Singapore 079906

Cambridge University Press is part of the University of Cambridge.

It furthers the University's mission by disseminating knowledge in the pursuit of
education, learning, and research at the highest international levels of excellence.

www.cambridge.org
Information on this title: www.cambridge.org/9781316515327
DOI: 10.1017/9781009019903

First published 2021

Printed in the United Kingdom by TJ Books Ltd, Padstow, Cornwall

A catalogue record for this publication is available from the British Library.

ISBN 978-1-316-51532-7 Hardback

To Peter Hennessy, my lifelong friend, colleague, and mentor, who has done as much to illuminate the office of prime minister as any figure in history.

Contents

Preface

This book may have been written during the COVID-19 lockdown in 2020, but it has been forty years in gestation since I wrote my first book on a prime minister, *Churchill's Indian Summer*, in 1981. Five years before that, I had asked my tutor 'Copper' LeMay what I could give him as a leaving gift from university, and he replied, '*The Office of Prime Minister* by Robert Blake' which had just been published. I was captivated, and have remained so for the rest of my life. At Oxford, I studied under David Butler and Vernon Bogdanor too, who became lifelong friends, inspirations and fellow travellers on this journey. In 1986, with Peter Hennessy, to whom this book is dedicated, I founded the Institute of Contemporary British History, in part to deepen the study of the prime minister. In the years since, I have edited many books on the effect that prime ministers have had, have written three on Number 10 and its staff, and six on different prime ministers, from John Major to Theresa May. These were each based on interviews with some 500 insiders, amounting to many millions of words of written record. The most valuable sources were always the civil servants who worked close to the prime minister: meticulous, objective, and retentive. These were the figures I asked to read over the books in draft, often many times to ensure accuracy and fairness, guided by Peter Hennessy's and my belief that the writing and study of contemporary history matters, and that it can be executed with its own kind of historical precision.

Certain questions have obsessed me all my life. Is the office of prime minister still the same over the years? Why did it emerge in 1721? How has it survived? Can and how should the office be strengthened? Why are only some PMs successful? Have political scientists been asking the wrong questions, e.g. has the office *become* presidential, and why don't they and historians of prime ministers talk more? Why do people want to be PM, and did the experience fulfil them?

Many of the most important events in Britain over the last 300 years that have shaped the lives of its people have of course occurred independently of the particular prime minister of the day: the economic upturns and downturns, the human and animal epidemics, the great technological advances, and social changes. Indeed, the figures who have influenced Britain more over the last 300 years have often been the scientists like Charles Darwin and Alan Turing, the social reformers like William Wilberforce and Emmeline Pankhurst, and economists Adam Smith and J. M. Keynes.

Occasional repetition is inevitable for the argument to make sense to those who alight just on individual chapters. I have tried to keep repetition to a bare minimum.

Chapter 1, which opens with an imagined dinner conversation in April 2021 between the first and the fifty-fifth prime ministers to celebrate the 300th anniversary of the office, asks how far it is indeed the same office, and explores the similarities between the jobs of Robert Walpole and Boris Johnson. While their tasks are more similar than many have thought, Chapter 2 looks at the vastly differently worlds they inhabit, and the fifty-three prime ministers in between them, due to economic, social, technological, and political changes. Walpole rarely left London, and when he did, he travelled no further than Norfolk: Johnson can travel to Berlin and back in a day. How has the arrival of rail, the car, and the airplane affected the prime minister, and equally the telegraph, the telephone, and the internet? Chapter 3, 'The Liminal Premiership', looks at the origins of the premiership, whether the chief ministers since medieval times, like Thomas Cromwell, foreshadowed the position, and how and why the post of prime minister emerged when it did in 1721. Following Walpole's departure in 1742, it examines how the office, which could have disappeared, survived until William Pitt the Younger in 1783, the figure who consolidated the position. After him, there was no going back.

Chapter 4 looks at prime ministers since Pitt the Younger's death in 1806, focusing on the six figures in the 215 years after him who have changed the agenda of British politics and left a long shadow under which their successors operated, trying to be either like them, or unlike them, but incapable of escaping their shadow. Chapter 5 discusses the power and the resources prime ministers have in their possession, not least the role of the spouse, an under-recognised support for the prime minister. Despite Britain having female monarchs for 45 per cent of the last 300 years, there have only been two female prime ministers, in office for less than 5 per cent of that time. The history of the premiership, and indeed those who have written about it, is almost exclusively male, as well as white, and socially exclusive, as the book explores. Chapter 6 looks at the constraints on the prime minister. These provide the key to why some prime ministers are successful: they maximise their advantages, and negotiate their way around these constraints, which have grown in number and complexity.

The next three chapters look at the prime minister in relation to three positions that have most affected the evolution of the office: Chapter 7 examines how, when and why the prime minister took over many of the roles and powers of the monarch; Chapter 8, the rise and fall of the Foreign Secretary, rendering the prime minister today, not the Foreign Secretary nor the monarch, the principal figure who represents the country abroad and decides its foreign policy; and Chapter 9 looks at the rise, and rise, of the Chancellor of the Exchequer since the job was separated from the prime minister's by Robert Peel in 1841, and how the Chancellor has emerged as the prime minister's greatest challenge. Finally, Chapter 10 looks at the position of the prime minister today. Why have more incumbents not achieved even their own ambitions, especially given the many advantages that prime ministers have in Britain over their opposite numbers abroad? These include leading a unitary rather than a federal country, not being constrained by a written constitution, having a head of state who is hereditary rather than elected, and an electoral system that usually guarantees a clear majority in Parliament rather than a coalition. It describes the ingredients that account for successful premierships, and explains, in contrast to say German Chancellors since 1945, why so many prime ministers have run into trouble. Finally, it recommends five changes to the office which will allow it to perform more successfully as it enters its fourth century.

Anthony Seldon

CHAPTER 1

The Bookend Prime Ministers

Walpole and Johnson

TÊTE-À-TÊTE OVER DINNER

Two well-nourished men, lit by a blaze of candles, are hunched over a celebration dinner in Downing Street for the 300th anniversary of the prime minister. They are engrossed in the conversation.

'I always liked this room. It was my favourite.'

'Not bad for a town pad above the shop.'

'I never thought the job would last long, but you tell me that it has lasted 300 years? It surprises me.' He surveys his host warily.

'Indeed it has. They say I'm the 55th prime minister. Ha! Imagine that: me as prime minister!'

'And what did you do to make yourself "prime minister"?'

'A good question. Many people ask. I was Mayor of London for eight years, and then Foreign Secretary. Before, I wrote newspaper articles.'

'The Mayor and journalism I know. But what's a Foreign Secretary?'

'He runs British foreign policy. Well, doesn't actually run it. At least not now. I do all the interesting stuff.'

'So when was it created?'

'. . . A long time ago. Didn't you have a Foreign Secretary?'

'Certainly not. Increasingly I did it. You've kept the Americans under your thumb I trust?'

'Not exactly.'

'Don't tell me you've let the buggers go.'

'Bloody North,' Johnson mutters under his breath. 'Tell me, what did *you* do to become PM?,' rapidly changing the subject.

'I saved the establishment of Great Britain when their greed threatened to overturn it all, returning order and good governance – of a kind. It helped that almost all those at Court who disfavoured me managed to disgrace themselves.'

'Ah yes, the South Sea Bubble, I learned about that at school - at Eton.'

'You went to Eton? So did I.'

'Yes. A King's Scholar, actually,' the host boasts, swallowing the last of his Beef Wellington with a satisfied burp.

'So was I. Destined for the Church, I was. At Eton I studied in Lower School, then Upper School, rebuilt shortly before I arrived.'

'*Mehercle!*[1] I was taught there too.'

'I boarded in Long Chamber.'

'So did I!'

'I ate in College Hall.'

'As did I!'

'I prayed in College Chapel and exercised in School Yard.'[2]

'*Ehem!*[3] Two British prime ministers, 300 years apart, nurtured in the same buildings and spaces.'

The common ground of their alma mater established, both men start to relax.

'So what keeps you awake at night?' the older man asks, adjusting his wig.

'The economy. I need money to "level up" the north.'

'Level up? I never went to the north. Barbarians. Have you tried taxing cider or putting up duties on imports from the American colonies? Sorry yes you said: you lost them. Bloody North indeed. What else troubles you?'

'Scotland. Nightmare. Damned nationalists want to break up the Union. Disaster.'

'We'd just unified Parliaments when I became the First Minister. The Jacobite rogues rose up in 1715 and tried to take over the country.'

'That's what the bloody EU have been trying to do for years!'

'The E U?'

'Yes, Europe. But I've fixed that now. We are free of them at last. Sovereignty reclaimed! Freedom to do what I will!'

'You think so? I tried to keep them on the other side of the Channel too. Though I had a German as my monarch who tried to be at the heart of everything. What else vexes you?'

'The epidemic ravaging our country. *Crapulentus sum!*[4]

'London was still suffering from the plague in my years. Then the Great Plague of Marseilles spread to England in my first year.'

'I nearly died of the illness: touch and go it was. I thought my number was up.'

'I nearly died in my first year too! The crows hovered! The dastardly Carteret – *bastard!* – was priming himself to take over. Damned business; Destouches, the French ambassador, gossiped everywhere about it.'[5]

'Never trust the French,' the host replies, rustling his unkempt blond hair knowingly.

There's a knock at the door. 'Are you coming up soon? It's very late,' says a young woman.

'In time, in time.' The door is closed, noisily.

'Who is that beauty?'

'Carrie.'

'Your wife?'

'Not exactly. Fiancée.'

'Ah-ha… well I had my mistress with me, Maria. 26 years my junior. Her?'

'Carrie is 24 years younger.'

'Aha,' says the guest with a new admiration. 'One needs one's distractions. It's hard being the man in charge,' he continues. 'Worst of it is that people are always plotting to get rid of you.'

'Touché! I got rid of my man next door early on, but no sooner had the new one arrived than he was after my office. They are the worst.'

'The man next door?'

'Chancellor of the Exchequer. Second Lord of the Treasury. He wants to control the money. Cheek. How was yours?'

'*I* was the Chancellor of the Exchequer.'

'*You* controlled the money?'

'I did!'

'Lucky you. But you didn't have to deal with the ghastly people in the press like I do: they're as bad as my MPs.'

'I had a livid sewer thrown at me daily from writers, journalists and cartoonists. So Parliament tough, too?'

'I never go there. Apart from when I am told I have to.'

'I had no option. I was Leader of the House of Commons.'

'Good grief! We are told the PM's job has become steadily more powerful. *You* weren't supposed to have had any real power.'

'Really? I could do largely what I wanted. Those unconvinced by my rhetoric would soon change their minds with a few payments from the Secret Service Fund.'

'No pushback on your leadership from the Lords?'

'Pussycats.'

'Judges?'

'Powerless pontificators.'

'Business?'

'In my pocket.'

'Devolved nations?'

'What?!'

'Municipal mayors?'

'Never heard of them.'

'The bloody Treasury?'

'Look, my friend, I *ran* the Treasury.'

'The Tory Party?'

'A troublesome lot, but in opposition. They were always awkward.'

A sigh. He drains another glass of Château Lafite.

'Look, my friend, you have to understand. I ran the government. I oversaw Parliament. I dispensed patronage. I spent the nation's finances, ran the elections, I kept us out of wars.'

'I'm exhausted contemplating it.'

'Oh it wasn't so bad. There were real compensations too.'

'Such as?'

'Power.'

'I'd like some more of that.'

'And an abundance of food.

'Yes.'

'Fine wines.'

'Yes, please.'

'Women and money.'

'Well . . . '

'Weeks away in the country, quite cut off from Downing Street: letters took two days to reach Norfolk. Bliss!'

Another sigh ... The older man shoots a look of sympathy at his host.

So we leave both men, talking late into the night.

Just an imaginary conversation, or is there any truth in their remarks? Despite the great differences in the office, and the periods in which they held it, are the similarities more striking than the differences? Let us now explore these questions.

Striking certainly are the similarities between the two *men* who occupied the office at the beginning and end of our time. Both came to power on opportunistic responses to national crises: for Walpole, the South Sea Bubble, where he posed as the defender of the political establishment against rampant greed and speculation, while for Johnson it was Brexit, capitalising on the widespread national frustration with the stumbling of his predecessor, Theresa May (54th, 2016–19), and offering a bold way through the impasse.

Walpole and Johnson were high-stakes chancers, revelling in their *coup de théâtre*: for Walpole had protected many of those who had let the South Sea Company get out of control, up to and including the king, adopting the 'skreen system', described as 'an extraordinary incidence of political nerve'.[6] For Johnson, it was challenging the establishment head on in forcing through the Brexit vote in Parliament, and his bravura in calling a make-or-break general election in December 2019.

Both prime ministers needed luck, and each enjoyed more than his fair share of it: for Walpole, many of his rivals for power were damaged by the South Sea scandal, like Charles Stanhope and John Aislabie, or died, like James Stanhope and James Craggs. For Johnson, Brexit undid those who had previously blocked his path to power, David Cameron (53rd, 2010–16), George Osborne, and, eventually, Theresa May.

Historians have highlighted the changes to *the office* of prime minister since 1721, and this book examines these in depth. But is the job that Johnson is doing in 2021 one that Walpole would have recognised, which justifies it being considered the same office, and how do their powers compare?

THE FIRST DAY FOR WALPOLE AND JOHNSON

Thursday 3 April 1721 was an unremarkable day in political London. No fanfare or ceremony surrounded the announcement by George I of his appointment of Walpole as First Lord of the Treasury, and Chancellor of the Exchequer. Merely a bald paragraph appeared in the press announcing: 'We are inform'd that a Commiſſion is preparing, appointing Mr Walpole firſt Lord Commiſſioner of the Treasury and Chancellor of the Exchequer.'[7] The appointment was not unexpected. Eight months earlier in June 1720, Walpole had been made Paymaster-General with the understanding he would become First Lord of the Treasury at the earliest opportunity.[8] But 1721 was not seen by contemporaries as in any respect a transformational year, like 1776 in the United States, or 1789 in France.

More public notice came when George II, who succeeded his father in 1727, offered Walpole Number 10 Downing Street as a personal gift. Initially he declined the offer, but later accepted it on the condition that it should 'be & remain for the use & habitation of the first Commissioner of his Majesty's Treasury for the time being'.[9] The *Gentleman's Magazine* recorded: 'Thursday, 20th July, 1732. Sir Robert Walpole, being an Inhabitant of the Parish of St Margaret's at Westminster, by having obtain'd a Grant of Count Bothmar's house in St James's-Park.'[10] Sitting tenants, Mr Chicken and Mr Scroop, had first to move out, and extensive work was carried out on the shoddy building, before it was ready for Walpole and his family to move into three years later. The *London Daily Post* duly recorded in September 1735: 'Yesterday the Right Hon. Sir Robert Walpole with his Lady and Family removed from their House in St James's Square to his new House adjoining to the Treasury in St James's Park.'[11] No one at the time could have foreseen that this move would prove of so much historic significance in defining the office and home of the prime minister. The acquisition further marked out Walpole's position against his other colleagues as the recipient of the king's special favour. No other minister was afforded the privilege of a central London home, so close to Westminster and the royal palace of St James's, from where George I and II conducted much of their business.

The lack of excitement surrounding Walpole's appointment contrasts with the high drama and international media hysteria which greeted

Boris Johnson's meticulously choreographed appointment as prime minister on 24 July 2019. On the day before, it had been announced that he had beaten his final competitor, Jeremy Hunt, and became leader of the Conservative Party by a margin of 66 to 34 per cent.

May spoke for her final time in the House of Commons as prime minister the following day at Prime Minister's Questions. At 2.30 p.m. she delivered her departing speech in the street outside Number 10, arriving at Buckingham Palace twenty minutes later to resign formally to the monarch, Elizabeth II. At 3.10pm Johnson arrived at Buckingham Palace to 'kiss hands' with the queen, when she constitutionally invited him to become her fourteenth prime minister. For those few minutes before, Britain had no prime minister, and all executive power had been invested in her. At 3.55pm Johnson spoke outside Downing Street, both to the crowd of journalists and to the watching world, delivering the message: 'The time has come to act, to take decisions, to give strong leadership and change the country for the better', and he pledged that Britain would leave the EU on 31 October 2019, 'No ifs, no buts.'[12]

Was Walpole given instructions by the monarch? No records remain. History cannot tell us what words passed between George I and Walpole on 3 April 1721, if any did, nor indeed will we know what precise words Elizabeth said to Johnson on his appointment 298 years later, beyond his indiscretion that she told him 'I don't know why anyone would want the job.'[13] We know better what the Cabinet Secretary, Mark Sedwill, the custodian of the British constitution, said to Johnson less than an hour later. The two men had conversed in the brief interval between Johnson's election as Conservative leader and his appointment as prime minister, to talk about the contents of a letter Sedwill wrote him, which opened: 'Tomorrow you will become the 55th prime minister of the United Kingdom.' It laid out the range of responsibilities, the main choices and decisions, that he would have to take early on in office. The official carefully outlined the principal national security issues, explaining what his roles as First Lord of the Treasury and Minister of the Civil Service entailed. When composing his letter, Sedwill had searched out the missive that his predecessor as Cabinet Secretary, Jeremy Heywood, had sent to Theresa May when she herself became prime minister in July 2016. Much was similar.

The secret Cabinet Office briefing expanded on the challenges he might expect in his first 100 days. It assured Johnson that the Civil Service was behind him and would give their very best to him. It branched out into Johnson's 'war powers', including his oversight as Chair of the National Security Council of the Intelligence Services, the National Command Authority, the nuclear deterrent, and the engagement proto- cols for 9/11-style attacks. These, and other duties it explained, were the prerogative functions he would be exerting on behalf of the monarch.

Johnson had not anticipated such a long and grave list. The briefing advised him that he would need to work closely with the Chancellor of the Exchequer if the government was to succeed. He paused at the long list of economic challenges, not an area of expertise. Nor was bureaucracy, so he flicked quickly through the paragraphs on his responsibility for the Civil Service, and for its top 200 appointees. He was more interested in his options for appointing Cabinet, and his choices on the structure of Cabinet committees. He perked up when reading about options for securing Brexit and Global Britain, the risks surrounding no deal, and preparing the Queen's Speech. At last, the moment he craved had arrived.

When Johnson returned from the Palace, Sedwill greeted him in Number 10's entrance hall before escorting him down the long corridor to the Cabinet Room. Then, he passed through that famous room into the adjacent office that has served as a study for prime ministers since Blair. Sedwill and he were joined by senior civil servants Peter Hill and Helen MacNamara, as well as members of his own team, including Eddie Lister, Lee Cain, and Dominic Cummings. Mark Spencer, whom Johnson had earmarked for Chief Whip, soon joined them.

In the study, he at last sat down for a cup of tea and his first meeting as prime minister. They used the Cabinet Office letter as an agenda. The civil servants told him how the prime minister, more than any other member of government, can personally shape the way they operate in office, because unlike other Cabinet positions, which have a full job description, his new job is much less prescribed. The PM, he was told, can operate in a loose way, as Ronald Reagan did as president of the United States during the 1980s, or could be very interventionist, like Gordon Brown (52nd, 2007–10).

Johnson then discussed his schedule for the next few days, which would focus on appointing his Cabinet. Other key duties would follow, including defence and security briefings, and the writing of 'Letters of Last Resort' to the commanders of Britain's nuclear-armed submarines, which provide instructions in the circumstances of the total destruction of British political and military command. Calls from world leaders, including those of Britain's NATO allies, needed to be placed in order.

As these discussions continued, in the study for his first time, while going through his duties as PM, observers saw the full weight of the office begin to dawn on Johnson. Before, it had been a dream, a lifelong ambition. Now, the heavy responsibility seemed all too real.

THE INHERITANCE IN 1721 AND 2019

Walpole and Johnson both came to office at moments of great national importance. For the former, financial consolidation was imperative after the Nine Years' War (1688–97) and the War of the Spanish Succession (1701–14), described by former Treasury official Nick Macpherson as 'the most expensive war Britain had fought to date, which more than doubled the national debt'.[14]

By 1719, it had reached £50 million, before the South Sea Bubble further jeopardised the national finances. Negotiating new tariff arrangements was an early claim on Walpole's time, as was finding a balance between the interests of the City of London and British companies. His task was to protect British business from foreign competition through a complex new tariff system, while ensuring that the tax burden was spread more fairly.[15]

The economy was equally central to Johnson. His most urgent task was securing Britain's exit from the EU with a trading relationship that would support British business and the City. Achieving a fairer distribution of economic activity across the nation, particularly in the Midlands and the North, where many traditionally Labour constituencies voted Tory for the first time in the 2019 general election, was another central concern. As an official said:

There were two very big issues that Johnson kept returning to from the outset, which saw his energy levels shoot right up: they were Brexit and 'levelling up' which encapsulated his view about what a modern Toryism was all about, socially as well as geographically.[16]

The Union was of existential importance to both prime ministers. While Walpole faced the Jacobite threat – supporters of the exiled Stuarts who dreamed of overthrowing the Hanoverians, and lingering discontent among Scots following the Union with England in 1707 – Johnson faced a different threat to the Union, not as violent, but no less serious. Walpole's task was to maintain Scotland securely in the Union; Johnson's task was to ensure that it didn't leave the Union entirely, a challenge made greater by Brexit and the SNP administration in Edinburgh pressing for a second independence referendum to reverse the result of September 2014. To help combat the risk, which he knew would prove fatal to his premiership, Johnson appointed himself the first 'Minister for the Union': 'To ensure that all of government is acting on behalf of the United Kingdom: England, Northern Ireland, Scotland and Wales'.[17]

Walpole came to office without any great relish for foreign policy, imagining he could leave it to other ministers. The task fell principally to Lord Townshend as 'Northern Secretary' (1721–30), who shared it with the 'Secretary for the Southern Department'. Walpole, though, found himself, as did his successors as prime minister, increasingly sucked into it. His claim to be undisputed First Minister became much stronger with the resignation of Townshend in May 1730. Likewise, Johnson too came to office with little relish for foreign affairs, partly due to his less than happy period as Foreign Secretary (2016–18). He, too, found himself getting drawn in once PM, finding the top global table the prime minister sits at much more congenial than the Foreign Secretary's lot. Walpole's foreign policy inclination was to promote peace with Europe at all costs, one of many stances he shared with his Tory adversaries. He remained pragmatically pacifist: he 'resisted the calls for belligerence to the very end. His defeat on the issue [over the War of Jenkins' Ear] signalled . . . a decline in his political power', wrote Reed Browning.[18] Johnson equally came to power seeing his mission after Britain left the European Union as building amity and trade with foreign powers.

THE POWERS OF THE PRIME MINISTER:
WALPOLE VERSUS JOHNSON

The powers of the prime minister have grown and changed over the 300 years. But the roles Walpole and Johnson filled have changed much less.

MAJORITY IN PARLIAMENT. The appointment of Walpole as First Lord of the Treasury ushered in a quiet revolution in British government. As historian Peter Jupp argues, it led to 'the establishment of a convention' that government from then on would be 'conducted in the Monarch's name by a group of ministers who had one acknowledged head, who would normally be First Lord of the Treasury, and leader of the House of Commons or House of Lords'.[19] The centrality of Parliament to the new office was embedded from the outset. Walpole's position may have been dependent on George I and George II in a way that Johnson's was not on Elizabeth II, but even in the eighteenth century, the monarch's choice for First Lord was heavily constrained by the state of parties in the House of Commons. Walpole's survival for twenty-one years owed as much to his power base in the House of Commons as it did to the monarch, as Walpole himself fully understood.

Maintaining a majority in the House of Commons was as fundamental to the task of Johnson as it was for Walpole. The experience of Theresa May from 2017 demonstrated the problems a prime minister faces without a parliamentary majority. The thirty-five years before 1721 had created a new political system, without which Walpole would never have emerged as the first recognisable prime minister. The Glorious Revolution of 1688, the Bill of Rights of 1689, and subsequent Acts had established the key principle of parliamentary supremacy or 'sovereignty'. The Crown recognised that the levying of taxes without parliamentary consent in future was illegal, and that Acts of Parliament could not be suspended except by Parliament itself, and that Parliament was to meet regularly. The Triennial Act of 1694 specified that there would be general elections every three years, amended by the Septennial Act of 1716 which said that they should be held every seven years (amended in 1911, to provide for five-year parliaments, until repealed in 2011). While the monarch in 1721 still retained some independent, if ill-defined, powers, Britain had gone a very long way to becoming a *constitutional* as opposed to an *absolute* monarchy. The monarch's real authority had begun to wither.

Jeremy Black regards the 1694 Triennial Act as the pivotal moment when Parliament became an indistinguishable feature of the political settlement. After it, the monarch would need a reliable figure to represent him, implanted securely within it to ensure a majority: 'Parliament didn't sit in 1682, 1683, 1684, 1686 or 1687, but after 1694 it becomes a permanent feature of the British constitution', he says, 'and the King needs his own person there to help ensure it does what he wants'.[20] The circumstances were thereby created for the emergence of an embryonic party system of Whigs and Tories, albeit, for much of the eighteenth century, with many parliamentarians remaining independent and eschewing hard labels. The two groupings centred around different sets of tendencies or beliefs: Tories held strong views on the preservation of the Anglican Church, and were more supportive of the monarchy and more hostile to military involvement in continental Europe than Whig politicians, who were at the heart of the Glorious Revolution and were the sworn enemies of the Stuart dynasty.[21]

The Act of Settlement in 1701 which ruled that no Catholic could ever become monarch again, further constrained the monarch with respect to Parliament, and established the independence of the judiciary, by making it clear that judges held office on the basis of their own good conduct, rather than on the word of the monarch. Descendants of Charles I (other than the safely Protestant future Queen Anne) were deposed, and Sophia of Hanover (granddaughter of James I/VI) became the next Protestant in line after her. The Act of Union of 1707 ended the independence of Scotland and the historic Scottish Parliament in Edinburgh voted to dissolve itself, a large Scottish representation then becoming Members of Parliament in Westminster. Two months before Queen Anne died in August 1714, Sophia died in Hanover, and her largely unknown son George inherited the succession. The Tory ministers Anne had favoured were promptly ejected from positions of influence. George I, as he became, preferred the Whigs, finding them more congenial and loyal to Hanoverians, and a prolonged period of 'Whig Supremacy' endured throughout his reign (1714–27) and George II's

(1727–60). What these first two Georges needed above all was a Whig on whom they could rely to ensure legislation and finances passed through Parliament. For this, Robert Walpole was their man.

Walpole's oversight of Parliament is recognisable today. As Leader of the House, he managed business in the Commons. He oversaw the general elections of 1722, 1727 (two years short of the seven-year span, due to the death of George I), 1734, and 1741, winning them all, albeit the last only narrowly. Fighting them stacked power even more heavily in the Whigs' favour, for as David Scott says, they had the spoils of office and the government slush funds at their disposal to pay the not inconsiderable costs.[22] Not the least of Walpole's parliamentary skills was to adopt Tory policies and lean into the centre-ground, a tack deployed when it suited him by Johnson.

MANAGING THE CABINET. Johnson's ability to appoint the ministers he wanted was evident in his preference for loyalist Brexit-supporters. In Walpole's day, ministers owed their appointment and allegiance to the monarch, and they had the right to discuss their department's business directly with the king. The early form of Cabinet was the 'Cabinet Council', which included Hanoverian courtiers, the Lord Chancellor and the Archbishop of Canterbury – confidants of the monarch rather than the PM. Hanoverians had particular interest in foreign and colonial policy, which entailed a close bond with the secretaries of the Northern and Southern Departments, which Walpole gnawed away at till he gained more influence over foreign policy following Townshend's resignation in 1730.

'Her Majesty's government' may be the correct form in 2021, but no one disputes that the ministers owe their allegiance and continuation in office to the prime minister. Walpole enhanced his personal authority by circumventing the large Cabinet Council, and operating a small 'Inner Cabinet' in which ministers owed their loyalty more to him. Over time, Walpole asserted his authority and put his stamp on the government. As J. H. Plumb wrote: 'A coherence emerged to government policy under Walpole, which coalesced around the ideas of peace, prosperity and a contented king and parliament, which led to questions about whether the government was in fact more Walpole's than the Monarch's.'[23]

Chairing Cabinet is a key task of modern prime ministers. They use the body to discuss policy, debate the most important decisions, and keep ministers in line. If a critical and controversial decision is to be made, such as over military action, policy of constitutional significance, or of major national economic and public health concerns, as with COVID-19, then it will likely be decided at the Cabinet table. For the more routine business of government though, the active decisions tend to be taken in committees, with Cabinet itself left to review, endorse, and adjust the direction of policy. It meets formally every week, at least when Parliament is sitting, and far more frequently at times of crisis. During the 2020–1 COVID-19 pandemic, it often met using conference call and video link facilities, simultaneously illustrating both the continuity and considerable changes that have taken place since Walpole's day. A monarch-free Cabinet has not meant a criticism-free Cabinet for the PM.

MANAGING THE MONARCHY. Johnson elected to manage Elizabeth II in a brusquer way than any of his thirteen predecessors as prime minister. Soon after coming to power, he attempted to prorogue Parliament during the Brexit crisis in late 2019, which was judged by the Supreme Court to be, 'improper' and therefore unlawful, resulting in an apology from Johnson to the queen. Johnson knew that the monarch had no effective control or power over him, and he could behave as he wanted, short of antagonising the powerful reservoir of press and public opinion fiercely loyal to the queen. Sedwill explicitly reminded him that the monarch still possesses the royal prerogative powers, which the prime minister only exercises in their name. Johnson shrugged, Cummings fumed.

Walpole could not take the monarch for granted, and the king was not bound to accept his advice. George I, when replacing Queen Anne's Tory ministers wholesale with Whigs, showed how powerful the post-1688 monarch could still be.[24] Despite a lack of familiarity with the English language, for his first few years George I convened and attended Cabinet meetings regularly, maintaining a keen interest in domestic as well as foreign policy.[25] Protecting the reputation of the monarchy during the South Sea Bubble – the king was a governor, and he had large holdings with the Company – had helped Walpole win his trust, as had helping patch up relations between George I and his son George, Prince of Wales, which reached a crisis point in 1721. But Walpole constantly had to use guile to retain the confidence of George I, and his position was far from secure. His sinuous ability to find his way into the affections of influential women at court underpinned his role, notably with George I's mistress, Melusine von der Schulenburg (Duchess of Kendal), and later with Queen Caroline of Ansbach, wife of George II.[26] 'For all his skill as a Parliamentarian, Walpole's supreme talent lay in managing the Royal Closet', Paul Langford wrote.[27]

Walpole was adept too at outmanoeuvring potential rivals, like Lord Carteret, among the few in Court who could speak German, and whose views were closer to George I on Hanoverian matters. So Walpole dispatched him to Ireland in 1723 as Lord Lieutenant. Squashing the nebulous 'Atterbury Plot' smartly in 1722, when the Bishop of Rochester, Francis Atterbury, was accused of trying to carry out a Jacobite coup d'état, strengthened his relations with George I. Walpole ordered the plotters arrested, deployed soldiers to Hyde Park from Ireland, suspended *habeas corpus* for a year, and had one member of the conspiracy executed at Tyburn. Thereafter, Walpole took control personally of 'Jacobite intelligence' and ensured both Georges knew it. Speaker Onslow (on Walpole's payroll) said that the Atterbury plot had 'fixed [Walpole] with the King, and united for a time the whole body of the Whigs to him'.[28]

Walpole proved deft too in managing the kings' long absences during the summer months when they went to Hanover every three summers or so, thereby enhancing the power and responsibilities of 'the emerging role of Prime Minister', as Andrew Thompson wrote.[29] Returning by carriage on uneven roads from Hanover to the Channel ports was slow, and once at the Channel, the royal party could be holed up for several days or longer, Black reminds us, if the winds were not favourable.[30]

A moment of extreme peril for Walpole came when George I died in 1727. Fearful for his future, he seized the initiative and travelled to Richmond Lodge where the new king was residing. On learning that George and Queen Caroline were taking an afternoon nap, he insisted that they be woken up so he could break the news personally and ask what they wanted him to do. The new George II was very clear what he wanted: Walpole's rival Spencer Compton to be First Minister, not him.[31] But Walpole was too quick, rapidly ingratiating himself with the new king by offering to help secure a £100,000 increase in the Civil List through Parliament.[32] Besides, unlike Walpole, Compton had little ability to control Parliament, and lacked Walpole's political talent. 'It was one of Walpole's most dangerous moments', says Daniel Finkelstein, ascribing his ability to survive the death of George I and remain prime minister as 'primarily because of his ability in Parliament. It was his relationship with Queen Caroline though which was responsible for him continuing for so long as prime minister.'[33] When Walpole moved into Downing Street in 1735, Caroline became a regular visitor, breakfasting with Walpole within a week of their move in October.[34]

We may ask whether the eclipse of the monarchy's political power was inevitable once a powerful First Lord had emerged. Nothing in history of course is destined. But what of the challenge posed by political scientist Patrick Weller?

> If the throne had passed on by lineage in 1714 to a Prussian or Russian [ruler] rather than Hanoverian, one could only speculate whether Frederick the Great (1740–86) or Catherine the Great (1762–96) would have been as prepared to yield as much to the demands of Walpole, or to any other prime minister. Frederick and Catherine had the ambition and political skills to have made far more of the British throne had it come their way. So one can interpret Walpole as filling a void: if the monarch will not rule, the first minister must, and Walpole does so willingly and effectively.[35]

The danger with such a view of Hanoverian impotence is that it underestimates the political acumen of George II in particular, and it underestimates the direction of travel of the British monarchy since 1688. The time for a monarch realising any absolutist tendencies had passed.

Walpole's leadership began seriously to falter in his seventeenth year in power, ironically, within eighteen months of his moving into Downing Street. In 1737, when his principal ally at Court, Caroline, died, it exposed him to the full force of opposition of the Prince of Wales, Frederick (who remained a powerful figure until his death from a lung injury in 1751, when his son, the future George III, succeeded him).

Behind the scenes, Walpole's long-standing foe, the Duke of Newcastle, who had long operated in his shadow, challenged him increasingly (and himself later became the PM in 1754). Walpole allowed himself to be dragged into war in 1739 (the War of Jenkins' Ear) which proved a costly failure, and he became increasingly mired in allegations of corruption, resigning after being defeated in a vote of no confidence. George II wept at the news and demanded to keep receiving Walpole's advice even after he stood down.[36]

Elizabeth II will be unlikely to weep when Johnson shuffles off his Downing Street coil. Johnson sees the queen for his weekly audience when she is in London, and he went to Balmoral in September 2019 for the annual PM's visit (COVID prevented it taking place in 2020). But he does not have to pick sides in Court intrigue, nor worry that he will be replaced on the accession of a new monarch. He does not agonise over whether he is in favour with the Prince of Wales, nor take a stand on Prince Andrew's private life, nor on the Duke and Duchess of Sussex's falling out with the royal Court. Nevertheless, as Peter Hennessy points out: 'Managing the relationship between the Government and the Monarch, and the Heir to the Throne' remains firmly top of their list, as the first duty of the Prime Minister's functions.'[37]

OVERSIGHT OF FINANCE. Johnson may remain First Lord of the all-powerful Treasury, but the Treasury is no longer a personal resource at his disposal. As Walpole would have been aware, the Treasury, and the office of Chancellor of the Exchequer, predated that of prime minister by several hundred years. The Treasury was established after the Norman Conquest: the Domesday Book in 1086 speaks of 'Henry the Treasurer'.[38] Older than any other department in Whitehall, except the Royal Mint, it was located from Henry VIII's time within the ramshackle Palace of Whitehall.[39] When William III and Mary moved to Kensington Palace following the Whitehall Palace fire in 1698, the Treasury relocated to the 'Cockpit' area, one of the few remnants of Whitehall Palace not burnt to the ground. In the 1730s, it moved into offices on the same site designed by architect William Kent, who was working simultaneously on upgrading Number 10 for Walpole. The Treasury remained within two hundred yards of the front door of Downing Street until it moved into its current offices in 1940 in the new

Treasury building on the corner of Whitehall and Parliament Square, opened in two phases in 1908 and 1917.

Walpole had been Chancellor of the Exchequer ('Second Lord of the Treasury') from 1713–15, returning to the post and combining it with First Lord of the Treasury in April 1721. Fundamental to his work and authority was his control over finance, underpinned by the enhanced role of the Treasury from the early eighteenth century. The rapid development of the City of London from the late seventeenth century, combined with the setting up of the Bank of England in 1694, helped ensure a favourable funding environment. Combining the office of First Lord with Chancellor greatly enhanced his strength. The Treasury provided him with capable officials, including John Scrope and Nicholas Paxton, significant Walpole allies and aides, especially as they sat in the House of Commons, helping ensure him parliamentary support.[40]

Johnson is in a far weaker position than Walpole over economic policy. He may be responsible for appointing the Chancellor of the Exchequer (and forcing his departure, as he did with Sajid Javid in February 2020), and be involved in budget planning, but Chancellor Rishi Sunak has his own views on economic policy. Within months of his appointment, differences began to emerge between Sunak's Treasury team, and Johnson and his Number 10 team who, like May and many PMs before her, wanted to cut back the Treasury's autonomy. Johnson can of course sack or move his Chancellor. But it would be very difficult to do so, so soon after the dismissal of Javid, and will in time become impossible with insufficient political capital. Dismissing Chancellors, unlike home or foreign secretaries, has dramatic impacts on the markets, financial and political. Well might Johnson envy Walpole.

PATRONAGE. How easy to believe that Johnson has far greater patronage powers than Walpole, because the Hanoverians retained so much authority over jobs. But do the facts confirm this? Johnson is certainly able to appoint and dismiss some twenty Cabinet ministers, and eighty more junior ministerial positions, whereas Walpole's heads of department and key figures within them owed their positions to the monarch. But Walpole possessed considerable influence over appointments, notably to the Treasury. The monarch's ministerial choices in contrast were limited to the ruling Whig party, in which the range of capable and loyal individuals to appoint was not wide. Modern prime ministers too, whilst theoretically able to appoint and sack any politician, need to ensure a balance of different factions, genders, ethnicities and regions within the party. Social diversity balance did not keep Walpole awake at night.

Walpole's and Johnson's patronage powers extend far beyond ministers. Johnson appoints the heads of the three security services, MI5, MI6, and GCHQ, though these are rarely political appointments, and he will generally accept the recommendations from within the security services. More than many prime ministers though, he has chosen to exercise his right to select top civil servants, dismissing several of Permanent Secretary rank, trying to replace them by figures deemed more sympathetic to his pro-Brexit, modernising agenda. He is responsible for a wide range of public sector appointments and regulators (numbering some 300 in 2021, down from over 2,000 in 1979),[41] a process that again he has been eager to influence, as in the appointment of the chair of the BBC.

Johnson has equally shown interest in the choice of the heads of the armed forces. During Walpole's time, George I and George II were keenly interested in military appointments, though Walpole did have some influence over the raising of regiments, because it involved spending Treasury money. Johnson, not known to be devoutly religious, though Carrie is a practising Catholic, is responsible for top ecclesiastical appointments. Since 2010 though, the PM has merely conveyed to the monarch the preference of the Church of England without comment; in 1721–42 the Church was a central part of national life.

Walpole milked the powers of patronage that he possessed to the full. Architect William Kent was enlisted to design his opulent Palladian country seat at Houghton Hall in Norfolk, which he used to host lavish entertainment. Every spring, it hosted ministers, politicians, and dignitaries for up to three weeks, known as the 'Norfolk congress'.[42] Housekeeping cost him some £1,500 a week: after one occasion, his wine merchant in London took back 500 empty cases of Château Lafite and Château Margaux. Walpole 'did not survive simply by telling backbenchers that he felt their pain', as Robin Lane-Fox put it.[43] Johnson, too, dispenses invitations to Downing Street or to Chequers, the country home of the prime minister since 1921, though shortage of time, and COVID, have heavily constrained this.

'Walpole worked hard to ensure that neither George I nor George II felt that they were being taken for granted. He never forgot that patronage is effectively at the disposal of the Crown, and took great care to exercise his influence over appointments in a way that didn't unsettle them', says Black.[44] His patronage regime became known as the 'Robinocracy' (Robin being a pejorative derivation of his first name, 'Robert'). With MPs not receiving a salary until 1911, it was common for inducements to be offered to them. The Secret Service fund was one of Walpole's nest-eggs: intended for espionage, he siphoned it off to help win elections and buttress support. Speaker of the House of Commons, Arthur Onslow, was just one of many on Walpole's payroll.[45] Sinecures, pensions, and some 'rotten borough' parliamentary seats were further gifts at his disposal. It was supposedly Walpole who commented about a group of MPs, 'all those men have their price'.[46] Harry Dickinson argues in *The Whig Supremacy* that 'Walpole remained in power for more than 20 years because he had an unrivalled ability to manage men, and a profound understanding of how the political system, which developed after 1714, actually worked.'[47]

Was Walpole corrupt, or was he merely playing by the rules of the day? Biographer Ed Pearce is in no doubt: 'Admirers must face the fact that Walpole was about power – acquisition of power, keeping of power, and getting rich by power. The fibre was always coarse, the vision low. Walpole did not invent English political corruption, but he turned it into a public company.'[48] Frank O'Gorman in contrast argues 'it has never been convincingly demonstrated that the British political nation became more corrupt under Walpole than it had been earlier'.[49] So there we have it, a corrupt regime, not in contrast to the norms of the day, though equivalent to many countries today, with Walpole simply playing the game.

The parliamentary 'Committee of Secrecy', set up after his fall in 1742, tried to build a case to prosecute him. His actions over the previous ten years were investigated, with his use of the Secret Service Fund a particular interest. But its inquiries were hindered by Walpole destroying many of his own papers – a great blow to historians. Aides like Scrope were uncooperative, refusing to answer questions or telling them that the Secret Service Fund was the king's business, and nobody else's. Nor was objectivity helped by some of Walpole's supporters being appointed committee members. Eventually, the committee's efforts petered out; too many important people had too much to hide. Thus, when his enemies thought they had finally got him, 'Cock Robin' managed to escape one last time.[50]

Later, a reform was passed preventing Treasury officials like Scrope and Paxton from again sitting in the House of Commons.[51] But while Walpole and Johnson exploited their patronage powers to the full and beyond, it is far from evident that it was a more powerful asset to Johnson than it had been to the first holder of his office.

NATIONAL LEADER. The final area of prime ministerial power is national leadership. Here at least we might imagine that Johnson would easily outshine Walpole. Johnson is, after all, demonstrably the legitimate *national* leader, rather than the monarch, leading at times of crisis, as during the COVID epidemic, and speaking directly to the nation about his decisions. The chief executive today is Johnson, rather than the monarch; the principal communicator to the nation in the media and House of Commons is Johnson, not the monarch; the chief determiner of government policy is Johnson, not the monarch; the significant intermediary with heads of government and heads of state abroad, and the person who ultimately declares war and would launch the UK nuclear strike, is Johnson, not the monarch.[52]

We would be wrong, however, to dismiss Walpole's role as a national leader. The 'Robinocracy' referred not just to Walpole's system of patronage, but the character it gave to the entire political system. It can be compared to 'Thatcherism', defining the political era in which both leaders were in office. Walpole was the most recognisable figure in the government, and the focus of both approbation and ire, not the monarch: it was his effigy angry mobs burnt during the Excise Crisis of 1733, when he attempted to increase duties. It was Walpole who was the subject of ridicule from some of the most prominent writers of his day, Jonathan Swift, John Gay and Henry Fielding. Gay's *Beggar's Opera* is a satire of Walpole's Britain. A short distance of travel only separates allusions to him in the line 'Robin of Bagshot, alias Gorgon, alias Bob Bluff, alias Bob Booty' from the puppet of Johnson in *Spitting Image* on television from October 2020.[53]

Nevertheless, Walpole had to compete with George I and II as, nominally at least, head of government. While it is true that the early Georgians had little of the presence and visibility of earlier rulers, Henry VIII, Elizabeth I or Queen Anne, they still set many key aspects of policy. King George II's support for war in 1739 undermined Walpole's position. Moreover, during Walpole's era, the existence of the Hanoverian monarchy itself was a controversial issue, with the exiled Stuart Court, and their domestic supporters, scheming for a restoration.

Today, Elizabeth II has a variety of constitutional, symbolic, and ceremonial roles, and she embodies the values of tradition and continuity. She is a symbol of national unity at a time when centrifugal forces are strong, and has authority across the Commonwealth. These are, however, just distant echoes of the time when the monarch was the real national decision-maker. All practical leadership functions may now be in the hands of the prime minister, but the monarch still retains considerable *influence*.

THE PRIME MINISTER'S DAY. Walpole may have had fewer responsibilities than Johnson, but as historians have stressed, he worked formidably hard, especially when Parliament was in session. His duties included:

> The reading of all the dispatches flowing in from the embassies and foreign courts; the perusal of reports from agents within the three kingdoms; formal meetings with members of the Privy Council, and outer and inner cabinets and the Treasury board; conferences with individual ministers; the delivery of speeches and the encouragement of supporters in Parliament; and, of course, daily audiences with the Monarch.[54]

This is not the programme of an amateur or part-time national leader. The team assisting Walpole may have been small in comparison to the 400 or so reporting to Johnson. Walpole, though, had MPs to help in addition to Treasury officials, including, at different times, senior politicians Henry Pelham (3rd PM, 1743–54), Thomas Winnington, Thomas Brereton, and Walpole's brother Horatio. Help came from several in the Lords too, such as from Edmund Gibson, Bishop of London, widely known as 'Walpole's pope', who brought him the votes of the twenty-six bishops.[55] The Duke of Argyll and Earl of Ilay helped him dominate Scottish politics in the 1730s, while in Ireland, then a British client state, Hanoverian business was aided by 'local Whig managers'.[56] A loose team of writers and journalists wrote supportive articles and propaganda, watered by the expenditure of £50,000 in his last ten years, as uncovered by the committee investigating his actions after his fall from power.

Walpole had more freedom on how he spent his day. Johnson does not have that luxury. His every hour is tightly choreographed by his Private Office and political team, who decide down to the smallest unit of time how he should optimise it. Prime ministers are initially surprised by how much of their day is taken up with tasks and meetings over which they apparently have no discretion. Walpole didn't have his own court, but since the Cabinet Secretariat was created in 1916 and the prime minister's office from 1964, the modern prime minister certainly does, with a retinue of staff with their own political climate, with some striking similarities to the monarch's court in the eighteenth and nineteenth centuries. 'The way Number 10 operates today has many similarities with the way the court operated under Henry VIII and Thomas Cromwell', says Rod Rhodes. 'There are obvious differences: Monarchs remain for life whereas prime ministers come and go. But the shenanigans, and the revolving door of key advisors who come in and out, is strikingly like the favourites in royal courts of the monarch in earlier centuries.'[57] And so, we finish with the monarchy.

SNIPPET OF A DINNER CONVERSATION BETWEEN KING GEORGE I AND QUEEN ELIZABETH II

Over a long candlelit table, attended on by smartly dressed courtiers, we find two distantly-related monarchs conversing in broken English:

> 'So you still have a First Minister in England, do you?' asks the Hanoverian.
> 'Indeed we do. I have had fourteen so far. Fourteen! We call them "Prime Minister" now.'
> '*Vierzehn!* Goodness! I had my hands full with just one. Sir Robert hated to being called that title.'
> 'I hope you kept him in order?'

'Indeed! But I could not have ruled without him in truth; he spared me a ... how do you say ... *schrecklich* embarrassment just before he became First Lord. After that, he saved my skin when there was a plot of murder against me in 1722. I owe him everything. And you?'

'Oh, they come and go. Huff and puff. "Full of sound and fury, signifying [often] nothing." But the state, the state, endures through it all.'

CHAPTER 2

A Country Transformed, 1721–2021

S O THE JOBS ROBERT WALPOLE PERFORMED FROM 1721 AND Boris Johnson from 2019 had much in common. But the country was *vastly* different. In this chapter, we explore some of the more momentous technological, political, cultural, and social changes that impacted on the office over the 300 years. Only by appreciating these factors, which have been perhaps under-considered in the literature on the office to date, can a rounded appreciation of it be achieved. The sheer pace and extent of these changes makes the survival of the office of prime minister over 300 years, and the adaptability of the individuals involved, even more remarkable.

THE THREE HUNDRED YEARS IN HISTORICAL PERSPECTIVE

The prime minister is a relatively new arrival in British history. It might be the longest-surviving office of political leadership in the democratic world, but many significant offices predate it. The Lord Chancellor dates back to 1066, the Chancellor of the Exchequer to the fourteenth century, the Chancellor of the Duchy of Lancaster to 1361, and the Speaker of the House of Commons to 1377 (although the Speaker of the House of Lords to just 2006, a position previously held by the Lord Chancellor). Many mayors date back considerably further, including the Lord Mayor of the City of London to 1189, and the Lord Mayor of York to 1217. Numerous ecclesiastical and academic positions have existed far longer, including the Archbishop of Canterbury, from 597, the Chancellor of the University of Oxford from c. 1201, and of Cambridge from 1215. Several east coast states in North America had governors appointed by the British monarchy before 1721, including the Governor of Virginia in 1607, Massachusetts in 1629 and Maryland in 1634. The Royal Mint has been in continuous existence from the time of Alfred the Great (king of the Anglo-Saxons c. 886–99). The Privy Council is descended from the *Curia Regis* (King's Court), which met first in 1066. The Treasury was in existence long before it became part of the Exchequer during the 1200s. The Admiralty had been operating since 1400, with the permanent office established in 1709. The Office of Works dates back to 1378, and the Northern and Southern Departments, which oversaw foreign and home affairs, were established at the Restoration in 1660. In Scotland, the Privy Council was meeting from the 1490s, while the Scottish Treasury settled in its Edinburgh location in 1584.

In the hundred and twenty years preceding 1721, three particular events led to the emergence of the British prime minister.

First, the accession of James I (and VI of Scotland) in 1603 saw the Union of the Crowns. The Union Jack flag was created, though James's dream of a political union with Scotland failed to materialise in his lifetime, the Union of Parliaments coming only in 1707. 'Great Britain' was born.

Second, a series of civil wars tore the country apart in the mid seventeenth century, including the Bishops' War (1639–40) in Scotland, and the Confederate Rebellion (1641–53) in Ireland, as well as the English Civil Wars of the 1640s and early 1650s. After the execution of Charles I (reigned 1625–49) in January 1649, a republic was formed under Oliver Cromwell (1653–8), but the Stuart monarchy was restored in 1660. Britain had its experience of political revolution: henceforth, evolution was to be its chosen way forward.

Third, in 1688, Whig parliamentarians invited Dutch Stadtholder William of Orange and his Protestant queen, Mary, to replace the Catholic James II (r. 1685–8). A war in Ireland followed, which was decided by Williamite victories at the Battles of the Boyne (1689) and Aughrim (1691). William's accession, known as the Glorious Revolution, ushered in parliamentary supremacy and thereby paved the way for the emergence of the PM.

For all these dramatic changes, however, in many ways the England of *1421* would have been far more recognisable, economically, politically, socially, technologically, and culturally, to Walpole than the Britain of

2021. We now turn to what has changed most in the last 300 years affecting the job of prime minister.

TRANSPORT AND COMMUNICATION

The most palpable difference between the working lives of the two prime ministers has been the impact of technology, which has shrunk Britain and the world. Walpole travelled and communicated at the speed of foot or hoof. Johnson travels at almost the speed of sound and communicates at the speed of light. Walpole was just eleven when Newton computed the speed of sound in 1687, while the first quantitative measurement of the speed of light had been in 1676, the year of his birth. Walpole inhabited a pre-Newtonian world: Johnson a post-Einstein one.

Walpole rarely travelled outside London, except to his country home at Houghton in Norfolk.[1] He therefore had no direct knowledge of vast tracts of the country over which he had jurisdiction, never travelling to Edinburgh and Cardiff, nor even to Manchester and Bristol. Few roads outside metropolitan London were paved, meaning uncomfortable journeys. Travelling to Norfolk could take him two or more days by horse-drawn carriage depending on the weather, an exhausting and time-consuming process, even in the most luxurious of carriages. His only way of communicating with colleagues in London was in person or by letter, and by handwritten dispatch on business matters with key figures across England, Scotland, Wales, and Ireland, as well as abroad, with often many days required for messages to travel back and forth. For Johnson, instantaneous communication with his opposite numbers and government officials abroad by phone, video, and texting is an unthinking occurrence, and he can visit fellow European leaders and be back in London within just a few hours of leaving Downing Street, with constant contact maintained with him by his team in London even when in the air.

Walpole's early successors, including Henry Pelham (3rd, 1743–54), Pitt the Elder (9th, 1766–8), and Lord North (11th, 1770–82), conducted their affairs much as he had done. In the 1750s, it took some ten days to travel from London to Edinburgh. Only with the onset of the transport revolution from the early eighteenth century, beginning with the rapid growth of turnpike trusts responsible for road maintenance, did road travel become quicker and more dependable. John McAdam began constructing solid roads using packed stones (for the first time systematically since the Romans) from the 1780s and 1790s, which revolutionised human movement. Thomas Telford then took the technology forward, aided by his mastery of bridge construction.[2] But even in 1786, it still took three days for William Pitt the Younger (14th, 1783–1801, 1804–6) to travel from London to Bristol.[3]

Within London itself, prime ministers travelled around by horse, carriage, or sedan chair: an estimated 400 sedan chairs were in operation in London at the time, compared to 500 'hackney' carriages.[4] Pitt the Elder was regularly conveyed around London in a sedan specially adapted to accommodate his gouty foot.[5] A contemporary drawing, from the late eighteenth century, shows a number of sedan chairs waiting in Whitehall, parked up like ranks of taxis at a modern railway station.[6] The limitations of contemporary travel and communications meant that North was having to take decisions of major historical importance in North America with only the haziest knowledge. Pitt the Younger, according to his biographer William Hague, rarely travelled outside London:

> He went abroad once in his life – and it was not as PM. He never made it west of Weymouth or north of Northampton, in his life. His world revolved around Number 10 and Kent where he had a second home, overlooking the Vale of Kent just below Bromley. As a member of Cambridge University throughout his life, he would travel to and from Cambridge on occasion, which would take just under a day. He would travel to Somerset, very occasionally and not even each year, where his mother lived.[7]

Eighteenth-century prime ministers never travelled abroad in office, though many had at other times in their lives. The Duke of Newcastle (4th, 1754–6, 1757–62) had done so as Secretary of State in 1750, and several others made 'grand tours', including Rockingham (8th, 1765–6, 1782), Grafton (10th,1768–70), and Shelburne (12th, 1782–3), when, as aristocratic young men, they had travelled to France and Italy. But they did not go abroad as prime minister nor meet their opposite numbers overseas. By the end of the eighteenth century, letters and dispatches were still taking a month or more to cross the Atlantic, and up to six months to reach India.

Change came only slowly in the nineteenth century. William Anthony Hay, biographer of Lord Liverpool (18th, 1812–27), says: 'He travelled by coach everywhere, and sometimes by boat along the River Thames.'[8] He too had made a grand tour through France, Italy, and the Low Countries as a younger man, and had spent time in Scotland overseeing cavalry. But as prime minister, he rarely travelled beyond his London residence at Fife House in Whitehall overlooking the Thames (demolished in 1869), Coombe in Kingston-upon-Thames, and Walmer Castle on the east Kent coast. A rare visit out of London was with George Canning to receive the Freedom of the City of Bristol, a journey that would have taken some twelve hours on the new hard road surfaces.[9]

Wellington (21st, 1828–30) famously rode up Downing Street on Copenhagen, his horse at Waterloo, to Number 10 in January 1828 when he first became prime minister. No lover of modern travel, he was forever put off the railway when statesman William Huskisson was killed in September 1830, mown down by Robert Stevenson's pioneering locomotive *Rocket* at the opening of the Liverpool and Manchester Railway. As Wellington biographer Elizabeth Longford wrote:

> Perhaps it was the tragic utterance of Huskisson – 'it's all over with me: bring me my wife and let me die' – or the piercing shrieks of poor Mrs Huskisson; or the roaring of a loud-hailer to stop the trains; or the cries from carriage to carriage to know what has happened; or the screams for surgical aid; or the tourniquet applied unavailingly by Lord Wilton; or the news of Huskisson's agonised death at 9 pm – perhaps it was a combination of all these horrors which prejudiced the Duke forever against railways.[10]

Lord Melbourne (23rd, 1834, 1835–41) equally was no lover of rail. 'People who talk much of railroads and bridges are generally Liberals', he muttered disparagingly to Queen Victoria, who, as his biographer David Cecil recorded, 'note[d] down this valuable item of political information'.[11] Melbourne was a proud horseman, and was famously painted with Victoria riding in the grounds of Windsor Castle.[12]

Travel by sea remained subject to the vicissitudes of wind and tide until the introduction of paddle steamers in the early nineteenth century. Technological innovation in the form of steam power, paddle wheels, then iron hulls, and screw propellers initially halved Atlantic crossings to thirty days, reducing it further by the end of the century to eight or nine days.[13] Capacity also increased, meaning more passengers and greater trade potential.

Robert Peel (24th, 1834–5, 1841–6) was the first to begin to take advantage of the new technologies. His biographer, Richard Gaunt, says 'Peel was in some respects a railway prime minister, though he did not exploit the railway in the way William Gladstone (30th, 1868–74, 1880–5, 1886, 1892–4) did later, either as a means of communication, or as an electoral aid, but he was certainly impressed by the impact of the railways on the country.'[14] Many parts of the country, even by 1850, still lacked the railway, and mid-nineteenth-century politicians tended not to travel far afield unless they had their constituency to visit, or their estate, or were staying with friends.

The sending of messages remained slow as well. Peel, described by David Brown as 'largely a manuscript prime minister',[15] was severely restricted in his ability to give instructions to the far-flung Empire, as he acknowledged in 1842:

> I feel very confident that your despatch to Lord Ellenborough [Governor-General of India] will be what it ought to be. It is impossible for anyone, writing at such a distance, to convey any other than general opinions. If positive instructions were sent, the lapse of time and change of circumstances might probably make them wholly inapplicable to the state of affairs at the moment of their receipt.[16]

When the Earl of Aberdeen became the prime minister (27th, 1852–5), a letter from London could still take two weeks to reach New York, thirteen days to Alexandria, nineteen days to Constantinople, forty-four days to Calcutta, fifty-seven days to Shanghai, and seventy-three days to Sydney.[17]

Historian Angus Hawkins says that for Lord John Russell (25th, 1846–52, 1865–6) and the Earl of Derby (26th, 1852, 1858–9, 1866–8): 'Their political world was primarily Westminster, Whitehall, the clubs of St James's and country houses during the parliamentary recess. Their sense of what is going on with public opinion is confined to the conversations they have in those places, and to some extent informed by newspapers.'[18] Russell made visits by train to the Midlands and the North, but they were not deemed successful. Hawkins says that, when in London, Derby enjoyed travelling by carriage and riding for pleasure in

Hyde Park. But from the early 1840s, he began travelling by rail when going to Knowsley Hall, the family stately home near Liverpool. Hawkins says he so enjoyed the experience, he had a special carriage as he got older in the 1860s.[19]

Biographer of Lord Palmerston, David Brown, confirms he also was no revolutionary in his use of the new technologies. After the Napoleonic Wars, he had travelled to France to watch battlefield re-enactments of British victories, and visited the Continent several times as Foreign Secretary in the 1840s and 1850s to help build alliances, meeting Napoleon III of France. These travels gave him the understanding he needed, as did the letters and dispatches he received, and hence he saw no need to travel abroad as prime minister. He used the railway to visit his country home of Broadlands in Hampshire, to see the slate mines in Wales, and to travel to the north of England in the 1850s and 1860s to make speeches. But he did not do so in the systematic way, Brown argues, that later Victorian PMs were to do:

> A large part of why he didn't travel as prime minister is down to time and age. Palmerston was 70 by the time he becomes prime minister, an elderly figure in many respects. While his reputation was one of vigour and energy, he had begun to ramble, and was caught napping in the House of Commons.[20]

The great change came with Gladstone after 1868, the first serious 'railway prime minister' to campaign across the entire country and make whistle-stop political tours, thereby gaining a far deeper, first-hand comprehension of the electorate and its concerns.[21]

The slow pace of sail, horse, and carriage had meant that being away from Westminster and Whitehall for too long was a risk for the prime minister. They might be challenged, or be absent in a crisis, unable to communicate, which was exacerbated by a lack of clarity about who would deputise for them. But by the late nineteenth century, technological advances in ships and railways opened up international travel for prime ministers. Benjamin Disraeli (29th, 1868, 1874–80) was the first to travel abroad when in office, when he went to the Congress of Berlin in June and July 1878. He took just four days to reach the German capital, leaving London on 7 June by train for the Channel to board a steamship, then another train from Calais to Brussels, where he dined with the Belgian king, before travelling via Cologne and arriving at the Kaiserhof Hotel in Berlin on 11 June. The speed and comfort of the journey meant that he was fresh enough to accept an unexpected invitation to call on German Chancellor, Otto von Bismarck, that same evening.[22] Disraeli biographer Edward Young says he was motivated to make the pioneering trip because 'he loved the theatre, it spoke to the novelist's love of high European politics, even though the feedback was he couldn't read a map'.[23]

Derby in the 1850s and 1860s was perhaps the last prime minister not to use any electronic means of communication, which was to transform the lives and work of the prime ministers in the late nineteenth century. He, like earlier PMs, had to rely on the capacities of the postal service which moved letters only as quickly as the existing technologies allowed. The first Royal Mail coach was set up in 1784, the first mail train ran in 1830, and in 1840, the first postage stamp, the 'Penny Black', was introduced.[24] Derby was a prodigious letter writer, leaving a vast archive of correspondence from his three periods as prime minister, providing a quality of insight, as into his complex relations with Disraeli, a mine which historians researching later less literary eras are denied.[25]

The telegraph began to transform the world of prime ministers and politics from the 1860s. The first demonstration that an electrical telegraph could be operated over a substantial distance had occurred as early as 1816, and by 1838 telegraph was installed on the Great Western Railway from Paddington to West Drayton. In 1857 a telegraph message from India, asking for urgent help against the Rebellion, still took forty days to reach London, because it had to be transported by ship from the coast of India, an undersea telegraph connection to London only being established in 1864.

In July 1868, the Telegraph Act paved the way for the government to purchase telegraph companies, and permitted the Post Office to set up telegraph services across the country. By 1870, 334 telegraph offices were in operation in London alone.[26] Gladstone was at his residence in North Wales, at Hawarden, in December 1868, when he received news of the election results by telegram: 'Very significant', he said, before continuing to chop wood.[27] During the 1870s, further cables were laid under the sea to the Far East, and then on to Australia and New

Zealand, completing by 1902 the so-called 'All Red Line' (the informal name for the system of electrical telegraphs connecting the entire British Empire) which circled the globe.[28] The completed circuit had a profound effect on the prime minister as well as the monarchy, and their relationship with the British Empire, with telegrams transmitted quickly and efficiently across the globe by the end of the nineteenth century. Paul Kennedy noted one downside: 'Far from increasing London's control of overseas events, the telegraph gave local officials the chance to exaggerate any crisis.'[29]

Typewriters were being developed from the mid nineteenth century, with Remington beginning production of its first model in 1873. Algernon West, Principal Private Secretary to Gladstone, would boast about his handwriting speed, but could not but be impressed by the speed and legibility of the new technology: 'These "typewriting women"', he said 'can beat me two to one in writing – and that shows the amount of work we can get from them.'[30]

The telephone followed hard on the heels of the telegraph and typewriter, with its first successful transmission of audible speech in 1876. The first telephone is believed to have been installed in Number 10 during Gladstone's second premiership of 1880–5 (at the same time as electric lights). Certainly he had a telephone installed at Hawarden at this time, describing it as 'most unearthly'.[31] Understanding the precise impact of the telephone on these first prime ministers to have access to it, including Gladstone, Lord Salisbury (31st, 1885–6, 1886–92, 1895–1902), and Lord Rosebery (32nd, 1894–95), is challenging. Hawkins says: 'Clearly the telephone is a very significant factor, but for historians, it's very difficult to nail it down because prior to the mid 1880s, unless a secretary was in the room with the PM or in the same building, the PM had to put what was said down on paper, and there's little or no primary evidence of calls recorded to base judgements upon.'[32]

Salisbury's biographer Andrew Roberts confirms that he had little taste for the telephone. Neither did Arthur Balfour (33rd, 1902–5), according to his biographer R. J. Q. Adams.[33] Andrew Bonar Law, Colonial Secretary then Chancellor of the Exchequer in the First World War, and later prime minister (37th, 1922–3), was another of Adams's subjects, of whom he says, 'I found no evidence that he had much interest in it.'[34]

Telegraph meant that for the first time, the prime minister in Downing Street could communicate with British forces in the field, initially during the Boer War of 1899–1902. By the time the First World War broke out, Number 10 was receiving news of military developments in real time, and could monitor and comment on the progress of armies on the front line as battles developed. Telegrams constantly flowing in and out made Number 10 a nerve-centre in the war, as captured by Frances Stevenson, aide and lover of Lloyd George (35th, 1916–22). In March 1917, she recorded:

> I can see LG standing in the large Drawing Room at No 10 on the afternoon in March 1917, reading a telegram which I had handed to him announcing the Russian Revolution. I can, without effort, recapture the silence after he had read the dispatch. Then he said: 'They will be no more use to us in this war.'[35]

A year later, during the German Spring Offensive of March 1918, she described how:

> A map in the Cabinet Room had the British line marked on it in red, and each day the line moved sickeningly back and back. One day in April I saw that the Germans had reached Bethune, near to where my brother was buried. 'They will soon be trampling over his grave', I thought.[36]

The war gave the use of the telephone a major impetus, for all the worries about security. Hawkins argues, 'There's a hell of a lot of conversation going on down the telephone, only a small part of which gets to being formally recorded, with notes kept.'[37] After H. H. Asquith (35th, 1908–16) and Lloyd George departed, use of the phone appears to have eased. Historian of Stanley Baldwin (38th, 1923–4, 1924–9, 1935–7) Stuart Ball says that he 'was very definitely not a "telephone prime minister" and neither was his successor [Neville] Chamberlain' (40th, 1937–40). Ball believes it was 'partly because of its lack of security, and partly because it was still not really "proper behaviour" to conduct official or important business by that means. But most of all, because Baldwin and Chamberlain always preferred face-to-face meetings, especially with colleagues.'[38] Historian David Dilks agrees: 'Neither Baldwin nor Chamberlain, nor indeed any of the other inter-war Prime Ministers, used the telephone a great deal. In times of crisis, that had to be done; but it was not their preferred method of transacting business.'[39]

Winston Churchill (41st, 1940–5, 1951–5) was much more comfortable with the telephone, though still liked to dictate long memos to colleagues. Security became a serious issue in the run-up to the Second World War, when hostile eavesdropping became an intense preoccupation of the British security services. During the war itself, Churchill was the first PM to communicate with an American president, F. D. Roosevelt, via a confidential communications system called 'The Scrambler', which unbeknownst to Churchill was being intercepted by German intelligence, but which was replaced in 1943 by the far more secure American-built SIGSALY.[40]

In 1958, as part of a UK–US defence agreement, a transatlantic telephone line was installed between the White House and Number 10, allowing both leaders to talk to each other in confidence. Number 10 was less than impressed:

> the Americans have pressed us to agree to the installation of a private line from the No 10 switchboard via US Air Force Headquarters at Ruislip direct to the Pentagon and thence to the White House. As the Americans were going to pay we agreed, and the telephone is now installed ... The whole thing is not really very useful and in any case it is completely insecure because the trans-Atlantic messages are relayed by wireless somewhere along the Canadian/New England coast and the Russians and everybody else probably pick messages up.[41]

What of transport in the twentieth century? Balfour was the first prime minister to bring a motor car to Downing Street, a De Dion-Bouton Voiturette, unreliable and reportedly breaking down every few miles. According to R. J. Q. Adams:

> There was something of Toad of Toad Hall in Balfour. He loved science and technology and was a very early adopter of electric light, bicycles, phonographs and motorbikes. He flew in a very early aeroplane, had automobiles from the earliest days, and ... travelled in a submarine.[42]

The Motor Car Act of 1903, passed by his government, introduced registration of motor cars and increased the speed limit to twenty-five miles per hour (from fourteen). Lloyd George's Budget in 1909 established licences for cars and petrol tanks,[43] and he, for his part, revelled in being driven around London and down to Churt in Surrey, his favourite retreat, being regularly chauffeured in style.[44] Chauffeur-driven cars for prime ministers paid for by the state, however, were not introduced until the Second World War (starting with a Humber Super Snipe), so those who could afford to do so before, like Neville Chamberlain, paid for their own driver and car, in his case an Armstrong Siddeley.[45] The car transformed the lives of prime ministers, allowing them to move around speedily and safely, and greatly enhancing their ability to get out to Chequers, the official country residence gifted to them in 1921.

If Gladstone was the first railway prime minister, Baldwin was one of the last. His father had been Chairman of the GWR, and he was a director; he was never happier than when travelling on a GWR train back to Worcester, or around the country, which he did 'very extensively, but not as often as he would like'.[46] By the 1940s, smoother roads, better car suspension, and more comfortable cabins combined to make it easy for the prime minister to conduct business on the road, reading papers and discussing business with aides, as Churchill did regularly during the war.

By that decade, flight became an option for the prime minister. Balfour and Churchill were the first prime ministers to embrace planes enthusiastically – Churchill had nearly killed himself flying in a reckless style even before World War I. Bonar Law, when Lord Privy Seal, had been a pioneer, flying to the Paris Peace Conference in 1919.[47] It was to be almost twenty years though before a prime minister was to use a plane in office, when Chamberlain flew in a Lockheed L10 Electra from Heston Aerodrome on 15 September 1938 to meet Adolf Hitler in Berchtesgaden.[48] He repeated the formula to see him at Bad Godesberg a week later, and again to Munich at the end of September to sign the agreement from where he returned to Heston waving his piece of paper, citing the words 'peace for our time' that Disraeli used on his return from Berlin exactly sixty years before. As Dilks records: 'Flying was known to carry a modest risk, but not more than that: Chamberlain dismissed that factor as being of no importance in relation to the immediate crisis, which demanded speed.'[49] Chamberlain wrote to his sister that the plane 'rocked and bumped like a ship in a sea' as they approached Munich.[50]

Ocean liners meanwhile also transformed the lives of prime ministers in the early twentieth century. By 1907, RMS *Lusitania* had cut the crossing of the Atlantic to under five days. Baldwin visited Canada, along with the Prince of Wales, in August 1927 to celebrate the sixtieth anniversary of the Canadian Confederation sailing on board RMS *Empress of Australia*,[51] and returning on the RMS *Empress of Scotland*.[52] The first prime ministerial visit in history to the United States came when Ramsay MacDonald (39th, 1924, 1929–35) travelled to New York in October 1929 aboard the White Star Line RMS *Berengaria* (a former German vessel, surrendered as part of war reparations). The last prime minister to use ocean liners as a mode of travel, for safety in the war due to its speed, then later out of sentiment, was Winston Churchill, travelling in splendour on board Cunard's RMS *Queen Mary*.[53]

The jet aeroplane made the liner redundant for the prime minister from the 1950s. Harold Macmillan (44th, 1957–63) was the first to fly in one, to attend negotiations over the future of Cyprus in Athens in 1958.[54] Margaret Thatcher (49th, 1979–90) insisted on using the RAF Vickers VC-10 on account of the fact it was a British aircraft, despite the fact that it was considered cramped and noisy, long after it had become functionally obsolete: 'Whenever the VC10 arrives in some far-off capital with the RAF Ensign fluttering proudly in the breeze,' she said, 'it makes us all just that little prouder of being British.'[55] Macmillan was also the first prime minister to use a helicopter when in power, lifted from Washington to Camp David when visiting President Eisenhower in 1959.[56] Harold Wilson (46th, 1964–70, 1974–6) used an army helicopter to visit Northern Ireland in 1974, while Thatcher also used helicopters to travel around the region. Subsequently, Tony Blair (51st, 1997–2007), David Cameron (53rd, 2010–16), and Theresa May (54th, 2016–19) used helicopters to visit forces in combat zones, enhancing the ability of the prime minister to visit troops speedily and safely in the front line.

Secure transmission remained an acute concern for post-1945 prime ministers, not least after computers were installed at Number 10 from the 1980s, and the internet was mainstreamed across all Number 10 computers in 1998.[57] John Major (50th, 1990–7), became the first prime minister to use an electronic diary and a video conference call in 1990, and these innovations only increased in frequency as internet capacity has improved, with a video conference suite installed in 2010.[58] Blair became the first prime minister to use a mobile phone regularly, and Cameron the first to use social media extensively.

POLITICAL CHANGES

All prime ministers operate in their own mini political climates which change even in the life of a short premiership. Compared to many countries in Europe and beyond, Britain was remarkably stable politically in the 300 years after 1721. It had no revolution nor civil war, neither did it adopt an elected head of state, a written constitution, proportional representation, nor a federal structure, which would have constrained prime ministerial power. But the political landscape still changed in significant ways.

First, the nature and stability of Great Britain. The Act of Union in 1707 did not end questions about Scotland's political future. Pro-Stuart and, often, anti-Union, Jacobitism remained latent. Pelham had to see off the Jacobite rebellion in 1745 when Charles Edward Stuart, grandson of James II, landed in Scotland, raised an army, and marched it down as far as Derby, before retreating to Culloden, near Inverness, where he was defeated in January 1746, ending the Stuart question.

The modern movement for Scottish independence emerged as a prime ministerial concern during the latter twentieth century and is tied to the fortunes of the Scottish National Party. The vote for the Union in the 2014 referendum did nothing to quiet the nationalists, and the Brexit vote in the 2016 EU referendum, in which Scotland voted 62% to remain, only heightened the pressure for an independent Scotland.

Wales, in contrast to its history before 1721, was far more peaceful, though demands for devolution came during the late twentieth century. A referendum was held in Wales, as in Scotland, in 1997. A Welsh Senedd, together with a Welsh administration, bought off some of the agitation. But Wales, with a smaller population (at 3 million, almost half that of Scotland), and lacking Scotland's economic and political importance, never featured very high in the prime minister's priorities.

Ireland most certainly did. It proved troublesome to eighteenth-century prime ministers, culminating in the Irish Rebellion of 1798, inspired in part by the French and American Revolutions. It was crushed by the British Army on Pitt the Younger's orders. The Acts of Union of 1800 ended the Protestant-dominated Dublin Parliament, with powers transferred to Westminster. The diagonal stripes of the Cross of St Patrick were added to the Union Jack, symbolically anchoring Ireland as an unalterable part of the United Kingdom. From 1801–1922, Ireland was governed by Parliament in London through a local administration based in Dublin Castle. Those who thought this would pacify Ireland were due for disappointment.

Ireland continued as a dominant concern for nineteenth-century prime ministers. The issue of Catholic emancipation prompted Pitt the Younger's resignation in 1801 and was resolved only in 1829. The Tithe war in the 1830s, the Great Famine of the 1840s, and renewed nationalist agitation for self-government from the 1870s ensured Ireland became a major preoccupation for Peel, Gladstone, Asquith, Salisbury, and Balfour. By 1914, Asquith's government feared civil war as the Ulster Unionists armed themselves and prepared to resist Dublin rule.

Irish nationalists took matters into their own hands. Over a dozen conspiracies, plots, and attempted uprisings aimed at ending British rule took place after 1800, culminating in the Easter Rising in 1916, and the Irish War of Independence in 1919. Lloyd George's solution of partition, with the Irish Free State gaining de facto independence as part of the Empire (until 1948), separated from the six counties of Ulster which remained within the Union under their own prime minister and administration, provided only a temporary solution. From 1969 to 1997 Northern Ireland returned as a major preoccupation of the British prime minister, with regular Irish terrorism spreading to mainland Britain for thirty years following a bomb in Aldershot in 1972. Brexit brought renewed pressure on the fragile peace settlement in Northern Ireland, negotiated by John Major and Tony Blair in the 1990s, bedevilling the task Theresa May and Johnson faced in leaving the EU, and causing the latter constant concerns.

The economic and political integration of Europe became a giant claim on the time of every prime minister from Harold Macmillan to

Johnson. Failure to gain entry in 1963 and 1967 damaged the premierships of Macmillan and Harold Wilson before Britain joined in January 1973 under Edward Heath (48th, 1970–4). Political parties became heavily involved in elections to the European Parliament from 1980, while a permanent place for the prime minister on the 'European Council' of leaders became another heavy drain on their diary. The move towards further integration in the 1980s, culminating in the formation of the European Union at the Maastricht Treaty in 1992, unleashed latent forces of Euroscepticism on the right of British politics. It became, along with the split over the repeal of the Corn Laws in 1846, and tariff reform in the early twentieth century, a prolonged Conservative chasm. Despite the hopes of all prime ministers from John Major onwards that the EU would not dominate British politics, it played a significant part in the downfall of all recent Tory prime ministers, Thatcher, Major, Cameron, and May. Johnson's continuation hinges on the success of Britain post-Brexit.

Britain's role in the world has been another constantly changing pre-occupation, as it rose and fell as a global power. During the eighteenth century, it was embroiled in a series of massive wars, invariably against France, including the War of the Austrian Succession, the Seven Years' War, the American War of Independence, and the French Revolutionary and Napoleonic Wars. For Newcastle, North, Pitt the Younger, and Liverpool, war-making would dominate their time as prime minister.

During the seventeenth and eighteenth centuries, the English and then British Empire had expanded in North America, only to receive a rude shock when the Thirteen Colonies seized independence during the American War of Independence. After that, Britain's imperial focus shifted eastwards, towards India and Australia during the late eighteenth century, and into Africa towards the end of the nineteenth century. Lord Salisbury, a keen imperialist, secured vast parts of the African continent during the 'Scramble for Africa' in the 1880s and 1890s. By the late nineteenth century, Britain was a global superpower, with the world's biggest economy, a network of naval bases all around the world, and a huge empire.

A final wave of imperialism after the First World War, when parts of the Middle East became British mandates, saw the Empire reach its greatest extent. But already, control over it was beginning to wane. The Dominions

(Canada, Australia, New Zealand, South Africa, Newfoundland) all received some form of self-government from the mid nineteenth century onwards. The African and Asian parts of the Empire had to wait for independence until after the Second World War, when the climate of opinion against colonialism from the United Nations and United States, the rise of protest within the colonies, the prohibitive cost of wars, and changing political mores in Britain saw a sudden impetus towards independence.

India in 1947 was the first to receive independence, a process driven personally by Clement Attlee (42nd, 1945–51), with Pakistan (including modern-day Bangladesh) created as part of its partition. The embarrassment of Anthony Eden's (43rd, 1955–7) disastrous Suez War in 1956 catalysed the process. Macmillan from 1957 accepted the end of empire, notably with his 'Winds of Change' speech in Cape Town in 1960, and within 8 years all, except breakaway Southern Rhodesia, had received independence.[59] What is surprising with hindsight is how comparatively easy British prime ministers found winding up the Empire, in comparison to countries like France and Portugal.

Britain retained some of the vestiges of world power status after 1945, including a permanent seat on the Security Council of the UN. It played a leading role in the creation of NATO (1949) and detonated its first atomic weapon in 1952, followed by a hydrogen bomb in 1957. But it soon became clear that Britain was the junior partner behind the USA in the Cold War with the USSR. It saw other countries – Germany, China, Japan – overtake it economically. Its relationship with the US, periodically special, never more so than in the 1980s with Thatcher and President Ronald Reagan at the helm, and its leading position in the EU, gave it a standing in the world. A major preoccupation for Johnson has been finding a place for Britain globally post-EU and with a cooler relationship with the US, exploiting Britain's continuing, and not inconsiderable, cultural 'soft power'.[60]

Turning our focus internally, the shifting coalitions within the Whigs and Tories preoccupied the eighteenth-century prime ministers. These groupings solidified from the late eighteenth century, but were always Westminster-focused, while the Conservative Party, created by Robert Peel in the 1830s, and the Liberal Party, which emerged during the

1850s from an alliance of Whigs, free-trade-supporting Peelites, and reformist radicals, looked outward across the entire country. The rise of mass political parties followed the Reform Acts of 1832 and 1867, which widened the electorate from 400,000 to 2.5 million. After that, the task of being the leader of a *national* party organisation with the need to campaign across the country placed extra pressure on the responsibilities of the prime minister, compelling Disraeli and Gladstone to behave in a very different manner to Derby and Russell. In 1893, the 'Independent Labour Party' was created as a political movement from trade unions and urban working classes given the vote in the Representation of the People Act of 1884. The Labour Representation Committee was established in 1900, which became the Labour Party in 1906. In the 1920s, it replaced the Liberals as the second party in the two-party system. Lloyd George was to be the last Liberal prime minister.

Swelling Labour and Conservative Party organisations added greatly to the prime minister's powers, but equally provided them with an additional challenge to their time and authority. Party divisions and splits caused constant them concern. For Conservatives, memories of Peel's splitting the party caused successive leaders regular anxiety. For Labour, the split in 1931 was the source of rancour for fifty years until the breakaway of the Social Democratic Party in 1981, and its bond with the Liberals to form the Liberal Democrats in 1988, caused new traumas. All prime ministers since Heath have been as exercised by splits within their own party as by the challenge posed by the official Opposition.

Walpole may not have had to contend with mass parties, but he certainly did with powerful interests, notably business, finance, the aristocracy, and Church. Organised interest groups waxed and waned over the following 300 years, few more insistent and successful than the slavery abolitionist movement which secured 103 petitions to Parliament in favour of abolition in 1773, rising to 519 in 1792 (the largest number in any session ever). The movement lost some momentum during the wars against France, but the slave trade was abolished by Parliament in 1807 and, far more significantly, slavery itself throughout the Empire in 1833.[61] Aside from the women's suffrage movement in the early part of the century, trade unions were the interest group of primary concern to prime ministers in the twentieth century, notably for Asquith and Lloyd

George during the First World War, for Baldwin during the General Strike of 1926, and for Wilson, Heath, and Callaghan in the 1960s and 1970s, until Thatcher's union legislation reforms in the early 1980s, and decline in their numbers, limited their ability to challenge the government of the day.

Mainland Britain might not have seen revolution in 300 years, as occurred in France, Germany, and Italy, nor civil war, as in the United States and Spain, but the threat of revolution and violence breaking out, as it had in Northern Ireland from 1969, was ever present in the minds of prime ministers. From the moment Walpole squashed the Atterbury Plot in 1722, prime ministers were constantly on their guard. On 6 June 1780, during the Gordon Riots, which saw four days of rioting across the city, an angry mob marched down Downing Street before being repelled by soldiers. The American and French revolutions, and the Irish rebellion in 1798, made prime ministers even more apprehensive at the turn of the century. The Peterloo Massacre of 1819 in Manchester was a consequence of establishment anxiety. The 1848 mass meeting held by Chartists in south London saw 85,000 special constables recruited to quell the risk of violence, such as was seen that same year on the Continent. Historian Theodore Hoppen points to a peculiar British reserve: 'although the widespread continental revolutions of that year formed a backdrop to events in Britain, no major Chartist leader saw himself in truly revolutionary terms'.[62] A nationwide General Strike was not repeated after 1926, but there were moments in the 1960s, 1970s, and 1980s when prime ministers and the security services feared the state was at risk from organised unrest.

Staying alive has been a constant concern. In 1803, a Colonel Despard had plotted a revolutionary 'United Britons' coup, inspired by the 1798 United Irishmen uprising, that might have involved the assassination of key figures, though little hard evidence was presented at his trial. In 1812, Spencer Perceval (17th, 1809–12) was murdered in the House of Commons by an aggrieved Liverpudlian merchant. The Cato Conspiracy of 1820 to kill Lord Liverpool and the Cabinet, though thwarted, was an icy warning. Peel only escaped being murdered in January 1843 because his assassin killed his senior official Edward Drummond in a case of mistaken identity. Irish terrorism added a new dimension. During the 1880s there were several high-profile assassinations by Irish nationalists.

During the Irish War of Independence (1919–21), barriers were erected in Downing Street, preventing public access for the first time, for fear that the prime minister was threatened.[63] Decades later, in 1984 and 1991, the IRA attempted to assassinate prime ministers, with a large bomb in Brighton during the Conservative Party conference, and then using an improvised mortar to drop three shells on Downing Street. Had one of these seriously wounded Thatcher or Major, medical advances might have kept them alive more successfully than the surgeon attending Perceval.

Counterterrorism became a constant preoccupation of the twenty-first-century prime ministers. During the early part of the century, there was a fear of Al Qaida-style terrorism following the 9/11 attacks on New York. Terrorism did indeed strike Britain in the 7/7 attacks on London in July 2005, which killed fifty-two and coincided with Britain's hosting of the G8 summit at Gleneagles, while a series of attacks in 2017 killed thirty-six. As the head of the nation's security apparatus, the responsibility to protect the country from terror attacks is never far from the prime minister's mind.

Central government was minuscule in size in the eighteenth century, and focused on finance – revenue, customs, excise, and war. In 1797, 84 per cent of officials worked on financial matters. At the end of the Napoleonic Wars in 1815, 20,000 officials were working in revenue departments, up from 2,500 in 1688: one radical MP described it as 'The Thing'.[64] Numbers rose in departments dealing with administration and defence too, from some 150 in 1688, to an estimated 2,500 in 1755. Yet in 1815, the Home Office had just 17 officials, the Foreign Office 30, the Board of Trade 20, and, in 1829, the Treasury had just 82.[65] Prime ministers before the mid nineteenth century had a very different range of duties, before social, economic, and imperial responsibilities were added.

The modern Civil Service, created by Gladstone in 1870 based on the Northcote-Trevelyan report,[66] ensured that the expanded central government overseen by prime ministers was run in a more meritocratic and professional manner. Central government swelled greatly during the First and Second World Wars, seeing a vast influx of statisticians, economists, and scientists, many who remained on after.[67]

Prime ministers continued to govern the country, and the Empire, from the same Downing Street building, albeit less dark, basic and unhealthy, into which Walpole moved in 1735. Few of his successors, though, lived there until Pitt the Younger resumed residency in 1783. Many opted not to live there again after Pitt, until Disraeli moved there in 1877, but only in 1902 did it become established as the permanent home of the prime minister. For much of the mid nineteenth century Number 10 had been dilapidated and was overshadowed by George Gilbert Scott's giant Foreign Office building which opened in 1868. In November 1900, American ambassador Joseph Choate nevertheless was moved to write: 'It is the smallest and at the same time, the greatest street in the world, because it lies at the hub of the gigantic wheel which encircles the globe under the name of the British Empire.'[68] Number 10 today, like the White House and Élysée in Paris, historical buildings also, is bursting apart at the seams, with staff crowded into small rooms if ultra high-tech.

Johnson's Cabinet still meets in the same oblong room overlooking the garden at the back of Number 10, that Walpole is believed to have used. After Cabinet emerged from the Privy Council and King's Council under the control of the monarchy after 1688, ministers slowly shifted their allegiance to the prime minister, with the emergence of the new doctrine of 'collective Cabinet responsibility'. In 1782, almost the entirety of North's government resigned with him, setting the precedent that the fate of the ministry was tied up with that of the *prime minister*. In 1870, the prime minister formally acquired the sole right to call Cabinet meetings, though this had been the custom, but their sole right to remove cabinet ministers from office was not formalised until under Arthur Balfour in 1903. The creation of the Cabinet Secretariat in 1916 under Lloyd George, and the formalisation of Cabinet minutes and agendas, gave the Cabinet a permanence, with the new office intended to serve Cabinet as a whole, rather than just the prime minister.

The legal and constitutional framework under which prime ministers have operated since Walpole has tightened considerably, particularly since 1945. Britain became subject to the European Court of Human Rights, established in 1959 by the Council of Europe, and when it joined the European Economic Community it became subject to a new set of laws. A whole series of constraints, including from devolved assemblies, elected mayors, the growth of judicial review, the House of Lords and House of Commons select committees, codifications including *The Cabinet Manual*, and constitutional watchdogs, hem in the twenty-first-century prime minister. Robert Hazell argues that all these changes have made life 'incredibly challenging' for the prime minister.[69] It is indeed a world apart politically and legally from that of Walpole.

ECONOMIC CHANGES

The economy shaped every single premiership. For Walpole, it was largely agricultural, with significant trading links to the Continent and the Americas. The population of London was estimated to be 675,000; only six other towns in 1750 had over 15,000; Bristol (45,000), Birmingham (24,000), Liverpool (22,000), Manchester (18,000), and Leeds (16,000).[70] London's population by 2010 had grown to 9.3 million and there were seven other cities with over one million.[71] Boris Johnson led a country hyper-connected with high-speed communications and transport. The vast majority were living in urban areas and cities, with only 17 per cent living in rural areas in 2015.[72] In 2021 Britain was the fifth-largest economy in the world, though it had been first for much of the nineteenth and early twentieth centuries.

The agricultural revolution in the mid eighteenth century provided the food which the steadily growing population needed to eat. Potatoes, brought by the Spanish from the New World in the late sixteenth century, were grown by British farmers from the eighteenth century, and were responsible for an estimated 25 per cent increase in population and urbanisation until 1900.[73] Crop rotation techniques created larger and sturdier crops and animal husbandry improved the quality of livestock: the average weight of a cow doubled in the eighteenth century to 800 pounds.[74] By 1850, the transport improvements meant that food and goods could travel more easily to feed urban populations. During the early nineteenth century, political divisions emerged over agricultural laws that favoured producers, including the Corn Laws, which blocked the import of grain and set artificially high prices. Robert

Peel's repealing of those laws during the 1840s was bitterly controversial, splitting the Tories, some of whom railed in defence of tradition and what Disraeli called the 'territorial constitution'.[75]

Over the nineteenth century, the Industrial Revolution transformed Britain into a global powerhouse. Coal production increased eight times to 150 million tonnes from 1750 to 1880, cotton processing for garments twelve times to over 600,000 tonnes, while the production of pig iron increased by twenty-five times to 7.8 million tonnes.[76] By mid century, steel was produced cheaply for steam ships, railways, civil engineering projects, and factory production. The new industries, concentrated in the Midlands, the north of England, London, and Glasgow, created prosperity, work, and higher wages, larger towns, and an industrial working class, with GDP per head rising from £13.85 in 1750 (roughly £1,400 today) to £29.61 in 1870 (over £3,000 today).[77] Once again, political debates were shaped by the changes wrought by industry. Disraeli articulated his concept of 'the Two Nations', divided by wealth and class. Parliament echoed to arguments about factory acts, child labour, regulation, and trade.

By the early twentieth century Britain's economy was losing ground to the growing economies of Germany, the United States, and Japan. From the 1930s, the country witnessed some de-industrialisation, the victim of its own early success, with growth in the new industries of car and aircraft manufacture, the electrical industries, and house-building. Attlee's government nationalised vast sections of the economy, including those that had led the Industrial Revolution: coal, iron, and steel, and the railways. But it and successive governments did little to make them competitive internationally, until in the 1980s Thatcher privatised them in a bid to make them more efficient, resulting in widespread unemployment and industrial strikes. Out of it was born Britain's post-industrial economy, with a thriving professional services and banking sector. Social and economic inequality increased from the 1980s, with rural areas, and towns that had earlier prospered in the Midlands, the north, South Wales, and Scotland suffering severe recession. The resentment helped spread disillusionment with government more generally and fuelled the vote for Brexit in the 2016 referendum and Johnson's determination to 'level up' across the country.

SOCIAL CHANGES IN POLITICS

Historians see power in the hands of a 'clique of propertied aristocratic families', perhaps seventy in number, continuing deep into the nineteenth century.[78] What struck Alexis de Tocqueville, author of *Democracy in America*, most when he visited Britain in the 1830s was the virile survival of its landed aristocracy. As historian S. J. D. Green put it, 'peers of the realm dominated at court. Men of rank prevailed in the King's government and over its representative institutions' well into the nineteenth century.[79] Three quarters of the House of Commons at the time of the second Reform Act in 1867 were aristocrats. Between 1721 and 1806, PMs sat in the Lords for only seventeen years, but between 1806 and 1902, they sat in the Lords for fifty-six years.

The composition of Parliament changed during the nineteenth century with each new Reform Act. The Parliament Act of 1911 gave MPs a salary for the first time (£400 a year), meaning that professional people without independent income could at last afford to stand. This, together with the emergence of trade unions over the late nineteenth century, broadened the composition of the House of Commons as more working-class MPs were elected. Upper- and middle-class influence, though, remained deep into the twentieth century and beyond. The radical government of Attlee had public school alumni in many dominant positions, including Attlee himself and all his three Chancellors. Churchill's government during the Second World War came from similar backgrounds,[80] while a third of the first Cabinet of Harold Macmillan were either related to him or had attended Eton, or both. Two of the five prime ministers since 1997 attended Eton, Cameron and Johnson, and one, Blair, the 'Scottish Eton', Fettes.

All PMs between 1964 and 1997 were state educated and two did not attend university at all (Callaghan and Major). Theresa May was educated at Holton grammar school, which turned into a comprehensive, Wheatley Park, while she was there (and was briefly educated at an independent, St Juliana's Convent). The recent trend does not therefore necessarily mark a clear pivoting back to the days of a privileged minority ascending to the office of prime minister. The Leader of the Opposition Keir Starmer also attended a state grammar school, as did Johnson's de jure deputy, Dominic

Raab. But Chancellor Sunak attended the independent school Winchester, and Gove the independent Robert Gordon's.

Walpole may have attended Eton, but he was from Norfolk minor gentry, not the wealthier aristocratic families like Cope, Townshend, or the Graftons. Pelham, Pitt the Elder, Fox, and Pitt the Younger were all second sons who didn't inherit the principal title, while Liverpool's father had been a civil servant.[81] Both Peel and Gladstone were provincials with Lancashire business antecedents and had country estates well outside the south east. Robert Blake divides prime ministers into 'insiders' and 'outsiders', with Canning, Addington, Peel, Disraeli, Lloyd George, and MacDonald cast as outsiders and, by implication, most others until 1975, his publication date, insiders.[82]

Despite Lloyd George and MacDonald coming from more humble origins, the grip of the establishment remained strong. Johnson was the twentieth prime minister to be educated at Eton (36 per cent of the total), while forty-two of the fifty-five went to Oxford or Cambridge (twenty-eight from Oxford alone), with nine educated at Eton and Christ Church, Oxford, the second richest college and the one with the strongest aristocratic connections.[83] Only ten prime ministers have been educated at non-fee-paying schools, including all five from the socially egalitarian era 1964–97. Henry Campbell-Bannerman (34th, 1905–8) was the first prime minister to attend a non-fee-paying school, the High School of Glasgow, the same school that Andrew Bonar Law attended (it became independent in 1976).

'There are three bodies no sensible man directly challenges', Macmillan is reputed to have said, listing the Catholic Church ahead of the 'Brigade of Guards' and the National Union of Mineworkers.[84] But for many years before Macmillan, prime ministers had ceased to regard religion in any form as a major concern, outside Ireland. Following the violent disputes of the sixteenth and seventeenth centuries, religious divisions had calmed in Britain by 1700, in contrast to many European countries. As Linda Colley has argued, national identity requires an enemy and an 'other': in Britain's case the 'other' increasingly was France, while the 'enemy' was Catholicism, which helped bind together Britain as a clearly Protestant state. Britain's island nature, with a strong navy rather than a mass army, and it being a 'metropole' were the other features of British identity which she argues united the nation and set it apart.[85]

Religious concerns for prime ministers after 1721 often centred on Ireland and Catholicism. The Test Acts of 1673 and 1678, which discriminated against non-Protestants holding office and gaining admission to Oxford or Cambridge, had fallen out of favour before being repealed in 1828. Anti-Catholic laws were being dismantled from the 1760s, this time with far more controversy, with Pitt the Younger having to resign over George III's opposition to plans for emancipation. Later, Wellington would work to pass the Catholic Emancipation Act of 1829 that removed most of the remaining restrictions on Catholics (though not all), despite hostility from both the House of Lords and the king.

Jewish emancipation also proved divisive. Pelham passed a law for Jewish emancipation in 1753, but anti-Semitic agitation caused him to repeal it the following year. Only gradually in the nineteenth century were laws against Jews holding office dismantled. Not until 1858 was Lionel de Rothschild finally allowed to sit in the Commons as the first Jewish MP: by that time, Disraeli, a baptised Christian of Jewish parents, was already an MP.

The bond between Anglicanism and the Tories/Conservative Party,[86] and between non-conformity and the Liberals, slowly waned in the twentieth century. While the latter dwindled with the eclipse of the Liberals, the former bond, with the adage that Anglicanism represented 'the Conservative Party at prayer',[87] lasted longer, while never very influential on policy formation.[88] James Beckford concludes that 'the fact that all major religious groups drew members from a variety of social classes and backgrounds ... helped to prevent religion from becoming a political issue in itself'.[89] Even as religious belief declined, prime ministers continued, for reasons of conviction and optics, to profess their faith, with Ramsay MacDonald a rare exception, declaring himself a humanist, and a supporter of the British Ethical Movement. In recent years, the decline in religiosity has accelerated, with 25.1 per cent of the English and Welsh population proclaiming no faith in the 2011 census, up from 14.8 per cent in 2001.[90]

Immigration profoundly shaped politics during the twentieth century, with ethnicity becoming a much more pressing concern for the British prime minister than religion. Whereas for Walpole immigration was effect-ively zero, for all prime ministers from Macmillan it was a major political issue, with 14 per cent of the UK population by 2020 from an ethnic minority background, and backlash never far away.[91]

The first major group to come into the UK in the last 300 years was Jews escaping from persecution in Europe during the late nineteenth century. The first legislation aimed at curbing immigration, the Aliens Act, was passed in 1905, allowing officials to bar entry to 'undesirable' immigrants.[92] There was a further wave of Jewish refugees during the 1930s. Large numbers of Poles fled from Poland during and after the Second World War. In the 1951 census the Polish-born population in the UK was 162,000, up from 45,000 in 1931. The British Nationality Act of 1948 passed by the Attlee government granted subjects of the British Empire the right to come and live and work in the UK. That year, the SS *Empire Windrush* arrived, bearing 693 migrants from the Caribbean, the beginning of a new phase of immigration. In 1962 tighter controls were placed on immigration from the Commonwealth, with an average of 72,000 p.a. coming throughout the 1970s, including a surge of East African-Asians from Uganda and Kenya. Immigration increased after 1998, peaking at 164,000 in 2004, and rose further again when eight Eastern European countries joined the European Union that year. By mid 2016, at the time of the EU referendum, annual net immigration had reached 330,000.[93] Even though only 55 per cent of these came from the EU, it was a powerful factor in voting in the EU referendum, with the desire to cut numbers a key theme of May's premiership (2016–19) as it had been of her time as Home Secretary (2010–16).[94]

Britain has yet to have an ethnic minority prime minister. Although supposedly Lord Liverpool had an Indian great-grandmother, Disraeli, who converted from Judaism to Anglicanism at the age of twelve, and Boris Johnson, with his Turkish great-grandfather, are the closest the country has come. Johnson's Cabinet in January 2021 contained four members from an ethnic minority background, including Chancellor Rishi Sunak, though just 10 per cent of the 2019 Parliament came from such a background.[95]

Women's issues had little direct impact on the PM for most of the 300 years. The Chartists from 1838–57 had pressed for universal *male* suffrage, but women's suffrage groups began to spread rapidly and campaign from the 1860s. Another fifty years passed before women gained the vote in parliamentary elections in 1918, and only on equal terms with men in 1928. Conservative aristocrat Nancy Astor was the first woman MP to take her seat in the House of Commons, from 1919–45, but with her anti-semitic and anti-Catholic views, had little to do with the prime minister. Constance Markievicz was the first woman to be elected, but as an Irish Republican, did not take her seat.

Margaret Bondfield was the first female Cabinet minister, appointed Minister of Labour by Ramsay MacDonald from 1929–31. It would be almost fifteen years before another woman was appointed to Cabinet, Ellen Wilkinson as Minister of Education from 1945–7, followed by Florence Horsbrugh, appointed as Minister of Education by Churchill (in error) in 1951.[96] Thatcher's own first ministerial experience was, indicatively, as Education Secretary (1970–4), the only woman in Heath's Cabinet.

Britain may have had only two monarchs out of fourteen since 1721 who were female, Queen Victoria and Elizabeth II, but they ruled for 133 years, well over a *third* of the life of the prime ministers. Britain's two female prime ministers, Margaret Thatcher and Theresa May, in contrast were in office for 14 years and 5 months, under 5 per cent of the time. The embedded maleness of Westminster proved resistant to change, even by Labour, which has yet to appoint a female leader. Prime ministers did little before Major to encourage women's promotion in Downing Street. When Caroline Slocock applied to become the first woman in Prime Minister Margaret Thatcher's Private Office, she learnt that a note had gone round Whitehall to say there was no point in submitting female candidates because she would not appoint them.[97] At the time, there was only one woman in the Number 10 Policy Unit, Carolyn Sinclair. Its head, Brian Griffiths (1985–90), wishing to hire another, asked the prime minister what her thoughts were: 'Brian, I think we should wait to see how the first one does, don't you?' Thatcher replied. 'Thatcher was comfortable in the male world of politics in which she had risen', Slocock remembers. 'She liked to work with men, particularly tall, military types with big voices who were like Denis [Thatcher]. She did argue publicly for more senior women but in practice she did not warm to them.' Major, who brought in Sarah Hogg as his policy head, was 'younger, more relaxed and you could tell instantly he liked working with women'.[98] Rod Rhodes says:

> Quite how far the two female prime ministers changed the position of women by dint of their gender is a moot point. It's a long-established political game at Westminster and Whitehall, where everyone knows the rules and learns them quickly, that the rules are written by men, and for women to succeed, they have to take on the behaviours and characteristics of their successful male counterparts.[99]

Nevertheless, there have been since the 1960s key female advisors in Number 10. One of the most influential was the first, Harold Wilson's powerful political secretary Marcia Williams (1964–70 and 1974–6). Anji Hunter (1997–2001) was senior advisor to Tony Blair, who referred to her as an 'outstanding operative' and 'solid voice for Middle England' in his memoir.[100] Kate Fall (2010–16) was known as Cameron's 'gatekeeper' and was Deputy Chief of Staff. By early 2021, Munira Mirza ran Downing Street's Policy Unit and Allegra Stratton was the PM's press secretary, and with Carrie Symonds also, women had never been in such a commanding position in Number 10.

John Major was responsible for appointing the first openly gay man to the Private Office in 1991, hitherto seen by the intelligence agencies as a security risk due to the potential for blackmail. Only in more recent years have openly LGBTQ employees become more common in Whitehall.[101]

Number 10 has not been at the forefront, either, of ethnic diversity. Cameron had Rohan Silva as his Deputy Chief of Staff, Ameet Gill as head of strategy, and Sam Gyimah as his PPS for a year. But progress to date of BAME people in senior posts, especially black people, has been glacial.

MEDIA AND CULTURAL CHANGES

Walpole's obsession with his public image, and his desire to influence it, were every bit as intense as Johnson's, even if the range of media forming an opinion of him, at home and abroad, was considerably narrower.

When appointed in 1721, there were an estimated twelve London news-papers and twenty-four provincial titles, which had flourished after the expiring in 1695 of the last Press Licensing Act of 1662. Newspapers were *local*: the first British daily newspaper, the *Daily Courant*, was not published until 1702, followed by the *Edinburgh Courant* in 1705. None of the outlets that scrutinised Johnson so minutely had been established, but they followed in rapid succession from Pitt the Younger's time with *The Times* (1785, published under the name *The Daily Universal Register* until 1788), *The Observer* (1781, the world's first Sunday newspaper), *The Scotsman* (1817), *The Manchester Guardian* (1821), *The Daily Telegraph* (1855), *The Daily Mail* (1896), and *The Daily Herald* (1912, renamed *The Sun* in 1964).[102] The era of the mass-circulation press, made possible by the railway, had arrived. It gave the press great power. Palmerston was the first prime minister to make cultivation of it a principal call on his time, while Colin Matthew dates Gladstone's first courting of the press, in the form of reporters from the *Daily Telegraph*, to the 1860s.[103]

Initially, government sought to discourage the press with prosecutions for libel and with stamp duties. Those who ignored the duty were pros-ecuted, and a campaign began to end the 'tax on knowledge', culminat-ing in Parliament removing the duty in stages during the 1850s and 1860s. Before then, *The Times* had been influential in the rise of Peel. Attempts to manage the press became an inevitable preoccupation of prime ministers, as ownership concentrated in the hands of a few wealthy (and opinionated) owners. Lord Northcliffe, owner of *The Daily Mail* and *The Daily Mirror*, was the first to attract widespread attention from the 1900s. He was uninhibited in seeing his titles reflect his views. A supporter of Lloyd George, he ordered his editors in December 1916 to publish the 'worst possible picture' of the failing Prime Minister Asquith, and 'a smiling image' of Lloyd George under the caption 'DO IT NOW'.[104] Pressure on Number 10 from proprietors was incessant in the interwar years, on topics as diverse as Empire, free trade, the General Strike, the abdication crisis, and the threat from Hitler and Mussolini.[105] Tony Blair may have said his number one opposition was 'the press', but any predecessor could have said the same in the previous hundred years.

Photography saw British inventors William Fox Talbot and John Herschel make significant advances in the 1830s.[106] This allowed prime ministers to become more recognisable figures in their own right, with wood-engraved images (sometimes based on photographs) appearing commonly in papers from the 1860s, and photographs from the 1880s.[107] As Bruce Coleman has put it, these images 'by the 1870s had taken the office of PM and its meaning beyond the old haunts of St James's, the Houses of Parliament and the great country houses out across the country'.[108]

The interwar years saw the rise of radio, another device that prime minsters sought to control. When Baldwin first became prime minister in 1922, there were 22,000 radio licences. By the time he left office in 1937, there were 8.5 million.[109] Hennessy pinpoints the beginning of the 'mediafication' of the British premiership to Baldwin's first radio broadcast in a general election, on 16 October 1924, as Leader of the Opposition. He also exploited his 'fireside manner' to great effect on radio as prime minister in the General Strike of 1926.[110] Nick Robinson writes that 'Stanley Baldwin was the first to appreciate that the [radio] gave him access to practically every voter in the country.'[111] The foundation of the BBC in the 1920s posed less of a threat to prime ministers, given its commitment, unlike the press, to impartiality. But it posed as great an opportunity for influence, which no successful prime minister could afford to ignore.

Cinema was expanding rapidly in parallel, affording fresh opportunities for influence. In 1929, the year before the first all-sound British film was released, 91 feature films were produced in Britain. By 1935 the number had risen to 225. By the 1930s, half the British public over the age of fourteen was going to the cinema at least once a week, with the number of cinema tickets sold weekly was twenty-five times that for football matches.[112] Newsreels had been first shown at the cinema between feature films from 1910, with *Pathé Gazette* and *Gaumont Graphic* producing silent films, and the first British sound newsreel, *British Movitone News*, appearing in June 1929. By the early to mid 1930s, the newsreel style had become established, offering listeners commentary with musical accompaniment. Baldwin was again the first prime minister to recognise the propaganda value of his appearances. They continued to be a popular and important source of mass news coverage until the mid to late 1950s, when television news began to take over.[113]

Broadcasting equipment was installed in Number 10 for the first time under Chamberlain in August 1938: 'These facilities both at Number 10 Downing Street and at the Office of Works are really for the purpose of enabling reassuring messages etc to be sent out by the Head of the Government in the time of emergency' declared an official document.[114] One year later, at 11.15 a.m. on Sunday 3 September 1939, Chamberlain sat in the Cabinet Room to read out on the BBC 'Home Service' his statement to the nation: 'This country is at war with Germany.'[115]

In 1931, MacDonald, who had suffered a terrible battering from the press in the 1923 and 1929 general elections, as well as in 1924 over the Zinoviev letter, decided he needed better protection, and appointed George Steward as Number 10's first 'press secretary'. Fixing times for Westminster 'lobby correspondents' to be briefed was one of his duties.[116] But the press advisor position did not become fixed until after 1945, when Attlee appointed Francis Williams, a journalist who had worked in the Ministry of Information during the war, as 'Advisor on Public Relations'. Williams defended his appointment to the Royal Commission on the Press in 1947: 'It is perfectly possible and proper for a Government to do what it can to secure newspaper ... support for its policies.'[117] When Churchill returned in October 1951, he was sceptical about the need – he had his own direct lines to the press lords Beaverbrook, Bracken, and Camrose – before eventually appointing Fife Clark as 'Advisor on Public Relations'. The post then became entrenched as 'press secretary' with Eden's appointment of William Clark (who resigned over Suez), and Macmillan's appointment of Harold Evans (not to be confused with the newspaper editor).[118]

Macmillan leant heavily on Evans's skill and understanding of television. During the 1959 general election, Evans ensured a broadcast of Macmillan opened with a panning shot of him at his Number 10 desk, to give the impression of a prime minister at ease with power.[119] Wilson was the first prime minister to arrive in Number 10 with a modern understanding of the power of the media, having seen first-hand Francis Williams operate under Attlee. He appointed journalist Trevor Lloyd-Hughes in 1964, and then the savvy Joe Haines in 1969, who returned to Number 10 with him from 1974–6. The most influential media advisors since have been Bernard Ingham, who served from 1979–90 throughout

Thatcher's period, Alastair Campbell, who worked with Tony Blair from 1997–2001, and Craig Oliver under Cameron (2011–16).[120] Johnson's appointment of Allegra Stratton in October 2020 to host an innovation of daily press conferences, in emulation of the White House, is just the latest attempt by the prime minister to shape the way the media report what they do to the electorate.

The rise of social media and the internet in the twenty-first century, with 96 per cent of households in the UK having internet access by February 2020, up from 57 per cent in 2006, required further adjustments in the way that prime ministers conducted themselves. By 2021, millions of Johnson's fellow citizens received news from alerts and websites on their phones, rather than from newspapers or television news.[121] Boris Johnson, like Blair and Cameron, was thoroughly at ease in the burgeoning world of 24-hour news coverage, unlike Major, Brown, and Theresa May, who were damaged by their lack of mastery of it.

Prime ministers have rarely been able to control their environments or external factors that have impacted on them, as we have seen repeatedly in this chapter. Those prime ministers who have flourished, in a Darwinian sense, have learnt best how to adapt and to turn these ever-changing factors to their advantage.

CHAPTER 3

The Liminal Premiership

From the Saxons to 1806

THE PRIME MINISTER WAS NOT PREDESTINED TO APPEAR IN British history in 1721. The job Walpole came to fill that year had been intermittently done for 750 years by forerunners, called here 'chief ministers' for simplicity's sake. First, we need to understand the similarities of this earlier post, and the differences, to the job of 'prime minister'. We then look at why events from 1688 are so critical to understanding why the job appeared in *1721*. Walpole's long period in office embedded the new post, but a certain contingency continued for four decades after he ceased to be prime minister. Only with the arrival of William Pitt the Younger (14th, 1783–1801, 1804–6) did the office of prime minister become a secure fixture in British politics.

CHIEF MINISTERS, 924–1688

Under King Aethelstan (r. 924–39), the first to rule over the whole of England, leading courtiers emerged as a kind of early medieval equivalent of government ministers, and so Dunstan can be considered the first 'chief minister', an unofficial term used by Clive Bigham who wrote about these figures during the 1920s. An influential force also with Aethelstan's successor, King Edmund (r. 939–46), Dunstan became Bishop of London and then Archbishop of Canterbury, before being canonised. As an advisor to the monarch, he helped oversee the conduct of government.

Bigham argues though that the supreme survivor Godwin had a greater claim to be considered Britain's first 'chief minister', rising meteorically to Earl of Wessex under King Cnut (r. 1017–35), and retaining his power for most of the period under Cnut's successors Harold I (r. 1035–40) and

Harthacnut (r. 1040–2), and then into the first ten years of the reign of Edward the Confessor (r. 1042–66).[1] But, to consider Godwin a 'minister' in any modern sense is to mischaracterise his role: Godwin was a powerful magnate, loyal to Cnut personally (rather than the Crown, 'England', or its people). Upon the king's death in 1035, Godwin chose to support Cnut's illegitimate son Harold, who became king until 1040, rather than his legitimate son Harthacnut, going so far as to murder another 'legitimate' claimant of the throne (Alfred, son of Ethelread the Unready), to curry favour with Harold.[2] It is a testament less to Godwin's office, and more to his power base and personality, that he was able to enjoy such leading status when Harthacnut came to the throne in 1040, and again with Edward the Confessor from 1042. Godwin even arranged for his daughter to marry Edward. Moreover, his son, having inherited the Wessex power base, seized the throne for himself in 1066, as Harold II (r. 1066), a move we have yet to see from any modern prime minister.

In Dunstan and Godwin, we see two very different kinds of leading courtier, models of which are seen throughout the medieval and early modern periods: on the one hand a cleric and administrator, lending advice from a bishopric (a minister); and on the other, a powerful magnate, looking to dominate a king as much as advise him (a lord). The Norman and Angevin periods saw a distinct new pressure upon kings, namely that they had lands on either side of the Channel and could not be in two places at once, so a competent and reliable 'deputy', who was a good financier and administrator, was required. The first leading example of this was Odo of Bayeux, half-brother of William I (r. 1066–87), whose ill-defined set of duties included sometimes filling in as regent of England, or otherwise accompanying William to the Continent if required. A warrior, a bishop, and an Earl, Odo was perhaps one of a kind in how he operated fluidly for the king's requirements, until he fell from grace in 1076 having defrauded the Crown, and was imprisoned for the rest of William's reign.[3]

Following Odo (perhaps *because* of Odo), a more formal role for the king's leading deputy developed, in the shape of what is more recognisably a chief minister. The Justiciar (later 'Chief Justiciar') emerged as a broadly equivalent position to a prime minister.[4] The first proto-Justiciars are considered to be Ranulf Flambard, Bishop of Durham, who served under William II (r. 1087–1100), and his immediate replacement, Roger, Bishop of Salisbury, who served under Henry I (r. 1100–35) and briefly under Stephen (r. 1135–54). Roger was definitively the most powerful figure below the king (despite being a cleric, not a lord), though never being called 'Justiciar' in his lifetime.[5] The role enjoyed a lifespan of nearly two centuries, with one of the last truly influential holders of the office demonstrating how tenuous the position still was: Hubert de Burgh was appointed Justiciar 'for life' under Henry III (r. 1216–72) in 1228 and then resigned six years later, with the office remaining empty until 1258, eventually disappearing for good from 1265.[6] Simon de Montfort, for a time de facto ruler of the country, can be considered the 'chief minister' despite not holding the title of Justiciar, from 1263–5, under Henry III. He was responsible for calling two famous parliaments in 1258 and 1265, the first stripping Henry of unlimited authority and the second including both knights and non-nobles from every county and major town in England for the first time.

From the high Middle Ages to early sixteenth century, the Chancellor was increasingly likely to be the chief minister. After all, he had substantial access to patronage, oversight of the Royal Clerks, and was Keeper of the king's 'Great Seal', which signalled his approval on official documents. Thomas Becket, Lord Chancellor from 1155 until he became archbishop of Canterbury in 1162, can be considered chief minister, overseeing the financial business of Henry II (r. 1154–89) and ensuring that his administration ran effectively. William of Wykeham was another Lord Chancellor (and cleric, as Bishop of Winchester) who effectively acted as chief minister under Edward III (r. 1327–77) and Richard II (r. 1377–99). Finally, the powerful Richard Neville, 'Warwick the King Maker', functioned as a chief minister for the first ten years of the reign of Edward IV (r. 1461–70, 1471–83), with his brother, George Neville, the Archbishop of York, as Lord Chancellor. This was during the 'Wars of the Roses' between the York and Lancastrian branches of the Plantagenets. Perhaps more in the image of Godwin than a ministerial Justiciar, or even a modern prime minister, Warwick fell out with Edward over the latter's secret marriage to the commoner Elizabeth Woodville. Warwick had favoured a marriage agreement with France, and Edward's decision had been kept from him. This, and the growing strength of the new

Woodville faction at court, eventually caused Warwick to depose Edward and restore Henry VI (1422–61, 1470–1) to the throne, before Edward seized power again, killing Warwick in battle in the process.

The 'Treasurer' gradually replaced the Chancellor from the mid sixteenth century, because of the expansion of trade and wealth, and a firmer establishment of Parliament, and the need of the king to have a powerful figure controlling royal finances. Whether called Justiciar, Chancellor, Treasurer, or simply first man in the kingdom, the position of the chief minister was perilous, as Bigham describes:

> Nearly always he was the friend of the King, rarely the champion of the people. His duties were arduous, his tenure insecure, his favour fleeting, his fate hazardous. Officially his post was never recognised nor were his privileges defined, though his penalties were only too well known. To run such risks required great rewards, and while few Chief Ministers abjured rank and riches, many met with an unhappy end. Yet they went on increasing in frequency, gradually forming a tradition which influenced those who worked with and those who came after them. At last they became a regular feature of the government until they were replaced by the modern Premiers.[7]

With the Tudor dynasty from 1485, we move into a new phase of chief ministers, edging, if only very slowly, closer to the prime minister as it emerged from 1721. Cardinal and Archbishop of Canterbury, John Morton was Lord Chancellor to Henry VII (r. 1485–1509), who charged him with building up the royal finances after the Wars of the Roses, and whose capricious tax policy ('Morton's Fork') proved remarkably successful at replenishing the royal Treasury.[8] His power was completely outstripped by Thomas Wolsey, also an Archbishop (of York), Cardinal and Lord Chancellor, who became all-powerful during his fourteen years as the chief minister, overseeing the finances, administration, foreign policy, relations with the Church, and love life of Henry VIII (r. 1509–47). He too was eclipsed, by his protégé Thomas Cromwell, effectively chief minister from 1532–40, serving as Principal Secretary, Royal Chancellor, Master of the Rolls, Lord Privy Seal, and Lord Great Chamberlain, an unprecedented achievement for a man who was neither noble, nor cleric, but simply a lawyer. Cromwell biographer Diarmaid MacCulloch is sceptical about seeing Cromwell as a proto-'prime minister'; he had some greater powers and others considerably less than prime ministers, including his utter dependence upon the monarch, and lack of a clear power base in Parliament.[9]

The range of Cromwell's activities in his eight years was nevertheless extraordinary, driving through the break with Rome and the Protestant Reformation, the dissolution of the monasteries, helping bring Wales into a union with England in 1536, and overseeing Henry's attempt to conquer Ireland by the Crown of Ireland Act in 1541, which declared Henry and his heirs to be kings of Ireland. Cromwell took great risks, acting as the henchman for the murder of many of Henry's enemies, building up his own factions, as with the Greys and the Seymours, and going behind Henry's back, as with the William Tyndale Bible and fostering the Zurich style of Protestantism, which Henry disliked.[10] Few prime ministers subsequently had his personal impact. Robert Tombs describes him as 'one of the most remarkable men to ever have held high political office in England'.[11]

Elizabeth I's (r. 1558–1603) chief minister, William Cecil, Lord Burghley, served from her succession in 1558 until his death in 1598. He was Secretary of State from 1588–72, then Lord High Treasurer for the rest of his life, combining the position of Lord Privy Seal for his last eight years. He shaped Elizabeth's entire domestic and foreign policy, notably completing the subjugation of Ireland and building an alliance with Scotland. His son, Robert Cecil, the first Earl of Salisbury, succeeded him as chief minister to Elizabeth, serving as Secretary of State from 1596, and Lord Privy Seal, remaining in office under the first Stuart monarch, James I (r. 1603–25), until his own death in 1612. George Villiers, the Duke of Buckingham, emerged as the king's favourite and chief minister from 1616, and remained with Charles I (r. 1625–49) until his murder in 1628. Charles I, unlike other Stuart monarchs, preferred to rule without anyone resembling a chief minister, apart from a brief period with Strafford, from 1638–40.

Oliver Cromwell is the only commoner, apart from his son Richard, in English history to be both head of state and head of government. As Lord Protector from 1653 until his death in 1658, he oversaw every aspect of politics, religion, and the military. Historian of Cromwell's regime, Paul

Lay, says: 'He is more like a prime minister than either a president or a monarch', and argues that he had more authority than the eighteenth-century prime ministers, given the tremendous centralisation of power into his person and hoarding of wealth into the centre, with all the opportunities for corruption it afforded.[12] Cromwell's regime was absolutist in comparison, with the judiciary marginalised, opponents jailed, and the 'Barebones' parliament purged in July 1653, before being dispensed with in December. There were limits, though, on Cromwell's power. The 'Instrument of Government', Britain's only written constitution, placed power in not only the 'Protector', Cromwell, but a small 'Council of State' as well, which was the governing authority, full of political and military figures, and operated under great secrecy. Cromwell's legitimacy was not derived from being head of state, nor did it come from Parliament, but rested upon his military leadership, and his belief, shared by many around him, that he was doing God's work.

Few imagined in the mid 1650s, when Cromwell's rule seemed so secure, that the Protectorate would not endure. Had it done so, Britain might have continued as a republic, joining Venice and the Netherlands in Europe, 120 years ahead of the United States, and 140 years ahead of France. But Cromwell's Protectorate lacked deep institutional roots, evident when he died, and his son Richard became Lord Protector. Without his father's talent, self-belief, and cold command, the essentially personal British republic unravelled. Civil and military factions fell out, Parliament divided over religion and the return of the monarchy, and, facing revolt, Richard Cromwell renounced power after nine months. And in 1660, the unthinkable happened: the monarchy was restored, with Charles II (r. 1660–85) becoming king.

But the monarchy that was restored was not the same. Never again would it exercise the authority of Henry VIII, or Elizabeth I, or James I, who in his *True Law of Free Monarchies* wrote of the 'Divine Right of Kings' that 'even by God himself they are called Gods'.[13] Periodically before 1649, but now here to stay, was the idea that the monarchy would rule in a balanced constitution with the Houses of Lords and Commons. In certain areas, the king could now only act with the consent of Parliament. Over his ministers, though, the king, not Parliament, had total authority: they were appointed by him, and responsible to him alone. 'Parliament looked upon the

Ministers with considerable suspicion ... they were enemies, not friends. They represented the King in any conflict over policy', wrote Byrum Carter.[14]

The chief minister post was restored too in 1660. Edward Hyde, first Earl of Clarendon, who had served as chief advisor to Charles I in the 1640s, became Charles II's Lord Chancellor until 1667. Like eighteenth-century prime ministers, he was *primus inter pares* among other ministers but did not have a great impact on the strong-willed monarch.[15] Clarendon too was deeply suspicious of the idea of a 'prime minister', believing it would be better if an absolute monarch returned, rather than Britain having a 'lawful monarch who ruled through a Prime Minister'.[16] Under him, a ministerial committee for foreign affairs was established, an important step towards the emergence of the Cabinet in the eighteenth century.[17]

THE ROAD TO THE PRIME MINISTER, 1688–1721

The 1688 revolution, the Bill of Rights of 1689, and subsequent Acts, as seen, were fatal blows to any lingering notions of absolute monarchy, making it clear that sovereignty lay in Parliament. The prime minister emerged as the direct consequence. The question is, why did it take over three decades for this to happen?

The answer lies partly in the two monarchs themselves, William III (r. 1689–1702) and Anne (r. 1702–14), who were both stronger and more assertive figures than George I (r. 1714–27) and George II (r. 1727–60) who followed them. William had accepted that the Declaration of Right was a prerequisite for his succession to the throne, enshrining a political system that required the king, the Lords, and the Commons to work together to govern. Nevertheless, William was an energetic and ambitious king, who continued in the belief of earlier Stuart monarchs that ministers were responsible to him alone, not to Parliament. He sought active control over government, attending many sessions of the emerging Cabinet Council, taking a keen interest in the appointment of ministers, and ensuring his will prevailed over them. He came to realise, however, that the post-1688 dispensation meant that, if he was to get his way, he should choose ministers best able to secure the support of Parliament.[18] Because of his determination to devise policy himself, Peter Jupp argues there was no single ministerial leader before Godolphin emerged in 1702, but rather 'dummy heads' such as Carmarthen from 1690–3, or collective leadership from 1693–1702, or 'duumvirs' of two men.[19]

Queen Anne from 1702 shared a similar outlook to William. She considered ministers to be personal servants, responsible to her personally and not to Parliament, and she too attended meetings of Cabinet Council, which began to meet regularly, often once a week. Many aspects of its operation, though, remained unclear, including what business came to it, which issues the monarch could decide themselves, and what the attendance at the meeting should be. Anne's first ministry was predominantly Tory and High Church, even though Parliament was predominantly Whig. She later brought in Whigs, but in 1710 they refused to serve in Cabinet with Tories, so she was compelled to form a Cabinet without them. This prompted the Whigs to coalesce into a more coherent unit while the Tories were undergoing the same process.

The Tory Lord Godolphin, who was Lord High Treasurer from 1702, emerged as Anne's leading minister, albeit in a duumvirate with Marlborough from 1702–8, and then on his own from 1708–9. He had some of the powers of a prime minister, exercising substantial control over patronage, some direction over the Cabinet Council, and took some decisions on his own. But on matters of foreign policy and key domestic matters, Anne herself decided. His power moreover remained wholly dependent on the monarch, not Parliament, nor was he ever in any sense in control of Cabinet. Anne summarily dismissed him in 1709: 'The many unkind returns I have received since – especially what you said to me personally before the Lords – make it impossible for me to continue with you any longer in my service'.[20]

Robert Harley, who was Chancellor from 1710–11, and then Lord High Treasurer until 1714, emerged as a more decisive figure than Godolphin, and was described by his contemporary Jonathan Swift as 'Prime Minister'.[21] He had more authority over appointments, and more responsibility than Godolphin for government decisions. But again, his power rested upon the monarch, as did the position and power of ministers. To circumvent it, he instituted a series of Saturday night dinners, allowing him to converse with senior ministers away from the queen, and decide who should be invited to this 'inner group' of ministers.[22]

Anne rejected any notion that she needed a 'prime minister': she regarded herself as her own prime minister, taking her own decisions, as when she vetoed the Scottish Militia Bill in 1708, or ennobled twelve Tory peers to ensure the House of Lords would assent to the Peace of Utrecht in 1711. The Whigs had strongly resisted the treaty, furious at a peace agreement with France that they considered overly lenient. She pursued, equally strongly, policies leading to the Act of Union of 1707, described as a 'personal triumph' for her.[23]

Had the dominating Anne not died in 1714, the Whig Walpole probably would not have emerged as prime minister seven years later. The Hanoverian succession was a major victory for the Whigs. The new king, not unfairly, suspected the Tories of having Jacobite tendencies, hankering after a return of the Stuarts. Therefore, George I was all the more dependent on just the Whigs, an essential prerequisite for the prime minister to emerge. George I, and his son George II, were not William III and Anne. Their royal house was alien to Britain, they spoke German, with a slender grasp of English, and remained emotionally attached to Hanover. They preferred to live in Kensington Palace, distant from Westminster, and the main home of the monarchy after fire destroyed Whitehall Palace during the 1690s.

Walpole, who, thanks to his Tory opponents, had spent six months imprisoned in the Tower of London during Anne's reign, was a beneficiary of George I's succession. Initially appointed chair of a committee to investigate the actions of the previous Tory ministry, he was promoted to Chancellor of the Exchequer and First Lord of the Treasury in 1715, though he resigned in 1717. An administration emerged led by Lord Townshend, then one led jointly by James Stanhope and Charles Spencer, Earl of Sunderland. Either might have become the first prime minister, were it not for a set of events in quick succession. A split in the Whigs helped Walpole, who led the faction out of power, then the South Sea Bubble saw the humiliation and departure of Sunderland, and then, with the death of Stanhope in 1721, the stage was clear.

Walpole's emergence has to be seen equally against the background of a number of long-term trends, including the weakening power of the monarch, the strengthening of Parliament, the rise of more cohesive political groupings, the greater coalescence of the Cabinet Council, and the slow formation of the United Kingdom. Monarchs in the past had periodically needed chief ministers to provide leadership for their government in their absence. But the money needed to fight the regular wars from the fifteenth to the eighteenth century led to the emergence of a financial and military apparatus in central government, which needed skilful oversight. Wars also required higher taxes, which could only be passed by Parliament, making leadership in the Commons vital. Financial institutions developed to facilitate this process, including the Bank of England (1694) and national debt, which gave new powers to the First Lord of the Treasury and Chancellor of the Exchequer as the key figure in government overseeing national finances. This process, the creation of what John Brewer called 'the fiscal-military state', played a vital part in the emergence of the prime minister.[24]

So what differentiated the chief minister from the prime minister? Put simply it was *autonomy* from the monarch. As we have seen, Walpole had a wide degree of independent authority. As Paul Lay encapsulates it:

> I wouldn't consider Thomas Wolsey or Thomas Cromwell to be prime ministers because they don't have the economic stability or independent power that Walpole and figures subsequently had. The Chief Ministers were there at the whim of the monarch and their job was to ensure the survival of the dynasty. That is the job of Wolsey and Thomas Cromwell and it is their failure to provide that which undoes them. These Chief Ministers might be important, but they're not remotely independent of the ambitions of the monarch, and their need to establish a succession.[25]

TWELVE INCOMPLETE PRIME MINISTERS: COMPTON TO PORTLAND, 1742–83

None of the twelve prime ministers from 1742 to 1783 between Walpole and Pitt the Younger approached Walpole in ability or authority. The figure who came closest, William Pitt the Elder (9th, 1766–8), lasted just two years and seventy-six days, and had been much more prominent as Southern Secretary from 1756–61. Walpole had survived all but twenty-one years in office, but none of his immediate antecedents, including Godolphin and Harley, had survived so long, and such a long period in office was entirely unexpected, not least by Walpole himself. The gnawing insecurity of his position, rather than any aura of permanence, contrasted with the monarch, who knew that he would hold office until death. Challenges from fellow Whigs, loss of confidence from the monarch, as when George II succeeded in 1727, and the constant threat of attack, illness, and incapacity stalked his premiership. A man more confident of his continuity might not have acted with a constant wariness, and the drive to charm, deceive, and manipulate, which were the hallmarks of Walpole's premiership.

No prime minister until Pitt the Younger came close to recreating Walpole's system. Walpole could rely on conditional support from the monarch. In the House of Commons, he exploited his position as Leader of the House to enhance his control, a control that was buttressed by his oratory and alliance-building skills, persuasion and manipulation. No one until Pitt had the same command over his party. Walpole understood clearly that 'his power was based upon party power, and that Cabinet government rested indirectly on the party system', as Carter said.[26] No prime minister was as adept as Walpole at manipulating patronage, using Treasury funds to ensure the selection of office holders and Whig candidates congenial to him. No one else before Pitt recognised the importance of combining the office of First Lord of the Treasury with Chancellor of the Exchequer, or used the Treasury so successfully to control all aspects of government spending and policy. None recognised how to work the Cabinet Council to ensure that it reached decisions which he wanted rather than his rivals or the monarch. Walpole's use of the device of an inner Cabinet anticipated the emergence of the modern Cabinet, free from the monarchical presence and will.

Spencer Compton (2nd, 1742–3), who succeeded Walpole, was the feeblest of all eighteenth-century prime ministers. Unwittingly, Compton established an iron rule for his successors as prime minister: don't follow in the wake of a giant. Indicatively, no full-length biography has been written of Compton: perhaps he doesn't merit the title of PM. George II had briefly turned to the Whig Compton upon his accession in 1727, because he had proved his loyalty overseeing the Royal Household. But, he quickly decided Compton was not up to the task, and so Walpole remained First Lord. George II turned to Compton again in 1742 because he wanted continuity, but he proved no more suitable than fifteen years before. This was a war ministry and the decisive figure was Secretary for the Northern Department, Lord Carteret, overseeing the War of the Austrian Succession, and scheming to redraw the map of Europe by promoting peace between Austria and Prussia to curb French power. Carteret spoke German and was close to George. But unlike Walpole, he believed that others should manage Parliament, thereby underlining the need for the First Lord to be able to command support in the Commons.

Compton was described by Rosebery (32nd, 1894–5) as 'the favourite nonentity of George II',[27] while Horace Walpole dismissed him as 'a great lover of private debauchery, who was thought to have fathered many children'.[28] Compton's undistinguished period had little impact at home, except the passing of the Place Act of 1742, which prevented MPs from being appointed to some public offices in the wake of the investigation into Walpole's corruption. He died in office in December 1743, a few days after George II had highlighted the monarchy's presence when he led his troops into action against the French at the Battle of Dettingen.

Henry Pelham (3rd, 1743–54), Walpole's protégé, survived ten and a half years, the sixth-longest continuous period in office in the history of the prime minister. It was far from assured. George II still preferred Carteret. But Carteret's continued disregard for Parliament, and diplomatic failures, led to his departure from government in 1744. Pelham's formation of a 'broad-bottomed' ministry (i.e. containing both Whigs and Tories) underpinned his own position. In February 1746, he survived a crisis when George II refused to allow him to appoint Pitt the Elder to the government, and Cabinet, to force the issue, resigned in support of Pelham. George proved no more successful than he had been in 1727 at advancing his own candidate, Lord Bath, and within two days he had to go back to Pelham. In 1751, when Pelham tried to resign, George prevailed upon him to remain, which he did for another three years before dying in office. 'Now I shall have no more peace', George lamented, while Horace Walpole wrote a more charitable epitaph: 'He lived without abusing his power and died poor.'[29]

Pelham was one of the most skilful of these incomplete prime ministers. He had shown himself a brilliant financial manager under Walpole, and used Parliament's finance-raising powers to help outmanoeuvre Carteret. Over the following years, he cut the national debt by reducing expenditure, despite the expense of foreign wars.[30] He then went for a general election a year early, in 1747, before Carteret's opposition had the chance to regroup, and handled it with consummate skill, as he did the general election in 1754, proving his skills as a party manager in the House of Commons and beyond. Having served as a captain of dragoons during the Jacobite rebellion of 1715, he saw off the last and most serious Jacobite uprising in 1745–6 until its bloody conclusion on the battlefield of Culloden. The 1750 Calendar Act introducing the Gregorian calendar, and an Act establishing the British Museum in 1753, were among his enduring domestic reforms. Pelham, however, did little to build the prime minister's permanence.

The prolonged political crisis from 1754–7, that followed Pelham's death, helped consolidate the position of the House of Commons. If prime ministers were not to sit in the Lower House themselves, it became evident that they would need to have a solid representation there. Pelham's older brother, the Duke of Newcastle (4th, 1754–6, 1757–62), had to give up in 1756 because he was unable to find a politician of quality to lead the House of Commons. Newcastle's first ministry, overshadowed by the Seven Years' War, is regarded as a failure because British forces suffered several serious defeats, and little clear war leadership was provided by the government.

Historians have, in general, been dismissive of Newcastle: 'it is hard in surveying the entirety of his career to find substantive arguments for regarding it as anything other than an exercise in political mediocrity', concluded Browning.[31] H. T. Dickinson is more damning: 'A Secretary of State without intelligence, a Duke without money, a man of infinite intrigue, without secrecy or policy, and a Minister despised and hated by his master, by all parties and Ministers, without being turned out by any'.[32] It is true, as Newcastle went on to prove, that he was better as a second-in-command – raising money, encouraging proteges, and negotiating loans for the government – than as a leader. His patriotism and dedication to the country were his saving graces.[33]

For 225 days, the shortest serving prime minister of the eighteenth century, the Duke of Devonshire (5th, 1756–7) served as a stop-gap. A man of duty from one of the great Whig families in England, but totally anonymous as prime minister.

Newcastle redeemed himself when he returned as prime minister from 1757–62, now in alliance with his erstwhile critic, Pitt the Elder as Southern Secretary. In 1758–60, British soldiers and sailors carried all before them, destroying the French empire in North America, seizing territory in Canada, sinking the French fleet in the Atlantic, and defeating the French army in Germany. 'The Pitt–Newcastle ministry was one of the most successful in British history. Under its direction, more battles were won and conquests made than in any other period of conflict', Middleton writes in his book on the Seven Years' War.[34] The government frayed from 1760 when George III (r. 1760–1820) succeeded his grandfather George II. The new king disliked Newcastle. In October 1761, Pitt the Elder resigned, and with his departure, the energy of the administration was lost, Newcastle following suit in May 1762.

The period from 1762–70 saw five prime ministers in seven years, the greatest churn in the history of the office. They were men of substance in the main, but none able to make an enduring impression on the position. Their brevity, and comparative powerlessness, owed almost everything to the new monarch. George became king in 1760, arriving with all the impatience of a twenty-two-year-old. He had been far from impressed by the relative passivity of his great-grandfather George I and grandfather George II: 'George III did have a model and it was neither of these. He regularly evoked William III. This is interesting, because of his status post Glorious Revolution. He was ambitious', says Andrew O'Shaughnessy, 'William III wielded much more power than any King subsequently. He wanted to see an *empowered* monarch.'[35] George subscribed to the idea of a 'Patriot King', independent in mind and dependent on no particular party.[36] As the Whigs had dominated government since 1714, this meant reducing their power. Exploiting his patronage power and funds at his disposal to engage in bribery, he built up a body of supporters, whom Edmund Burke, a critic, named the 'King's Friends'.[37]

These were 'in-between' years when the prime ministers were dealing with the fallout from the Seven Years' War, making a protracted peace, dealing with the consequences of the considerable debt, and then having their attention increasingly taken by problems in their expanding colonies in North America, which erupted in war in the mid 1770s.

John Stuart, Earl of Bute, (6th, 1762–3), had been the tutor to the young George, in whom he nurtured a belief that his Hanoverian predecessors had allowed royal prerogatives to slip into the hands of greedy Whig families. Bute, for all his intellectual qualities, was ill-suited to be prime minister. The new King George III nevertheless appointed him a minister, and then prime minister after the waning Newcastle ministry burnt itself out, the first Tory to hold the position, and one of only three in the eighteenth century (alongside North and Pitt the Younger). Bute was widely disliked: by the Whigs, by Pitt the Elder's supporters, critical of his peace treaty concluding the Seven Years' War, by many of the English, who disliked him for being a Scotsman and for imposing a tax on cider, and by parliamentarians for his lack of understanding of either House. His appointment had one historical importance, as Daniel Finkelstein highlights: 'It was one of the last attempts by the British monarch to install a prime minister who lacked any parliamentary base.'[38] George, distressed when Bute decided that he could take no more abuse and resigned, wrote to him to say, 'my D. friend must not be surprised that seeing him resolved to quit the scene of business is the most cruel political blow that could have happened to me.'[39]

George had no option but to turn back to the Whigs and ask George Grenville (7th, 1763–5), in many ways a happy choice. He 'brought order to all aspects of government policy and administration',[40] wrote his biographer Philip Lawson. 'He did not view the unfunded debt or budgetary deficit as an integral part of the nation's economic structure, but evils to be remedied if the country were to prosper.'[41] Grenville viewed critically the 4 per cent of government budget allocated to the British army in North America, so had the apparently bright idea of asking the American colonies to help pay by a Stamp Act on legal transactions in 1764. The colonists took a different view, declaring 'no taxation without representation'.[42]

Grenville was fearless in standing up to George III, as were the two most senior figures in the ministry, Lords Egremont and Halifax, who were united in their distaste for the king's continued reliance, even if exaggerated, on the hated figure of Bute.[43] Grenville increasingly clashed with George, reaching a high point in the crisis over a draft regency bill in 1765. George sought to dismiss him, but failed to do so, emboldening Grenville to agree to continue only on the condition that two of George's favourites be relieved as ministers: 'Never again would [the King] suffer such humiliation, allowing his ministers to dictate the terms of service, and he would do all in his power to keep [Grenville] from taking office again.'[44] George became even more determined to find a successor to Grenville: but first Pitt the Elder, then an ailing Newcastle, turned him down, before Newcastle recommended his protégé, the Whig Lord Rockingham, who duly replaced Grenville in July 1765.

Rockingham (8th, 1765–6, 1782) however, proved no more biddable than Grenville. He was determined to be a party leader of the Whigs first, and a government leader, prime minister, second. George rapidly became disillusioned, angered at his failure to provide money from the Civil List for his three younger brothers. So he moved swiftly against him, this time succeeding in persuading Pitt the Elder. Rockingham served less than a year and a half in two separate periods (he came back in 1782 for a final ninety-six days before dying). His importance to history is, as Finkelstein argues, 'maintaining essentially an ideologically-based political grouping all the way through the period, thus helping create the modern idea of a political party, as well as a cohesive opposition, in place of the more fluid party system before'.[45] His qualities included foresight about the American colonists, counselling moderation in their treatment, and at home, as Walter Bagehot wrote, 'exercising a guiding and restraining control' over his fellow Whigs.[46] Rockingham has real claim to being considered Britain's best short-serving prime minister in his brief second spell: in 1782, he tried to tackle corruption at home, set about making peace with the Americans, and granted greater measures of self-government to Ireland.

Pitt the Elder (9th, 1766–8) is the outstanding politician of the mid eighteenth century, even if his historical importance owed far more to his work before he became prime minister. So prominent had he been in the Pitt–Newcastle ministry of 1757–62, that contemporaries often referred to him as 'prime minister' even though Newcastle was the senior figure as First Lord. His skills as an orator made him stand out in his attacks on corruption under Walpole in the 1730s, subsidies to the Hanoverians in the 1740s, and peace with France in the 1760s. His oratory helped draw large numbers of MPs to him and keep them onside, giving him considerable authority in the House of Commons. Because his speeches were not published, and records were not kept, it will never be known what exactly he said.[47] Parliamentarians were expected then to speak without notes. 'The abilities of Pitt were primarily parliamentary', writes Richard Middleton. 'His brilliant if bombastic oratory mesmerised the members and captivated a large proportion of the nation.'[48]

Today, Pitt would be called a 'strategic visionary' (though the word 'strategy' only entered the English language long after he had died). His campaigns, advocating British greatness and expansion of the Empire, his ferocious antagonism towards Britain's rivals, France and Spain, his opposition to corruption, and his support for the American colonists in the 1760s and 1770s, gave him a broad popular appeal. 'Pitt was unique among leading politicians in his time in the extraordinary interest he evoked outside Parliament, at least from the late 1750s, and in the way he shaped people's images of himself as Britain staked its place on the international stage', says his biographer, Marie Peters.[49] He is indeed the first prime minister to have a popular appeal in Britain and abroad. He was considered a hero in the American colonies for his part in the Seven Years' War, and many places in America are still named after him, notably Pittsburgh.

Despite this, his ministry of 1766–8 was unhappy. With the Duke of Grafton ensconced as First Lord of the Treasury, Pitt chose to become Lord Privy Seal, and was ennobled as the Earl of Chatham, accepting the peerage he had refused all his life, which had resulted in the affectionate monicker 'the Great Commoner'. Having sacrificed his Commons power base for the much smaller House of Lords stage, he failed to manage his ministers, or give a clear lead. 'Chatham's priority was policy, not man management – and first and foremost foreign policy', says Peters.[50] Unable to stamp his authority on Cabinet, and outvoted on his pressing for an inquiry into the East India Company, his health broke down and he had a prolonged nervous breakdown in 1767.[51] In his absence, Chancellor of the Exchequer Townshend passed a Revenue Act, which included imposing customs on tea and other goods, leading to further strains with the American colonists.[52]

Pitt the Elder's public standing is reflected in the unusual credit for a prime minister of being given a monument in Westminster Abbey which states that 'he exalted Great Britain To an Height of Prosperity and Glory Unknown to any Former Age'. He was a great man in history, but not a significant prime minister, and he added nothing to the office. Nor was he an adept manager of party, or Cabinet, or government, beyond his own interests in foreign policy. He was a one-off.

The record of Pitt's successor, the Duke of Grafton (10th, 1768–70), is proof of his lack of enduring impact. Only thirty-three when he, with customary reluctance, accepted George III's invitation to become prime minister, he is the second youngest prime minister (after Pitt the Younger) in history. But unlike him, Grafton was conspicuously lacking in the attributes for office, including moral seriousness. Evergreen Horace Walpole dismissed him as 'an apprentice, thinking the world should be postponed for a whore and a horse race'.[53] Cabinet overruled him on expelling the radical MP John Wilkes from the House of Commons, and on imposing harsh measures against the American colonists, exacerbating the unrest still further.[54]

By 1770, George III, aged thirty-two and considerably more experienced than when he came to the throne, had come into his own. 'George clawed back quite a few powers, appointing army officers and bishops, and was perfectly happy to do so without referring to the First Lord of the Treasury', says his biographer Andrew Roberts.[55] Having quarrelled with a succession of Whig prime ministers, he turned to a Tory, hoping for more than from Bute. Indeed, in Lord North (11th, 1770–82), George found, initially at least, the figure he desperately needed: a capable administrator happy to be subservient to him, and who could run business as he wanted. The prestige and autonomy of Cabinet and its ministers were promptly diminished, as George III 'tried to be his own Prime Minister, and to control and direct Cabinet personally'.[56] The Whigs saw George trying to control Cabinet, patronage, and government action from in the House of Lords, and did not like it: as the Whig statesman Charles James Fox wrote, 'his Majesty was his own unadvised minister'.[57]

North should not be dismissed as a lightweight, as history has tended to do because of his role in the loss of the American colonies. Highly intelligent, dedicated, and principled, he spoke several European languages. Like many aristocrats of the era, he had made a continental tour in his youth, which encouraged a broad range of interests. His grasp of detail and oratory gave him a command in the House of Commons, all the more impressive because 'he faced one of the most brilliant parliamentary oppositions of all time in terms of sheer oratorical ability, with politicians of the calibre of Fox, Burke and both Pitts'.[58] The historian Edward Gibbon was a keen supporter and dedicated the fourth and final volume of *The Decline and Fall of the Roman Empire* to North.[59] O'Shaughnessy highlights North's Treasury reforms, built on later by Pitt the Younger, as 'testimony to North's abilities that Britain remained solvent while France was bankrupted by its participation in the American War of Independence'.[60] North biographer Peter Whiteley writes, 'his understanding of the nation's finances was never bettered by any of his predecessors, and his impact on Treasury administration was both beneficial and lasting'. He highlights too his deep morality: 'in the often unedifying world of eighteenth century politics North shone as a beacon of decency, conscientiousness and competence; and when the time came for his departure, he left with dignity and honour'.[61]

North, though, lacked the killer instinct and savvy of a Walpole or Pitt the Elder, and could be indecisive and unwilling to impose his will on others. This other side of North is seen in his uncertain leadership during the American War of Independence. A hawk in favour of coercive measures in the 1760s against the Thirteen Colonies, once he became prime minister, he became more conciliatory, removing the Townshend duties except, fatefully, on tea. After the Boston Tea Party in 1773, he introduced the Coercive Acts, but, with little consistency, pressed for a royal commission to explore peace, which George III opposed. The Conciliatory Acts which North introduced in 1775 gave the colonists some of what they wanted, but it was deemed 'too little, too late'.

Having failed to prevent war, when it broke out in 1775 he repeatedly asked George if he could resign. In November 1778, he wrote to him (referring to himself in the third person):

> The public business can never go on as it ought, while the Principal & most efficient offices are in the hands of persons who are either indifferent to, or actually dislike their situation ... Lord North ... therefore, thinks it his duty to submit the expediency of his Majesty's removing him as soon as he can,

because he is certainly not capable of being such a minister as he has described.[62]

George stood by North, even after the defeat at Yorktown in 1781. But by early 1782, his majority in the House of Commons had evaporated, and he wrote again to George imploring him to let him resign:

> The Parliament have altered their sentiments, and as their sentiments whether just or erroneous must ultimately prevail, Your Majesty, having persevered so long as possible, in what you thought right, can lose no honour if you yield at length, as some of the most renowned and most glorious of your predecessors have done, to the opinion and wishes of the House of Commons.[63]

The dependence on the monarch to assent to the resignation of the PM highlights the subordinate position of the office. The king was the destroyer as well as the creator of the prime minister. What are we to make of North's twelve years? He contributed to stabilising the position of the office after so many brief interludes following Newcastle's departure. He gathered into his one person several key aspects of the role of the emerging prime minister. An idea of what the job involved in the 1770s can be seen in this letter to George in which he describes what an ideal premier might do

> To perform the duties of the Treasury, to attend the House of Commons at the rate of three long days a week, to see the numbers of people who have daily business with the first Lord of the Treasury, and to give all thought to the principal measures of government in this very looming crisis is enough to employ the greatest man of business, and the most consummate statesman that ever existed.[64]

At the same time, North was having to deal with trivia himself, such as a personal letter from the wife of a German commander in Canada, asking for his permission for her carriage to be admitted duty-free into England.[65] Cabinet too, for all George's intrusions, became more institutionalised under North, with minutes taken and the notion of collective action taking firmer root: achieving it 'certainly strengthened the hand of the prime minister when dealing with the King, and indeed when

dealing with Parliament'.[66] Blake highlights another historical importance of North, the first 'clean sweep' of associated ministers departing
with the prime minister in 1782. 'With the exception of the Lord
Chancellor the new administration under Lord Rockingham consisted
entirely of new men.'[67]

Instability returned after North, with three Whig prime ministers following in 1782–3, and with the Tory Thurlow, the long-serving Lord Chancellor
(1778–92), proving to be effectively 'His Majesty's Opposition' in the House
of Lords.[68] After North, George returned to his old tricks of 1760–70 of
stirring up dissent amongst the Whigs, divided between the followers of
Rockingham and the (now dead) Chatham. When Rockingham died, after
his short spell, George turned to one of the 'King's Friends', Shelburne
(12th, 1782–3). No fool, he had ambitious plans for enhanced free trade, for
parliamentary reform, and for a new sinking fund to repay the national debt.
Abroad, he oversaw negotiations to conclude the American War, culminating in the Treaty of Paris in 1783, ratified after he fell from power, in which
he successfully argued that a generous peace with the United States would be
best for long-term relations, a judgment that would be proven in time.[69] But,
like many successors, he suffered because he never learnt the craft of the
prime minister. His model was Chatham: 'He regarded the members of his
administration not as colleagues, but as underlings who just had to carry out
his policy.'[70] William Grenville (the future 16th, 1806–7) commented wryly
of the Shelburne method, 'you will certainly think the mode of keeping
a cabinet unanimous by never meeting them at all is an excellent one'.[71]
John Cannon's damning verdict is that 'no politician who held office with
Shelburne wished to do so again',[72] and concluded 'Shelburne's failure
was all his own. He had no concept of man management, either in theory
or in practice. He remained in many ways a strange visitor to the
Westminster Parliament.'[73]

After Shelburne was driven from office, George alighted on Portland
(13th, 1783) as the nominal prime minister in the unstable Fox–North
coalition. The position of Fox was destroyed by the presence of North in
the Cabinet, and meddling by George spelt its downfall. 'Portland was an
absolute cipher. The King even stops him from creating peers which
utterly cuts him off at the knees in terms of political power', said
Roberts.[74] George loathed Fox, a mutual feeling, and this antipathy

made Fox, however powerful his parliamentary position, unacceptable to George as a potential prime minister. So often in history, the success of one party or politician has hinged on the unacceptability of the 'other'. In desperation, George III turned to the decidedly anti-Foxite William Pitt the Younger, confident that he could control him.

WALPOLE'S LONG SHADOW: THE CHARACTERISTICS OF THE IMPERMANENT PM, 1742–83

Not until December 1783, when William Pitt the Younger first became prime minister, was there an incumbent with the grasp of the job, the autonomy, and the vision of Robert Walpole, or whose example would, like Walpole's, reshape the premiership for decades after him. None of the twelve prime ministers between these two giants inhabited the office as these men did, and neither did they change the nature of the office. All twelve operated under the shadow of Walpole, some deliberately trying to emulate him, others to be unlike him. Pitt was the first prime minister not to be born when Walpole was in office, and the first to be fully free of him. Before considering Pitt's tenure, we review the characteristics of the impermanent premiership over these forty-one years.

TREASURY-FOCUSED. The Treasury had become by the early eighteenth century the prominent department, largely free from the grip of the monarchy, even before it moved into its proud new Kent-designed offices at the end of Downing Street in the 1730s. Prime ministers were First Lords of the Treasury from 1721 to 1783, with the exception of Pitt the Elder, when Grafton was the First Lord, succeeding him as prime minister in 1768. The Treasury provided the power base for these prime ministers, giving them staff to execute their business in Parliament, and helping with patronage and the management of government affairs. When George II in 1755 complained to Hardwicke, the Lord Chancellor, that 'the Duke of Newcastle meddles in things he has nothing to do with', Hardwicke's response was that 'the head of his Treasury was indeed an employment of great business, very extensive, which always went beyond the bare management of the revenue; that it extended through both Houses of Parliament, the members of which were naturally to look thither'.[75]

Financial concerns lay at the heart of the prime minister's work: the Chancellor of the Exchequer was clearly subordinate to them. 'Pure financial policy lay at the centre of [the First Minister's] strategy until such a time as unanticipated emergencies blew them off course' Peter Jupp asserts.[76] Bute was thus determined to conclude the Seven Years' War so he could focus on restoring national finances and root out corruption. Grenville's premiership had financial reconstruction and tightening colonial administration as its centrepiece. North was above all concerned with improving the national finances until the American War, while Shelburne 'envisaged a peacetime programme, a financial reconstruction, a revision of trading agreements and administrative reform'. Rockingham stands out as the rare exception of a prime minister whose primary concern was *not* the state of the national finances. This day-to-day financial burden did not end in 1783, and indeed lasted until the mid-nineteenth century, when it became the Chancellor's primary responsibility, as discussed in Chapter 9.[77]

CONTINUING MONARCHICAL AUTHORITY. George I and George II might have been much less dominant figures than William and Queen Anne, but a second characteristic of this period is the continued authority of the monarch over the prime minister, above all over their appointment and dismissal, and over other ministers. George I was the least dominant of the three monarchs in this period, and it is significant that Walpole staked out the territory of the office in the six years in which they overlapped. George II was more forthright and his longevity –he survived until the age of 77 in 1760 – was 'very important to the stabilisation of the old Whig system'.[78]

George III is by far the most dynamic of the first three Hanoverians, and it was a measure of Pitt's success that he managed to contain his ambition, and did not allow him to prevent the office of prime minister emerging as preeminent. Assertive prime ministers could in this period force the monarch to rethink, as happened in 1746 when Pelham's Cabinet submitted their resignation, forcing George II to accept their ultimatum, or in 1765, when Grenville put pressure on George III to accept his choices for Cabinet. George II complained when forming the Newcastle–Pitt ministry that 'ministers are Kings in this country'.[79] But the prime minister could only exert authority on specific occasions, and often at a price. George III conspired to have Grenville's government dismissed shortly after the showdown, and he brought down the Fox–North ministry in 1783, paving the way for Pitt the Younger. In the spring of 1755, George II vetoed a promotion for Pitt the Elder, who wrote:

> The weight of the irremovable Royal displeasure is too heavy for any man to move under, who is firmly resolved never to move to the disturbance of Government; it must crush any such man; it has sunk and exanimated me; I succumb under it, and wish for nothing but a decent and innocent retreat ... by being placed out of the stream of Cabinet Council promotion.[80]

Pitt the Elder remained as Paymaster of the Forces, but within two years he was appointed Southern Secretary, the post where he made his name.

The monarch remained the more important figure too in the almost constant wars throughout this period. The war against the American colonists from 1775 was very much driven by George III, as we see in Chapter 8. Monarchical authority did not, of course, end suddenly with Pitt the Younger's appointment in 1783: Pitt later resigned in 1801 due to George III's concerns over Catholic emancipation. But Pitt's premiership was critical in the rebalancing of power from monarch to prime minister.

CABINET FLUIDITY. Cabinets for Pitt were periodically difficult to manage, as they have been for all his successors to the present day. But Cabinet management for a prime minister before 1783 was far *more* uncertain. The Cabinet Council met only irregularly, its exact remit and membership was imprecise, the ministers were largely autonomous of the prime minister, owing appointment and dismissal to the monarch, and they saw themselves and their departments as working for the monarch. The sheer size of the Cabinet Council made it unwieldy, and J. H. Plumb wrote that every one over William III's and Anne's reigns 'rapidly disintegrated into faction; their composition rarely [remaining] stable for more than a year'.[81]

Post-1688 legislation helped the emergence of the Cabinet by repealing previous statutory provisions. In 1705, legislation was repealed that had made ministers responsible individually for their advice, thereby allowing the development of a notion of a 'collective responsibility' for advice. Legislation was also repealed that had prevented ministers from sitting in the House of Commons, thereby enabling Cabinets to consist of members from *both* Houses of Parliament. This prevented the emergence of a true separation of branches of power, as occurred in the United States, where the 1787 US Constitution prevented the heads of government departments sitting in Congress.[82]

At the beginning of the eighteenth century, Cabinet's composition was tilted heavily towards the monarch and royal Court. In 1701, Sunderland wrote that it included: 'Archbishop, Lord Keeper, Lord President, Lord Privy Seal, Lord Steward, Lord Chamberlain, First Commissioner of the Treasury, Two Secretaries of State; the Lieutenant of Ireland must be there when he is in England. If the King would have more, it ought to be the First Commissioner of the Admiralty, and the Master of the Ordnance.'[83] Long before 1783, Cabinet had established itself as the place where the heads of the major departments met, including the Secretaries of the Northern and Southern Departments, and the Treasury. Cabinet had also taken over from the large and unwieldy Privy Council, claiming the ear of the monarch. In 1739 the Duke of Argyll had complained about the multiplicity of different bodies: 'My lords, it is not being in privy council, or in cabinet council, one must be in the minister's council to know the true motives of our late proceedings.'[84] The decline of the Privy Council was accelerated by its appointment of members for life, hence it contained Whigs and Tories, which was out of tune with the increasingly polarised politics in the eighteenth century. Cabinet's emergence was facilitated too, as we have seen, by the device that Walpole, as several of his predecessors like Harley, fell upon, of having an 'inner Cabinet', which might meet in their London or country home. Collective responsibility took longer to emerge. Moments of Cabinet unity, as under Pelham, vied with times when the monarch packed Cabinet with 'King's Friends', denting attempts by the prime minister to establish a collective voice.

Cabinet had still to establish itself by 1783 as the essential decision-taking forum. Weighty matters could be discussed, as in mid 1746, when the Cabinet decided the fates of Jacobite prisoners after the Forty-five Rebellion, and in January 1775, when Cabinet agreed to restore parliamentary authority in the Thirteen Colonies by force: 'To take the most effectual methods to enforce due obedience to the laws and authority of the supreme legislature of Great Britain'.[85] But at other times, the admittedly patchy records from the period suggest vital decisions were taken away from full Cabinet, or that Cabinet was being drawn into matters of no great import, as when at the height of the war with America the records show it:

> agreed that as Mr Moncrieff has done such signal service during the siege of Charleston and has been so strongly recommended by Mr Henry Clinton for some distinguished mark of His Majesty's favour it is humbly submitted to his majesty that it is the opinion of this meeting ... that Mr Moncrieff do receive an immediate and distinguished mark of his majesty's approbation.[86]

Cabinet thus evolved little between Walpole and Pitt the Younger. Jeremy Black sees it as still a very fluid part of the constitutional apparatus: 'When you had a good, effective prime minister, then they are able to get a degree of cohesion. But at other times, the PM can find it very difficult if their opponents in Cabinet are able to appeal above their head to the King. We can talk about Pelham and North having "a Cabinet", but only in the sense that we understand that the ministers owed their loyalty primarily to the crown'.[87] The institution of Cabinet had to await Pitt the Younger to truly solidify, a process that was integral to the evolution of the office of prime minister itself.

THE IMPORTANCE OF THE HOUSE OF COMMONS. The House of Lords (or 'Upper House') was in theory, and in constitutional documents, the senior House in Parliament. The House of Lords emerged out of the 'Great Council' or *Magnum Concilium* that had advised the monarchy since at least the reign of Edward I, composed of the nobility, bishops, and landowners.[88] It merged into the Lords and had its position restored in 1660 and confirmed in 1688. Despite the continuing hold of the aristocracy, the House of Lords lost further authority relative to the Commons in the eighteenth century. The frequency with which Britain was at war from 1688 to 1815 gave the Lower House a particular authority as it held the power of the purse. The Commons was also more difficult to manage than the smaller and more biddable Lords, so took more attention, and when prime ministers, like Devonshire in 1756–7, tried to govern without a majority, they struggled to find cohesion.[89] Even though a majority was important in both Houses – as Lord Waldegrave said to George II in 1757, after George had suggested he form a government: 'nothing could be done for the public service, without a steady majority in both Houses of Parliament'[90] – securing a majority was much easier for prime ministers in the, then smaller, Lords than in the Commons. The most significant prime ministers in this interim period after Walpole, including Pelham and North, sat in the Commons, whereas Shelburne, Rockingham, and Grafton all led from the Lords, without great success. Pitt the Elder's decision to become a Lord at the beginning of his premiership in 1766 was widely seen as a significant error.

Prime ministers were traditionally the Leaders of either the Commons or the Lords, depending on which house they sat in, highlighting the continuing centrality of Parliament to their work, though some, including Compton, Chatham, and Rockingham (for a total of under four years), were not. But it was in these years nevertheless that the centrality of the House of Commons, and its greater importance to political life, including the life of the prime minister, became established.

One development which aided this process was the ending in 1771 of the tradition that publication of speeches by parliamentarians in either house constituted a breach of parliamentary privilege. Increasing public interest in politics, and the growth of newspapers, created a new climate, and records of speeches began to appear printed under the name 'Hansard' from 1812.

Historian John Clarke says that 'the eighteenth century had a mixed constitution, with proper roles for the monarchy, the Commons, the aristocracy and the people. If any one of these elements tried to enhance their power too much, they would be brought back a bit.'[91] Finkelstein adds that 'the critical role was for the prime minister to hold the bridge between the monarch and the House of Commons at this time'.[92]

AN UNREFORMED, SMALL STATE. The size of the state in this period was similar to the sixteenth and seventeenth centuries, with fewer than 300 officials working at the centre of government in Whitehall, and only some 7,500 civilian officials working across the country, mostly in military, customs, and excise, and inspection positions.[93] Jupp contrasts Britain with those European states which saw periodic overhauls of the bureaucracy on the orders of the monarch, including Peter the Great in Russia, William I of Prussia, and Maria Theresa for the Habsburg Empire. Britain had neither a monarch, nor indeed a prime minister, who instituted a top-down reorganisation. Not until the second half of the nineteenth century did this begin, with central government taking over roles undertaken hitherto locally.[94]

'A modern prime minister speaks of their role in terms of leading and changing the whole of society', says William Hague, biographer and former Foreign Secretary. 'But in the eighteenth century, they had a far more limited view of the role of government. They saw themselves as in office on the basis of being the most effective person to conduct the King's government.'[95] The most significant bureaucratic change in these years was the creation of the Home and Foreign Offices in 1782, from the former Southern and Northern Departments, which had been created at the Restoration in 1660. But significantly, the work of these two new departments continued much as before, amateurish, small-scale, and with promotion on the basis of patronage and preferment.

THE UNIMPORTANCE OF GENERAL ELECTIONS. Just six general elections were held between 1742 and 1783, following the seven-year cycle ordained by the 1716 Septennial Act, (in 1747, 1754, 1761, 1768, 1774, and 1780). The elections, though lively and controversial, tended to confirm governments already in office. When the monarch appointed a new ministry, the custom, especially if they lacked a majority in the Commons, was to call a general election to provide that majority. Because of the Crown's influence and the patronage that ministers could bring to bear on constituencies, and the people that controlled them, the system worked.[96] The election that Pitt the Younger called in his first full year, in 1784, was significant precisely because it gave him a personal mandate which his immediate Whig predecessors before 1783 lacked.

Prime ministers in this period thus did not need to be national figures, still less popular: any ridicule and disdain they endured did nothing to undermine their continuation in office. Pitt the Elder can be considered the first 'popular' prime minister, recognised during the war with France as the symbol of Britain himself, rather than the monarch. Waldegrave, famous for being First Lord for just four days in 1757, cited 'the popular cry without doors [i.e. outside Parliament] was violent in favour of Mr Pitt' as the reason why George II should appoint the Pitt–Newcastle ministry instead.[97] Bute cited his own widespread unpopularity as a reason for his departure in 1763, but it did not necessitate it, least of all with the king's continuing support.

Few politicians of this era aimed for genuine popularity amongst the wider population. Portland captured the mood of the age when he said, 'the idea of courting popularity by any means I have always reprobated ... the possession or enjoyment of it has always something in it very suspicious, and I hardly know any act or measure vulgarly or commonly called popular which has not originated in a bad cause, and been productive of pernicious effects'.[98]

THE FLUIDITY OF THE PRIME MINISTER. The identity of the prime minister is thus far from fixed in this period. Before Pitt the Younger, it is still not established whether the government will be led by the First Lord of the Treasury, or by another minister: only that the government has to have *a* leader. The dominant figure in a ministry was not always the First Lord. Sometimes duumvirates (as Pitt–Newcastle in 1757–62) or even triumvirates, where several figures were in charge, were the norm. This was particularly likely when the First Lord of the Treasury sat in the House of Lords and they had a powerful figure in the House of Commons, or where a powerful and experienced personality eclipsed the first minister. Carteret, the Lord President, dominated Compton's ministry in 1742–3 and oversaw foreign and war policy during the War of the Austrian Succession. When Newcastle was First Lord during the Seven Years' War, Pitt the Elder was the dominant figure leading the war in his capacity as Southern Secretary. In the latter stages of the American War, Lord George Germain, Colonial Secretary of State, was often more dominant than North himself. In 1783, the prime minister, the Duke of Portland, paled into insignificance, justifying it being known as the Fox–North coalition. After Pitt the Younger, such fluidity was the rare exception, not a norm.

PITT THE YOUNGER, 1783–1806

Pitt the Younger was the most important single figure in the history of the British prime minister after Walpole. A precocious intellectual, he went up to Cambridge at the age of fourteen; was a witness at nineteen when his father, by then Lord Chatham, collapsed whilst speaking in the House of Lords (he died just over a month later); was twenty-one when he entered the House of Commons and delivered a sparkling maiden speech within a month; was Chancellor of the Exchequer at the age of twenty-three, and prime minister at twenty-four. He was dead at forty-six, an age that would be considered young for a prime minister to start their premiership today, having given his entire adult life to his job, which he performed with a dedication to hard work and integrity that makes a point about the importance of character and moral seriousness in successful leadership.

Pitt was in office at a time of considerable national unrest. The Gordon Riots of 1780, inspired by anti-Catholic sentiment, had seen several days of rioting and looting, including attacks on the Bank of England, and threats to Downing Street itself, with the mob surging towards Number 10, only repelled by soldiers. Edmund Burke described it as a 'wild and savage insurrection' that 'prowled about our streets in the name of reform'.[99] The prospect of more violence and even revolution was very real in Britain. 'If in 1783, you'd asked which country was the more likely to experience revolution before the end of the century, Britain or France, most people would have said: "Britain". After all, 'Britain had lost its colonies and appeared in a total mess.'[100] Pitt stabilised the nation and saw off the closest moment that Britain came to having the revolution that afflicted its neighbours.

Spreading prosperity was key to this success, achieved by strengthening the economy and harnessing it to the Industrial Revolution. New budgetary measures were devised to enhance the yield from custom and excise, and he created the sinking fund in 1786, to pay down the national debt. In the 1780s, it had stood at £243 million, but by 1792 he had already reduced it to £170 million.[101] Pitt was responsible for commercial treaties with France and freeing up Irish trade, exploiting to the full his position as Chancellor of the Exchequer which he held throughout his time in power. His economic successes alone would have made him one of the great prime ministers. But there was so much more.

Loss of the American Colonies had left the country isolated – Britain has not had to experience loss in a major war since – and it left a deep scar on national self-confidence. The old order had been roundly discredited. The king had considered abdicating. Pitt restored confidence. The mental instability of the monarch added to his burdens, especially as in 1788, when it first manifested, his great Whig rival Charles James Fox saw it as his chance to unseat Pitt. Fox wanted his friend the Prince of Wales (the later George IV, r. 1820–30) to be named as 'Prince Regent', arguing that the prince had a 'hereditary right to the regency'. Pitt seized his opportunity, declaring, 'I'll unwhig the gentleman for the rest of his life.' As the architects of the 1688 revolution, Whigs held dear the principle of parliamentary sovereignty which Fox overlooked by denying the right of Parliament itself to decide the future succession. Thus did Pitt address the double threat – the King's instability and the challenge from Fox – and calm duly returned.[102] Pitt rallied Cabinet to get behind his Regency Bill, which proposed placing the king's person and property in the hands of the queen, and which passed the Commons with a healthy majority in February 1789. Defence of George III, who had become a popular figure, further boosted Pitt's image.

A moderate reformer rather than a radical, he introduced a bill in 1785 to remove the representation of thirty-five 'rotten' boroughs, and to make a minor extension to the franchise. But he lacked the support in Parliament to see it through, and he made no further attempt. Hague argues Pitt's parliamentary reforms were simply intended to make the old system work better, not to overhaul it entirely.[103] Pitt equally made tentative steps to abolish the slave trade, declaring a debate in the Commons in April 1792, calling it 'this curse of mankind ... the greatest stigma on our national character which ever yet existed'.[104] But Parliament did not abolish the slave trade until the year after his death, 1807, and slavery in the British Empire was not abolished until 1833.

Ireland proved another major concern. In 1798, Irish Presbyterians, inspired by ideas from the French and American Revolutions, and angry at being excluded by the Anglican establishment, rose up against the British. Catholics, seeing the opportunity, joined forces with them, and a French army, ominously for London, landed on the west coast of Ireland. Pitt responded quickly and aggressively, and British forces put down the rebellion. The Act of Union of 1800, which unified both countries, followed, motivated as much by the desire to rein in the reactionary Protestant ascendancy as to punish the Irish, and to try to inoculate Ireland against further French influence, with the hope of enlisting Irish support in the wars against France. Pitt convinced himself of the need for Catholic emancipation. John Bew argues he and Irish Secretary Castlereagh 'showed a willingness to go for *raison d'état* [national interests] above and beyond royal edict'.[105]

Pitt threw himself into foreign policy, concerned with making Britain into a great power and building up its empire. The India Act of 1784 reorganised the East India Company, creating a Board of Control, and centralised British rule in India. When no longer possible to send convicts to the Americas after the war, he looked to the southern hemisphere, and in 1786, his government took the decision to settle them in Australia, with the colony of New South Wales proclaimed in 1788. In the Constitutional Act of 1791 he divided the province of Quebec into a French 'lower' Canada and a predominantly English 'upper' Canada, thus solving another growing problem. His decision to rebuild the navy in the 1780s after the humiliations of the American War helped prepare the country for the French wars from 1793.

In 1793, four years after the outbreak of the Revolution, France declared war on Great Britain, and Pitt became a war leader. The rest of his premiership (with a brief hiatus when he was out of office from 1801–4) would be predominantly concerned with war and foreign policy. During the late 1790s, Britain faced the threat of invasion, a threat that was renewed with the outbreak of the Third Coalition War in 1803, this time with France led by the aggressive and opportunistic Napoleon Bonaparte.

Only Churchill from 1940 was in power at a moment of greater national peril. Indicatively, that year, he published and wrote the foreword to a book on the wartime speeches of Pitt.[106] Pitt rallied the nation under the very real threat of invasion, passed laws creating militia and volunteer units, and cracked down on French sympathisers, deploying coercive powers some considered excessive. He introduced income tax from 1799 in his 1798 budget to pay for the war. 'For personal purity, disinterestedness and love of this country, I have never known his equal', William Wilberforce said of him.[107] The Napoleonic subjugation else-where in Europe lacked the brutality of what Hitler would have done to Britain had he invaded in 1940, but a French invasion would have been a profoundly distressing and unpredictable event in British history.

Pitt resigned in February 1801, having failed to convince George III of the need for Catholic emancipation. Soon afterwards, George had another attack of mental illness, brought on he believed by his worry over Catholic emancipation. As Roberts points out, 'Addington had not yet been appointed, but Pitt had resigned so there was no prime minis-ter. Yet they managed to coalesce and work it out together.'[108] Henry Addington (15th, 1801–4) negotiated the Treaty of Amiens in 1802 and ended the income tax which Pitt had introduced in 1799. War broke out again in 1803, driven by Napoleon, which lasted until 1815. Addington's unsuitability was soon evident to all. Pitt by now was lonely, depressed, and unwell, suffering from the health ramifications of the multiple bottles of port he was drinking each day. He appeared in the Commons, having retired from public life, and spoke so brilliantly that demands for his return in 1804 became unstoppable. Tory states-man George Canning memorably wrote:

> when our perils are past, shall our gratitude sleep?
> No, – here's to the pilot that weathered the storm.[109]

At the end of 1805, news came to London of Napoleon's great victory over the Austrians at Ulm, opening the road to Vienna, but also Nelson's victory at Trafalgar, putting paid to Napoleon's hopes of a successful invasion. Soon after, Pitt was toasted at the Lord Mayor's Banquet as 'the saviour of Europe'.[110] But his strength was sapping, and in January 1806, news came of the Battle of Austerlitz, in which Napoleon crushed the Austrians and Russians. Pitt is supposed to have uttered, 'Roll up that map; it will not be wanted these next ten years.'[111] He died soon after on 23 January 1806.

Pitt is one of only eight first-rank prime ministers who shaped the country and their successors for years afterwards. As Tombs wrote, 'for nearly half a century, from 1783 to 1830, England was almost a one-party state, run by William Pitt, and his 'Pittite' heirs, professional politicians who had built up an invincible body of support based on patriotic defence of the country, king, Church, constitution and property, and a reputation for efficient and even (so far as war allowed) economical government'.[112] Castlereagh biographer Bew believes, 'Castlereagh saw himself as the heir of Pitt's vision. When peace comes in 1815, it is Pitt's peace.'[113]

Pitt further changed the stature and nature of the office of prime minister. His longevity in office – just ten days short of nineteen years, the second-longest-serving after Walpole – was significant as it helped groove a successful model of governing into the political psyche. He had initially signalled his intention to be a decisive leader by asking the monarch to dissolve Parliament in March 1784, only four years after the previous general election, and won almost seventy seats, vanquishing the Whigs, including figures like Fox and Burke. Precipitating a general election and gaining a personal mandate from it was entirely new. 'The victory gave him immense personal authority. At that time, the prime minister came into office by manoeuvres of factions in Parliament or the request of the King. But the 1784 general election gave Pitt personal authority which he retained for most of his time in office. It put him in an entirely different situation', writes Hague.[114] Pitt can thus be considered 'the first Prime Minister who actively sought to mould public opinion to reinforce his position in Parliament and with the court', according to Leonard.[115]

The key moment in Pitt's eclipsing of George III came when he insisted that Lord Thurlow, the Lord Chancellor, one of George's favourites, be dismissed in 1792. Pitt wrote to Thurlow with brutal candour to say: 'I think it right to take the earliest opportunity of acquainting your Lordship that being convinced of the impossibility of His Majesty's service being any longer carried on to advantage while Your Lordship and myself both remain in our present situations, I have felt it my duty to submit that opinion to His Majesty, humbly requesting His Majesty's determination thereupon.'[116]

Pitt was the first prime minister to have oversight of *all* government departments, which saw a significant weakening of the tradition of departmentalism, where ministers saw themselves as autonomous, running their office on behalf of the monarch. 'Pitt deliberately exerted a control over other ministers that his predecessors had neglected to do', argues Hague, aided in this by financial oversight in his capacity as Chancellor of the Exchequer, to ensure that 'not much happened in government without his agreement'.[117] By 'strengthening the coordination of government departments ... he fortified the British state for a lengthy war and against the buffetings of social discontent through the industrial revolution, while helping to prepare for the management of an empire which would encompass a quarter of the globe'.[118] Pitt built up Cabinet from a low point when he first became prime minister, with his 'mince-pie administration', so called because it was not expected to last beyond Christmas. Cabinet became a group of capable ministers who accepted his leadership and a growing sense of collective responsibility for their decisions. George III became increasingly content for ministers to look to Pitt rather than to himself for guidance: he realised he had no option but to rely on Pitt, not least if the alternative was Fox. Pitt leant on lieutenants, none more so than Henry Dundas, Home Secretary and then War Secretary. But unlike earlier eighteenth-century prime ministers, this was not in any sense a 'duumvirate'.[119]

The prime minister's office was still not the finished article on Pitt's death – indeed, it never became the finished article. But in all these ways he sharpened, defined, and enhanced what the prime minister can do.

SLOW EVOLUTION OF THE TITLE 'PRIME MINISTER'. When, in the 1950s, an official delved into the national records to ascertain the origins of the office of prime minister, he drew a blank, reflecting what Peter Hennessy refers to as 'the continuing imprecision about the origins of the premiership'.[120] We see this in the words of leading Whig, Samuel Sandys, when he tore into Walpole for his accumulation of power, protesting that: 'According to our constitution, we can have no sole and prime minister'. Rather, Sandys claimed that the constitution (which he did not define) dictates that Britain should have 'several prime ministers or officers of state', each with their own department, and 'no officer ought to meddle in the affairs belonging to the department of another'. Walpole, though, he alleged, had 'obtained a sole influence over all our ... public affairs, but has got every officer of state removed that would not follow his direction'.[121] Walpole replied forcibly: 'I unequivocally deny that I am sole and prime minister'.[122] Suspicion of the words 'prime minister' owed much to the idea that the monarch should be their own 'prime minister', which explains Newcastle's criticism of Robert Harley, one of Queen Anne's favourites, for trying to act as the 'premiere minister'.[123]

Eighteenth-century prime ministers before Pitt were uncomfortable with the term. In 1761, Pitt the Elder described a 'prime minister' as an 'abomination in a free country'.[124] North, the following decade, would not allow anyone to call him 'prime minister', insisting 'there was no such thing in the British constitution'.[125] Lewis Namier thus said, 'it is often difficult to say who . . . was the prime minister or, to use the contemporary expression – *the* minister'.[126]

Pitt the Younger explained the need for such a position in a conversation with Dundas, who recorded his belief that Britain required 'an avowed and real Minister, possessing the chief weight in counsel and the principal place in the confidence of the King. In that respect there can be no rivalry or division of power. That power must rest in the person generally called First Minister'.[127] Pitt made the case for there being just one minister, though indicatively, he used the term 'First Minister'. Nevertheless, Blick and Jones found that *The Times* began to use the phrase 'prime minister' while he was still in office, with two articles in May and June 1805 employing the term, describing Pitt the Elder as 'the father of the present prime minister'.[128] Indicatively, the title 'prime minister' began to be used in contemporary parliamentary debates as a neutral description, rather than a term of abuse.[129] On 29 April 1805, Castlereagh, then President of the Board of Control, described Pitt as having had 'perhaps the longest political life ever enjoyed by any Prime Minister of this country'.[130] The following year, in a House of Lords debate, Lord Holland referred to 'the constitution, which abhorred the idea of a Prime Minister'.[131] The term 'premiership', however, only appeared later, with the first use believed to be in 1835, and regular mention from the 1850s.[132]

The 'office of prime minister' was first referred to specifically in Parliament in 1822, and again by Peel in 1827. Blick and Jones speculate that the term was increasingly used after Liverpool's departure in 1827 because of rapid leadership changes, first Canning (19th, 1827), then Goderich (20th, 1827–8), then Wellington (21st, 1828–30), with the last, as a military hero, generating considerably enhanced national interest.[133] The first prime minister to use the term *about themselves* would appear to be Peel, who on 12 June 1846 said, 'I, in my place as Prime Minister of this country, am charged with the proposal and conduct of more important measures than have ever perhaps been submitted to the Legislature of this country.'[134] He was most certainly not the last prime minister to assert, though, that the problems afflicting them were greater than for any of his or her predecessors.

The first official use of the term 'prime minister', and thus recognition, came at the time of the Treaty of Berlin in 1878, where Disraeli signed himself as 'First Lord of the Treasury and Prime Minister of Her Britannic Majesty'.[135] But the term wasn't 'known to law', according to Jupp, until 1905 when Edward VII issued a warrant giving the PM precedence in ceremonies over the Archbishop of York.[136] Others believe the term 'prime minister' began to be widely used from the late nineteenth century when, most unusually, three figures who were not prime minister occupied the office of First Lord of the Treasury during Salisbury's (31st, 1885–6, 1886–92, 1895–1902) tenure: Lord Iddesleigh (1885–6), William Henry Smith (1887–91), and Arthur Balfour (1891–2, 1895–1902).

During Salisbury's premiership, the term 'prime minister' had become widely established, and Hansard used it to describe him from 1895.[137] The first meeting of the Committee of Imperial Defence, in December 1902, recorded 'the prime minister' as present, perhaps the first use in government documents, while the august 'Imperial Calendar' (the predecessor to the *Civil Service Yearbook*) referred for the first time in 1904 to Balfour as 'prime minister and First Lord of the Treasury'.[138] The first mention in statute was not until the Chequers Estate Act of 1917 which specified that the gift was for the use of the premier.[139] Not until the late twentieth century did the *Civil Service Yearbook* refer specifically to 'a Prime Minister's Office'.[140]

With the lack of clarity about terminology for the prime minister, and with no written document specifying the powers of the office, we have to rely upon what prime ministers *did* to understand the evolution of the office. How five men and one woman prime minister in particular built on Walpole's and Pitt the Younger's achievement is the subject of the next chapter.

CHAPTER 4

The Transformational Prime Ministers, 1806–2021

THE PRIME MINISTER CANNOT BE UNDERSTOOD FROM STUDY-ing a list of powers written down in laws or documents but only by looking at what they did in flesh and blood. Not all prime ministers are equal. Chapter 3 established that only two of the fourteen prime ministers between 1721 and 1806 left an enduring impact on the office, and in this chapter, we consider the other six who defined the office as 'agenda changers'. They are the creators of the evolving office of prime minister. All eight – two in the eighteenth century, three in the nineteenth, and three in the twentieth – carved out what the office of prime minister means, and shaped the office in their own image. After these 'agenda changers' ceased to be prime minister, their successors over the years that followed either tried to be like them, or tried deliberately to distance themselves from them: but none could escape their long shadow.

Prime ministers come to office desiring to be many different things, but united in just one common aim: not to be like their predecessor. Since 1900, Lloyd George wanted to be a galvanising prime minister, unlike Asquith; Bonar Law and Baldwin distanced themselves from the sleaziness of Lloyd George; Churchill wanted to provide a clearer patriotic lead after the appeasing Baldwin and Chamberlain; Attlee had a very different conception of a business-like office to the frenetic Churchill; Macmillan consciously distanced himself from Eden after Suez, as Wilson did from the aristocratic Macmillan and Home; Heath abhorred Wilson's seamy side as prime minister, while Thatcher set herself up in direct opposition to the corporatist Heath, Wilson, and Callaghan. Major made it clear from day one that he would govern in a less high-handed manner than Thatcher, while Blair deliberately ridiculed Major's woebegone style; Brown scorned Blair's sofa government and aloofness from the Labour Party, while Cameron had obvious contempt for the Brown hectoring style of Government, as May did for the entitled chumocracy of Cameron, as Johnson most definitely did for the vacillating May.

But the 'change-maker' prime ministers go far beyond merely distancing themselves from their predecessors. They protect the Union, and bolster the country's reputation. They seize their historic opportunity. They recast the mould in which the office of prime minister was formed. All eight, revealingly, were considered by contemporaries to be Britain's first modern prime minister, leaders who redefined the office. We now examine why some are in the top tier, and why others are not.

ROBERT PEEL (24TH, 1834–5, 1841–6)

Walpole and Pitt the Younger had no equal until Robert Peel, who first became prime minister in 1834. Few of the eight prime ministers between Pitt and Peel made any more impact than the twelve prime ministers between Walpole and Pitt the Younger. Henry Addington (15th, 1801–4), concluded the Treaty of Amiens in 1802, but he failed to distinguish himself as a war leader, and is best known for his Home Secretaryship from 1812–22 (as Lord Sidmouth), the longest continuous spell in history, when he oversaw a repressive regime against advocates of an extension of democracy. Neither Lord Grenville (16th, 1806–7) nor Portland, when he returned to power from 1807–9, distinguished themselves , bar the former legislating for the abolition of the slave trade. The abstemious and fecund (he had thirteen children) Spencer Perceval (17th, 1809–12) was right on most issues, but was assassinated after only two years and seven months, the only incumbent to suffer that fate, and the only Solicitor or Attorney General (he was both) to have become prime minister.

Lord Liverpool (18th, 1812–27) might be considered a candidate for the top tier as the second-longest continuously serving prime minister (after Walpole) at fourteen years and ten months. The Napoleonic Wars were concluded successfully by him in 1812–15, he steered the country towards peace and prosperity, he saw off threats, albeit harshly, from radical agitation. The Peterloo Massacre in 1819 is a rare example of tensions boiling over into violence.

Norman Gash considered Liverpool's Government 'The last of the great eighteenth-century administrations in its structure and duration [and] the first of the great nineteenth-century administrations in its problems and achievements'.[1] The first part of his statement is the more accurate: he did little to anticipate the new century, and nothing to change the office of prime minister to prepare it for it. A successful consolidator but not an innovator, his chief concern, as William Anthony Hay describes, was 'directing the King's government first in wartime, then in the disruptive period after Waterloo. He thought of his role as managing the state and protecting the interests of the state.'[2] First-tier prime ministers need to achieve more than that, especially with so long in office. Liverpool can be understood as a mirror image of the long-serving Tory peer who was prime minister at the end of the century, Salisbury: both capable, patriotic, and principled administrators who embraced the status quo but had no great desire to change it with altered circumstances.

George Canning (19th, 1827) had been an exceptional Foreign Secretary and Viscount Goderich (20th, 1827–8) a capable Chancellor: but they served less than a year between them as prime minister. Canning was the shortest-serving prime minister in history (119 days before he died), while Goderich, incapable of holding together his coalition of Whigs and Tories, resigned after 144 days (the shortest for a PM who did not die in office). The Duke of Wellington (21st, 1828–30 and 1834) oversaw the passage of Catholic emancipation, and resisted parliamentary reform, but left no enduring mark on the office. Wellington's premiership is the only example in British history – in contrast to the US – of a military hero making it to the top.

Earl Grey (22nd, 1830–4) was the outstanding figure between Pitt and Peel. He brought the Whigs back into office after a gap of fifty years, and championed reform, overseeing the passage of the Reform Act of 1832 and the abolition of slavery in the British Empire in 1833. After being excluded from office for most of his active life, he 'was out for revenge' as Coleman puts it.[3] No other peacetime prime minister achieved so much in such a short period. His bold move to ask the king for the creation of new peers in the Lords to scare them into passing the Reform Bill was a major change in the relation between the Crown and prime minister, and Asquith, (35th, 1908–16) employed a similar tactic with George

V over the passage of the 1911 Parliament Act. In both cases an influx of new peers was avoided and the Lords acquiesced. But that aside Grey did not fundamentally change the nature of the prime ministership.

Still less did Lord Melbourne (23rd, 1834, 1835–41), though he served almost exactly twice as long as Grey. He is best known for his tutelage of the young Queen Victoria and as being the last prime minister to be dismissed by a monarch in 1834. He toughed it out and returned to power for a second spell, another shift in the power dynamic between monarch and prime minister. He enjoyed being prime minister, particularly flirting with the young queen and other married women, but grew bored when she married Prince Albert, 'offered no meaningful leadership' in Cabinet, and lacked the gravitas needed for a PM.[4]

So we come to Robert Peel (24th, 1834–5, 1841–6), who, like all in the first tier, had considerable experience of politics and government before he came to the office. An MP first in 1809 at the age of thirty-one, he served under Liverpool as Chief Secretary of Ireland (1812–18), and as Home Secretary twice, initially under Liverpool (1822–7) and then under Wellington (1828–30). In that capacity, he played a key role in the Catholic emancipation but is best remembered for setting up the Metropolitan Police, known thereafter as "Bobbies" or "Peelers" after his first and second names.

His brief four-month induction as prime minister in 1834 was followed by a stint as Leader of the Opposition from 1835, before returning to Downing Street in 1841. In 1839 he had refused to form a government and take over from Melbourne during the 'Bedchamber Crisis', when Queen Victoria refused to appoint any Tories to her Royal Household. The decision ensured that when Peel did become prime minister again, it was after a general election victory, ensuring that his legitimacy came from the electorate rather than the monarch. Peel embodied elements of the Pittite system, but far more, he looked forward into the nineteenth century and the era of professionalised politics and administration.

He was to transform the office of prime minister. The general election in July 1841 was the first in British history where an opposition party triumphed and replaced a sitting government with a previous majority, and the last where the monarch openly took sides. Melbourne's Whigs had been struggling in the Commons for several years, and in May 1841, their Budget was defeated. In its wake, Peel demanded a vote of no confidence, winning with a majority of one. Whigs and Conservatives quarrelled over whether such a defeat required a prime minister to resign. Victoria's advice from the statesman Lord Brougham was that she needn't dissolve Parliament unless an election would end with the government strengthened. Melbourne clung on, but his Cabinet realised the cause was lost and Victoria reluctantly dissolved Parliament in June. Aghast at the prospect of losing her beloved prime minister, and the Conservatives winning the general election, she provided money from the Privy Purse to support Melbourne's cause. But with a swing of 4 per cent, Peel's Conservatives triumphed with 367 seats, up 53 from the 1837 election, against Melbourne's Whigs who won 271, down 73. This was the first general election that returned a party against the wishes of the Crown. Modern electoral party politics was born.

Peel was to contribute greatly to the formation of the modern Conservative Party: first in the 1830s by helping the political group coalesce and then by breaking it in two in 1846.[5] The 'Tamworth Manifesto', which Peel had issued in December 1834 in his constituency as a way of distancing himself from the Toryism of Wellington, and outlining his own new brand of Conservatism, became a foundational text. It was in truth modest in its ambitions, accepting that the Reform Act of 1832 was irrevocable, and promising that the Conservatives would reform in future as necessary, but without making radical promises. The Manifesto nevertheless was published nationally, and was seen as a first statement of aims by a party leader to the electorate. 'It is the first time that someone contending to be prime minister is establishing some form of contract with the electorate of what they will do when they're in power', said Robert Crowcroft.[6]

Peel became the first prime minister to complete a sweeping agenda of domestic reform in just one ministry. In less than five years, from 1841–46, the government banned women and (most) children from working in mines, introduced rudimentary protection for factory employees, and passed minimum standards for railway passenger travel. Peel also cut tariffs to stimulate trade and introduced income tax in 1842 for the first time on a permanent basis (it had been introduced during the French and Napoleonic Wars, but was abolished in 1816). Peel, in contrast to his predecessors, 'took a systematic approach' to solving problems, whereas earlier prime ministers tended to be reactive, says Jupp. Having identified a series of problems, public finances, protective tariffs, and Ireland, he 'devised solutions that reconciled the discordant interests of the agriculturist, the manufacturer and the indirect and direct taxpayers for at least a generation'.[7] This was new and very significant.

Peel became the first prime minister sitting in the House of Commons not to serve simultaneously as Chancellor of the Exchequer. Losing the services of the Treasury proved a significant moment in the evolution of the premiership, and one we explore in greater detail in Chapter 9. The growth of the Treasury's political and financial power, particularly in the twentieth century, allowed the Chancellor to emerge as a growing threat to the prime minister's preeminence. Blick and Jones rightly regard it as one of the most significant moments in the evolution of the prime minister.[8] No subsequent prime minister combined the job with Chancellor of the Exchequer, with the exception of Gladstone from 1873–4 and again from 1880–2, and then Baldwin from May to August 1923.

Peel's decision was recognition that, by 1841, the job of prime minister had become 'full-time' (though prime ministers continued to be Leader of the House of Commons or House of Lords until the twentieth century). Whereas Peel released himself from the humdrum 'day-to-day business of the Treasury',[9] he still took all key financial decisions himself, with his Chancellor of the Exchequer, Henry Goulburn, 'permanently overshadowed'.[10] Peel introduced the Budgets, notably in 1842 and 1845, and the fiscal innovations mentioned earlier. Jupp considers Peel 'the only Prime Minister [of the 1721–1848 period] who had clear control of his government's agenda'.[11]

Peel was a ferocious worker – not all prime ministers have been – with a determination to keep on top of his Cabinet. He attacked the time-honoured notion of 'departmentalism', where ministers saw themselves as sovereigns in their own domains, replacing it with a clearer sense of collective responsibility, which had started to emerge under Pitt the Younger. Over the previous six years, Melbourne's Cabinet had been described as a 'Republic', over which he had little control.[12] Peel, as prime ministers do, reacted against his predecessor, but with good reason.

Peel's correspondence shows him ranging over vast areas: economic and social policy, the army, the war in Afghanistan, the Canadian border, and the governance of India (on three occasions he chose a Governor-General).[13] His appetite can be glimpsed in this letter written to one of the three, Lord Ellenborough, in August 1843:

> You will see that we have an extraordinary combination of difficulties to deal with at home – Ireland and Repeal agitation; a terrible schism in the Church of Scotland; civil war in Spain; increasing jealousies of the Church on the part of Dissent, leading to formidable and successful organisation against our Education scheme; trade still depressed, and revenue not flourishing.[14]

In August 1845, Peel wrote about his mounting exhaustion fulfilling all his duties:

> I defy the Minister of this country to perform properly the duties of his office – to read all that he ought to read, including the whole foreign correspondence; to keep up the constant communication with the Queen, and the Prince; to see all whom he ought to see; to superintend the grant of honours and the disposal of civil and ecclesiastical patronage; to write with his own hand to every person of note who chooses to write to him; to be prepared for every debate, including the most trumpery concerns; to do all these indispensable things, and also sit in the House of Commons eight hours a day for 118 days.[15]

His attempts to legislate to lower food prices by repealing the Corn Laws (a protectionist measure blocking imported food and grain and designed to keep grain prices high to favour domestic producers) led eventually to his resignation as prime minister. He had succeeded in abolishing the Corn Laws, but at great cost; splitting the Conservative Party he had helped forge.

Bloody, but unbowed, he resigned in June 1846. Four years later, whilst riding on Constitution Hill in London, he was thrown from his horse, and died of his injuries three days later. He was memorialised with a white marble statue in Westminster Abbey in 1852, another statue in Parliament Square in the 1870s, and memorials across the country. Historians have revered him as 'the great Conservative patriot; a pragmatic gradualist ...

a conciliator who put nation before party and established consensus polit-ics', in the words of Boyd Hilton.[16] To Gash, he was the 'chief architect' of the transition from 'the age of revolt' to 'the age of stability', who softened 'class and religious animosities', ushering in the twenty years of stability and prosperity of the mid Victorian era, including 'the long Indian sum-mer of aristocratic parliamentary rule'.[17]

Peel's impact on the psyche of the Tory party was to be greater than that of any other Conservative prime minister. Gladstone and Aberdeen, his President of the Board of Trade and Foreign Secretary respectively, led his 'Peelite' followers into a fusion with the Whigs to form the Liberal Party. Not until the election in 1874 did the Conservatives again win a working majority, a gap of twenty-eight years. 'Don't split the Party' was etched on every Tory successor, including High Tory Salisbury, who loathed him for hurting the Party.[18] Balfour and Baldwin, who fought to keep the Party together in the early twentieth century over similar debates on free trade against protectionism, were still deeply affected by his legacy. His long shadow stretched indeed down the long century, even to Major, Cameron, and May, for whom party unity over Europe remained their primary priority.

Peel's promotion of free trade, as in the repeal of the Navigation Acts and Corn Laws, was a happier legacy. The thirty-six-year-old William Gladstone spoke about continuing and completing Peel's free trade policies in his landmark Budget speeches of 1853–4 and 1860–6 as Chancellor.[19] 'We cannot forget that Peel and Mr Gladstone were in the strict line of political succession', wrote Liberal John Morley.[20] Thatcherites looked back to Peel, and to Gladstone, for inspiration for her free trade policies. His hyperactivity in office discouraged some of his mid-century successors, or was used by them as an excuse for inactivity. Gladstone in contrast celebrated and emulated his activism in govern-ment. Peel's overriding of Cabinet colleagues provided another caution-ary tale. Disraeli was selective about his involvements as prime minister, and took care to carry Cabinet with him, as did Salisbury.

Peel was not the complete prime minister. Unlike Pitt, Lloyd George, and Churchill, he did not serve at a time of war, nor did he oversee a social revolution, like Attlee. He looked backwards as well as forwards: 'Peel sees himself as similar to Liverpool and earlier Hanoverian predecessors, as the principal servant of the Monarch', says Hawkins, and in his explicit disregard for his parliamentary party 'can be seen the last vestiges of the idea of a prime minister in the mould of a monarchical executive'.[21] Gladstone said to him in the months after he fell from power in June 1846 that he thought he had exercised more personal authority as prime minister than any holder of the office since Pitt the Younger, adding: 'Your government has been not carried on by a Cabinet', Gladstone told him, 'but by the heads of departments each in communication with you'.[22] A presidential PM indeed.

VISCOUNT PALMERSTON (28TH, 1855–8, 1859–65)

Palmerston's statue is also to be found with Peel's in Parliament Square, one of only seven British prime ministers to be so honoured (along with Canning, Derby, Disraeli, Lloyd George, and Churchill). Palmerston was not a great administrator, like Peel, nor a great war leader, like Churchill, nor did he help found a political party, like Derby, nor introduce innovations to the office of prime minister, like Lloyd George, nor was he responsible for significant economic or social reforms, like Attlee. His claim to be one of our landmark prime ministers is because he was the first nationally known and popular prime minister (though Chatham came close), anticipating what became an essential requirement, who presided over the country at the peak of its international confidence and prowess, exemplifying national pride in Britain. More than any predecessor too since Walpole, he shamelessly manipulated the press. All prime ministers after him were affected by his legacy: from now on, it was the PM more than the monarch who articulated the views and spirit of the nation.

Jumping to Palmerston has meant passing over three prime ministers, none insignificant. Lord John Russell (25th, 1846–52, 1865–6) was one of the most intellectual and idealistic of British prime ministers, who worked with a statue of his hero, the radical Charles James Fox, on his desk. No other prime minister had a novel by Charles Dickens, *A Tale of Two Cities* (1859) no less, dedicated to him. Much of Russell's reforming zeal and energy had, however, been spent by the time he became prime minister, supporting electoral reform and the elimination of rotten boroughs, and the repeal of the Corn Laws. He proved a mostly reactive, disappointing prime minister, responding with little dynamism or compassion to the Irish Famine, which saw a million die of starvation. Nor did he respond particularly well to the Chartists, with their demands for political and social reform, culminating in their 1848 demonstration. Admittedly, political realities necessitated a strong response to any potential revolutionary behaviour given revolutions unfolding on the Continent in the same year.[23]

Lord Derby (26th, 1852, 1858–9, 1866–8) was the longest-serving leader of the Conservative Party in history (1846–68), fitting between the great Tory beacons of Peel and Disraeli. Hawkins appropriately named his biography *The Forgotten Prime Minister: The 14th Earl of Derby*.[24] He was one of the most talented of the nineteenth-century prime ministers, but never had a Commons majority or a long ministry whilst also being stuck in the Lords when he might have been much more effective in the Commons. Derby saw 'the importance of rehabilitating the Conservatives as moderate, responsible, and therefore a credible party of government, away from it being an atavistic party of rural protest, into which it was in danger of descending by the late 1840s'.[25] His first government became known as the 'Who? Who?' Cabinet because those were the words used by the elderly, deaf Wellington to greet each ministerial name when they were read out in the House of Lords in February 1852.[26] Disraeli may have claimed for Derby, when unveiling his statue in Parliament Square in July 1874, that 'he abolished slavery, he educated Ireland, he reformed Parliament'.[27] But politicians are inclined to exaggerate the truth on such occasions, no doubt hoping that such charitable eulogies will be delivered about themselves. There are good reasons why Derby is largely forgotten today.

Derby showed no such generosity when he tore into Lord Aberdeen (27th, 1852–5) during the Crimean War. Aberdeen's undistinguished premiership was ended when Russell, who thought he should have been prime minister, resigned, bringing down the entire coalition government. Aberdeen had only remained in office because Victoria had insisted he carry on because the alternative was Palmerston. Now Palmerston had his opportunity, for which he had to wait till the age of seventy.

Like all first-order prime ministers, Palmerston (28th, 1855–8, 1859–65) had a long political grounding, first as a Tory MP from 1807, appointed almost at once as Secretary at War, a position he held from 1809–28. From there, he oversaw the army, but not foreign or war policy, and he was not promoted to Cabinet till 1827 by Canning. Foreign Secretary under three prime ministers (Grey, Melbourne, and Russell) from 1830–4, 1835–41, and 1846–51, he became Home Secretary in the Aberdeen government of 1852–5. Palmerston had been an admirer of Canning and one of the Canningite Tories to form a coalition with moderate Whigs in 1827–8, explaining his transition to the Whigs from 1830.

In the post-1832 era, recognition across the nation had begun to matter. Palmerston's 'presidential' impact was demonstrated in the 1857 general election, when the question posed to voters was, effectively: 'Are you, or are you not for Palmerston?'[28] 'Lord Palmerston was almost certainly the most popular politician in British history' wrote ex-politician Roy Hattersley. 'It just so happened that for most of his sixty years in the House of Commons he said and did what most Englishmen would have said and done. He spoke for England, and, in consequence, England loved him.'[29] 'The immense popularity he enjoyed throughout the country as a whole was one of the main reasons for Palmerston's political longevity', wrote Laurence Fenton. 'He was "the people's darling".'[30] His claim to be the embodiment of the nation was boosted by the death of Prince Albert, in December 1861, and Victoria's prolonged withdrawal from the public scene, which Palmerston exploited.

His prominence would not have been possible without shameless manipulation of the rapidly spreading national press. Several titles 'were effectively in his pocket, including the *Morning Post*, *The Globe*, the *Morning Advertiser*, *The Daily News* and the newly launched *Daily Telegraph*'.[31] Editors, journalists, and owners were royally dined and entertained, not least at receptions hosted by Lady Palmerston at Cambridge House in London's Piccadilly.

His biographer, David Brown, reflects on the factors that shaped his premiership:

His notion of being prime minister was *not* to be Aberdeen, not to be timid as he saw it, nor to be overly cautious, but to offer a clear narrative, a strong patriotic lead. He was equally clear he did not want to be like Russell: he saw himself as cementing his claim to be the leader of parliamentary Whiggery. He viewed the shortcomings of his predecessors as prime ministers, and rivals, and simply felt he could do a better job, almost by dint of being himself, by being a strong personality, and being someone around whom government ministers and the country could coalesce. An idea almost.[32]

Palmerston, like Pitt and Peel before him, displayed elements of earlier epochs, while also anticipating the future. Historians differ about how far he prepared the ground for the social and economic reforms of the later nineteenth century. He was certainly no believer in parliamentary or constitutional reform. Steele argues that his administrations should be seen as more than 'an interlude between the aristocratic ministries that worked the 1832 settlement, and the democratic politics that arrived with the reform bills of 1866–7'. Palmerston, he argues, was a 'conscious introduction to the new era'.[33] Indeed, we best understand him as a populist, a patrician, and an egotist, who strode the global stage, and largely avoided controversial domestic reforms.

In his focus on foreign policy, Palmerston clearly anticipated the focus of future premierships, of Gladstone, Disraeli, and Salisbury, and indeed of many prime ministers from Lloyd George, after whom no prime minister was able to avoid foreign policy becoming a major element of their premiership. He was the first prime minister to believe in the merits of an ideological and moral, as well as a commercially minded, foreign policy; Palmerston's predecessors had let purely economic and national self-interest determine their foreign policies. It was Wilberforce, an independent MP, who drove the abolition of the slave trade in 1807 and of slavery outright in 1833. Prime ministers had not seen abolition as a major priority. So Palmerston's arguing for liberal constitutional progress, and for the promotion of self-government for free peoples against despotism, was fresh, shown in his support of constitutionalists in the Iberian peninsula in the 1830s to 1840s, the Poles in the 1840s, the Italians in the 1850s, and the Danes in the 1860s. As prime minister during the American Civil War (1861–5), though his instinct was to back the Southern states, arguing: 'If the Southern Union is established as an independent state it would afford a valuable and extensive market for British manufactures.'[34] But he also saw the Southern secession as another example of 'self-determination against a dominant power' despite personally being an abolitionist; so his idealism *and* commercialism informed his feelings.[35] Ultimately, after waiting for the military balance to change, he chose to remain neutral in the conflict, hoping to keep Britain's future options open. Basing his electoral appeal on nationalism and patriotism, as he did over the contemporarily highly popular Opium War of 1856–60, beat a direct path to more recent examples of flag waving populism.[36] After Palmerston, in peace as in war, prime ministers came to be seen as the embodiment of Britain: to the extent that they succeeded, the public and the popular press loved them and gave them their support.

When Palmerston died in 1865, he received a state funeral at Westminster Abbey. It was a measure of his public standing that he was one of only a handful of commoners, and the first for his ministerial achievements, to receive a state funeral in the nineteenth century (Nelson, Wellington, and Gladstone being the others).

WILLIAM GLADSTONE (30TH, 1868–74, 1880–5, 1886, 1892–4)

None of our first-tier prime ministers before 1868 had modernised the apparatus of the British state, mobilised the power of government to attempt to resolve the great economic and social issues of the day, or run a modern democratic election campaign. All these, and more, Gladstone was to achieve. This puts a perspective on the rival claims of his great protagonist Benjamin Disraeli (29th, 1868, 1874–80). Disraeli was three times Chancellor of the Exchequer, once preceded by Gladstone, and twice succeeded by him, although never once approaching his prowess in the post. Disraeli shamelessly ingratiated himself with Queen Victoria, making her Empress of India in May 1876. She in turn showered him with gifts and praise. But he did not try to rewind the royal clock back before Palmerston to the era of that other great Victoria-flatterer, Melbourne. Indeed one of Disraeli's actions limited the royal prerogative: when he lost the general election in 1868, he immediately resigned before the House of Commons even met. Up until then, results in general elections would be tested in the House of Commons, with a vote to clarify party support: 'But Disraeli changes that, Gladstone isn't keen on it but reluctantly follows in 1874, and by the 1880s, it has become almost a convention', writes Coleman.[37]

Gladstone and Disraeli 'defined political rivalry in the nineteenth century', wrote John Campbell in his study of two hundred years of gladiatorial political contests.[38] They also defined the future of the premiership. They were not grandees, and 'neither played the game as it had been understood', said Coleman.[39] Rather, they were a new breed of *professional* politician: neither would have turned down the premiership as several grandees did in the century, including Wellington, Althorp, Lansdowne, the 15th Earl of Derby, and Hartington. They exploited rail travel to reach the electorate enfranchised in the 1867 Reform Act, especially in the cities, and they milked the press, facilitated by Gladstone's repeal of paper duties in early 1861 (for which he received a honeymoon from them).

With Gladstone coming to power in 1868, they both shared and refined the evolution of party politics. For the first time since 1846, both party leaders were in the same House of Parliament. Not since Pitt and Fox had two such clear opposites both sat in the House of Commons. Their long rivalry did something to 'enhance the celebrity' of the other.[40] Before 1832, general elections had strengthened the nominated ministry. However, the three general elections from 1868 to 1880 all led to changes in the governing party, with Gladstone defeating Disraeli twice (in 1868 and 1880), and Disraeli the victor once (in 1874), consolidating the idea of the 'swing of the pendulum' in national elections, with significant majority governments for the first time becoming the norm. Both men were known nationally as the leaders of their parties, more widely recognised – bolstered by photographs, mugs, decorative plates, party paraphernalia, and cartoons (such as by John Tenniel, principal political cartoonist in *Punch*) – than any previous party leaders in history.

Disraeli however has less claim to historical significance. He believed he was too old (sixty-nine) and unwell to capitalise fully on his Commons majority in 1874,[41] but led a moderately reforming government till 1880 which passed two Trade Union Acts, a Public Health Act, and a Factory Act, building on the work of the first Gladstone government of 1868–74. For all his pontification on social reform, he wasn't deeply engaged in it. Rather, he took care with making good appointments, expecting ministers he appointed, notably Home Secretary Richard Cross and Chancellor of the Exchequer Stafford Northcote, to do the work. Foreign policy was what interested him, especially Europe and the Near East. But he was always bigger on showmanship than substance, revelling in the romance of foreign travel and big, dramatic gestures. 'Disraeli was interested in a foreign policy aimed at making Britain great', Black contends, highlighting that he 'counters the creation of a unified Germany under the Hohenzollerns by making Victoria Empress of India. These are key issues for Disraeli.'[42] He rode roughshod over his Foreign Secretary, Lord Derby (son of the prime minister), and insisted on buying a controlling share in the Suez Canal for £4 million in 1875, writing triumphantly to Queen Victoria, 'It is settled; you have it, Madam!'[43] He engineered his appearance at the Congress of Berlin in 1878 to make it look like his triumph, though much of the work was put in by Salisbury, his new Foreign Secretary, after Derby had resigned.[44]

He was at his best in the Commons, where he 'excelled in the art of presentation. He was an impresario and an actor manager', wrote his biographer Blake, 'He was a superb parliamentarian' with a 'mind like a Catherine wheel shooting out sparks'.[45] But he lacked Gladstone's, or indeed Palmerston's stamina, and sank rather than rose once in the post of prime minister. He accepted an earldom in 1876, and began withdrawing further from day-to-day domestic policy, while in his last eighteen months he 'waited upon, rather than shaped, events'.[46] The Congress of Berlin proved his last hurrah: agricultural depression, reversals in colonial wars, and Irish problems all mounted against him thereafter. Roundly defeated in the 1880 general election, he led the Conservatives in opposition, publishing his last novel *Endymion* shortly before he died at the age of seventy-six under a year after leaving office. Victoria, respecting convention, did not attend his funeral at Hughenden, but sent primroses, his favourite flower, and visited the burial vault a few days later. Gladstone, whose intense dislike of Disraeli was no secret, absented himself from the funeral, but spoke subsequently in the House of Commons in praise of his personal qualities, but pointedly, not his policies. Even Blake conceded that Disraeli was 'a great character, but not a great Prime Minister'.[47]

Gladstone's long preparation took him through the conventional Eton and Christ Church, Oxford, graduating with a double first in mathematics and classics, before entering Parliament in the 1832 general election as a high Tory and a supporter of slavery (his grandfather was a slave owner). After the 1846 split, he joined the Peelites, making his name as Chancellor of the Exchequer under Aberdeen (1852–5), Palmerston (1859–65), and Russell (1865–6). 'Gladstonian Liberalism' emerged as his doctrine, emphasising free trade and equality of opportunity as opposed to protectionism and protection for the status quo.

Gladstone's political energies were fired by a deep religious zeal that shaped his moralistic view of the world and ferocious industry and hard work. In a deeply religious time, even areligious politicians like Palmerston and Disraeli knew how to manipulate religious sentiment to their advantage. Gladstone saw his political work as a religious zealot might see their 'mission'. He sought to create a nation of 'morally autonomous individuals' all contributing and active in society.[48] Just as the Conservative Party became the home for Anglican voters, Gladstone helped the Liberal Party appeal to non-conformists.

This remodelling of the British state into one that aimed to serve the interests of all in society, not just the aristocracy and the prosperous middle classes, marks him out as a great prime minister. He wanted to remove the inefficiencies and the inherited constitution which prevented all people performing to their best, believing a smaller and more economic state would result. Reform and retrenchment went hand-in-hand for him, as historian Richard Aldous has highlighted.[49]

Years of pent-up thought, frustration, and nervous energy exploded in Gladstone's first ministry of 1868–74, inspired by the legend of Pitt the Younger, and the legacy of Peel. The Municipal Franchise Act of 1869 gave unmarried rate-paying women the right to vote in local elections for the first time. Army reforms tackled entitlement head on, centralised powers in the War Office, abolished the purchase of officers' commissions, and set up reserve units around the country, thereby modernising the army. While these were led by the War Secretary, Lord Cardwell, many of the other reforms were driven by Gladstone himself, not the ministerial heads of department. The Irish Church Act of 1869 disestablished the Anglican Church in Ireland, which he followed up with the Irish Land Act of 1870. In 1870, he finally implemented the Northcote-Trevelyan proposals he had initiated in 1854, establishing a permanent and politically neutral Civil Service. Education reform encouraged local School Boards to allow 'every child up to the age of twelve . . . a free place, accelerating the opportunities for working-class children to be educated, and to enhance prosperity and social mobility in Britain'.[50] Local government reform took responsibilities for public health and local government away from the Home Office, and abolished the Poor Law Board, giving responsibility to local government on the ground. The Trade Union Act of 1871 made it legal for the first time to join a trade union. University reform removed religious discrimination, allowing Catholics, non-conformists, and non-Christians to take up professorships, fellowships, and studentships at Oxford, Cambridge, and Durham, a further Gladstonian boost for nonconformity. The Secret Ballot Act of 1872 tackled bribery and 'redefined the vote as the private act of individual conscience rather than a public declaration of opinion'.[51] In 1873, Gladstone established the Supreme Court of Judicature and remodelled the English court system. It was a breathless list of legislative reform: only the Labour government of Clement Attlee from 1945–51 can compare with it for the sheer volume of legislation.

More than any other single prime minister, Gladstone advanced representative democracy in Britain. The Second Reform Act of 1867, which doubled the number of men voting to 2.5 million and extended the franchise to all male ratepayers and lodgers above a certain level of rent, had actually passed under the Conservatives and had been opposed by Gladstone for going too far. Yet, he was the first prime minister fully to understand its implications. His second administration passed another Reform Act in 1884, increasing the electorate to 5.7 million though still falling far short of universal adult suffrage, with 40 per cent of men and all women excluded, to be followed by the 1885 Redistribution of Seats Act, equalising the size of constituencies.[52] His vision, as he said in 1884, was the enfranchisement of 'capable citizens',[53] arguing that a thriving country depended on them being actively involved in politics.

His 'Midlothian campaign' of 1878–80, taking its name from the constituency in Scotland which he won in the 1880 election, is seen as the first modern political election campaign. Harold Wilson described it as 'perhaps the greatest series of political speeches in our history'.[54] In a coruscating attack spread over four addresses, he tore into Disraeli's government for its neglect of domestic reform, its financial incompetence, and mismanagement of foreign affairs since 1874. Gladstone's moralism again came to the fore; he saw Disraeli's pragmatic unwillingness to condemn the Ottoman Empire for the 'Bulgarian Horrors' (atrocities committed by Ottoman forces in suppressing an 1876 Bulgarian rebellion) as a failure of Christian values. The speeches were for Gladstone therefore another Christian endeavour in a life utterly dominated by them. The Midlothian campaign reunified the Liberal Party under him, and set the tone for the general election in 1880 that defeated Disraeli and brought Gladstone back to power for his second government.

In his first term, Gladstone had worked from his London home, 11 Carlton House Terrace, selling it in March 1875, after he resigned the Liberal leadership. When he returned to power in 1880, he moved into Number 10.[55] Gladstone and Downing Street have been long associated in the public mind with his bringing back night-time prostitutes for reforming conversation, which he did innocently, if naively and often in the company of his wife. But there was a far more important dimension of Gladstone's use of Number 10. He was the first truly professional prime minister. Disraeli had decided to move into the long uninhabited Number 10 in 1877, but he had merely lived there. Gladstone turned it into a powerhouse. It is no coincidence that it was Gladstone who introduced the 'unearthly' telephone and electric lighting into Number 10.[56] For the first time in its history, the building was organised with an attention to detail and efficiency that set the tone for those to follow. 'Gladstone … ran an embryonic "Cabinet Office", probably more formally organised and certainly more fully recorded than any of his predecessors', writes Colin Matthew. Record-keeping was much more systematic, he says, than for any previous prime minister in history, reflecting partly Gladstone's recognition of the importance of good administrative order, but also 'with an eye to his place in history'.[57]

Algernon West, Gladstone's private secretary (1861–94), unburdened himself in his diary about the work:

> Though unknown to the theory of constitution, the Prime Minister looms large in the eyes of the public. This means an enormous letter-bag to deal with, which is the first task of the Prime Minister's day ... even after the foolish and impertinent letters have been weeded out, the mass of correspondence remaining to be dealt with is very large. At one time, Mr. Gladstone was conscientious almost to absurdity in answering such letters.[58]

Gladstone had travelled even more in his final fourteen years in politics after 1880 as trains improved. No prime minister before had been seen in as much of the country, including Northern England, Wales, and Scotland, polarising opinion as he went and derided in music-halls, but widely revered too as the 'People's William', 'an image constructed by the Liberal press and himself'.[59]

Gladstone returned to office in 1880 with no overall legislative programme in mind, but merely the intention to improve the existing structure of government.[60] Ministers complained he held himself too aloof, and that Cabinet did not meet often enough. As with his first ministry, and Disraeli's, it unravelled towards its end. He kept trying to drive policy forward, but with less and less success. Peel had been the first prime minister who saw himself as 'the originator of many of the legislative measures of his administration' but he was something of an outlier. As Matthew wrote, 'it would not have occurred to Melbourne, Aberdeen or Palmerston that his duty as Prime Minister was personally to stimulate, far less to draw-up, bills through Parliament, or that his government should be judged by legislative achievement'.[61] But a problem with Gladstone's excessive nervous energy, as Coleman highlights, was that when his measures backfired, he took the blame.[62] Placing so much reliance on himself as a generator of ideas also posed the question: what was to happen when the well began to run dry, as it did after 1880?

This helps explain why Ireland became his great final crusade. He addressed himself to the question 'which challenged the next century in almost every decade: how far was the unitary constitution of the United Kingdom of Great Britain and Ireland sustainable?'.[63] His launching of

Home Rule in 1885 without consultation split his senior colleagues and the wider Liberal Party. He finally ran into the sand, when his faltering final ministry of 1892–4 was defeated over his Home Rule proposals. Ultimately, Gladstone's Irish policy was a failure, with war and division to be Ireland's fate, though had it succeeded, some of the bloodshed of the following century might have been avoided.

Gladstone's legacy runs wide. His attempts to realise an ethical foreign policy for Britain, concerned less about the abstracts of great power politics and self-interest than about the human beings caught up in history, left a long mark.[64] But they were not always popular at the time and Gladstone was seen by many contemporaries as a 'failure' on foreign policy. His infamous delay in sending reinforcements to Khartoum, leading to the death of General Gordon in Sudan in 1885, was a clear low point in his political fortunes. It allowed the Conservatives to call him '(G. O. M. = M. O. G.: Grand Old Man = Murderer of Gordon) . . . an ace, to be played at convenience for the rest of Gladstone's career and beyond'. The episode was a major political scandal: the government's majority was reduced to just fourteen after a censure motion, and Gladstone almost resigned, coming within a 'whisker', according to Colin Matthew.[65]

He left a long shadow. David Marquand sees the Labour Party from the mid 1920s as the direct heirs of Gladstone, advocating 'a more moral foreign policy, of right against might'.[66] Labour Foreign Secretary Robin Cook (1997–2001) saw himself in the Gladstonian tradition, as did Blair in his criticism of 'a traditional foreign policy view, based on a narrow analysis of national interest and indifferent unless that interest is directly engaged'.[67] Labour has been short of heroic figures to cite as inspirations, at least prior to Attlee, and so has often claimed Gladstone as their own. Equally, Conservative anti-statists see much to admire in his championing of small, efficient government and his extolling of the virtues of honest hard work and meritocracy.

Not everyone admires Gladstone. Attlee himself disliked his overly ideological and moralising approach, regarding him as 'a dreadful person' and a 'hopeless leader' who 'showed complete blindness in relation to social problems'.[68] Some historians are 'wary' of him and find him 'too self-righteous for a politician, unwilling to compromise, and not always realistic, as over the Bulgarian atrocities'.[69] But after Gladstone, the job and the office of prime minister, party politics, Whitehall and Downing Street, and general elections were never the same, and that is the mark of a great incumbent, even if, like so many of the top tier, his premiership ended in failure and bitterness.

DAVID LLOYD GEORGE (36TH, 1916–22)

A gap of twenty-two years, and five prime ministers, separates Gladstone from the next top-tier prime minister, David Lloyd George, in part because his successors, learning from his example, wanted to avoid his presidential, highly personalised style of leadership. The main absentee from our list is the Marquess of Salisbury (33rd, 1885–6, 1886–92, 1895–1902). Serving for thirteen years and eight months, the fourth longest, his absence may be a surprise, as was the exclusion of Lord Liverpool, who served a year longer. Roberts makes a strong case for Salisbury's greatness in his biography, subtitled 'Victorian Titan', dedicated to Margaret Thatcher.[70] But Salisbury added nothing enduring to the office of the prime minister (nor did he live at Number 10), nor to its ambitions, nor to its image; nor did he change the relationship of the prime minister to Cabinet, nor to Parliament (he sat throughout in the House of Lords), to the Civil Service, to the nations of the United Kingdom, nor to the electorate. He chose to be Foreign Secretary for all but a little over two years of his time as prime minister, a precedent that only Ramsay MacDonald followed subsequently in 1924. His belief 'that whatever happens will be for the worse, and it is therefore in our interest that as little should happen as possible', appealed to those of a conservative disposition and satisfied a desire for stability and order, leading to great electoral success, but meant he had no great ambition beyond some mild reforms to change or utilise fully the office of prime minister.[71]

Salisbury had a pre-Gladstone notion of being prime minister, and because he remained a foreign policy specialist throughout, the politics of being a prime minister seemed to be a bit of a bore for him. It is hard to disagree with Paul Smith: 'Salisbury seems to belong to a distant and antipathetic tradition, the last grand aristocratic figure of a political system that died with Victoria, or even before, a great whale irretrievably beached on the receding shore of the nineteenth century'.[72] He was not comfortable with late Victorian innovations of electricity, telegraphy, or cars, and was at a loss with how to deal with the urban poor, having little impetus towards resolving the many glaring inequalities of the era. His many admirers are chiefly to be found on the right of politics. He inspired the *Salisbury Review*, a Conservative magazine founded by philosopher Roger Scruton during the 1980s.

We need not linger on Lord Rosebery (32nd, 1894–5), counted out on grounds of brevity and total unsuitability for the office at the time, despite being seen as a 'prince over the water' for the imperialist 'Liberal League' from 1902–10 and a successful writer after his premiership. Arthur Balfour (33rd, 1902–5) was tough and creative on Ireland and one of the architects of the Entente Cordiale with France in 1904, but his most important work came before and after he was prime minister. Liberal Sir Henry Campbell-Bannerman (34th, 1905–8), who served for two years and seven months – 'CB', as he was known – guided the Liberal Party to a landslide victory in the 1906 general election, and presided over the first social reforms of the prewar Liberal governments, including the Pensions Act of 1908. But he was under the shadow of his talented senior ministers, Chancellor of the Exchequer H. H. Asquith, Foreign Secretary Sir Edward Grey, War Secretary Richard Haldane, and, increasingly, President of the Board of Trade, Lloyd George. His contributions were mostly ephemeral: the first lift in Number 10,[73] and the only prime minister to hold the position concurrently with 'Father of the House' (the longest continuously serving MP), he suffered increasingly from ill health, dying seventeen days after resigning in April 1908. Too ill to be moved, he was the last prime minister to die inside Number 10.

H. H. Asquith is a far more significant omission. A brilliant intellect, he too added little to the conduct or image of the office, while the domestic achievements of the government owed much more to his Chancellor of the Exchequer Lloyd George (1908–15). His premiership was overshadowed by crises over Ireland, trade unions, women's suffrage, and the constitutional crisis of 1909–11, only the last of which he resolved satisfactorily, besting the new King George V, whilst his leadership during the First World War in its first twenty-seven months, including controversies over the introduction of conscription and the 'shell scandal', was increasingly inadequate: 'He was not qualified to run the war', concluded biographer John Grigg.[74] The failures mounted: the Dardanelles in 1915, the disappointment of the Battle of Jutland in 1916, the disaster of the Somme, which saw the death of his son Raymond, all overwhelmed him. He failed to provide the leadership the country badly needed.

David Lloyd George (36th, 1916–22) was the first prime minister of modest origin (his schoolteacher father died when he was aged one and he was raised by his mother and her shoemaker brother in rural Wales), and paved the way for prime ministers not from affluent backgrounds in the era of universal suffrage. His personal command and vision of the prime minister at home and abroad set a new standard, reaching beyond that of even Gladstone. No one before him, utilising the crisis of wartime, had built up the structure at the centre of government and across Whitehall enabling the modern state to expand into new areas of economic and social life.

He had an extensive career in politics before reaching Number 10. An MP at the age of twenty-seven in 1890, he held his South Wales seat for the next fifty-five years. As Chancellor, his People's Budget of 1909, decision-taking during the constitutional crisis, and his stewardship of the National Insurance Act of 1911, which helped establish the welfare state, stand out. As Minister of Munitions from 1915, and then War Secretary, he provided the urgency which Asquith did not, and then engineered a crisis in confidence in him which culminated in his succession as prime minister in December 1916.

He arrived in Number 10 with pent-up energy and high on self-belief: he set out to be a dominant prime minister. Colossal doses of adrenaline were injected into Whitehall: by the time he took a holiday in August 1917, his War Cabinet had met 222 times. 'Almost every nut and bolt of Britain's war making machinery saw his involvement and he entertained a stream of visitors both inside and outside of government', says David Woodward.[75] Prevailing over his military commanders, who sidelined his attempts to attack Germany away from the Western Front, and who got their way over the third Battle of Ypres ('Passchendaele') in 1917, was difficult. He did however force a reluctant Admiralty to adopt the convoy system, significantly boosting the effectiveness of the Atlantic supply route,[76] and overruled the service chiefs in unifying the Allied armies on the Western Front under one command in March 1918, which helped provide operational coherence in the final months of the war. He had the foresight to bring the Empire behind the war effort, and set up the Imperial War Cabinet.

The creation of the Cabinet Secretariat in December 1916 (later renamed the 'Cabinet Office'), headed by Maurice Hankey, the first Cabinet Secretary, reshaped the work of the prime minister more than any other innovation during the century. It professionalised Cabinet, circulated papers and agenda beforehand for the first time, oversaw proper records, and followed up on them. The Cabinet Secretary emerged as the most important official in British government: none of the thirteen holders of the office to date served as long as Hankey (1916–38).[77] Lloyd George wanted still more support, and so in early 1917, set up his own personal secretariat in a collection of huts outside the Number 10 back entrance, nicknamed 'the Garden Suburb'.[78] Helping him with policy-making, and liaising with ministers and departments, were its principal purposes. It was headed by W. G. S. Adams, an Oxford political scientist, who became known as 'Principal Secretary', and worked closely with the other leading figure in the secretariat, Philip Kerr (who later became the Marquess of Lothian and British ambassador to the United States till his death in 1940). Together, they determined the secretariat's organisation and allocation of work, which ranged from improving agriculture and addressing the Irish Question to raising the school leaving age and postwar reconstruction. Disbanded at the end of the war in 1918, it set a pattern of bringing outsiders with expert policy advice into Number 10 which later prime ministers were to follow.[79]

Lloyd George established more Whitehall departments than any other prime minister, including the Ministries of Food, Shipping, Pensions, and Labour in 1916, the Ministry of Reconstruction in 1917, the Air Ministry and Ministry of Information in 1918, as well as the Ministry of Health in 1919.[80] The Ministry of Information, to take just one, was established in February 1918 under the leadership of Lord Beaverbrook, proprietor of the *Daily Express*. It set about its work with prodigious energy, organising newsreels, photographs, and propaganda to assist government. It was disbanded in November 1918, partly because of fears by MPs that press barons would formally be implanted at the centre of Whitehall.[81] They had the measure of Lloyd George in this, as he 'paid particular attention to press lords', very much in the tradition of Palmerston and Gladstone.[82]

Not even Gladstone came close to Lloyd George's remodelling of the machinery of central government. Morgan argues that Lloyd George replaced the creaking Victorian machinery he had inherited with 'a new leviathan of state power'.[83] Biographer Hugh Purcell believes his reforms, including conscription, labour relations, pricing, and profits, on top of these changes 'pushed a democratic society as far as it could go'.[84]

Scandal scarred Lloyd George's premiership and helped precipitate its end. His dalliances with his mistress and personal secretary, Frances Stevenson, did not stop her being awarded an OBE in 1918, nor accompanying him to Paris for the peace conference in 1919. Prime ministers had mistresses before and after Lloyd George, but others were less brazen. Implicated for buying shares with insider knowledge in the Marconi Scandal of 1913, he became increasingly cavalier in moral issues, and his style of government after 1918 alienated Cabinet colleagues. 'His remote presidential methods, his long absences from Parliament, his private links with the press and with wealthy donors to his fund made his regime look like a constitutional perversion', wrote Morgan.[85] His creation of peers and knights en masse in return for political donations, albeit devices many of his predecessors had used before, caused mounting upset, with cronies of little distinction finding their way into the Upper House. He 'preside[d] over a corrupt style of government reminiscent of the days of Walpole. The stench of bribery and dishonour surrounded [the coalition], and indeed the very idea of coalition, for decades to come.'[86] Few prime ministers have risen so high, the so-called 'Man who Won the War', to have fallen so low so quickly, as Lloyd George. Prime ministers after him, consciously or unconsciously, took more care to ensure their conduct was above reproach, seeing the damage that it had caused him politically and personally.

Lloyd George's successes though continued after war. The Representation of the People Act (1918), which gave all men over twenty-one and women over thirty with property qualifications the vote, bore fruit in the 'coupon' election of December 1918, a landslide for the coalition government he headed. Domestic policy achievements included the Ministry of Health in 1919, the Housing Act allowing local authorities to build subsidised housing in 1919, and the Unemployment and Insurance Act of 1920, which extended national insurance to an extra 11 million workers. The postwar financial crisis, unemployment, trade union unrest, and retrenchment prevented the election sentiment of 'a country fit for heroes to live in' from materialising. But the settlement of the Irish War of Independence, which granted dominion status to the Free State of Ireland, with most of the accoutrements of independence, while the six predominantly Protestant counties in the north remained in the UK, was a very significant personal achievement which 'resolved' the 'Irish Question' for nearly fifty years. His close involvement at the Paris Peace Conference of 1919, particularly in the Treaty of Versailles, helped ensure that the punitive attempts of French prime minister Georges Clémenceau were tempered, but that left the treaty arguably halfway between sufficiently lenient or decisively onerous, which played its part in the rise of Hitler. The Allies would not make the same mistake in 1945.

The Chanak Crisis in September 1922, where he argued for war with Turkey, against Cabinet which overwhelmingly did not, precipitated Conservative MPs to pass a motion at the Carlton Club in October in favour of breaking away from him and fighting the next general election alone. Lloyd George then resigned. Bonar Law duly led his Conservatives to an election victory in November. Later, Lloyd George led a diminished Liberal Party from 1926–31, became an apologist for Hitler, turned down a Cabinet post offered by Churchill in May 1940, and died in March 1945. A disappointing post-premiership: but a great if badly flawed prime minister nevertheless.

What of his legacy? 'He laid the foundations of what was and still is the structure of the twentieth-century prime ministership. Many of those improvisations were enduring, and created the template for modern government', says biographer John Campbell.[87] Morgan agrees: 'Lloyd George had a wider view of the role of prime minister than any previous prime minister, with the nation and across the world. In this sense, you could argue that he was the most significant prime minister that Britain had.'[88] Political scientists have long debated whether Margaret Thatcher or Tony Blair made the office presidential. They overlook history. Lloyd George was not even the first presidential prime minister, though few were more so than him. Harold Laski, Chair of the Labour Party in 1945, was in no doubt, 'his power increasingly resembled that of the president: Lloyd George's premiership was a presidency in all but name'.[89]

CLEMENT ATTLEE (42ND, 1945–51)

Twenty-three years and five prime ministers separate Lloyd George and Attlee. None of them, not even Churchill, meet all our requirements for the top tier. Andrew Bonar Law (27th, 1922–3) was a politician of the first rank as Leader of the Opposition (1911–15) and Chancellor of the Exchequer (1916–19). But he was prime minister for barely seven months, the shortest-serving PM of the twentieth century, succumbing to throat cancer that killed him five months after he resigned in May 1923.

Stanley Baldwin (28th, 1923–4, 1924–9, 1935–7) was the dominant political figure in the interwar years, who found a language of nationhood to reach across social divides, and was the first to master radio broadcasts, notably during times of crisis – such as the General Strike of 1926, the abdication crisis of 1936, and the rise of the dictators – to soothe and reassure the nation.[90] A businessman, he was a late entrant to the Commons (forty-one), and briefly ran the Board of Trade and Treasury in 1921–3 before being catapulted into Number 10, but was not a prime minister who sought to direct Whitehall departments himself. Biographer Philip Williamson says: 'He did not regard it as his job to help run departments ... he felt no inclination to write policy or administrative memoranda and letters.'[91] He saw himself as a coordinator in a way nineteenth-century prime ministers, apart from Peel and Gladstone, would have recognised. Stability was his aim, and cleaning up the messes left by Lloyd George, not unpopular objectives after the First World War, notes historian Stuart Ball.[92] He was a successful prime minister, who led the moderate and reforming administration of 1924–9 which extended the welfare state, and who during the 1930s began to rearm the country, and deftly oversaw the abdication crisis. But he lacked dynamism, and failed to properly anticipate the threat from the dictators, or to lead the economic modernisation the country needed.

Few figures were better equipped to be prime minister than his successor Neville Chamberlain (40th, 1937–40), thrice an activist Minister of Health, and twice Chancellor of the Exchequer for a total of six years. Far more vigorous than Baldwin, highly intelligent and ambitious, 'a remarkable peacetime administrator', he expected to be in power a long time.[93] But he was blown away by the foreign policy crisis in the run-up to the Second World War before he could make a significant domestic mark on the premiership as he had on his earlier departments. His premiership ended in May 1940 in failure, but he remained a loyal member of Churchill's War Cabinet for four months after May 1940, before dying of cancer that November.

Ramsay MacDonald (39th, 1924, 1929–35) proved Labour could be a legitimate and responsible party of government, but again, beyond this, did not add to the office of prime minister. He presided over a ten-month minority government in 1924, the second Labour Government of 1929–31, brought down by the financial crisis, and he remained on for four years as an increasingly ineffectual prime minister at the head of the National Government of 1931–5, in which the powers behind the black door of Number 10 were Conservatives, Baldwin and Chamberlain. His legacy is less that of prime minister than the leader of the Labour Party who built on the work of earlier Labour leaders Keir Hardie and Arthur Henderson, and brought the party to power. But it is largely a negative legacy, with Labour not back in power alone for fourteen years after 1931, a similar impact to that of Peel on the Conservative Party. Labour leaders after him had etched into their psyche that they must not split the party. As late as the IMF crisis of 1976, Callaghan was fixated by the fear that he might become another Ramsay MacDonald.[94]

Winston Churchill (41st, 1940–5, 1951–5) is regularly rated by academics and historians as the best or second-best prime minister in British history.[95] Churchill was a greater war leader than either Pitt, Palmerston, orLloyd George. His oratory inspired and epitomised the fighting spirit of the nation. To achieve victory, he introduced a small and streamlined War Cabinet, brought brilliant outsiders into Whitehall, like Frank Lindemann as his scientific advisor, centralised power in Number 10 and the Cabinet Office, and made himself the dominant figure in the conduct of war policy. But none of these were innovations, with the exception of appointing himself 'Minister of Defence' in 1940, of importance in facilitating direct and constant communication with the Chiefs of Staff, and ensuring the civilian and military sides of government worked together better than in 1914–18. 'Although some have attempted to distinguish Churchill and Lloyd George's methods, the similarities are plain.'[96] Andrew Roberts believes 'Churchill took over when a lot of the powers had already been aggregated at Number 10 to win the war, and he continued with that. He attached new labels to things.'[97] Crowcroft agrees: 'the British state during the Second World War ultimately performs in a similar fashion to the First World War, because there was an institutional memory'.[98]

In the 1945 general election, Churchill was portrayed as a presidential leader. Again, not new. So was Gladstone in 1880 and Lloyd George in 1918. Churchill had more claim to be an innovative prime minister, paradoxically, when he returned to Number 10 for his widely but wrongly derided final 'Indian Summer' spell in October 1951. He insisted on bringing back his wartime Private Secretary, Jock Colville, retaining Norman Brook as Cabinet Secretary, and, through a constitutional innovation, grouped a number of departments under 'overlord' ministers. He initially became Minister of Defence, as he had been in 1940, but only for a few months, and not Leader of the House of Commons, as he had been in title at least up to 1942. He acted as de facto Foreign Secretary, despite appointing the vastly experienced Anthony Eden, grabbing the 'best' bits of foreign policy, relations with US presidents, Truman then Eisenhower, and policy in the Cold War post the death of Stalin in 1953.[99] After he left in April 1955, no prime minister after him sought to emulate him. He was sui generis.

Mild Clement Attlee (42nd, 1945–51) in contrast was an innovator. He presided over an historic peacetime government, oversaw the growth of the British state, and created a modern system of government that lasted; he drove through the most ambitious domestic policy agenda since Peel in 1841–6 and Gladstone in 1868–74, and achieved far more in foreign policy than either; he provided an alternative model for his postwar successors by being a coordinator, not a presidential prime minister, and he was one of the last prime ministers to understand the importance of the House of Commons. He was also one of the most diversely experienced to have come to the office, having served as a barrister, an academic, a frontline soldier in the First World War, a volunteer in the East End, and mayor of Stepney, before being elected MP in 1922. A minister under MacDonald in the governments of 1924 and 1929–31, he became deputy leader of the party in 1931, and leader in 1935. He served throughout the Churchill coalition government from 1940, initially as Lord Privy Seal and then deputy prime minister from 1942 overseeing postwar plans for domestic policy. His experience showed when he eventually became prime minister at sixty-two.

While Lloyd George's plans after 1918 of creating a 'fit home for heroes' suffered from lack of funds and know-how, Attlee made certain not to repeat the same errors.[100] The British Civil Service, he claimed, was the 'envy of the world',[101] and he ensured it had the money, the backing, and the personnel to do the job, with the result that it recruited some of the ablest graduates, while retaining or bringing back many of the brilliant minds that had come into it during the war, like Oliver Franks, whom he made ambassador to the US. Edward Bridges, Churchill's Cabinet Secretary during the war, was appointed Permanent Secretary to the Treasury, while Norman Brook became the new Cabinet Secretary, establishing a systematic structure of Cabinet committees that underpinned the frenetic policy agenda.

The postwar reconstruction work that Attlee oversaw during the war, inspired by J. M. Keynes and William Beveridge, made possible what was the biggest one-ministry social revolution in British history. Some landmarks stand out: a mixed economy, with coal, electricity, and railways nationalised; pensions, unemployment, sickness, and child benefits to all contributors in the 1946 National Insurance Act; trade unions reformed, with Baldwin's 1927 Trade Disputes Act repealed; the National Health Service (NHS) set up in July 1948; and national parks and new towns created. Abroad, with the support of the formidable Foreign Secretary Ernest Bevin, the government played a leading role in the creation of the United Nations in 1945 and NATO in 1949. Britain became the third nuclear power in the postwar world, after the USA and USSR, with his 1946 decision, made in secret with no Cabinet discussion, to build a British atomic bomb, thereby committing the country to a nuclear deterrent. The 'Truman Doctrine', to counter communism worldwide, and the 'Marshall Plan' to rebuild Western Europe with American money, were strongly encouraged by Attlee, a vigorous Cold War warrior.[102] He and Bevin strengthened the 'special relationship' with the US as an anti-communist alliance. These were considerable historic achievements and they set the direction of British policy for over 50 years.

The Attlee government also gave independence to India, Burma (now Myanmar), and Ceylon (now Sri Lanka) in 1947 and 1948, and ended Britain's mandate in Palestine in 1948, which led to the creation of Israel. However, the decolonisation process was rushed, and conflicts quickly broke out in both India, which led to partition, and the Middle East.

Attlee showed that prime ministers can act as leaders of their team, allowing ministers to take the lead and gain the credit. Bogdanor considers Attlee's premiership 'the high point of Cabinet government'.[103] 'Attlee modelled his style as prime minister on being mayor of Stepney,' says John Bew. 'He saw himself as chair, with utter control of the process. He never did anything without being absolutely on top of every single detail.'[104] Some believe that Attlee was more successful at team-building than any prime minister in recent history.[105] He was fortunate of course to have a team that included Bevin, Hugh Dalton, Herbert Morrison, and Stafford Cripps, who had held senior positions during the war, and to whom he added Aneurin (Nye) Bevan at Health. They were old and tired maybe, and didn't prevent the loss of momentum and cohesion after 1947, and nor did the younger figures like Hugh Gaitskell and Harold Wilson whom he promoted into the Cabinet. Attlee's skill as an arbitrator ensured that senior Cabinet colleagues, including Bevin and Bevan, from polar opposite wings of their party, and Herbert Morrison who hated both of them, worked well in a team together. Attlee was as good a dismisser as an appointer, both vital attributes for the prime minister. Hennessy describes how Cabinet colleagues 'all feared the summons to Number 10 that might eject them once more onto the backbenches. Unlike most of his predecessors and successors, Attlee didn't wrap his dismissals up.'[106] Indeed, even Thatcher, who emulated Attlee's grasp of detail and intolerance of evasion, lacked his killer instinct for telling ministers what they didn't want to hear.

Attlee, unlike Disraeli and Lloyd George before him, and Thatcher and Blair after, was not detached from Parliament. Although the first prime minister not to take up the Leadership of his House, he invested considerable time and energy in the Commons and speaking to MPs: 'He never developed a reputation for being distant or aloof, except in the sense that his personality was very crisp', says Adonis.[107] Fellow Labour MPs were proud of him and showed him palpable respect, bolstered by his regularly outsmarting Churchill, as when he defended himself in a censure motion in December 1945, or when he defended Bevin for his foreign policy.[108] He pushed the Parliament Act of 1949, which amended the 1911 Act and reduced the House of Lords' power of delay to one year, further entrenching the authority of the Commons. The 'Salisbury Convention' was also set under him, whereby the House of Lords agreed not to block or wreck measures that had been included in a governing party's election manifesto.[109] No prime minister did more to entrench and legitimise parliamentary democracy postwar than Attlee.

Like all our first-tier PMs, he finished unhappily. He stayed on too long, turning his landslide victory of 1945 into almost a loss in 1950, and a defeat to the Conservatives in 1951. He bequeathed a party divided without a clear sense of momentum or direction. He committed the country to high levels of expenditure, central planning, and nationalisation which arguably dogged the country's economic and industrial progress postwar, in contrast to Germany, Japan, and the United States. And he left a legacy of trouble by scuttling out of the Indian subcontinent and the Middle East so quickly. But his impact on the office of prime minister, showing how to work with Cabinet, Parliament, and the Civil Service to achieve historic change, threw down the gauntlet to subsequent prime ministers.

MARGARET THATCHER (49TH, 1979–90)

Six prime ministers served in the twenty-six years between Attlee's defeat in October 1951 and the election of Margaret Thatcher in May 1979. Two made minimal impression on the office because of brevity, Anthony Eden (43rd, 1955–7) and Alec Douglas-Home (45th, 1963–4). Two prime ministers were associated each with just one major event: Edward Heath (47th, 1970–4) and James Callaghan (48th, 1976–9). Heath came to office with the most comprehensive plan for government of any Conservative prime minister, worked up in five years in opposition.[110] But hard-fought attempts to reform local government, trade unions, and central government, and to find a solution to the deteriorating situation in Northern Ireland, all failed. Only one event made an enduring impact: leading Britain into the European Economic Community (EEC) on 1 January 1973. By doing so, his biographer Philip Ziegler claims that he changed the lives of British people more fundamentally than any prime minister since Churchill: 'By securing Britain's entry into Europe, he reversed almost a thousand years of history.'[111] An orthodox prime minister in his relations with Cabinet, the Civil Service, and Parliament, he relied increasingly on a coterie of close advisors in Number 10. The end was unorthodox, a premiership overwhelmed.

Harold Macmillan (44th, 1957–63) is often derided as a backwards-looking prime minister, 'the last Edwardian at Number 10', but, in fact, he was mostly effective.[112] He was so much more than the image, crafted in part by himself, and he anticipated, if not always completed, bold departures for the country, the Conservative Party, and the prime ministerial office. He decided in 1960 that Britain's future lay in the EEC, established three years before, though the application was rejected by President de Gaulle of France in January 1963.

In February 1960, he told parliamentarians in Cape Town the unwelcome news that a 'wind of change' was sweeping across the continent of Africa, and that self-government was on the march: he accelerated the pace of the decolonisation of the British Empire, with relative speed and lack of rancour. He became the first jet (and helicopter) prime minister, travelling to more overseas conferences, meetings, and destinations than any prime minister before. In July 1962, he sacked seven members of his Cabinet in one fell swoop in what became known (after Hitler's 1934 coup) as the 'Night of the Long Knives', including Selwyn Lloyd, Chancellor of the Exchequer. Coleman regards it as a key moment establishing the right of the prime minister, not the monarch, to dismiss Cabinet ministers.[113] He was aware that Britain was becoming a 'stagnant society' but did not know how to modernise the economy, nor society.[114] He anticipated Wilson in building up a personal staff within Number 10; but he did not add enduringly to the stature, perception, or substance of the prime minister. The Profumo Crisis of 1963 made Macmillan look weak and out of touch and the 'Magic Circle' elevation of Douglas-Home as his anointed successor tarnished his reputation, leading the Conservatives to introduce party leadership elections in 1965.[115] The last prime minister to be born in the Victorian age (1894), to have fought in World War One, to read novels at leisure in Number 10, while dying (in 1986) in the early days of the internet, he fell just short, as did Baldwin, of being an agenda-changing prime minister.

Harold Wilson (46th, 1964–70, 1974–76) has often been considered one of the better prime ministers, and he was, technically, Labour's most successful electorally, winning four elections. He was definitely one of the ablest intellectually to hold the office, having acquired a first in Politics, Philosophy and Economics (PPE) from Jesus College, Oxford: Roy Jenkins writes, 'academically, his results put him among Prime Ministers in the category of Peel, Gladstone, Asquith and no one else'.[116] A lecturer at Oxford at the age of twenty-one, one of the youngest in the twentieth century, when Attlee appointed him to the Cabinet in 1947 he became, as he liked to remind people, the youngest Cabinet minister since Pitt the Younger.[117] As prime minister from 1964, he introduced the most fundamental reform of the Civil Service since Gladstone, with the 1968 Fulton Report, which made the PM officially responsible for the Civil Service. He attacked the Treasury head on, creating the Department of Economic Affairs in 1964 as a direct challenge to its near monopoly on power. He created an image of himself on television, which shaped the premiership more than any other new technology since radio and news-reels in the 1930s. He sold himself, perhaps too hard, as in tune with the age of the sixties. To beef up his personal resource, he operated a 'kitchen Cabinet' of close advisors to guide him in Number 10, and in March 1974, when he returned to power, he introduced the Policy Unit in Downing Street. To round it off, he resorted to the first national referendum in British history, in June 1975, on whether Britain should continue its membership of the EEC.

But closer examination of Wilson's innovations suggests a less rosy picture. Prime ministers had been de facto if not de jure heads of the Civil Service since the nineteenth century, many Fulton reforms failed to bite, the Civil Service Department was disbanded by Thatcher in 1981, and the Department of Economic Affairs was dissolved in 1969 while he was still PM. Wilson may have been the first prime minister deeply to understand television with a comfortable and reassuring presence, but Baldwin had blazed the trail with the new media technologies in the 1920s. Wilson even copied pipe-smoking from him (while privately puffing on cigars). Macmillan, besides, was the first television prime minister, 1959 being the first television general election, a year before the first presidential television election in the United States in 1960. Wilson did bring in his own team in 1964, introducing special advisors (SpAds) into Number 10, including Marcia Williams, and his favourite economists Thomas Balogh and Nicholas Kaldor. But Lloyd George's secretariat had anticipated Wilson's Policy Unit, while every prime minister since Chamberlain relied on their own close advisors in Downing Street: for Churchill, Colville and his son-in-law Christopher Soames; for Macmillan, three officials, Tim Bligh, Freddie Bishop, and Philip de Zulueta, and his close friend John Wyndham, Baron Egremont.[118] Like Macmillan in 1959, Wilson won a landslide election in 1966: both men struggled to realise the potential it gave them.

Not even holding the first national referendum can be considered groundbreaking, as an earlier referendum had taken place in March 1973 in Northern Ireland on whether it should remain part of the United Kingdom, albeit boycotted by nationalists and therefore uncontested.[119] Wilson's aims of improving Britain's long-term economic performance, forging ahead with science and technology, and reducing inequality, remained largely unfulfilled. Like Macmillan, he tried to find a postcolonial role for Britain in the world, which included a second unsuccessful attempt to join the EEC, again rebuffed by De Gaulle. His most defiant foreign policy stance was his resistance to American president Lyndon Johnson, who wanted Britain to commit forces to Vietnam, a decision that needs to be set alongside Blair's decision to support President Bush on invading Iraq in 2003. Wilson's final term in 1974–6, with the exception of his clever ploy to have a referendum to hold his party together, was a disappointment. Pimlott contrasts the vibrancy of the 1964 manifesto with the one in 1974 which was 'at best, a shopping list, at worst a collection of slogans'.[120] Overall, Wilson's policy achievements pale beside Attlee's and Blair's.

Certainly, though, there were significant reforms, including the decriminalisation of homosexuality and abortion, abolition of theatre censorship, reform of divorce laws, changing the legal age of adulthood and therefore voting to 18, abolition of the death penalty in most cases, and the creation of the Open University in 1969.[121] But the social reforms were the achievement of his brilliant Home Secretary Roy Jenkins (1965–7), and Wilson failed, like Macmillan, to solve Britain's deep-seated economic and labour problems. Lack of principle, both ideological and personal, was the ultimate undoing of Wilson; he proved more successful as a pragmatic party leader than prime minister.

The next Labour prime minister was James Callaghan. His challenge was to hold the government together in the IMF loan crisis of 1976, despite a tough economic backdrop. During the 'winter of discontent' in 1978–9, his government was severely damaged by the trade unions, which he had resisted reforming in 1969, and was finished off by a vote of no confidence in March 1979. Despite being the only PM to have held the other three great offices of state (Chancellor of the Exchequer, Foreign Secretary, and Home Secretary), he had added little to any of them. Attempts to rehabilitate his historical reputation as PM have not convinced.[122] Unlike Attlee, who also left his party in distress, Callaghan had little to show for his years at Number 10.[123]

If Heath was clear on strategy but poor on tactics, and Wilson strong on tactics but vague on strategy, Thatcher (49th, 1979–90) excelled at both: 'She had an idea of what she wanted to do and largely did', as Steve Richards encapsulates it.[124] Few gave her much credit when she became an MP in 1959 and a junior minister under Macmillan and Douglas-Home from 1961–4. She came to national prominence as Heath's Secretary of State for Education and Science from 1970–4, before becoming a surprise challenger to her boss in February 1975. Four and a quarter years as Leader of the Opposition saw her stamp her mark as a leader totally unlike him, Wilson or Callaghan. They were conciliators, and corporatists; she a conviction politician, and an anti-statist. In the 1970s, she became fired up by the liberal values espoused by think tanks like the Institute for Economic Affairs and Centre for Policy Studies, which pumped out academic and heterodox tracts, in sharp contrast to the consensus framework of policy established by Attlee.[125]

Her historic importance emanates from her emphatic, self-confident style, her winning three general election victories in a row, her serving eleven-and-a-half years, the longest since Liverpool, her upending the politics that had dominated British policy for the previous thirty years, her impact on the global stage, greater than any peacetime prime minister in the century, challenging the boundaries and the objectives of the state, changing the operation of Cabinet government forever, and, not least, for being the first female prime minister.

Style matters. The most commanding prime ministers of the twentieth century before Thatcher, Lloyd George and Churchill, in both cases were because the existential crisis of a major war focused public attention on them. Thatcher established a similar presence in peacetime, much harder. 'Throughout her premiership, she was the dominant figure in British public life, and not only made the political weather, but went some way to changing the political climate, too', writes David Cannadine. 'For much of her time as Prime Minister she commanded the Cabinet, the Civil Service, the Commons, and parts of the country to a degree, and for a duration, which no other Prime Minister in modern times has rivalled.'[126]

No other prime minister since 1945 has had an '-ism' appended to their name. 'Thatcherism' became a widely accepted moniker to describe not only a range of coherent policies, but a style of government.[127] She took time to gain in confidence as PM. Until 1981, she was faced by a Cabinet that had many personal and ideological sceptics, and her almost total inexperience abroad showed. A Cabinet reshuffle in 1981, victory in the Falklands War in 1982, and general election success in 1983 boosted her confidence.[128] Biographer Charles Moore describes her approach: 'her "housewife economics" directly challenged the postwar orthodoxy that the state could run the economy. Countries cannot become richer, freer or even fairer, she asserted, if the government and trade union leaders controlled labour, forever increased public debt, nationalised the main means of production, and sought to manage demand. Individual liberty was both an economic and moral imperative.'[129] Thatcher systemically pulled apart the building blocks of the postwar settlement, privatising vast tracts of the economy, ending the government's commitment to full employment, and removing powers from trade unions. Not everything changed: the NHS, education system, pensions, and universal welfare were substantially unaltered. Political scientist Dennis Kavanagh, who popularised the notion of the 'postwar consensus', nevertheless sees 'Attlee and Thatcher as the two bookends of postwar British politics: one set up the policies on which the consensus was based, the other deconstructed them'.[130]

Needless to say, Thatcher was controversial. Throughout the 1980s, and beyond, people defined themselves as either with her or against her. Many people were inspired to enter politics for the first time, simply to oppose her. Nor did everyone benefit from her economic policies, with the consequences of deindustrialisation being unemployment and deep social problems. One of her hopes was that she would create a more moral society, and yet the materialistic and self-centred 1980s culture that her liberal economic policies often encouraged was the antithesis of her aims.[131] Old-style liberals were upset too when her government allowed the passing of Section 28 which made 'promoting homosexuality in schools' illegal.[132]

Thatcher quickly made foreign policy her own, so by 1990, 'on the international stage, she possessed a star quality which no world leader in her day could equal, and which no twentieth century British premier has attained, with the exception of Churchill'.[133] No American president has ever deferred to a British prime minister in peacetime as much as President Reagan, himself a considerable figure in history, so much so that his successor George H. W. Bush was advised by aides to keep a distance from her.[134] Every world leader wanted to beat a road to her door. She was the iconic world figure of the 1980s, facilitating the dialogue between Reagan and Mikhail Gorbachev of the Soviet Union that helped to end the Cold War. After years of talk of decline after 1945, the achievement was historic.

She had less sense of history herself though than perhaps any of the great PMs: a chemist by education and barrister by occupation, her ferocious work rate left her little time for reading or for the arts. 'Year Zero was 1940 for her', writes Thatcher specialist Chris Collins. 'The great Victorian and Edwardian figures did not register much. Margaret Thatcher never made anything of Peel, nor was Disraeli a particular favourite.'[135] Nevertheless, we may say Thatcher was at her most *Gladstonian* in her desire for a small state, even if her success was uneven. The 1979 manifesto had given a clear commitment to curb the growth of unelected bodies: but they soared in number in the 1980s, specifically 'quasi-non-governmental organisations' ('quangos'), executive agencies covering education, health, and other services. Simon Jenkins argues thus that, despite her intentions, power became increasingly centralised in central government.[136] She abolished the Civil Service Department and drove for a smaller and more efficient Civil Service, but was unable to reduce the size of the state. Crowcroft describes how

> Thatcher attempted to use the office of prime minister to transform the size of the state, and bring about a transformation of the electorate's values. Even though she succeeded often only at the margin in reducing the size ..., she stands out as being only the first prime minister since Salisbury to try to reduce dependency on the state and to boost the private sector.[137]

Thatcher respected tradition, the constitution, and the Crown. But she marginalised Cabinet and Parliament, cashing in on her large majorities in the House of Commons after 1983 and 1987, and asserting her power to drive through change and to avoid discussion, which she considered a distraction. 'She established a new convention', says Philip Norton. 'Rather than summing discussion up at the end of the Cabinet, she would sum it up before. This isn't necessarily a sign of strength. She was dominant in Cabinet, but never had a purely Thatcherite Cabinet, which perhaps explains why she acted as she did.'[138] Cabinet increasingly became a forum where decisions were *reported*, with the important discussions taking place in the labyrinth of Cabinet committees or in ad hoc meetings.[139] In the end, as with Gladstone, Lloyd George, and Churchill, her aloofness from her colleagues brought her down in November 1990. The successor, John Major (50th, 1990–7), tried in his first two years to show that he was a different style of leader by consulting Cabinet. It didn't last. It rarely does. Tony Blair (51st, 1997–2007) and all prime ministers since, whatever their initial collegiate intentions, have taken the key decisions outside Cabinet, except when parliamentary position or national importance dictated that they had no other choice.

Thirty-one years have passed since Thatcher ceased to be prime minister, and six prime ministers have arrived at Number 10 full of high hopes about how they would be free to change the country as they wished, and five to date have left disappointed, at moments not entirely of their choosing. All six lived under her shadow, as did the three Conservative

Party leaders who never made it into Downing Street, William Hague (1997–2001), Iain Duncan Smith (2001–3), and Michael Howard (2003–5). If Major tried desperately to be unlike her and found himself increasingly undermined by her and her acolytes, Blair made abundantly clear his admiration for her style.[140] New Labour's 'abandonment of socialism and nationalisation, and its embrace of the free market, free enterprise and wealth creation' owed much to her.[141] Gordon Brown (52nd, 2007–10) disowned Blair both before and after he became prime minister, but he too made a show of inviting Thatcher to tea at Downing Street: Number 10's press release spoke of a meeting of minds between two 'conviction politicians' in their two-hour meeting.[142] Bonar Law and Baldwin would no more have celebrated having Lloyd George at Number 10 for tea, than Heath would have invited Wilson. That is a measure of the Thatcher effect, and of her long shadow.

The continued celebration of Thatcher after 1990 by the Murdoch, the *Mail*, and the *Telegraph* groups of newspapers, and their leading commentators, played a significant part in prime ministers wanting to defer to her, and to be seen to be like her. Her continuing influence on Euroscepticism was felt after her death: no prime minister had more influence on the 2016 referendum result than Thatcher. Nor would any would-be prime minister after her, serious about winning a general election, propose giving powers back to trade unions, renationalising industry en masse, or having high rates of direct tax. David Cameron (53rd, 2010–16) searched for a form of softer Conservativism than Thatcher's, but happily supported a 'ceremonial funeral' for her at St Paul's Cathedral when she died in 2013.[143] Boris Johnson (55th, 2019 to present) cannot escape being considered 'heir to Thatcher' in breaking from the EU and freeing Britain of restrictions to develop a capitalist economy post-Brexit, like Singapore, and in projecting an image across the country of a strong and decisive prime minister.

Thatcherism may by 2021 be coming at last to an end with, as Bogdanor argues, the credit crunch of 2008 discrediting unbridled capitalism, the expenses scandal spreading mistrust of politicians, and COVID challenging the viability of a small state: to which we could add environmentalism.[144] But her long shadow explains why Blair, for all his transformation of the constitution, making him effectively the last British prime minister to run Scotland, his three election victories, his domestic reforms, and his presidential manner at Number 10, does not qualify as an agenda-changing prime minister at the level of the 'big eight'.

But with a new decade, the door is wide open for the next candidate. Supporters of Boris Johnson, and the man himself, as did so many of his predecessors, believe he will make the cut. He certainly has the opportunity, and the powers, as we see in the next chapter.

CHAPTER 5

The Powers and Resources of the Prime Minister, 1721–2021

P RIME MINISTERS COME TO OFFICE DIZZY WITH IDEAS ABOUT how they are going to make Britain a better country and outperform their predecessor, but with only the haziest idea about how to be PM. Is it a surprise that many underperform?. 'Reality only fully dawns', says Mark Sedwill, one ex-Cabinet Secretary, 'when they go to see the monarch, and walk through the front door of Number 10 for the first time.'[1] Their first words to the nation uttered on the doorstep of Number 10 say more about them than the job to begin moments later. 'Where there is discord we will bring harmony', said Thatcher, quoting Francis of Assisi. 'A country that is at ease with itself' was Major's aspiration. For Blair, it was to govern not for 'the privilege of the few but the right[s] of the many' and to 'rebuild trust in politics'. His school motto inspired Brown to promise the nation that 'I will try my utmost.' Fighting 'burning injustices' was May's intention, while Johnson was going 'to restore trust in our democracy' by 'uniting our country' and 'answering at last the plea of the forgotten people' by achieving Brexit and 'level[ling] up across Britain'. Gus O'Donnell, who patiently waited as Cabinet Secretary to greet two incoming prime ministers, made a study of these first speeches, and notes how similar are the aspirations of the virgin prime ministers.[2]

Premierships can go by in a blur of frenzied activity. Prime ministers typically only reflect fully on the powers and resources they possessed *after* their period in office is over, when they are writing their memoirs, ruefully reflecting on what might have been. That doesn't mean that there aren't precise powers, some formal, others informal, accumulated over the years, and it is these that we consider in this chapter. The most successful prime ministers, like Thatcher, knew, by study or osmosis, how to use them.

Andrew Turnbull, her last Principal Private Secretary and later Cabinet Secretary, captured an essential truth: 'There was no codification of her powers at all. By the time I took over as her PPS, she had been in office for nine years. She had a well-structured modus operandi. None of it was written down. But everyone *knew* very clearly what the prime minister did and was expected to do. There was no dispute about it.'[3]

PRIME MINISTERS COMPARED: THREE MODELS ABROAD

Because so many prime ministers have failed to live up to even their own hopes on entering office, we begin by noting that they have *more* powers and potential authority than most prime ministers abroad. Several political systems have been based directly upon the Westminster model, our first type, their origins lying in colonial government, with a Governor-General as the queen's representative fulfilling the monarch's function. Australia's constitution thus vests executive power in the monarch, and in the Governor-General as the monarch's representative, but does not mention the prime minister by name.[4] The prime minister has emerged however to the point where he or she is 'the first among equals':[5] they chair the Cabinet, determine its agenda, and oversee the work of the government, supported by the 'Department of Prime Minister and Cabinet'. They appoint ministers, albeit under some constraints, decide election dates, are the public face of the country abroad, and the principal focal point for the media within the country. The similarities with the way that the British PM has developed are striking.

The prime minister of New Zealand has a similar position, although the country does not have a written constitution. Instead, as in the UK, it has laws and treaties that lay out the precedents which define the powers of the prime minister. The documents say: 'The person who leads the political party or group of parties (coalition) with a majority of seats in the House becomes the Prime Minister' and 'The Governor-General must always act on the advice of the Prime Minister or Ministers who have necessary support of elected representatives in Parliament.'[6] In recent decades, the prime minister in New Zealand has emerged as the main spokesperson for the government, both within and outside Parliament.[7] As a unitary country, New Zealand is perhaps closer to

Britain than any other, though its electoral system rarely throws up prime ministers with a simple majority, which is why the New Zealand experience became of such interest to the keepers of the British constitution as Britain faced the prospect of coalition governments in the early twenty-first century.[8]

Westminster-*influenced* political systems provide another model. In India, while the president has been the head of state since the country became a republic in January 1950, the prime minister is the head of the executive branch, and exercises most executive powers. Officially, prime ministers act as advisor to the president, but as the latter is largely ceremonial, similar to the British monarch, the prime minister has had the real power ever since the first PM, Jawaharlal Nehru, down to the fourteenth, Narendra Modi. The prime minister can be a member of either house in Parliament, with Manmohan Singh serving as PM (2004–14) from the Rajya Sabha (Upper House), not seen in Britain since Salisbury ceased to be prime minister in 1902, whereas Modi is a member of the Lok Sabha (Lower House). The prime minister allocates portfolios amongst the ministers, using the Cabinet Secretariat, modelled on the British office, to help do so.[9]

The Republic of Ireland is modelled closely on Westminster too, with the obvious difference that since April 1949 an apolitical president is head of state, after Ireland formally became a republic. The post of prime minister, known as *Taoiseach* (meaning 'prime minister'), was inaugurated by Éamon de Valera in the 1937 Constitution of Ireland, replacing the post of 'President of the Executive Council of the Irish Free State' from 1922. The Taoiseach advises the president to dismiss ministers and dissolve Parliament on his or her own authority. Under the Irish Constitution, the Taoiseach is both de jure and de facto chief executive, whereas in most other parliamentary democracies, the head of state remains the chief executive, at least in name. Brendan O'Leary writes that the post is 'potentially more powerful than any other European Prime Minister, with the exception of the British counterpart'.[10] The powers of the president should not be disregarded, with two living former presidents, Mary Robinson (1990–7) and Mary McAleese (1997–2011) continuing as members of the Council of State.

The French prime minister is the least influential in this second category. Appointed by the president of the republic, who is executive head of state, the prime minister is head of government and shares significant powers with the president, though clearly subordinate. In principle, the president can appoint whoever they like as prime minister, but in practice it needs to be someone acceptable to the National Assembly. 'Cohabitation' can result, with a president and prime minister from different parties, as between 1986 and 1988, when the Socialist president François Mitterrand served with conservative Jacques Chirac as prime minister. The office of president had been largely ceremonial under the Third French Republic (1870–1940) and the Fourth Republic (1946–58), but the constitution of the Fifth Republic (1958 to present) transformed its power, consolidated when the 1962 referendum voted to make the president directly elected by universal suffrage, not by the French Assembly. The president is Commander-in-Chief, decides whether or not France goes to war (e.g. President Chirac's opposition to the war in Iraq in 2003), rules at times of national emergency, and can govern by decree, as did the first French president of the Fifth Republic, Charles de Gaulle, during the Algerian War. But the French prime minister is not without powers, and constitutionally 'directs the actions of the government', which relieves the president of much of the day-to-day work that dogs the British PM. Significantly, the French PM is not 'primus inter pares', hence not technically superior to other ministers.

European federal models constitute a third model. Germany provides the most illuminating comparison, given the country's success, and its desperate starting point in the late 1940s. It has both a presidential and a *federal* state, with considerable powers in the hands of the sixteen partly sovereign states or *Länder*, a system initially established at the creation of the Federal Republic of Germany in 1949, and extended with the reunification of Germany in 1990. Seven German chancellors served from 1949 until Angela Merkel succeeded Gerhard Schröeder in 2005. The *Grundgesatz*, the Basic Law for the Federal Republic, provides the federal chancellorship with its strong power base: the right to form and chair the federal Cabinet, and to propose and dismiss candidates from ministerial office, and to establish the guidelines of government policy for federal ministers to enact, albeit with the 'principle of ministerial autonomy' giving them certain freedoms of action.[11] The chancellor is accountable to the Bundestag, the federal Parliament, designed by the Constitution for consensus, not confrontation. The Chancellor must abide by decisions agreed with coalition partners, based upon the state of the parties within the Bundestag.

Eight chancellors have served since 1949, on average nine years each, the system ensuring stability and strength, underpinned by the stable German economy, which helped absorb the shock of reunification. The German president has wide-ranging ceremonial obligations, and some significant reserve powers, but does not eclipse the chancellors, all of whom, as John Kampfner argues, have made an enduring impact, notably Konrad Adenauer (1949–63) and Helmut Kohl (1982–98) alongside Merkel herself.[12] We can well ask: why they have consistently achieved more than their opposite numbers in Number 10?

The power of the Italian prime minister, in theory, is comparable to the British PM. The Italian Constitutional Charter of 1947 confers considerable power on the PM as head of the executive, placed at the centre of government, directing policy, maintaining political and administrative capability, and coordinating the work of ministers.[13] Endemic corruption, though, has tainted the operation of the office and the trust it inspires. In the First Republic (1946–94) Christian Democrats were the senior party, and the Communists the principal opposition. The dominant figure was the serially corrupt Giulio Andreotti, seven times prime minister between 1972–1992. The assassination of former prime minister Aldo Moro by the Red Brigades was a nadir of domestic Italian politics in May 1978. The Second Republic after 1994 was dominated by the differently corrupt Silvio Berlusconi, three times prime minister. The 1947 Constitution baked instability into the system by providing for two co-equal houses in the legislature, and proportional representation, designed to prevent tyrannical excess as under Mussolini, but producing instability instead, with twenty-nine prime ministers since 1945, and over sixty different governments, albeit most from the Christian Democrats.[14]

Proportional representation (PR) electoral systems abroad produce coalition governments which limit the powers of prime ministers. 'If the prime minister's own party has a minority of seats in the legislature, then the ministers are enabled to go their own way, and departments are viewed as the property of the party whose minister is their chief', says Dennis Kavanagh. 'So the prime ministers in such cases are under severe restraint. The only party they can call on for discipline is their own.'[15] The Italian experience is often cited to counter PR, long advocated as the solution to Britain's adversarial political system.

So how does the power of the British PM compare to those abroad? Their average length of service from 1945 to January 2021, with fourteen prime ministers serving an average of four years and eight months, matches New Zealand, Australia, and India, all averaging four years and six months, but is markedly shorter than the French president's (seven years and four months) and German chancellor's (eight years and ten months).

Patrick Weller, the academic impresario of comparative political leadership, is unequivocal: 'the British prime minister is more powerful than any other'.[16] The New Zealand PM he places second, in part because of the country's unitary constitution. Australia follows, where a potentially powerful prime minister is limited by the country having a federal government with independent state powers. Canada comes fourth, where the provinces have even more autonomy than Australian states. Then the Netherlands and Denmark, where the prime ministers are 'safe within their own parties, but not safe in Parliament, because coalition partners can walk out and bring the government down, resulting in coalitions regularly being reworked'.[17] In countries where the position of prime minister is most fragile, as in Italy, the incumbent needs to be constantly responsible and reasonable, or corrupt Walpole-style, to ensure they are taking coalition partners with them.

In Britain, the prime minister, as long as he or she has a majority in Parliament, can take major decisions without taking Cabinet with them, beyond their own small inner circle in Number 10 and key Cabinet ministers, above all the Chancellor. This power is boosted by the country being a unitary not a federal state, by the head of state being hereditary not elected, and by the non-proportional electoral system generally producing a government with parliamentary majorities. With so much going for them, why has prime ministerial performance not been stronger? Our thesis is that they often squander their authority by not fully taking stock of the powers at their disposal at the outset, evaluating their historic opportunity, and setting a realistic strategy. So what exactly are these powers and resources?

SOURCES OF THE PRIME MINISTER'S POWER

The prime ministers' 'formal' powers have only recently been written down, albeit in a far from complete or unambiguous way. But these powers only become fully effective when the prime minister knows how to exploit them.

ROYAL PREROGATIVE POWERS. 'The royal prerogative itself is a notoriously difficult concept to define adequately', said the Select Committee on Public Administration in 2004.[18] Indeed it is. *The Cabinet Manual* of 2011 has this to say about the royal prerogative: 'The residual power inherent in the Sovereign, and now exercised mostly on the advice of the Prime Minister and Ministers of the Crown'. Ministerial powers, in contrast, 'derive from legislation passed by Parliament, the royal prerogative and common law ... Ministers now exercise the bulk of the prerogative powers, either in their own right or in the advice that they provide to the Sovereign, which he or she is constitutionally bound to follow.'[19] Even in 2021 the queen's advisors still look to late Victorian constitutional theorist, A. V. Dicey, who described the royal prerogative as 'the remaining proportion of the Crown's original authority and ... therefore ... the name for the residue of discretionary power left at any moment in the hands of the Crown, whether such power be in fact exercised by the Queen herself or by her Ministers'.[20]

The monarch retains some *constitutional* prerogatives, above all the right to 'advise, encourage and warn ministers' *in private*, as identified by Walter Bagehot in his book *The English Constitution* (first published in 1867).[21] The *legal* prerogatives of the Crown in contrast contain mostly obsolete remnants, which include the right of the Crown to certain swans and whales, and the right to press men into the Royal Navy. The final type of royal prerogative though, the *executive powers*, are very much alive. By convention, the monarch acts on ministerial advice, with powers delegated to them. These royal prerogative powers include the conduct of diplomacy, including the recognition of states and the governance of Britain's overseas territories; the deployment and use of armed forces overseas, or in Britain to maintain peace; appointing and removing ministers; peerages and honours, patronage appointments, and the appointment of senior judges; recommendations for honours and the granting of pardons, all of which are still of importance today. Parliament had not been directly involved in that transfer of power until recently when the Constitutional Reform and Governance Act 2010 gave Parliament statutory powers to ratify treaties and also statutory footing on the organisation of the civil service. The Fixed-Term Parliaments Act of 2011 took the power of dissolution away from the monarch and placed it in the hands of parliamentarians, but the repeal of the Act, planned in 2021, will place the prerogative power back in the hands of the monarch.

CODIFIED POWERS. Britain might have had a Cabinet Secretariat at work since 1916, but much of the remit of the prime minister was left up in the air. Not until newly appointed Cabinet Secretary Norman Brook (1947–62) instructed talented Treasury official William Armstrong (later head of the Civil Service, 1968–74) to institute some order, was a first attempt made to codify the powers of the prime minister and Cabinet. Britain did not have to cope with defeat in 1945, as did Germany and Italy which adopted new constitutions postwar which defined the jurisdictions of their leaders. This was a British makeshift response instead. Armstrong had been a wartime Private Secretary to Cabinet Secretary Edward Bridges and in 1946 became responsible for keeping the 'Cabinet Committee Book' up to date. He regularly bombarded his bosses with memos suggesting improvements, which included drawing up a 'Precedent Book', which became a permanent feature of the British state. Kevin Theakston describes it as 'a collection of material covering constitutional and procedural contingencies, kept in loose-leaf binders in the Cabinet Secretary's office and regularly updated up to the 1990s'.[22] Another Armstrong initiative was to compile a compendium of directives and papers issued by Downing Street on how to conduct Cabinet business, which became known as 'Questions of Procedures for Ministers (QPM)'.

A year later, Armstrong composed the first official list of the functions of a prime minister and his staff, later incorporated into the 'Precedent Book', which Peter Hennessy found buried in the National Archives at Kew in the late 1990s when researching his book, *The Prime Minister*. The

Armstrong document is of seminal significance to our understanding of the prime minister, and states the following:

> The office of the Prime Minister is not founded on any statute and does not carry with it the charge of any Department. The Prime Minister has no statutory power. His powers derive primarily from the fact that he is normally the chosen leader of a political Party with a majority in the House of Commons, and that as such he has been asked by the King to be Head of the Government. The extent to which the powers latent in this position are made real depends on two things:
>
> The personal influence of the Prime Minister over the Ministers who make up the Government ... deciding whom to recommend for the various offices ... power to recommend the moving of a Minister from one office to another, or his dismissal from the Government altogether ... [and] by his own resignation ... [to] bring about the resignation of the whole Government. These powers are great ... But if they were used arbitrarily or harshly the influence of the Prime Minister and the cohesion of his administration would suffer greatly.[23]
>
> [Second,] the Prime Minister's Chairmanship of the Cabinet and some of its most important Committees, particularly the Defence Committee. Responsibility for the Government's policy as a whole is borne, not by the Prime Minister himself, but collectively by all Ministers.[24]
>
> The Prime Minister is also normally First Lord of the Treasury ... day-to-day work is under the charge of the Chancellor of the Exchequer and the Prime Minister is not directly concerned. Nevertheless, the Prime Minister does derive one very important power from his position as First Lord, namely his ultimate power of control of the Civil Service.[25]
>
> ... for appointments to the highest permanent posts in Departments the consent of the Prime Minister is required. In this matter the Prime Minister is advised by the Secretary of the Treasury. This arrangement ensures that the information available in the Treasury regarding the Civil Service is put at the disposal of Ministers in making these appointments, so that the highest administrative posts may be filled by the best men [sic] from the whole Civil Service and not merely by promotion within each Department.[26]

The Cabinet Manual of 2011 is a second codification of ministerial powers. Gordon Brown came to power as prime minister in 2007 intent on initiating a written constitution. As the 2010 general election approached, with it the likelihood of a hung parliament, the queen's Private Secretary, Christopher Geidt (one of the three-person 'magic circle', along with the Cabinet Secretary and the senior official at Number 10) went to New Zealand to examine how their political system adapted to hung parliaments and coalitions. Gus O'Donnell, the Cabinet Secretary, took this quest forward when he attended a meeting of Westminster-model Cabinet Secretaries in New Zealand shortly before the general election. Discussions with officials there convinced him of the importance of Britain having its own *Cabinet Manual* to prepare the ground should a hung parliament ever materialise.[27] 'Britain's top officials were anxious to prevent a repeat of what had happened in 1974, where there was confusion among political players and the public about what was going on, so they wanted publicly to establish the basic principles', says Andrew Blick.[28]

As the most recent authoritative statement, it is important to lay out some of what *The Cabinet Manual* says. It summarises the PM's power thus:

> The Prime Minister is the head of the Government and holds that position
> by virtue of his or her ability to command the confidence of the House
> of Commons, which in turn commands the confidence of the electorate,
> as expressed through a general election. The Prime Minister's unique
> position of authority also comes from support in the House of
> Commons. By modern convention, the Prime Minister always sits in the
> House of Commons. The Prime Minister will normally be the accepted
> leader of a political party that commands the majority of the House of
> Commons.[29]

The *Manual* underlines the importance of collective responsibility, with Cabinet 'the ultimate arbiter of all government policy',[30] despite the doctrine being deeply frayed since the 1990s. The prime minister's responsibility for national security is highlighted, overseeing the three security services, MI5, MI6, and GCHQ, while acknowledging that the Foreign Secretary, the Home Secretary, and the Northern Ireland Secretary have statutory powers to authorise specific operations. As Catherine Haddon notes, however, a problem with *The Cabinet Manual* is that writing down and trying to codify powers can raise more problems than it resolves.[31] What is put in, and what is left out? Several of the powers listed in this chapter are omitted, while some that are included are marginal. O'Donnell is emphatic that *The Cabinet Manual* was never intended as a list of the prime minister's powers. It was also very deliberately '*The Cabinet Manual* and not the *Prime Minister's* manual'.[32]

A further document discussing the powers of the prime minister is the *Ministerial Code*, starting life as *Questions of Procedure for Ministers* under Attlee, but changing name in 1997. All incoming prime ministers issue their own *Ministerial Code*. The 2019 version mentions the 'Prime Minister' many times, specifying, for example, 'The Prime Minister's written approval must be sought where it is proposed to transfer functions: between ministers in charge of departments; and between junior ministers within a department.'[33]

All six surviving Cabinet Secretaries agree there is still no single document that fully defines the power of the prime minister, and most believe that, even if such a document were to be produced, it would be far from complete and satisfactory. Indeed 'as we go into the fourth century of the prime minister in Britain, there is still no single document writing down all their powers' concludes O'Donnell.[34]

THE PRIME MINISTER'S POWERS

The British prime minister has considerable power and surprising freedom to be and do what he or she wants. 'Prime ministers can take unto themselves informal powers. They can simply announce that something is in their remit. They can just decide they're going to do something, and they are able to have that power, even if there is no constitutional backing for it', says O'Donnell.[35] Their powers contrast sharply with those of their Secretaries of State, whose powers are largely based upon statutes, and much more constrained. Nor is the UK prime minister as constrained as many prime ministers abroad, as seen above, who deal with regular challenges from their judiciaries and legal systems if they have written constitutions, all of which take precedence over convention. The prime minister is indeed in an enviable position.[36] So what are their powers?

SETTING THE AGENDA. This is the most important power prime ministers have. As their first words on the Number 10 doorstep show, they pitch up with ambitious sentiments but little detailed work on how to make it happen. Prime ministers have a choice: they either set the agenda themselves, or have it set for them by others or by events. Judgement will come on whether they executed a clear agenda that took the country forward, and on how well they responded to events – wars, economic crises, pandemics – thrust upon them. Prime ministers before Peel, with the exception of Pitt the Younger, saw their job as financial management and keeping the country safe. But from Gladstone, most had a sense of an agenda, a trend strengthened by general elections becoming contests between rival parties with competing programmes for office.

Prime ministers since Balfour have came to office with their ambitions and plans laid out in election manifestos, which became formalised over the twentieth century. The Civil Service, during the campaign, then fleshes out these manifestos with details on how to implement them. But few prime ministers have seen their agendas fully enacted. To be successful, they have to catch a tide of public and intellectual support, as Attlee and Thatcher enjoyed, but MacDonald and Major did not. They have to be able to convince their colleagues in Cabinet and the party of the merits of their case, as Heath did but May did not, and find the money to deliver it, as Lloyd George and Wilson did not. They have to avoid being blown off course by events, as Eden was with Suez, Callaghan by the financial and union crises, and Major by 'Black Wednesday'.

To enact their agenda, or respond effectively to the external events that impact upon them, they have to utilise their powers: over appointments, Cabinet, the Civil Service, the House of Commons, their party, and over their own time: and they have to bring a perfect set of skills that are sine qua non for their office. We now examine these in turn.

PATRONAGE AND POWERS OF APPOINTMENT. At the halfway point between Walpole and Johnson, Walter Bagehot wrote in 1872: 'The highest patronage of a Prime Minister is, of course, a considerable power', but he continues: 'though it is far less than it seems to be when stated in theory, or looked at from a distance.'[37] The appointing power is indeed formidable and ranked at the top of the most pressing decisions

Johnson had to make when he first became prime minister in July 2019. If a prime minister appoints the right ministers to the right jobs, they will be a long way down the road to a successful premiership. Indeed, this will make or break it.

It is a surprise then how little close attention prime ministers often give to the full range of appointment and, indeed, dismissal powers at their fingertips. The most significant appointments may have been in the mind of a would-be prime minister for many months or years, but when the result of the general election is declared at dawn on a bleary Friday morning and they have had a night without sleep, PMs can rush out appointments to feed the hungry press. Few leaders were as confident of victory as Blair in 1997, but he was reluctant to tempt providence and not all appointments had been finalised in advance.[38] Prime ministers are never more powerful than in the first month after a general election victory, or after they have come to power mid parliament. Yet few seem fully to realise it. They are, after all, at their greenest.

When Theresa May succeeded Cameron in July 2016, her two weightiest appointments were her Chancellor and the Foreign Secretary. Yet to the former, she appointed Philip Hammond, who spent the next three years blocking much of what she most wanted to do on the economy and Brexit, while to the latter, she appointed Boris Johnson, whom she hoped to mentor. Some hope. Unfamiliar with many MPs in her parliamentary party, a not uncommon trait amongst prime ministers, she let junior ministers be selected on the advice of her special advisors and whips, and for top posts, leant heavily on Cabinet Secretary Jeremy Heywood.[39] When Johnson became PM in July 2019, he left out or dismissed many experienced ministers. Being a good sacker can be very important for a PM. 'Monitoring and firing' are, however, often not undertaken by PMs with the seriousness they merit. They give less attention to it than the chief executives of companies and organisations at large, and the 'criteria for success' are far less clear. Performance management of ministers has often been the most amateur part of Number 10's work. Cabinet reshuffles are more often shambolic than not, and rarely achieve the hoped-for lift-off or restart for the premiership.

Prime ministers' appointment powers reach far beyond ministers. Johnson paid more attention than any predecessor to top Civil Service appointments, inspired by his chief aide, Dominic Cummings (2019–20), whose impatience with traditional Civil Service thinking had been evident for many years. Departing top officials included Simon McDonald from the FCO, Philip Rutnam from the Home Office, and Jonathan Slater from the Department for Education, alongside several other Permanent Secretaries, replaced by figures deemed more in tune with the Johnson/Cummings philosophy. Most significant was the departure of Mark Sedwill who had inducted him, replaced in 2020 by forty-one-year-old Simon Case as Cabinet Secretary and head of the Home Civil Service, and by David Frost, a Johnson loyalist, who took over Sedwill's job as National Security Advisor. Mistrust of the Civil Service had been a feature of several incoming prime ministers before, notably Thatcher in 1979 and Blair in 1997, who brought two senior figures, Jonathan Powell and Alastair Campbell, into Number 10 with power to give instructions to civil servants. But Johnson's mistrust went far further than any.

Johnson used to the full the power to make political appointments to the House of Lords, notably in 2020 former cricketer Ian Botham, a campaigner for Brexit, and, against the advice of the Lords Appointments Commission, businessman Peter Cruddas, an illustration of 'the power of the prime minister to make appointments that indicate their values', as Philip Norton put it.[40] The last ideological Conservative prime minister before Johnson was Thatcher, whose impatience with the status quo is shared by Johnson. Ideological prime ministers will always seek to influence political and public sector appointments more than others.

Political honours, including knighthoods, are a powerful reward. Whips of all stripes since Walpole have been shameless in the way they parade enticements before the eyes of potential troublemakers. Major and Blair used this power extensively: Heath, in contrast, was casual at exploiting it.[41] Prime ministerial hospitality is another carrot: receptions are held on many evenings in the state rooms on the first floor of Number 10, while lunch and dinner invitations to Downing Street, or to Chequers, indicate who is in favour, and who not. Prime ministers, flushed with the excitement of office, start out with fine intentions about displaying their largesse, but find all too often the crushing demands of office prevent them being realised.

USE OF CABINET AND ITS COMMITTEES. Having put the right people in the right places, the prime minister needs to ensure they have a Cabinet system which works for them, freeing them up from routine business and ensuring their own will is carried through. 'The ability to chair meetings of Secretaries of State and to sum them up without a vote is critically important. It is the other great role of the prime minister', says Richard Wilson.[42] Cabinets contain the big beasts, of whom many think they should be PM. Cabinets might not be full of the PM's friends, in the way that eighteenth-century Cabinets were of the 'King's Friends': but they are *necessary*. The prime minister decides if and when Cabinet meets, for how long, what issues are discussed there and how, how the minutes are recorded and distributed, and what Cabinet committees there should be and what they should decide. Weak prime ministers have been subdued by their Cabinets: strong ones, without exception, and by a variety of methods, dominate them.

Relying on an inner Cabinet has been one such ploy, all the way back to Walpole. The fluidity of the constitution has played strongly into the prime minister's hands. During periods of strife, as during the Napoleonic and Crimean Wars and the First and Second World Wars, prime ministers have operated with a small group of trusted advisors. Sometimes they use an official committee of Cabinet: more often, an informal grouping around them.

Only from Pitt the Younger does Cabinet emerge as a resource for the *prime minister* as opposed to the monarch. Even in the nineteenth century, though, Cabinets lacked precision and a clear remit. They usually ceased to exist when the prime minister resigned, fell, or died. They rarely took major collective decisions and could be regularly ignored. When in 1875, Home Secretary R. A. Cross wanted a bill to liberalise trade union activities, Disraeli pushed it through Cabinet despite universal opposition. Well does Richard Aldous write that he could be 'quite cavalier with Cabinet'.[43] Measures requiring legislation would often go to Cabinet because the PM needed ministers' support in Parliament, but foreign policy much less so, especially when the big beasts, Palmerston (1830–4, 1835–41, 1846–51), Salisbury (1878–80, 1887–92, 1895–1900), and Grey (1905–16) were Foreign Secretary.[44] Cabinet could prevail over prime ministers if it felt taken for granted or bounced, as it did against

Gladstone over Irish Home Rule in 1885–6 and against Salisbury in 1900, when it was partly responsible for convincing him to no longer combine being Foreign Secretary with prime minister.

Nineteenth-century prime ministers used Cabinet for collective strength in standing up to the monarch, as Wellington did to prevail over George IV on Catholic emancipation, or Gladstone over army reforms in 1870–1. Cabinet at its most powerful could even insist on the choice of a PM with the Crown, as it did with Queen Victoria in 1855 and 1859, pressing her to accept Palmerston. It was gloriously fluid.

By 1914, Cabinet had become an *irregular* decision-taking body, with a growing number of committees, ad hoc since the eighteenth century and formalised with the Committee of Imperial Defence from 1903, taking some decisions.[45] But prime ministers still regularly took key decisions on their own, or with two or three colleagues. Asquith effectively ran a duumvirate with his Chancellor of the Exchequer, Lloyd George, charting the course through the constitutional crisis of 1909–11, until they fell out from the summer of 1915. The Cabinet system remained in flux in the twentieth century.

The creation of the Cabinet Secretariat, when Lloyd George became PM, ushered in a new phase with Cabinet, from 1916–39, becoming the acknowledged *decision-taking* body, albeit with those decisions increasingly taken in committees, given the expanded social and economic business to conduct. Strong prime ministers like Lloyd George took major decisions outside Cabinet. The growing requirement for secrecy during the Second World War, the advent of nuclear weapons, the Cold War, and war against terrorism have all been reasons for decisions being removed from full Cabinet. Intelligence is the PM's secret weapon. 'The Second World War was the time the prime minister began having regular access to the heads of the intelligence agencies' says John Kerr. 'The prime minister's main task was to win the war. That's when the bond between the PM and the intelligence community really took off.'[46]

From 1945 until 1976, Cabinet, meeting twice a week, became the principal *decision-ratifying* body, with the committee system reaching a high point of precision under Norman Brook (1947–62) and Burke Trend (1963–73) as Cabinet Secretaries, both sticklers for form. With government growing exponentially after 1945, decisions had to be taken there, then presented for ratification (if not always discussion) to ministers in full Cabinet. Callaghan's meticulous use of full Cabinet during the IMF crisis in 1976 can thus be seen as a late flowering of the phase when full Cabinet was sovereign, before leaking impacted on it. When prime ministers in this period lost the full support of their Cabinet, as Attlee did in 1951, Churchill after 1953, Eden after 1956, and Macmillan after 1962, life became much harder for them. The prime ministers in their most successful phases, Attlee until 1947, Churchill until 1953, Macmillan until 1961, Wilson until 1967, and Heath until 1973, knew how to play Cabinet to maximise their authority. None managed it better than the last, who held his Cabinet together without splits, resignations, or leaks during three tempestuous years.[47]

From 1979 until 1997, prime ministers turned Cabinet into an *information-giving* and *discussion* body. Reduction in the number of meetings to one a week in 1977 was significant, still more so Thatcher's progressive spurning of the Cabinet/Cabinet committee system from 1983.[48] Her ministers started to complain increasingly that they learned about Cabinet committee decisions from minutes sent to their Private Offices. Cabinet returned for a brief time under Major, from 1990–2, to the decision-ratifying body it had been until the late 1970s. But the increasingly hostile atmosphere in it after Britain's ejection from the ERM in September 1992, and leaking, meant Major could trust Cabinet ministers less and less.

Blair, from 1997, recognising Major had lost traction, took Cabinet government in a much more personalised direction. Margaret Beckett, a minister throughout, recalled: 'Tony didn't do business in full Cabinet: he preferred to hold discussions with individual Cabinet ministers or in small groups. Such business was faithfully reported to Cabinet, but not discussed there in detail.'[49] There was more fluidity under Blair, and less reliance on set procedures than at any point in the twentieth century. Blair's first three Cabinet Secretaries, (Robin Butler (until 1998), Richard Wilson (1998–2002), and Andrew Turnbull (2002–5), were left to manage the implications of his 'sofa government' style of sidelining Cabinet government. Based in his 'den', the oblong office at the end of the Cabinet Room hitherto occupied by the Private Office, 'denocracy' slowly became the norm.

The early twenty-first century, post-Blair, has seen a hybrid Cabinet system emerge, which demanded a different tack from PMs. On items of major political or national significance, full Cabinet would discuss and, if necessary, decide. At more routine times, Cabinet meetings review, endorse, and adjust decisions taken elsewhere, without themselves determining the direction of policy. Brown had little time when Chancellor (1997–2007) for the views of his Cabinet colleagues, and likewise as prime minister from 2007; he established the National Economic Council (NEC) as a response to the Global Financial Crisis, which for a time supplanted Cabinet's Economy Committee, the body for senior ministers to discuss, if not always decide, economic matters.[50] Prime ministers had chaired the Overseas and Defence Committee after 1945, which morphed into the National Security Committee from 2010, bringing together foreign, defence, and security personnel. Meetings of the COBR (Cabinet Office Briefing Room) Committee, which first met in 1972 during the miners' strike,[51] provide another opportunity for the PM to lead, and be seen to lead, at times of crisis, including natural disasters and terrorism. Blair was particularly good at seizing control and the limelight, as during the fuel protest strikes in 2000 and foot and mouth in 2001, a style Brown emulated after the failed terrorist attacks in London and Glasgow in 2007.

Cameron had to use Cabinet and its committees after 2010, less from personal choice than the necessity of being in a coalition government with the Liberal Democrats. But the key cross-party body was not the Cabinet Committee set up to bring together top figures in the coalition, but 'the Quad', consisting of Cameron, Osborne, Liberal leader Nick Clegg, and Treasury Chief Secretary Danny Alexander.[52] That said, the most important decisions of his government, including to hold a referendum on the EU, were taken just with trusted advisors around Cameron and Osborne, who met in the PM's study, still the same 'den' Blair had used, twice daily, at 8.30 a.m. and 4.00 p.m.

May's premiership divided into two clear halves. In her first year, she kept some decisions over Britain's Brexit strategy away from full Cabinet, but tried to ensure a balance of viewpoints was represented in the key Brexit committees. In her final two years, considerably weakened by the 2017 general election result, she had no option but to coax Cabinet, deeply divided on the way ahead, behind a common line.[53] Starting with an all-day Cabinet at Chequers in July 2018, she held regular lengthy meetings in an ultimately vain search for agreement. Cabinet came to the fore under May also in April 2018, after a chemical weapon attack had been carried out in Douma, Syria, debating whether the UK should join the US and France in a series of reprisal military attacks. It was less involved though in decisions after the Salisbury poisoning in March 2018, May's finest hour as prime minister.

Johnson resorted to the command and control style, deciding many key issues with his tight-knit group in Number 10, or in discussions with his Cabinet Office minister Michael Gove, and Chancellors Sajid Javid and, from February 2020, Rishi Sunak. COVID planted Cabinet back centre stage, with Johnson needing to ensure it supported major decisions. During 'lockdown', meetings took place via video link, even at weekends when, for the first time, virtual assemblies had the status of a full Cabinet meeting. The COVID Cabinet committee dealt with the detailed work, the other principal Cabinet committee under Johnson, besides the NSC, being the Brexit committee. Johnson was fortunate to have a Cabinet more in tune with him than Thatcher or Major, and his command over them, despite the pressures, remained strong in early 2021.

Prime ministers have all struggled to find their ideal modus operandi with their Cabinets, not helped by the growing complexity, volume, and pace of government decisions. The need to respond to a media that will not wait until the next Cabinet has added fresh challenges. Leaking started in earnest under Wilson in the 1960s, was reined back under Heath, but took off under Major and Blair in the 1990s, adding to the difficulties. Johnson has adapted the Cabinet system in his own inimitable way, showing how flexible the system is. The fact is that, after 300 years, the Cabinet system is still evolving. Difficult to define it may be: but mastery of it is sine qua non.[54]

POWER OVER THE CIVIL SERVICE. Prime ministers are the country's de facto chief executive, and the Minister for the Civil Service. But they can arrive in office unsure how to make the Civil Service work for them. This has not been helped by the lack of familiarity with it. The last five prime ministers, including Johnson, served in just three government roles before becoming PM, averaging 0.6 apiece. The five PMs before that served in 29 different roles, an average of nearly six. That's a considerable difference. They possess several powers over Whitehall, rarely used by some, and inappropriately used by others. They can create departments, merge and abolish them, change the culture, reform the Civil Service ground up, if they want to, and give themselves any positions they wish. Walpole could hardly be an innovator with the monarch still very clearly in charge. The creation of the Foreign and Home Offices in 1782 though was an early example of politicians influencing the shape of what was still *His Majesty's* government. Departments stayed relatively unchanged in the nineteenth century, but the expansion into social and economic policy after 1900 led to many changes. Lloyd George created the Ministry of Labour in 1916, among many other departments, while Churchill established the Ministry of Reconstruction in 1943, and May two entirely new departments in July 2016, the Department for Exiting the EU (DExEU), and the Department for International Trade (DIT).[55]

Prime ministers have most wanted to gain more personal control over the Treasury, which has entailed several raids on its powers, as discussed in Chapter 9. Defence and foreign affairs have seen more PM activity than some areas. Macmillan set in train a process that led to the unified Ministry of Defence created in 1964, absorbing the historic War Office, Admiralty, and Air Ministry. No area has been more politicised than overseas aid. Wilson created a Ministry of Overseas Development in 1964 to signal the importance Labour attached it. Heath incorporated it back into the Foreign Office in 1970, and when Labour returned to office in 1974, Wilson once again established a separate Ministry of Overseas Development. In 1979, Thatcher again transferred the Department back within the Foreign Office, while the Minister for Overseas Development was demoted to below Cabinet rank. When Blair came to government in 1997, he established it again as a separate department with its own Cabinet minister, Clare Short, a position that Cameron retained when he came to office in 2010 with his passionate commitment to overseas aid, ushering into law the UN target of 0.7 per cent of national income. But in September 2020, Johnson merged DfID back into its mother department, renamed the Foreign, Commonwealth and Development Office (FCDO).

Departments representing the different nations within the United Kingdom reflect shifting political pressures on the prime minister. A Scottish Secretary was established with the Act of Union in 1707, and abandoned in 1746 after the Jacobite Rising. Gladstone created a Scottish Office in 1885, with its head upgraded to full Secretary of State rank by Baldwin in 1926. Wilson created a Secretary of State for Wales in October 1964, with a Welsh Office established the following year. Johnson appointed himself 'Minister for the Union' in 2019, albeit without a new department, to show his commitment not least to Scotland.

Prime ministers can change the culture and size of the Civil Service. Gladstone was fired by reformist zeal as Chancellor of the Exchequer and as prime minister, with the Northcote-Trevelyan Report embedding the apolitical culture of the Civil Service. Wilson sought to make it more efficient and open to specialists with the Fulton Report. Thatcher came in with a fervour to change it and make it more businesslike, open to the disciplines of the private sector, believing that efficiency gains would enhance the quality of public service. She appointed Derek Rayner (from Marks & Spencer) whose Efficiency Unit resulted in £170 million of savings, and the axing of 16,000 positions.[56] Major from 1990 rowed back on Thatcher's privatising zeal, and in his Citizen's Charter of 1991 wanted to celebrate public services while attuning them better to the needs of users. Blair after 1997 returned to the Thatcherite determination to enhance performance, establishing a Delivery Unit and an Office of Public Service Reform. In 2012, Cameron launched a Civil Service reform initiative designed to boost performance management and efficiency. May and her Chief of Staff Nick Timothy wanted to introduce farseeing change across Whitehall, but changed little, while Johnson and Cummings came to office with a determination to succeed where Thatcher and Blair hadn't in changing the entire culture by making it more open to outsiders, to experts, more business-like, and more digitally aware.

ACQUIRING NEW OFFICES AND POWER. Prime ministers can reward themselves with any titles they desire. Salisbury thus appointed himself First Lord of the Treasury for only six months of his second term, handing over to William Henry Smith, and then to Balfour in 1895 for the rest of his premierships. After him every PM became First Lord. The prime minister from 1905 became a constitutionally recognised position, with a rank in the official order of precedence. It was not until the Ministers of the Crown Act in 1937, however, that they received a salary for the first time. Salisbury chose to appoint himself Foreign Secretary until November 1900. Ramsay MacDonald in his first period in power in 1924 did the same, and only reluctantly handed it to Arthur Henderson when he returned in 1929–31. No one prime minister has held more positions than Wellington, who, as caretaker prime minister for two weeks in 1834, was concurrently Foreign Secretary, Home Secretary, and Secretary of State for War and Colonies, as well as First Lord and Leader of the House of Lords. Spencer Perceval, in addition to Chancellor of the Exchequer and Commons Leader, was Commissioner of the Treasury for Ireland (1810–12) and Chancellor of the Duchy of Lancaster.

Several prime ministers, like Disraeli from 1876–8, adopted the title 'Lord Privy Seal', traditionally the *fifth* of the great offices of state (after the Lord High Steward, now vacant, the Lord Chancellor, the Chancellor of the Exchequer, and the Lord President of the Council).[57] One of the oldest offices, dating back to 1307, it has long ceased to be keeper of the monarch's personal seal and become a sinecure. Balfour was the last PM to hold it, and as it carried a salary and ranking, it was a useful title for PMs to hold till the job became paid and recognised after he stood down.[58] Since Attlee, the post has frequently gone to the Leader of the House of Lords or House of Commons, though it does not confer membership of the House of Lords: one-time holder Bevin remarked that he was 'Neither a Lord nor a Privy nor a Seal'.[59] Prime ministers have used the Lord President perch for their deputies, especially in coalitions: Baldwin from 1931–5, and Nick Clegg (who was officially deputy prime minister also) from 2010–15.

Churchill appointed himself Minister of Defence throughout his period as prime minister from 1940–5, and Attlee retained the position for a year and a half until December 1946. When Churchill returned to office in October 1951, he insisted on taking the job again until persuaded, five months later, to relinquish it, appointing instead one of his favourite generals from the war, Lord Alexander of Tunis, whom he promptly bossed around.

Prime ministers don't have to give themselves new titles to be the dominant force in a policy area. Blair acted in effect as Education Secretary in addition to being PM (Andrew Adonis tried 'very hard', to persuade him to take the formal title).[60] Many have acted as if they were Chancellor of the Exchequer, not least the former incumbents Lloyd George, Macmillan, and Gordon Brown. Palmerston carried on as de facto Foreign Secretary after he relinquished the title, and many prime ministers, as they survive longer at Number 10, become increasingly involved in foreign affairs, to the irritation of their Foreign Secretary. Prime ministers often bear the impression of the last office that they held: May as PM never entirely relinquished her mindset as Home Secretary (2010–16); Johnson in contrast did not try to continue as the Foreign Secretary, but did become in effect 'Minister for COVID', during the pandemic. In theory, however, there is nothing stopping him announcing that he is Health Secretary, Education Secretary, Foreign Secretary, or even Chancellor. In the British constitution, anything goes: almost.

MANAGEMENT OF THE HOUSE OF COMMONS. Walpole's supreme mastery of the House of Commons was integral to his success as prime minister. 'Walpole enjoyed being in the Commons, and he was good at it. He was *extremely* good at it. He was witty, clever, and a great speaker for the government from the Treasury bench', says Black.[61] North's, Chatham's and Pitt the Younger's ability to persuade MPs was equally vital to their success. Prime ministers need to be able to command, or at least manage, the House of Commons, a much more complex task than leading the House of Lords, as eighteenth- and nineteenth-century prime ministers in the Lords found. When PMs were in the Lords, they ensured one of their ablest ministers was appointed Leader in the Commons. Lloyd George was the first commoner PM not to be Leader of the Commons, handing it to Bonar Law from December 1916 until March 1921, as the Conservatives were the largest party in Parliament. In February 1942, Churchill, under pressure from war duties, handed the leadership to Stafford Cripps, not a success, and from November 1942, to Eden. Salisbury, the last peer PM to sit in the Upper House, was Leader of the House of Lords throughout his entire period as prime minister until July 1902, appointing Balfour Leader of the Commons from October 1891.

Prime ministers since Thatcher have attended the Commons much less, but this is not a new phenomenon, with Balfour being attacked for the irregularity of his attendance.[62] Those who do not command the House, like Douglas-Home, whose political career had been recently spent in the Lords until renouncing his peerage in 1963, find life harder. It mattered to Douglas-Home because the Conservatives were under fire from Wilson, the most formidable opposition leader of the century, until Blair. Thatcher largely escaped undamaged from her Commons absenteeism, partly because her opposite numbers, Michael Foot (1980–3) and, to a lesser extent, Neil Kinnock (1983–92), were politically ineffective, but Major suffered grievously when facing John Smith (1992–4) and Blair (1994–7). All prime ministers this century, Blair, Brown, Cameron, May, and Johnson, have been criticised by their parliamentary parties for being remote. All emitted periodic promises about how they were going to host receptions and reach out to the troops as never before: but none carried through to satisfy expectations aroused. By 2021 it was clear that prime ministers had little time for Parliament on top of their other burdens: as long as they had a big majority they were relatively safe, if not entirely so. PMs, provided they can count on a clear majority, now regard Parliament less as a power, than as a chore and even a bore.

PARTY LEADERS. The leadership of their political party gives the PM further strengths, and is the gateway to becoming PM. After the Whig and Tory factions began to coalesce in the eighteenth century, mass-membership parties formed from the nineteenth century. Balfour failed to provide leadership, as R. J. Q. Adams says: 'An intellectual, a philosopher, and a man of supreme self-confidence, he was neither equipped nor willing to be a successful party leader.'[63] National party organisations with large London headquarters sprouted up to supply the prime minister with a steady stream of talent to recruit into Number 10, research and policy ideas to filter into policy, and the funds and means to fight general and other elections. The annual party conference, and series of regional conferences that the parties put on, provide the platform for the prime minister to speak, grandstand, and thank the party faithful. Their speech to the annual conference in the early autumn is the biggest in the PM's year, and staff at Number 10 start gathering ideas for it typically from early summer. It is the closest the PM has to the annual State of the Union address given by the US president. Recognition from the party faithful, as beleaguered PMs like Churchill found in 1953, Thatcher in 1990, and May in 2018, can be useful in reminding their Cabinets and MPs very visibly that they are still wanted and needed.

SEVEN PRIME MINISTER SKILLS

Prime ministers require many diverse skills. No one human being can possess them all. But seven are utterly essential, and a prime minister will fail to maximise their powers if they do not exhibit them.

PERSUASION. Personal charisma and the ability to charm have always been a vital ingredient in the arsenal of the prime minister. The command-and-control style of a Wellington only took a prime minister so far, while an insipid personality, as possessed by Wellington's predecessor, Goderich, didn't work either. Lack of persuasive skill and charm hampered Heath, Brown, and May. Lloyd George, Wilson, Cameron, and Johnson all had it, though few mastered the skill better than Blair: 'His forte was one to one, but he had extraordinary persuasive power in small groups', says Richard Wilson. 'He much preferred that to larger groups of ministers.'[64] 'Blair had always believed that he could conquer the world with charm', writes Andrew Rawnsley.[65] 'He invested huge faith in his ability to talk his way out of trouble, round problems, through dilemmas and into alliances.' Liberal leader Paddy Ashdown added a caution: 'One of Blair's failings is to overestimate the power of his charm.'[66] Hubris is an ever real danger for prime ministers. Prime ministers don't have to be extraverts to persuade: Attlee was famously monosyllabic, but he won round his MPs by his obvious interest in them personally and his passion for their common cause. Major was wooden with a big audience, but lit up small groups: he recognised this, when, during the 1992 general election campaign, he stood on a soapbox in Luton without amplification. Prime ministers have to find their own voice to charm, persuade, and cajole their many audiences. Richard Neustadt argued in *Presidential Power* that while the power of the US President is restricted, the 'power to persuade', using the incumbent's reputation, style, and charisma, is all-important.[67] Personal magnetism and charisma are equally essential for the prime minister.

One facet prime ministers can do nothing about is their *height*. Height can be used to create an impression of power to aid in persuasion. Physical presence matters. Callaghan made very effective use of his 6' 1" stature. In the US, Abraham Lincoln, Lyndon B. Johnson, and Donald J. Trump are presidents who famously relied on their physical presence. Though perhaps height did not matter much in the pre-television age; Lord John Russell and Churchill were the two shortest prime ministers, but do not seem to have suffered for it. Male PMs in the television age since Wilson have all tended to be tall. Major and Blair were six feet, with Brown an inch under and Cameron an inch over. Salisbury (the tallest PM at 6' 4") with his beard created the aura of power. Johnson overcomes his shorter height (5'8") by using his hair and his mannerisms with a performer's skill to define his public persona.

ORATORY AND STORY-TELLING. Prime ministers who are natural orators make speeches that command the attention of the media and country. No other government minister (except the Chancellor) has their potential: the media might be interested if they are making a controversial speech, but they lap up every word a prime minister utters. When used well, as Peel, Gladstone, Lloyd George, Churchill, and Blair did, it boosts their standing in Westminster and beyond. Philip Williamson emphasised how central speeches were to Baldwin's 'chief function and achievement'. They went far beyond short-term announcements, going to 'unusual depths ... [articulating] an analysis of the nation's and the world's fundamental problems. They used history, topography, literature, art, economics, ethics, religion and politics both to deploy social and political criticism and to suggest and appropriate social and political order.'[68] Few recent prime ministers have been natural speech-makers, or have uttered memorable phrases that have endured in the public memory. Wilson was the first to use a 'speech writer' in the form of his press secretary Joe Haines. Thatcher benefited greatly from the skills of playwright Ronnie Millar, who wrote her best line, 'the lady's not for turning', at the October 1980 party conference, having previously said 'u-turn if you want to', a pun on a play title by Christopher Fry. Brian Jenner, an authority on the subject, says she was the best orator of the modern era, never more effective than at PMQs.[69] Since her, prime ministers have relied increasingly on speech writers for phrasing. Attlee had little talent for oratory, and neither had Heath or Callaghan. Johnson does have oratorical skill and writes many of his own phrases, unusual for a modern premier. Whether or not they are phrase-makers, or natural orators, prime ministers need to rapidly learn that they are 'teachers' to the nation. They must be able to tell a story, to appear in command, empathetic and articulate. Performing convincingly as the 'public face' of the government is essential for the modern prime minister. Churchill was the supreme story-teller.

ENERGY LEVELS. Today, it is unlikely that a prime minister who is not fit and energetic will succeed. Thatcher had more of the qualities required to be a successful prime minister than almost any incumbent, including the ability to work formidably hard. Turnbull puts her command down to three qualities: 'She worked harder, she'd been there longer, and she briefed herself so well there was nothing she couldn't answer at PMQs twice a week. The amount of work she put in to her boxes and parliamentary briefings kept her on top of everything: she was never blindsided by the fact that she had not read all the papers.'[70] Macmillan is rightly seen as the last prime minister who could read long books in office, and not since MacDonald have PMs been able to take long leisurely holidays. The 1960s and 1970s changed all that, with Wilson taking the 'garden room' staff on holidays to the Isles of Scilly, and Heath in regular contact with Number 10 when captaining his yachts. The job of prime minister since Thatcher – famous for her five hours' sleep at night – has become relentless, with no uninterrupted breaks in the evening, weekend, or holidays. Incumbents have to have outstanding levels of stamina. No modern prime minister has needed more stamina than Theresa May, who endured the most relentless and hostile battering for her final twelve months of any incumbent since Eden.

INTELLECTUAL ABILITY. Prime ministers require razor sharp intellects to process all the material hurtling towards them. Cabinet ministers have material on a defined range of subjects, at considerably less volume, and are called on to react at speed for less. Wilson said that the authority of the prime minister depends on him 'Being in touch with what's going on and not going on . . . the more things you take an interest in, the more information comes back to you. A Prime Minister governs by curiosity and range of interest.'[71] A university education does not necessarily denote intellectual ability. Forty-seven prime ministers attended one; the eight who didn't included some of the most intelligent, Disraeli, Lloyd George, Churchill, and Major. Neither does being awarded a double first, as Eden was (in oriental languages) act as guarantee of success; so fluent was he as a linguist, he conversed with Hitler in German in 1934.[72] Forty-two went to Oxbridge (twenty-eight to Oxford, fourteen to Cambridge), but only one completed a doctorate, Gordon Brown, one of the most intellectual of all. Intelligence is multifaceted, including social and personal intelligence, as the Harvard academic Howard Gardner has taught us.[73] Intellectual brilliance, possessed by Russell, Gladstone, Rosebery, Balfour, and Asquith, is no guarantor of success as a PM. Politics is strewn with brilliant figures who never made it to the top, including Charles James Fox in the eighteenth century, Lord Randolph Churchill in the nineteenth, and Roy Jenkins in the twentieth.

TEMPERAMENT. Prime ministers need a certain kind of temperament, notably the ability to keep calm in crises, a quality in which Peel and Cameron excelled. North, Goderich, and Heath did not, and suffered for it. But having an equable temperament, as Callaghan and Douglas-Home had, is no guarantee of success. The pressures and demands of being PM accentuate the worst behaviour traits of a prime minister, and colleagues and the media are unwilling to make allowance for it: indeed, often the opposite. The scrutiny of their every slip is one reason prime ministers retreat into the bunker of trusted advisors: like the besieged British soldiers at Rorke's Drift in the film *Zulu*, one of Major's team once confided. It requires a very special quality to live each day under acute pressures, to palm off the attacks, humiliations, and betrayals, and to know the cameras never leave them alone when outside Number 10. To absorb shocking news, election defeats, and policy reversals, but to come out composed in front of the world's media, as Cameron had to do the morning after the Brexit defeat, requires very remarkable human gifts.

RUTHLESSNESS. If a prime minister lacks this quality, they will fail. High politics requires tough decisions. Cabinet and ministerial posts are limited, and some people will not make the final list. Scandals need to be lanced by a resignation or a sacking. Former allies have to be dispatched to the backbenches disappointed. Without some ruthlessness, a prime minister will not flourish in Westminster's harsh environment. In September 1981, Thatcher decided on a major reshuffle, purging many ministers who did not share her economic views, much to their anger and shock. She promoted ideological allies and later wrote that the reshuffle brought harmony to the Cabinet, leaving it 'on my side'.[74] In September 2019, Boris Johnson controversially expelled twenty-one Conservative MPs who had voted against a no-deal Brexit from the Conservative Party; including several party grandees and many promising younger MPs. The measure demonstrated Johnson's determination to deliver Brexit to party and public, and paved the way towards his election victory just three months later.

But too much ruthlessness can come back and bite a prime minister. Theresa May fired George Osborne at the beginning of her premiership, surprising many, not least Osborne, by telling him to 'get to know the Conservative Party better'.[75] He repaid her with his venomous editorship of the London *Evening Standard* over the years that followed.

OPPORTUNISM AND POPULISM. Prime ministers need to understand when to seize advantage of a political opportunity and how to use it for the highest popular effect. After the inconclusive 2010 election, David Cameron was able to take the political initiative by making a 'big, open and comprehensive offer' to the Liberal Democrats, ultimately allowing him to convert a disappointing election result into a stable government. Harold Wilson, knowing his party was divided by Europe, sidestepped the issue entirely with a referendum in 1975 that turned out to his advantage.

Pitt the Elder and Lord Palmerston made their names as great patriots by championing forthright foreign policy stances and achieved enormous popular affection in doing so. Later, Lloyd George moved quickly for an election in December 1918 and fully leveraged his reputation as a war leader to achieve a huge victory for his coalition, before the harsh costs of the conflict began to sink in. In 1983, Thatcher was able to wrap herself in the Union Jack after victory in the Falklands the previous year and it helped her to win a landslide victory.

THE PRIME MINISTER'S RESOURCES

The prime minister's task would be impossible without the *resources* at their disposal. The post lacks a mighty Whitehall department behind it, like the Foreign Office, Ministery of Defence, Treasury, or Home Office. But it has considerable, and not always well-utilised, resources.

NUMBER 10 AND CABINET OFFICE. After the prime ministers lost the Treasury in 1841, it took several years for them to build up the personal staff to allow them to fulfil their tasks. The prime minister's Private Office began to cohere in the first Gladstone ministry after 1868, with Algernon West and Edward Hamilton as 'Principal Private Secretaries' directing the PM's business.[76] Disraeli's decision to move into Number 10 in 1877 accelerated the process: most PMs after this lived in Downing Street, where the office took root. By the early twentieth century, a recognisably modern Private Office organising the prime minister's paperwork, diary, and relations with ministers was up and running.

Lloyd George's 'garden suburb' secretariat and the Cabinet Secretariat greatly enhanced his support from December 1916. After the Treasury's and the Foreign Office's attempts to strangle it after 1918, it morphed into the permanent fixture that is the Cabinet Office. The vast expansion of responsibilities of the PM after 1918 would not have been possible without it. It vies with the Treasury as the most important office at the centre of Whitehall: but, unlike the Treasury, it is always loyal to the prime minister. Hence prime ministers' dependence on it not only to smooth out their working life but also to get a grip on the government machine and decision-taking in Cabinet.

Churchill, Eden, and Macmillan all reshaped Number 10 to give them the personal staff and support they needed, but Wilson from 1964 took it to a new level, bringing in outsiders as special advisors, including Marcia Williams as his Political Secretary in 1964, and setting up the Policy Unit on his return to Downing Street in March 1974. Thatcher fiddled rather than made grand gestures of reform, comfortable to rely increasingly on just three key aides, press secretary Bernard Ingham, her Foreign Affairs Private Secretary, Charles Powell, and, periodically, economics advisor Alan Walters, none of them elected politicians. She also relied greatly on Lord Whitelaw, her de facto deputy until his stroke in December 1987. Blair oversaw a considerable expansion in the shape and size of Number 10 staff from 1997, as has Johnson since 2019.

So what does Number 10 offer a prime minister today? The Private Office still lies at its the heart, headed by the Principal Private Secretary, and with specialist officials under him (no female holders yet) overseeing economic, foreign, home, public services, and parliamentary affairs. It connects the PM to Whitehall, to the rest of the country, and to the world. The Policy Unit provides the PM with specialist advice and ideas on their agenda and on proposals put forward by ministers. The communications team, including the Press Office, oversees their external messaging. An events and visits team ensures that their travel and meetings run smoothly. A Political Secretary and their Parliamentary Private Secretary connect them to the party, its MPs and peers, while the Director of Legislative Affairs provides support on handling government business in Parliament. The National Security Advisor briefs the PM on intelligence, defence, foreign, and terrorism matters. Number 10 today is overseen by a Chief and Deputy Chiefs of Staff, and by a Permanent Secretary. The Cabinet Office, based at 70 Whitehall in the building the Treasury occupied until 1940, steers the PM through Cabinet business, allowing them to get a grip on government.

There is little discernible correlation between the size of the Downing Street empire and the effectiveness of a prime ministership. Britain's two strongest since 1945, Attlee and Thatcher, both operated with small Number 10s, working closely with the Civil Service.

POLITICAL CAPITAL. A prime minister might be supremely talented, and have a very clear agenda, but unless they possess political capital, they will not be effective. A prime minister can be compared to an elegant

Ferrari – they might be able to make a dazzling impression at speed, but without the fuel of political capital, they will go nowhere. As Richard Wilson, who saw several prime ministers close up, put it:

> What matters to a prime minister is whether they are in a strong or a weak position with their colleagues, their party, Parliament, the press, and public. If they are strong, they will be powerful. If they are in a weak position, they will not be powerful. So what matters for the power of prime ministers is the political context in which they operate. All power is fluid. End of proposition.[77]

Before the extensions to the franchise after 1832, political capital came to the PM through the affirmation of the monarch, credibility with Cabinet, and their proficiency in Parliament. Since mass democracy, the electorate has become king, or queen. 'Power is fundamentally given by the electorate. If a prime minister has a strong mandate, then they are going to be powerful. With an electoral mandate, the prime minister can tell Cabinet ministers that they are there because of you as the leader. Gladstone did that, Disraeli did that, Campbell-Bannerman did in 1906, and Attlee in 1945. It is the key factor', as Bogdanor puts it.[78]

Politicians, back to 1721 and before, have never been naturally loyal beasts. They lend their support to a leader conditionally, for as long as they think he or she will best serve their interests. If a PM wins a significant general election victory, it earns them a personal mandate they lacked before, and often a honeymoon period, as Lloyd George found after 1918, Attlee after 1945, Macmillan after 1959, Wilson after 1966, Thatcher after 1983, and Blair after 1997 and 2001. But it wanes rather quickly as Johnson has found.

The timing and the winning of general elections have thus become *all*-important, which is why so many PMs say in private that election timing, a power denied to many leaders abroad, is their loneliest decision. This power was modified by the Fixed-Term Parliaments Act of 2011, which took away the PM's ability to ask for a dissolution of Parliament without Parliament's consent. However, as 2017 and 2019 proved, if a prime minister was set on an election, they would likely secure it. Cameron disappointed Conservative MPs by not winning an outright victory in the 2010 general election, but they stayed mostly loyal to him because his personal popularity was higher than the party's and he was seen as a winner, as he proved in the 2015 general election. Brown in contrast squandered his political capital when he failed to call a general election in late 2007, while May's unprompted calling of one in June 2017 led to a catastrophic loss of seats. Johnson knew he was taking the biggest gamble of his life in calling a general election in December 2019. If he had lost it, he would have gone down as not just one of the shortest, but worst prime ministers in history.

HUMAN CAPITAL. The prime minister has greater convening power than anyone in the country. No one, almost, turns down an invitation from the prime minister or Number 10, even unpaid, to offer advice, join a working group, attend a meeting, or lend support to a good cause. Nobel Prize winners, celebrated artists, world-famous entrepreneurs, and ultra-composed sportspeople turn to jelly if the summons with the embossed envelope arrives on their doorstep (or inbox). Prime ministers have on tap the best brains and top talent in the country and beyond. They are superstars, the more so the longer they are in office and retain their political capital. The most savvy prime ministers – Lloyd George, Wilson, Blair, Cameron, and Johnson – knew it and exploited it. As well as the romance of an invitation to visit Number 10, the most famous political address in the world after the White House, they have Chequers, the country house in Buckinghamshire, an often under-utilised resource. World leaders flock to it – President Nixon in 1970, Vladimir Putin in 2001, and Chinese premier Wen Jiabao in 2009. So do they to Number 10, drinking in the history of every room, a history that serving prime ministers are often too busy to absorb.

SECOND IN COMMAND. The prime minister can invite anyone in their Cabinet to step up as their official or unofficial deputy, which gives them a considerable extra resource. Constitutional documents had not acknowledged such a deputy position – although *The Cabinet Manual* now refers to it[79] – but neither do they prevent the prime minister appointing one. Countries with written constitutions sometimes refer to an official deputy; the US Constitution mentions 'Vice President' eight times, while the French constitution has no mention of one. John Adams, the second president of the United States, and its first vice president, memorably dismissed the position in a letter to his wife in 1793 as 'the most insignificant Office that ever the Invention of Man contrived or his imagination conceived'.[80]

Sharing the monstrous burden is the most important reason why prime ministers have chosen official or unofficial deputies, and is why we argue that the post should become regularised: an overburdened prime minister will not perform at their best. The ever-present fear of a terrorist attack taking out the prime minister, or the lesser likelihood of nuclear attack, are further reasons for the position being formalised. In the event of a nuclear strike, the 'first nuclear deputy' is the Defence Secretary, whereas for a terrorist attack, it is the Home Secretary. Theresa May thus spent much of the 2012 Olympic Games in London sitting in a windowless room, several floors below Downing Street, in case a major terrorist attack on the Olympics killed the prime minister: 'She was the designated ministerial authority' to decide 'if kinetic action was required, for example if a rogue aircraft was coming inbound for the centre of London', said a senior official.

If escalating international tension is deemed such a high risk that a nuclear exchange is possible, then the prime minister, the nuclear deputies, and the Defence Secretary, following a meticulous predetermined plan, are taken at speed to different locations with separate command structures to allow them to direct hostilities, if necessary. Because Britain has a Cabinet system, if a prime minister is assassinated (as Spencer Perceval was in 1812) or otherwise dies in office, then Cabinet becomes the ultimate executive authority, and it is Cabinet that must decide on an interim successor. Rodney Brazier, the leading constitutional authority, notes that existing documents, including *The Cabinet Manual* and the *Ministerial Code*, are 'silent on the subject' of the exact procedure for the appointment of a successor in the event of the death of a PM.[81] In the US with its presidential system, the Twenty-Fifth Amendment spells out the succession; and with four American presidents assassinated (Lincoln, Garfield, McKinley, and Kennedy), they are perhaps right to be cautious. The tradition of a 'designated survivor' in the event of the senior figures being taken out is thus far more deeply embedded in the US national psyche.[82]

The protocols in the UK were severely tested when, in April 2020, Boris Johnson fell ill with COVID-19 and for a few days his survival was in question, as it had been in September 1918 when Lloyd George caught Spanish flu and nearly died.[83] Dominic Raab, the Foreign Secretary, had been appointed 'First Secretary of State' in July 2019, and on Johnson's word, was given the nod to deputise for him, including chairing Cabinet, and the nuclear and security responsibilities of the PM, and would have taken over *pro tem* had Johnson died. The Cabinet Secretary Mark Sedwill would then have convened Cabinet and told them: 'You now need to make a recommendation to the queen of who should be appointed as the new prime minister.' While Johnson was out of action, Sedwill ensured that everyone referred to Raab as 'First Secretary' at Cabinet, not as 'Foreign Secretary', to help ministers understand psychologically that he was now in a very different position. Cabinet would then have been charged to ascertain if there was a clear candidate on whom they all agreed. If they had, and no one wanted to stand against him or her, it would then have needed to be squared with the 1922 backbenchers' Committee, to see if any MPs wanted to stand. The next PM would be the Conservative Party's choice, and whether there would be a leadership election, as there was in 2019, would depend on whether there were multiple candidates. Considerable questions remained. What would have happened if Cabinet hadn't agreed on a common candidate? If a leadership election had been triggered, how long would Raab remain, and in what capacity: as acting prime minister or 'full' prime minister? If Raab himself was the choice of Cabinet, would he have continued to chair it or would that have given him an unfair advantage in a national party poll, in which case, who would take over from him?

Existential reasons might be the most urgent justification for formalisation of the role of deputy prime minister, but support to allow prime ministers to do their job more effectively is the ongoing need. Prime ministers from Walpole onwards have turned to senior colleagues to confide in and to share the burden of work. Pitt the Younger had Henry Dundas, Disraeli had Stafford Northcote, Asquith had Lloyd George, and Attlee had Bevin. The position of 'Deputy Prime Minister' (DPM) was formalised when Churchill appointed Attlee 'Deputy Prime Minister' in February 1942. Attlee was given the ministerial position of

Dominions Secretary, which carried a salary, unlike the Deputy PM position. The choice of Attlee was because Churchill wanted to demonstrate the importance of the second party in the Wartime Coalition and was not an indication of an intended successor. Indeed Churchill had left written advice to the king that Eden should succeed him in the event of his death. During the First World War, Lloyd George had similarly given the Conservative Lord Curzon the title of Lord President of the Council and Leader of the House of Lords, whilst Bonar Law was given the Chancellorship and the leadership of the House of Commons. Nick Clegg held the position of 'Deputy Prime Minister' in the 2010–15 coalition government, a clear continuity with the titles held by Attlee in the previous coalition when it ended in 1945.

Attlee appointed Morrison his deputy in 1945, the first use of the title in peacetime.[84] When Churchill returned in 1951, he wanted it as an additional honour for his Foreign Secretary Eden, in part as a sop given his increasing impatience to take over the top post.[85] George VI objected on the grounds that it would prejudge the monarch's prerogative power to choose the prime minister's successor. The feelings of another minister, in this case Rab Butler, were in part responsible for Macmillan's decision to create a new position in 1962 of 'First Secretary of State', which indicated that the incumbent was highly favoured, and second in command, without upsetting the Palace as a re-use of DPM might have done. The First Secretary of State title caught on, if more as an ego-massager than for functional reasons. Wilson appointed George Brown, whom he had beaten in the leadership election the year before, in October 1964. Unlike Butler, George Brown did not receive even the unofficial designation of 'Deputy Prime Minister'. Wilson latched onto the title, conferring it on Michael Stewart in 1966 and then Barbara Castle, still the only female holder, in 1968, after which the position went into formal abeyance until 1995.

Had he not died shortly after taking office, Chancellor of the Exchequer Iain Macleod might have emerged as deputy prime minister under Heath. As it was, the moniker, if cynically, was given to William Armstrong, by now Head of the Civil Service, drafted by Heath into Number 10. The burden broke him, and a nervous breakdown removed him from action. Thatcher after 1979 avoided formal titles, but chose the

Deputy Leader of the Conservative Party, Whitelaw, as her de facto deputy. Finding time for the task on top of his ministerial duties, he filled precisely the role expected of him, helping mediate in disputes between ministers, and smoothing Thatcher's path, allowing her to concentrate on the topics of most importance to her. She missed him when he retired following a stroke in December 1987. When, at a dinner in his honour in August 1991, she allegedly uttered the words 'every prime minister needs a Willie', she spoke a fundamental truth about the life of the modern PM.

The title 'Deputy Prime Minister' made a return in October 1989, for all the Palace's concerns, when she reluctantly acceded to Howe's demand for the title, in addition to making him Lord President of the Council and Leader of the House of Commons. Her initial impatience with him when Chancellor had grown to profound irritation by this time, but her feelings turned to deep anger when she wrote in her memoirs: 'It is a title with no constitutional significance and in practical terms it just meant that Geoffrey sat on my immediate left at Cabinet meetings.'[86]

Major avoided formal titles when he became prime minister in November 1990, but his very clear deputy and chief confidant was Chris Patten, the party chairman, until he lost his seat in the 1992 general election,[87] after which Major came to rely increasingly on Tony Newton as the de facto deputy, Lord President, and Leader of the House of Commons.[88] By the summer of 1995, Major's life had become intolerable, with his Cabinet deeply divided over Europe; after he triggered a contest amongst Tory MPs about whether they wanted him to continue as party leader, it became clear that he needed more ballast. So he appointed the biggest beast in Cabinet, Michael Heseltine, as 'First Secretary of State', a title not used for twenty-five years, as well as 'Deputy Prime Minister'.[89] Heseltine was the perfect choice, 'fixing' the Cabinet, chairing a number of Cabinet committees, and giving the prime minister the space that he needed, as Whitelaw had done for Thatcher.

SPOUSES. Prime ministers have a formidable resource in the spouse, often relegated by writers on prime ministers to a footnote in history, in part because their impact is often hidden. Yet for much of the history of the premiership, spouses have been enormously influential. Forty-five of the fifty-five prime ministers were married, five have been widowers

(Devonshire, Melbourne, Aberdeen, Rosebery, and MacDonald), four never married (Compton, Pitt the Younger, Balfour, and Heath), and two had their husbands in Downing Street (Denis Thatcher and Philip May). Spouses have no official status as in the United States, where "FLOTUS' (the First Lady of the United States) has a considerable office, and her own independent role. Not all prime minsters' spouses have moved into Downing Street: Catherine Walpole, the Duchess of Wellington, and Mary Wilson are just three who did not. 'I'm starting to understand why the WPM [wife of the prime minister] feels so tricky', wrote Sarah Brown, wife of Gordon. 'I have no exact status, no official position, masses of conflicting expectations both internally and externally, and a terrible suspicion that at any moment, a great mistake will be made by ME!'[90]

No other politician in the UK has their spouse living with them as part of the package. Some Chancellors live at Number 11 with their wife (no female Chancellors yet), but expectations of them, and public interest, are minimal. The partner is one figure on whom the PM can, in the last analysis, totally rely. The position of women in society may have been transformed from Catherine Walpole to Carrie Symonds, the fiancée of Boris Johnson, but many of the expectations placed on the spouses have changed far less. They are required to keep an orderly and quiet home, to live above the shop in Downing Street, whether or not they like the idea, and, with increasingly younger prime ministers, look after young children, as did Cherie Blair, Sarah Brown, Samantha Cameron, and Carrie Symonds. They are expected to be seen in company with the prime minister at official occasions, receptions, and dinners, but are not supposed to offer any political comment. At times of crisis they are required to be seen in public with their spouses, offering reassurance to them and to the nation. Their Downing Street flat has officials and other visitors coming into it all hours of the day. Weekends and holidays are never private; ubiquitous if discreet 'garden room' staff and duty clerks are with them all the time, and their sleep is often disturbed by urgent calls to the PM. Spouses travel abroad with the prime minister on longer trips, in part in the vain hope of spending some quality time with them.

In the fraught life of a prime minister, the spouse is an asset of considerable importance to the prime minister's emotional and physical well-being, and to the skill with which they exercise their job. Hester Pitt, married to Chatham, was one of only two women to be both the wife and the mother of a prime minister (Elizabeth Grenville was the other). Contemporaries noted how well she coped with the erratic emotional behaviour of Chatham, while being a considerable intellect herself: Horace Walpole said that women like her should 'take the government upon themselves instead of their husband',[91] while banker Thomas Coutts described her as 'the cleverest *man* of her time in politics and business'.[92] When Chatham's health deteriorated during his administration of 1766–8, she took over his correspondence and acted as a link to Cabinet. In October 1768, George III encouraged the Duke of Grafton to discuss with her the removal from office of Lord Shelburne. In recognition of her importance, she was created Baroness Chatham in her own right (not universally popular, some called her Lady Cheat'em). On Chatham's death in 1778 (she was thirteen years his junior), she threw herself into the life of her unmarried son William, playing a crucial role in shaping this most influential of prime ministers. Their voluminous correspondence, in which she offers him ample personal and political comfort, shows her influence. She died in 1803, only three years before her beloved son.

Julia Peel, wife of Robert, provides a different model: she kept away from politics, oversaw her husband's domestic affairs, looked after their two capacious homes, at Tamworth and Whitehall Gardens, and exchanged letters with him every day they were apart. The early 1840s Chartist agitation thrust her into the spotlight when she feared their home, Drayton Manor Park, in Tamworth, would be attacked. Julia Peel was a cavalry officer's daughter, and evidently had great confidence in her ability to defend herself:

> My own dearest love, during the whole of this tumultuous scene and expected attack I felt anxious only to save you from an alarm for us ... Our arrangements were quickly and vigorously made and should have been equal to an attack from two or three hundred till assistance had come. But then we expected three or four thousand. I am confident, however, that no men actually attacking doors and windows here would have left this place alive ... when you come from the station do so as quietly as possible. I shall take care not to say when I expect you.[93]

Emily Palmerston was the grandest hostess of all the spouses: 'The sister of one Prime Minister [Lord Melbourne], the wife of another [Palmerston] and the close confidante of both, she had as much political influence as any woman of her time.'[94] David Brown writes how 'through her soirées and her management of access to Palmerston [she] did much to influence his public career'.[95] Despite Palmerston's repeated and public acts of infidelity, their marriage was a happy one.[96] 'Lady Palmerston made her husband happy, as he did her, and she was a political power in her own right. In the last and most successful decades of Palmerston's life, she was his best advisor and most trusted amanuensis. Theirs was one of the great marriages of the century', wrote biographer Gillian Gill.[97] Lady Palmerston held regular Saturday parties during the season at Cambridge House, Piccadilly, from 1855, 'packed with politicians, diplomats, and courtiers, peers, bishops, and office-seekers as well as a smattering of carefully selected journalists, notably John Delane of The Times [editor 1841–77]'.[98] Courtier Henry Greville recorded in his diary that no 'other human being than his wife share[d] his confidence'.[99] She survived him by only four years, and was placed beside him in Westminster Abbey. She alone shows how incomplete any study of the prime minister is which excludes spouses.

Mary Anne Disraeli and Catherine Gladstone, as might have been predicted, provide very different models. The former made herself constantly available and so great was Disraeli's need for her that he would turn down official invitations to spend time with her. An important celebration at the Carlton Club was thus refused because 'Mary Anne ... was waiting for him with a bottle of champagne and a pork pie from Fortnum and Mason.'[100] Catherine Gladstone was never totally herself at Number 10, but 'in an age when the public position of women was fast changing, Catherine Gladstone was an important icon, her own commemorative plate next to her husband's on many a sideboard'.[101] She bore eight children, two of whom died young, and immersed herself in social causes, supporting orphanages, refuges, and retirement homes. Colin Matthew records how assiduously Gladstone kept her in touch with the details of critical developments, and how greatly he relied on her at moments of stress. As the children grew up, she became increasingly involved, providing him with little bottles of egg-and-sherry drink to consume while giving long speeches in the Commons ('one for an important speech, two for an exceptionally long one'), waving to onlookers from train windows when he was too tired to do so, and liaising with press reporters about his speeches.[102] During the Midlothian campaign, she 'broke precedent by sitting by her husband in the centre of the platform, rather than in a special 'ladies' section' and occasionally spoke herself.[103]

Margot Asquith and Margaret Lloyd George provided different models again in dealing with their emotionally wayward husbands. Three years after his first wife Helen died of typhoid, Asquith married Margot, their wedding register signed by four prime ministers: himself, Gladstone, Rosebery, and Balfour. Margot was as intellectually strong as her husband and even more self-assured. She lectured George V: 'You see sir, you only see fashionable Tories and not very clever ones.'[104] She begged the Chief Whip in November 1910 to hold a general election before the year was out (as happened), and in June 1915, she summoned Lord Kitchener to persuade him to withdraw a parliamentary question. She insisted on visiting the Western Front, despite being told by Edward Grey, the Foreign Secretary, it was pure self-indulgence.[105] But she did not succeed in warding off the political ambitions of Lloyd George, and was beset by rage and bitterness when he finally ousted her husband. Nor did she deter her husband from writing amorous letters during Cabinet and other meetings to Venetia Stanley, close friend of their daughter Violet. Between 1910 and 1915 he wrote to her up to three times a day.[106] Asquith was mortified when Venetia married one of his protégés, Edwin Montague, in July 1915, and his agonies redoubled when his beloved son Raymond died on the Somme in September 1916.[107]

Margaret Lloyd George had to cope with the knowledge that her husband was sleeping with his secretary, Frances Stevenson, in Downing Street. He thought he needed the company of both women. As Mark Hichens has described: 'his role as a bigamist … suited him nicely. On the one hand, he had a gentle, wise maternal figure, soothing and steadying. On the other he had an attractive, totally devoted, compliant younger woman who was also a highly efficient secretary.'[108] Margaret died in 1941: Lloyd George married Frances two years later, and died in 1945.

Ramsay MacDonald's social reformer wife, Margaret, died of blood poisoning in 1911 before he became prime minister, and it was left to their daughter Ishbel to provide much of the support that a wife had customarily given the PM. This entailed going to the Oxford Street sales together in January 1924 when, having moved into Number 10, they learnt that incomers were expected to bring their own cutlery and crockery.[109] She was with him until he resigned as prime minister in 1935, later buying a public house, Ye Olde Plow Inn near Chequers, which she ran until 1952, employing some of those who had been in her father's service. Lucy Baldwin proudly called her gentle husband 'tiger Baldwin', and was ambitious for him: it was said of her 'that she had more influence upon him than he on her'.[110] Anne Chamberlain was another devoted wife and skilled hostess, who had encouraged and supported Neville's every step up the political ladder, and who had grand designs for a hopefully long stay in Downing Street. Sadly for them, it was not to be.

The course of the Second World War might have been very different had Clementine Churchill not encouraged her husband through his difficult interwar years, then offered him tireless support from 1940-5. Three of their four children caused them concern, notably Randolph's drinking and gambling, and the break-up of daughter Sarah's marriage. But she never wavered, visiting air raid shelters often on her own and regularly reporting back to him. She could tell him truths no other could, as when she wrote to him in 1940, saying that he was becoming overbearing, and staff were becoming frightened to tell him the truth. In 1941, she became Chair of the Red Cross Aid to Russia fund, known as 'Mrs Churchill's Fund'. From March to May 1945, at the invitation of the Russian Red Cross, she visited the Soviet Union, travelled widely, and was received by Stalin. After the war ended, she failed to persuade Churchill to stand down as party leader, but supported him selflessly through his physically fraught final years in Number 10 from 1951-5.

Postwar prime ministers with the exception of bachelor Heath were all heavily bolstered by their very different spouses and partners, from the retiring but ultra-loyal Violet Attlee, Audrey Callaghan, and Norma Major, to the razor sharp barrister Cherie Blair and campaigner cum public relations supremo Sarah Brown, to the thirty-nine-year-old fashion businesswoman and mother Samantha Cameron, who held the family together when their son Ivan died in 2009, and had a child, Florence, in Number 10,[111] and the thirty-three-year-old political strategist Carrie Symonds who joined Johnson in Number 10 in July 2019, peppering him with ideas on the green agenda, animal rights, and his choice of advisors.[112] Just as Macmillan was the last old-style PM (bar the short-lasting Douglas-Home), so too his wife Dorothy was at the end of the line (bar Elizabeth Douglas-Home) of a Chatelaine overseeing Number 10. As her husband said of her, 'she filled it with children ... filled it with flowers ... with a sense of friendliness among all the staff and servants ... like a family gathering in a country house.'[113] That was not what Mary Wilson felt she had been signed up for in 1964.

Prime ministers have often married ambitious people, increasingly with their own careers, and with strong ideas that chimed with their own. Britain's two female prime ministers, by their own admissions, could not have managed to negotiate the challenges they faced without their extraordinarily devoted and self-negating husbands, Denis[114] and Philip.[115] It is perhaps not coincidental that Heath and Balfour, two bachelors, were so poor at understanding not only their own feelings, but those of their parties. It could be that the spouse, the ignored figure in the life of the prime minister, is their most *important* resource.

The prime ministers who have performed best in office have bent the powers, and resources, at their disposal to their advantage, and exhibited to a high level the core seven skills. Robert Blake concluded at the end of his book on the prime minister: 'The truth is that the powers of the Prime Minister have varied with the personality of the Prime Minister.'[116] Or as Asquith memorably put it: 'the office of Prime Minister is what its holder chooses and is able to make of it'.[117]

But what of the *constraints* on the prime minister, and why have they hemmed in some more than others? That is the subject of the next chapter and it takes us into the heart of the art of the prime minister.

CHAPTER 6

The Constraints on the Prime Minister,
1721–2021

NO PRIME MINISTER OPERATES WELL AS A GENERAL GIVING orders to troops (though some come to Number 10 thinking they can). They are all playing chess on a multi-dimensional board, prey to challenges that vary in type and intensity over time, some of which are new and growing, and others constant. The most skilful negotiate their way through these constraints, turning them to their advantage, and refuse to be defined by adversities. The least able are swallowed up by them. We first consider the institutional restraints, the checks and balances they face, some dating back to 1721, before considering *variable* constraints, which have made and destroyed premierships, and rendered even the best-qualified incumbent a cornered animal.

INSTITUTIONAL CONSTRAINTS

THE MONARCHY. George I was powerful in 1721, but was not *all* powerful. Elizabeth II in 2021 has symbolic authority, but not *merely* symbolic. The Hanoverian dynasty had less power than monarchies in pre-revolutionary France or in eighteenth-century Russia or Prussia. Its standing had been reduced progressively after the Restoration in 1660, the Glorious Revolution of 1688, and the ascent of the Hanoverians in 1714. But deep into the nineteenth century and beyond, it remained *His/Her Majesty's* government in far more than just name. The slow emergence of the prime minister as the chief executive and shaper of the monarch's prerogative powers is a major subject, and one we consider in depth in the next chapter.

PARLIAMENT. The other principal restraint on the prime minister dating back to 1721 is Parliament. Walpole captured the relationship with the House of Commons towards the end of his time:

> A seat in this House is equal to any dignity derived from posts or titles, and the approbation of this House is preferable to all that power, or even Majesty itself can bestow: therefore when I speak here as a minister, I speak as possessing my powers from his Majesty, but as being answerable to this House for the exercise of these powers.[1]

Walpole knew his precarious position rested on his ability to secure a majority in the House of Commons for the monarch. Parliament, though, had real *independent* power, the principle of parliamentary supremacy established after 1688 as a permanent feature of the constitution, with regular general elections (initially every three years from 1694 and then every seven from 1716), making its position far more solidly entrenched than Walpole's own. Much has changed since Walpole's time: 'But the relationship between Westminster and Downing Street would be more recognisable [to him] ... locked in a historic embrace, prime ministers and parliaments have yet to escape each other. Theirs was a reluctant match at the outset and perhaps remains so to this day. But marriages do not have to be made in heaven to serve their purpose', as Langford elegantly put it.[2]

The management of the House of Commons remained crucial for Pelham, Newcastle, Chatham, and North. The House of Lords' support could be largely taken for granted: smaller, easier to manage, and under government sway for much of the eighteenth century. The principle that the prime minister was Leader of the House of Commons or House of Lords was integral to the way they exercised authority, depending on which house they sat in. Wellington eventually came to believe that the prime minister 'Should always be Leader of the House of Commons'.[3] The nineteenth century, though, saw more prime ministers leading from the Lords, including Wellington, because it was the house where the most senior member of the party resided, and into which long-serving figures were promoted, as was the case with Disraeli (as Lord Beaconsfield). National political parties emerging from mid century equally made the job of managing the Commons less difficult, which Black says explains why more prime ministers were based again in the House of Commons.[4] The prime minister remained Leader of the House of Commons, if only nominally, until Lloyd George and then Churchill relinquished the post in their coalition governments, by which time the 'leadership' role had become much less important to their power.

Votes of no confidence struck terror and continued to underline the prime minister's dependency on the House of Commons, and they allow us to chart its potency over the 300 years. First used to defeat Walpole in 1742, twenty-one votes of confidence have been successfully passed thereafter against the prime minister and government. North's defeat in 1782 saw the entire Cabinet resign for the first time after a no confidence vote. Pitt suffered the same fate in February 1784, but refused to follow the precedent to resign, retaining the support of George III and the House of Lords, though he called, and won, an election soon after. When Wellington was defeated in one in November 1830, he submitted his resignation to William IV, who invited Lord Grey to form a government.

The nineteenth century saw the high point of House of Commons power, with the convention firmly established that a defeat on a significant motion obliged a government to resign or seek a dissolution so a general election could be held. Peel had such a defeat in April 1835 which precipitated his resignation and William IV's invitation to Melbourne to form a government, and another 'no confidence' motion in June 1846 led to his final resignation and Russell forming a Whig government. Melbourne was defeated twice, in June and then August 1841, which prompted a reluctant Victoria to invite Peel to form a government. Russell had the dubious distinction of three such defeats, in February 1851 and again in February 1852, and in 1866.

Derby, who succeeded him after his February 1852 defeat, suffered the same fate himself that December, and again in June 1859, when Palmerston formed the first Liberal government. Aberdeen was defeated in June 1855, which saw Palmerston become prime minister in the first place, before he himself was defeated in March 1857. Gladstone was defeated in 1873 and 1886, Salisbury's government in January 1886 and 1892, Baldwin in 1924, and MacDonald at the end of 1924. Governments after that tended to have comfortable majorities. The longest gap in history between 'no confidence' motions then occurred after 1924, before Callaghan's minority government was defeated in an official no confidence motion in March 1979, which forced a general election won by Thatcher that May.[5] Since the 1980s, the convention has been that defeat on a major item of government policy can prompt a '*confidence* motion' in the government, as Major engineered in 1993 when defeated on his Maastricht policy on the EU, and May did in January 2019 after she had been defeated on her EU Withdrawal Bill.

Prime ministers were thus relatively secure in the House of Commons from the 1920s to 1970s, as long as they could command majorities. Prime ministers didn't have to take great notice of MPs, 'who were more deferential to the leadership'.[6] But habits of disobedience began to grow from Heath's time.[7] Thatcher's government, despite the increasing majorities in her three general elections, suffered four defeats in her eleven years, while Callaghan suffered thirty-four defeats in his three years in power. Major was defeated six times in six and a half years, Blair four times in ten years, Brown three in three years, Cameron ten in six years, and May an extraordinary thirty-three times in just three years, including the biggest defeat (by 230 votes, January 2019) and the fourth biggest (March 2019) in House of Commons history (MacDonald notched up the second and third biggest defeats, both in 1924, when leading not even the biggest party in Parliament).[8] On one day, 3 April 2019, May suffered five Commons defeats, the most in history on a single day.[9] Boris Johnson was defeated repeatedly during his first six months until the general election in December 2019.

Fear of defeat in the vote on COVID lockdown on 30 November 2020 and subsequently in 2021 led to Johnson making concessions and investing considerable personal capital to win round his backbench MPs. Independently minded MPs who have become more rebellious, as monitored by Philip Cowley and Mark Stuart on their dedicated websites, act as a significant constraint on government.[10] The emergence of the so-called 'political class' in the modern era, career and free-thinking politicians who lack either an alternative professional background or local government experience before entering Westminster, has contributed to this. Tim Bale identified that of the ninety-seven Tory MPs who joined in December 2019 at least nine had worked previously as special advisors.[11]

What of declaring war? The royal prerogative theoretically gives the prime minister and ministers the power to act when there is no statute in place, including to deploy troops and make international treaties.[12] A select committee report in 2004 recommended reforming the prerogative 'to enact statutory safeguards' around the exercise of power.[13] Ambiguities remained, and in 2013, Cameron's team in Number 10 debated whether Parliament's agreement was required before military action in Syria, following chemical weapons use by the Assad regime. It was recalled, and Cameron was defeated.[14] In 2018, when their use was repeated, Parliament was not consulted, but May was careful to get full Cabinet approval. War-making is not the only fuzzy area.

In 2019 Johnson attempted to use the royal prerogative to prorogue Parliament for six weeks. This was challenged in the Supreme Court and declared unlawful, not least on the grounds this 'exceptionally long' prorogation would have prevented parliamentary scrutiny. The issue has unsurprisingly 'revived debates about whether prorogation (like dissolution) should be put on a statutory footing'.[15]

Select committees developed in the 1960s as Parliament's response to the perceived weakness of the House of Commons in the era of more powerful executive government and tight whipping. The modern system of cross-party committees, shadowing government departments, began to operate in 1980, and are potentially a challenge for the PM. Their impact can vary wildly. Notable successes have been Andrew Tyrie (2010–17) at the Treasury Select Committee, which pressured government to be more accountable for its public spending, Tom Tugendhat (2017 to present), Chair of the Foreign Affairs Committee, on government policy towards China, and Frank Field (2015–19) on the Work and Pensions Committee on the operation of universal credit.

Parliamentary committees may have impinged only marginally on prime ministers, though Hazell argues they have become more assertive after the public bill committees gained the power from 2006 to take evidence, and the Wright reforms in 2010, which introduced direct election of select committee chairs and gave backbenchers a voice through the Backbench Business Committee: previously the only days outside the control of government were the twenty days allocated each year to the opposition.[16] Significantly, it was turbulence from a rebellion of eighty-one Conservative MPs on a backbench committee motion on EU membership in 2011 that helped convince Cameron he could no longer resist holding a referendum.[17] By 2017 around fifty top public appointments were systematically scrutinised by select committees too.[18] The Liaison Committee, composed of the chairs of all select committees, is the only Commons committee with power to question the prime minister, usually three times a year. Johnson repeatedly refused to appear before it until questioned by it in September 2020, answering questions about COVID-19 testing, national lockdown, and the plan for Brexit.[19]

Prime minister's Questions (PMQs) are the most visible aspect of the House of Commons' power to hold the incumbent to account. If they're seen not to be agile and convincing, prime ministers can lose support with their own MPs. Until the 1880s, questions to the prime minister were on the same basis as for other ministers: they could be asked on any day without notice. In 1881, as a courtesy to the seventy-two-year-old Gladstone, questions began to be asked at a fixed point on up to four days a week and placed at the end of the list of questions to ministers, so he could arrive late: sometimes time ran out.[20] The frequency was reduced to just two days, Tuesdays and Thursdays, for the even more elderly Churchill in 1953.[21] Under Macmillan, an experiment began in 1959 with questions in two slots of fifteen minutes each, on Tuesdays and Thursdays, which became a permanent feature from October 1961. Televising Parliament in 1989 gave PMQs even more prominence. The gladiatorial clashes between the Leader of the Opposition and the prime minister were highlighted, with their audience not just MPs, but the whole nation. Thatcher was wounded by constant probing on her feuds with Cabinet, as was Major with his Cabinet, while Cameron hit Blair hard with his line 'He was the future once', in December 2005.[22] Blair reduced the two sessions down to just one of thirty minutes in 1997, initially at 3:15 p.m. on Wednesday, but moved in 2003 to noon, which Campbell said saved him a day or more of 'prep'. No regular event that the PM undertakes is more taxing than PMQs. Super-calm Macmillan confessed they could make him 'physically sick'.[23]

The Fixed-Term Parliaments Act of 2011 limited the prime minister's personal power by removing the prerogative to request the dissolution of Parliament to call a general election, ostensibly brought in by the coalition government to provide 'a certain amount of stability as it created an expectation that Parliament would run for a full term', and to remove 'the right of a Prime Minister to seek the Dissolution of Parliament for pure political gain', requiring a two-thirds majority in Parliament to call an early election (votes of no confidence were unaffected).[24] Brazier believes it was right to remove 'the prime minister's unfair power to choose an agreeable election date'.[25] The two-thirds mechanism was used by May to trigger her early general election in 2017; however, in 2019 Johnson lost on three attempts to do so, only managing to call an election by passing a separate act. The Act's forthcoming repeal will restore the PM's power to call an election.

What of the House of Lords? The Great Reform Act had been blocked by it, and only passed in 1832 when Tory peers abstained after learning that Grey had asked William IV to create sufficient Whig peers to secure the passage. Gladstone's second attempt at Home Rule was blocked by it in 1893, after the Government of Ireland Bill had passed the Commons. When the Conservative-dominated House of Lords rejected the Liberal Party's 'People's Budget' in November 1909, and after the two 1910 general elections, Asquith and Lloyd George acted. Asquith obtained George V's agreement to create as many Liberal peers as necessary to pass the legislation. Then, the Parliament Act was passed in August 1911 removing the power of the House of Lords to reject money bills and replacing its veto over other bills with merely a power of delay. The balance between both Houses was further altered to the benefit of the Commons by the reduction of maximum length of a parliament from seven years, as it had remained since 1716, to just five, which increased the frequency of general elections. The 1949 Parliament Act, passed by the Attlee government, further reduced the delaying power of the Lords from two years down to just one. Finally, during the 1945–51 Labour government, the Salisbury Convention was negotiated, stating that the House of Lords would not reject any government policy that appeared in a party's manifesto. The convention reflected that, although the Lords was dominated by Conservatives, it was a Labour government that had been elected and they should have the right to enact their manifesto. It took its name from the Leader of the Lords, Lord Salisbury (grandson of the namesake prime minister).[26]

So is the Lords now unimportant? By no means. It retains the ability to wound government and more, having defeated government legislation 39 times in the 2019–20 parliament alone.[27] It emerged as a significant challenge to the Labour governments of 1974–9, inflicting 126 defeats in its first full year, and 78 in 1977–8, and continued to challenge the Thatcher governments, albeit less intently, inflicting a high point of 22 defeats in 1985–6. It returned to a higher volume of defeats when Labour was returned to power in 1997, with 88 defeats in the 2002–3 session, and 45 in 2006–7. A stunning fact is that from 1997 to 2010 the Labour government was only defeated in the Commons seven times; in the same period it had 528 defeats in the Lords.[28] Blair's reforms after 1997 removed all but ninety hereditary peerages, with new hereditary peers elected to the House by their fellow hereditaries. With their 'stigma of illegitimacy', as Hazell puts it,[29] removed, the Lords became more assertive. This prompted an important 2008 study concluding that 'the Lords is already playing a significant role in the policy process in Britain'.[30] May had no peace from it either: with Brexit to the fore, it defeated her legislation 69 times in the prolonged 2017–19 session.[31]

Prime ministers should thus be wary of its potential, especially in the era of the reformed House of Lords when 'a Lords "win" [has been shown to be] more likely on a major than a minor policy issue'.[32] It is necessary to note too that many Lords wins 'occur under the media's radar, partly because it is in the government's interest to compromise quietly rather than being seen to climb down', says Meg Russell.[33]

Parliament has found many fresh ways to challenge and test the prime minister, different in form, but no less potent for Johnson than they were for Walpole. Parliament, both houses, is still an active constraint for the prime minister in 2021. Number 10 has become very careful, as seen again in 'lockdown' policy in 2020–1, with Johnson anxious not to put forward proposals that will run into trouble in the legislature.[34] And that is a prime minister with a majority of eighty.

CABINET. Cabinet ought to be a huge resource for the PM. Prime ministers have almost limitless 'power over its remit, operation and composition', says Lord Butler, Cabinet Secretary to three PMs. 'Much depends', he adds, 'on the personal political position of the prime minister at the moment, but it's a very real power in the hands of the prime minister'.[35] Surely Cabinet is a total boon, as the PM enjoys vastly greater powers over it than opposite numbers abroad? Well no, and here are four reasons why.

Prime ministers' ability *to appoint* their first choices to it is heavily constrained. Pimlott says that Wilson in 1964 felt he had no choice but to appoint a Cabinet 'largely composed of his enemies who – because the PLP had voted them onto the parliamentary committee – were there by right'.[36] May in 2016 had her options again significantly limited by the need to find a balance of remainers and brexiteers in her Cabinet, so she appointed Hammond as Chancellor and Johnson as Foreign Secretary, neither of whom proved loyal to her.[37]

Prime ministers' ability to *dismiss* is heavily circumscribed also. They tended to keep their Cabinet ministers in post much longer in the nineteenth century. In Peel's 1841–6 ministry, the Foreign Secretary, Home Secretary, and Chancellor of the Exchequer all remained unchanged, while in Palmerston's second ministry from 1859–65, Gladstone stayed put as Chancellor, Russell as Foreign Secretary, and Charles Wood as Secretary of State for India. Asquith, who said about such matters that 'there are always more horses than oats', retained Lloyd George as Chancellor and Grey as Foreign Secretary. Baldwin kept fourteen members of his Cabinet appointed in November 1924 through to June 1929; an extraordinary achievement. Churchill kept Eden as Foreign Secretary for all except the first seven months of his first ministry and throughout his last. As ministerial life became much shorter, problems mounted with dismissed or bruised ministers becoming dry tinder. Turnbull highlights the weakness:

> If a US president gets rid of a Secretary of State for Transport, that person disappears into history. If the prime minister sacks a cabinet colleague, they go onto the backbenches and cause trouble. Over time, the parliamentary support gets tainted by the increasing numbers of has-beens and never-weres who think they're owed something, or could have had something. The longer a prime minister is in office, the more likely his or her support will dwindle because of them.[38]

Macmillan hoped to inject new energy when he sacked seven Cabinet ministers in 1962, and his authority never recovered. Thatcher resorted to reshuffles to keep her government fresh and ministers on their toes: 'she viewed them as a weapon to consolidate her power', said Butler, 'but I viewed them as very damaging to continuity'.[39] She was fatally damaged by the departures of Lawson and Howe in 1989 and 1990, as Major was by Lamont's dismissal in 1993, while Blair never felt he had the political capital to move Brown from Treasury to Foreign Office.

Prime ministers suffer because of *resignations* following scandals or disagreements. When Ernest Marples remained as Macmillan's Minister for Transport after 1959 despite his brushes with scandal (both in accusations of corruption and his prodigious use of prostitutes), officials thought 'it was remarkable how ministers could stay in their position regardless of what had happened'.[40] But change followed swiftly, with the Profumo scandal in 1963 rocking the government. As the media felt empowered to probe ministerial life, the numbers of resignations shot up. Not even Heath could avoid being damaged by the resignations of Lords Lambton and Jellicoe following sex scandals in 1973. When John Major declared in his party conference speech in 1993 that he wanted to get 'back to basics', it was an open invitation to the media, and a series of ministerial resignations were triggered by scandals. Twice Peter Mandelson, Blair's principal loyalist in Cabinet, resigned following scandals, in 1998 and 2001.

Each resignation prompts an unwelcome reshuffle, taking time and expending the prime minister's political capital. By the early twenty-first century, Number 10 staff came to dread phone calls from papers on Saturday evening giving advance warning of horrors in the Sunday press. May's premiership saw ministerial departures, mostly over policy disagreements, reach historic levels: thirty-five outside reshuffles.[41] Johnson, drawing from the experience, resolved to hold his Cabinet together in a much tougher style, but resignations soon came, including Work and Pensions Secretary Amber Rudd and even his brother Jo Johnson, with more coming after the December 2019 general election, including Chancellor Sajid Javid. His insistence on standing by Home Secretary Priti Patel in November 2020, following the inquiry into bullying by his Standards Advisor, who resigned after his refusal to dismiss her, shows his determination to fight.

Finally, and most importantly, the prime minister's power over Cabinet is *conditional*. As long as he or she retains the initiative, is popular in the polls, and able to impart a clear sense of direction, they retain its allegiance. If not, the Cabinet, composed increasingly of enemies, is waiting to pounce, as we see repeatedly in these pages.

THE EXECUTIVE. The executive, which again should be an unqualified asset for the prime minister, so often has not been. It's not just the Chancellor of the Exchequer, and the mighty Treasury, which have emerged as the biggest checks on their authority (as discussed in Chapter 9). Powers of execution are invested by statute in the ministerial heads of department, not in the prime ministers, as they quickly learn. Oversight of the executive and the work in departments have often proved more a restraint than an additional power to the prime minister. The most precious commodity a prime minister possesses is time, and executive oversight eats up vast chunks of it. Often with little reward. Prime ministers regularly use the analogy of pulling levers and expecting Whitehall to respond: but little or nothing happens.

Some PMs take the job of chief executive more seriously than others, while some prefer to avert their eyes. Churchill decided in 1951 to have a series of 'overlords' supervising departments, a plan abandoned in 1953,[42] while Wilson set up the Fulton Committee, which in 1968 recommended a number of innovations, including more specialists in the Civil Service, many of which came to nothing. Managerialist Heath created a series of 'super ministries' after 1970, including the Department of Trade and Industry (DTI), while Thatcher tried to reduce the overall size of the Civil Service. Blair, with his Delivery Unit, and Cameron sought to make it more efficient and responsive, while Johnson has been as ambitious as any, trying to make it more open to fresh ideas, digitally responsive, and to recruit more figures with specialist technical knowledge.

It is far from clear whether much political benefit has accrued to prime ministers for all the exhausting effort expended trying to oversee and improve the executive branch. Blair memorably described how he had 'scars on his back' from his efforts to reform the public services.[43]

THE QUALITY OF NUMBER 10. Compared to the offices of heads of government and state abroad, Number 10 is small, constrained by the physical size of the building into which Walpole moved in 1735. The

Cabinet Office from 1916 has compensated for the physical limitation, especially after it moved into the adjacent Old Treasury building on Whitehall, with an interconnecting door. For all the accretions of new functions, such as the Policy Unit from 1974 and the vastly expanded communications hub, Number 10 remains low on brainpower, especially against the Treasury: 'Number 10 is underpowered, lacks analytical resource, doesn't have direct levers of power, comparatively few civil servants in the building, and with the political team quite mixed', says Rupert Harrison.[44] Political aides at Number 10 tend to be young or inexperienced, coming in with massive zeal and commitment, but little knowledge of 'what works', which explains why so many have not lasted, including Steve Hilton (2013), Nick Timothy and Fiona Hill (2017), and Dominic Cummings and Lee Cain (2020). The traditional response of prime ministers to the underpowered Number 10, including by Blair and Johnson, is to expand the size. But doing so creates further problems of managing their own staff and their rivalries.

THE JUDICIARY AND JUDICIAL REVIEW. The prime minister is subject to the law and is not above it, and actions of the government have to be within it. This is a real constraint. The doctrine of *parliamentary* sovereignty, however, means the judiciary will be more limited in its powers of judicial review than constitutional supreme courts in other countries, notably in the United States. The judicial branch of government has thus not been the powerful presence in the UK for much of the life of the PM that it has often been elsewhere. Judges in Britain today are not politically appointed, which helps further to depoliticise the judiciary. As one of Blair's constitutional reforms, the Supreme Court was established in October 2009, taking over the traditional judicial function of the House of Lords exercised by the twelve 'Law Lords'. The powers of the British Supreme Court are limited: it cannot overturn primary legislation made by Parliament, though it can overturn secondary legislation, and following the Human Rights Act of 1998, it can declare legislation incompatible with the European Convention on Human Rights.

So here is a comparatively new and growing constraint. Until the mid twentieth century, the courts did not regard it as their business to challenge the government. Eden's actions in the Suez crisis may have disturbed his Attorney General, Reginald Manningham Buller, while Minister of State at the Foreign Office Anthony Nutting resigned. But Eden was not unduly troubled by the legality of what he was doing, any more than such thoughts had concerned Asquith, Lloyd George, or Churchill in their conduct of the two world wars. Internment of 'aliens' in both wars, chemical weapons use by British forces from September 1915, and the bombing of enemy cities, all happened without mass raising of legal eyebrows.

From the 1960s a sequence of cases, notably *Ridge* v. *Baldwin*, developed modern public law principles, greatly extending the scope of judicial review of government decision-making, and a simplification of the rules in 1978 led to a steady increase in the number of cases brought against the government (and other public authorities). In the 1970s, following a number of cases where judges, including Master of the Rolls Lord Denning, came out in favour of the police and government against trade unions, a perception took hold that the judiciary was overly sympathetic to government. J. A. G. Griffiths wrote a celebrated book, *Politics of the Judiciary*, at the end of the decade alleging establishment bias and politicisation in the judiciary.[45] Entry into the EEC, when 'European law took precedent and the courts could strike down UK law', prompted further judicial activism, argues Norton.[46] In the 1990s, in a series of cases the judiciary seemed to turn *against* the government. Most significantly, in a deportation case in 1993, the House of Lords in *M* v. *Home Office* held for the first time that injunctions could be granted against ministers of the Crown.[47] When going to war in 2003 in Iraq, Blair took great trouble to ensure that Attorney General Peter Goldsmith was giving advice that indicated that the actions were legal, as did Cameron when he intervened in Libya in 2011.[48]

Concerns about an overly intrusive judiciary rose to fever pitch following two cases initiated by British businesswoman Gina Miller, an opponent of Brexit. *R* v. *Secretary of State for Exiting the European Union* argued successfully that the British government could not trigger Article 50 without approval from Parliament, and in September 2019, Miller successfully challenged the government's prorogation of Parliament. Brazier highlights the 'severe blow' suffered by Johnson, following hard on the heels of Theresa May's 'suffering a setback from the same source'.[49] Outrage followed about judicial activism constraining the 'will of the people', notably from Brexit-inclined commentators and press. Green, however, injects a welcome note of perspective: 'Other than the two exceptional Brexit cases associated with Gina Miller that ended up at the Supreme Court, it is difficult to think of a significant recent case where the province of public law and judicial review has been extended.'[50]

Criticism of 'inappropriate' judicial activism did not go away, and reached a new height in late 2020, with Johnson and Priti Patel criticising 'activist' and 'leftie human rights lawyers' for obstructing immigration controls, thereby 'hamstringing' the criminal justice system and the freedom of government to operate as it thinks it should.[51] Lord Kerr of Tonaghmore, the longest-serving Supreme Court Justice, responded that 'a healthy democracy', as in the UK, requires the judiciary to provide 'a vouching or checking mechanism for the validity [of] laws ... the last thing we want is for government to have access to unbridled power'.[52]

What are we to make of all this? A lively debate has taken place among academic lawyers about 'whether the Supreme Court has been more activist than the Law Lords', but Hazell believes that while 'the Supreme Court has a higher profile so people are more aware of it', it has been no more activist.[53] Judicial review cases can nevertheless cause problems for the government. Although they cannot influence the activities of Parliament itself, and nor can primary legislation be ruled invalid, 'the courts can make a "declaration of incompatibility" in some human rights cases and can "disapply" primary legislation if it is contrary to EU law'.[54] As Hazell concludes, 'anyone working in government will tell you that judicial review is a significant restraint'.[55]

POLITICAL PARTIES. Again, a putative strength for the prime minister can turn out anything but. Retaining support of their colleagues in the Whig or Tory party in the eighteenth and early nineteenth centuries, alongside that of the monarch, was essential for the prime minister remaining in power. When they lost it, and without strong monarchical backing, they fell, as Devonshire did in 1757 and Goderich in 1828. Party backing could not be taken for granted.

The advent of mass political parties during the mid nineteenth century led to a new era. After that, prime ministers could count on a more formal party structure to help them at elections and keep the MPs in line. Effective practitioners, like Palmerston and Salisbury, could stay in office for a long time. However, party could quickly become a weakness if disunited. Melbourne in 1834, Peel in 1846, Russell in 1852 and 1866, Gladstone in 1886, and MacDonald in 1931 as Labour prime minister were all brought down by splits in their own parties.

Mass democracy from 1918 created a situation where prime ministers became even more vulnerable to the whims of their parties, who viewed their leader through the lens of their ability to lead the party convincingly, and to win the next general election. Conservative prime ministers have been particularly vulnerable, with party pressure, as mediated by the big beasts, playing its role in easing out Churchill in April 1955, Eden in January 1957, and Macmillan in October 1963. They came under still greater pressure when Tory MPs began voting for their leader from 1965, engineered by outgoing party leader Douglas-Home. Popularity with MPs was responsible for propelling in his successor Heath as leader in 1965, and unpopularity with MPs ousted him in 1975. Thatcher lost the support of her parliamentary party and Cabinet in November 1990, and though Major narrowly won a leadership election to remain in office in July 1995, he was wounded in his final two years after it, while May lost the confidence of her party long before she was forced to resign in June 2019. Only the absence of an agreed and willing alternative in the deeply polarised Brexit Cabinet accounted for her survival until Johnson took over.

Traditionally, the Labour Party has been more respectful of its leaders, though its first prime minister, MacDonald, was never forgiven for leading a rump of its MPs into the National Government in 1931. Attlee (till 1951) and Wilson (till 1976) were allowed to stay on as prime ministers long past their best, aided by the near impossibility for Labour of ejecting a sitting prime minister. Blair and Brown suffered from increasing unrest from their own parties, Blair at the hands of Brown and his supporters, and Brown himself from the centre-right of the party, with David Miliband principal cheerleader, who pulled back only on the very brink of a direct challenge.[56]

Party management is a major concern for every prime minister. Recent prime ministers – including Blair and Johnson – have periodic rude reminders not to take their MPs for granted, even in the circumstances of a large majority. But, for those with a smaller majority or no majority, like Major, Cameron, and May, there is additional pressure to take party views into account, not least over Europe. Another headache for Conservative PMs is dwindling membership, last counted at 180,000 in 2019 and declining, which is two-thirds male, half over 65 years old and nine-tenths middle class.[57] Number 10 often has a low regard for party concerns, which they feel are irksome and parochial, and the figures in the PM's court who act as a bridge to them are often not high-rankers. Dominic Cummings, Johnson's most influential aide, was brazen about his disregard for MPs. Many were shocked. But he expressed an opinion many PMs themselves would not dare utter.

In Parliament, backbenchers club together to magnify their voices against a Number 10 that is often perceived as distant. For Conservative prime ministers, the powerful 1922 Committee articulates these views, and frequent visits to 'the 22' are an unloved part of the job. The Committee was established in April 1923 by a group of new Conservative MPs from the November 1922 election.[58] During the Brexit crisis of 2016–20, Conservative prime ministers also had to cope with the noisy European Research Group, a parliamentary group containing purist Brexiteers. For Labour prime ministers, the worry is the Parliamentary Labour Party (PLP), which will regularly summon them to answer questions. In the circumstances of a hung parliament or a small majority, these groupings can become extremely powerful indeed, eking out conditions from a weakened prime minister who cannot do without their support.

Prime ministers may be content enough to attend the annual party conference, but are universally relieved when their bullet-proof car whisks them off after their keynote speech at its conclusion, back to the seclusion of the Downing Street world where they are again in control. Most attend fundraising and party dinners through gritted teeth, regarding receptions for party faithful as akin to reunions with distant relatives they have left behind long ago, and regard visitations to the Commons for 'socialising with the troops' or interrogations by their backbenchers as a peculiar form of masochism.

INTEREST GROUPS AND FUNDING. No prime minister relishes being fundraiser-in-chief, a necessary evil for them since the nineteenth century and fraught with hazard. Fighting general elections nationally has always been expensive, and the more money that is raised, the more likely a successful outcome, and the leader being in Downing Street. National party organisations and regional structures eat money, as do fighting regular by-elections. Finance comes from membership fees, (recently) state funding for administrative costs, and party donations. It is the last of these which has proved so contentious for the prime minister. The first attempt to regulate them came soon after the 1867 Reform Act, in the Corrupt and Illegal Practices Prevention Act of 1883, designed to rule on constituency expenditure, followed by the Prevention of Abuses Act of 1925 to regulate honours after the furore surrounding Lloyd George's activities.

While the Conservatives have since 1900 attacked Labour for its dependence on trade union funding, Labour has returned fire on business funding of the Tories, notably wealthy donors, whose reasons for giving and rewards for doing so have aroused suspicions. A host of rich businessmen, from James Goldsmith in the 1990s to Lord Ashcroft in the 2010s, had a significant impact on Tory prime ministers. Concerns were not allayed by the Act in 2000 which established the Electoral Commission, requiring all parties to register and set limits on donations. The Committee on Standards and Public Life in 2011 made a number of further recommendations to address the more egregious concerns. These concerns reached new highs over money raised for Johnson's leadership election in June–July 2019, and the general election that December. An Open Democracy report found that 'an awful lot of the Tories' funding comes from a very few, very rich individuals', with one dining group, it said, responsible for £130 million in the previous decade.[59]

Tory leaders can no more ignore the views of business and finance than Labour leaders can trade unions. Len McCluskey, General Secretary of Unite the Union, the largest union affiliated to the Labour Party, might lack the clout of Jack Jones, General Secretary of the Transport and General Workers Union, and voted the most influential person in Britain in 1977 in a Gallup poll, ahead of Prime Minister Callaghan. But his influence and that of his fellow union leaders on a future Labour government would be significant. Raising money is perilous territory for prime ministers, as Walpole was the first to find out.

Prime ministers can be forced to change direction by pressure from popular or insistent individuals without money too. William Wilberforce headed the campaign against the British slave trade; William Willett, the builder, campaigned tirelessly for 'daylight savings', eventually introduced after his death in 1916; actress Joanna Lumley pushed the Brown government into agreeing that Gurkhas could settle in the UK; and footballer Marcus Rashford forced the Johnson government into a U-turn on free school meals twice in 2020.

THE NATIONS OF THE UNITED KINGDOM. The United Kingdom has been a *unitary* rather than a *federal* country, with sovereignty remaining in Westminster, though reforms since the late 1990s have challenged this on the margins. Federal countries, where sovereignty is shared, see far greater constraints on the power of the leader at the centre. The prime minister thus has real and enviable authority across all four nations. True? Not entirely. So why has nationalism been so often a constraint? While Scottish prime ministers like MacDonald were recognised as such in Scotland, rarely have prime ministers convinced the non-English nations they are truly one of them. It has not helped that since Douglas-Home ceased to be prime minister in October 1964, all prime ministers have been English (with the exception of the three-year tenure of Scottish Gordon Brown) and many have been very obviously from the southeast of England. They are more than the prime ministers of *England*, even if foreigners and some incumbents themselves have seen the job in that light, so dominant has England been in the Union.

Scotland edged its way slowly back up prime ministers' priorities from the 1970s, as nationalism flickered into life. Blair came to power in 1997 with a promise of creating a devolved institution in Scotland, affirmed in the referendum in Scotland in late 1997. The Scottish Parliament was duly created in 1998, with considerable powers to make primary legislation in all areas not expressly 'reserved' for the UK government in Westminster, including tax-raising, constitutional, foreign, and defence policy. During the 2010s (partly in response to the Scotland referendum in 2014), further powers in tax, welfare, transport, and energy were devolved to the Scottish Parliament.[60]

Wales by contrast has been relatively benign, with less demand for greater autonomy. The proposal to create a devolved Assembly in Wales was supported only narrowly in a referendum in 1997 (50.3 to 49.7 per cent), and the National Assembly established in 1998 had only limited law-making powers. These were gradually increased in the Government of Wales Acts (2006, 2014, and 2017), and in 2020 the National Assembly was renamed *Senedd Cymru* or Welsh Parliament.

Finally, Northern Ireland has had a devolved administration since 1921. But that was suspended in 1972, and abolished entirely, along with the Northern Ireland Parliament, in 1973. A new power-sharing Northern Ireland Executive was created by the Good Friday Agreement in 1998, which specified that government positions be divided between parties with the largest share of votes, in practice meaning joint unionist and republican governments. The first Democratic Unionist Party–Sinn Fein government was duly created in 2007 and has governed since (with an exception of 2017–20 when the Executive was in a caretaker mode). As with the other devolved administrations, some powers continue to be reserved to Westminster.

What this has meant for the prime minister is that large areas of the UK effectively have their own government and policy made at Westminster does not affect them, and they are often making policy for England alone. This has only become more acute when the government in Westminster is a different party to that or those governing in Holyrood, Cardiff, and Belfast. With the formation of the Conservative–Liberal Democrat coalition in 2010, this situation occurred for the first time, with entirely separate government in Westminster to the parties in the devolved administrations. The Brexit crisis since 2016 has put more pressure on the prime minister's freedom to act in this respect. Scotland's vote to remain in the EU has led to a situation where an unapologetic and forthrightly anti-Brexit SNP administration in Edinburgh regularly attacks the prime minister.

This has become a massive constraint on the PM. Very few, even in Number 10, foresaw the forces diminishing the PM's power that were unleashed by Blair's reforms. Hazell argues they 'will hammer more nails into the coffin of parliamentary sovereignty', and to survive 'Westminster may become more of a gearbox than a powerful engine'.[61]

LOCAL GOVERNMENT. Local government has become another signifi-cant worry for the PM. It has its origins in the Anglo-Saxon period, which gave birth to the shires and local responsibility for the provision of some services. It thus long predates its 'junior' partner, central government. By the time Walpole became prime minister in 1721, it was taking responsi-bility for roads, bridges, prisons, public buildings, licensing, and raising local taxes. The Municipal Corporations Act of 1835 standardised bor-oughs, and, with ratepayers electing its members, its concerns included public health and poor law relief. Further Acts from 1888–94 set up County Councils, including London, creating a system of local govern-ment in England that lasted nearly 100 years until the reforms instituted by the Heath government in 1972.

Several prime ministers, Neville Chamberlain and Attlee for example, had their roots in local government: they knew and understood it. Major has been a rare exception since 1951 in coming out of its stable, with Johnson, Mayor of London for eight years till 2016, another. Margaret Thatcher was the first prime minister to run headlong into it, facing some of her strongest opposition from Labour-controlled local councils. Her Local Government Act of 1980 tried to tighten local government fund-ing, and she took powers away from various councils, including London Docklands and Merseyside, deploying Environment Secretary Michael Heseltine to provide regeneration from the centre rather than from the localities themselves. Liverpool, Sheffield, Islington, Lambeth, and Haringey were councils who strongly resisted, which determined her to abolish the Greater London Council in 1986, and the Inner London Education Authority in 1990. She met her nemesis though when she instituted the community charge (or 'poll tax') that year as part of her plan to provide an independent source of local taxation. In that sense, one could say that local government helped bring about her demise.[62]

Again, few anticipated how the Local Government Act of 2000, which instituted the first directly elected mayors, the first being that of Greater London, would form a direct challenge to the prime minister's authority. The Localism Act of 2001 permitted referendums for elected mayors in the largest cities, and in 2014 it was announced that Greater Manchester would elect its first mayor. By the time Johnson became prime minister in 2019, fifteen directly elected mayors were operating in England (though none in

Wales).[63] Some of his greatest challenges have thus come from elected mayors, less, oddly, from his successor in London, Sadiq Khan, than from Labour Mayor Andy Burnham in Greater Manchester and Conservative Mayor Andy Street in the West Midlands. The moment that directly elected mayors appeared, the potential for discord with the prime minister was created on issues that conflicted with Westminster, as mayors, representing their own electoral base, could claim 'an authority if they wanted to stand up to the prime minister that they are the leader of a city, directly, rather than indirectly, elected'.[64] Increasingly, the PM is hemmed in.

THE EUROPEAN UNION. The EU, to which Britain belonged from 1973–2020, enhanced but also diminished the prime minister's authority. It did both before Britain joined, as it will do now Britain has left. At least Brexit frees up the PM, or will it? Its forerunners, the European Coal and Steel Community in 1951 and the European Community itself in 1957, threw down a gauntlet to prime ministers Attlee, Churchill, Eden, and Macmillan as they puzzled through what Britain's future relationship with this emerging body might be. After two de Gaulle rebuffs in 1963 and 1967, British prime ministers struggled once inside to find a settled place. Undoubtedly PMs saw benefits to being in the EU: Thatcher, standing alongside Heath in 1975, declared, it 'does more trade and gives more aid than any group in the world', giving Britain 'peace and security in a free society', poignant in a century that had seen two world wars; moreover these benefits were mutual for both Britain and the EU.[65] Nevertheless, as Steve Richards puts it: 'Membership of the EU created a special form of hell for each prime minister.'[66]

No prime minister since Heath, with the exception of Callaghan, has avoided the EU becoming a major draw on their time and political capital. Wilson sidestepped a coming furore over membership within his party by offering the country the 1975 referendum. Thatcher signed the Single European Act in 1986, but became progressively critical of EU supranationalism in her final years, notably in her Bruges speech in 1988, and alienated her Cabinet, which (together with the poll tax) cost her the premiership. Major was stymied from his first year in office by divisions within the Conservative Party over the Maastricht Treaty and its aftermath. Blair saw himself, as the first prime minister born after the end of the Second World War, as free to view the relationship with Europe with fresh eyes. He hoped that Britain would join the single currency, an objective thwarted not by the EU itself, but by the man next door, Gordon Brown, his Chancellor. Cameron vowed that he would never allow the EU to predominate over his premiership: but he could not escape the rise of UKIP and mounting Tory dissent, so he called the referendum which did for him. May knew from day one that her premiership would be dominated by it, but not even she anticipated the torture and humiliations it meant for her personally, as she battled to find the way out of the EU maze. Johnson's premiership was overshadowed by the EU from his doorstep speech until an even greater crisis, COVID, took over. One can only speculate what all of these prime ministers might have been able to achieve without the rancour over the EU flooding in wave after wave through Downing Street.

The European Convention on Human Rights (ECHR) entered into by Wilson (and part of the Council of Europe, not the EU) proved a particular cause of ire amongst Conservatives, as it submitted Britain for the first time to the jurisdiction of an international court, including on immigration, prisoners' rights, and family law.[67] Conservative Party fury was focused too on repealing the 1998 Human Rights Act, which gave legal effect to the protections of the ECHR in UK law, and replacing it with a 'UK Bill of Rights'.[68]

The sheer time that the EU took prime ministers cannot be overestimated. On top of their already over-crowded diaries, they had to add attendance at European Council meetings with the heads of government of all EU states, together with the presidents of the EU Council and EU Commission twice a year or more. When Britain held the six-month presidency, as it did six times, its last in 2005, it was an additional burden, not least on top of NATO summits, the UN General Assembly, and G7 and G20 meetings. The EU Council might be preceded by several days in which prime ministers would fly to see their opposite numbers, principally in Berlin, Paris, the Hague, Rome, and Madrid, for bilaterals. Following the Council meetings, they would often have a flight back from Brussels arriving at London's RAF Northolt in the early hours, with a statement to be prepared for them to deliver the next day in Parliament. Whatever the benefits of EU membership, it has played a part in the fall of every Conservative prime minister since 1979 and proved a headache for every Labour one since 1964. A special kind of hell indeed.

THE MEDIA. Prime ministers arrive in Number 10 thinking they can control the media which had savaged their predecessors but cannot in their first weeks get enough of them themselves: but they all end despising it. Managing it was a concern for all prime ministers following Walpole, though Colin Matthew argues that Gladstone was the first politician fully to recognise the political value of newspapers, courting reporters at the *Daily Telegraph* in the 1860s, and the celebrated John Delane of *The Times* in the 1870s.[69] Palmerston even before him had seen the potential to exploit it, though the 1870s and 1880s were the decades when 'The newspapers became increasingly national and gave an extraordinary amount of print space to politics, Parliament and the work of government. Handling it became another key new element in the view from the prime ministerial chair', as Hawkins says.[70] The spread of new media forms from the early twentieth century convulsed Number 10 and led successive prime ministers to have to adapt. From then on, successful prime ministers without fail, such as Lloyd George, Baldwin, and Churchill, were masters of the media.

Baldwin was not by any means the only prime minister to wilt under its power, but he was the first to express the concern every successor has shared when he unleashed this broadside:

> The newspapers attacking me are not newspapers in the ordinary sense. They are engines of propaganda for the constantly changing policies, desires, personal vices, personal likes and dislikes of the two men [Lords Beaverbrook of the *Express* and Rothermere of the *Daily Mail*]. What are their methods? Their methods are direct falsehoods, misrepresentation, half-truths, the alteration of the speaker's meaning by publishing a sentence apart from the context ... What the proprietorship of these papers is aiming at is power, and power without responsibility – the prerogative of the harlot through the ages.[71]

The speech was widely reported in the British press on the following day, but not those papers owned by Beaverbrook and Rothermere. Churchill dictated that the press was tightly controlled during the Second World War, and when he returned to power in 1951, his press proprietor friends, Beaverbrook, Camrose (*The Telegraph*), and Bracken (*The Financial Times*) were supportive of the government and colluded in downplaying the seriousness of his stroke in the summer of 1953.[72] Churchill took on a press secretary in Number 10, reluctantly: what need had he of one when he could go straight to the boss?

No prime minister since Churchill has been able to afford to disregard how their decisions and policies might be received in the press, though none subsequently has had his high-level influence. In the early twenty-first century, the big press beasts, Rupert Murdoch (*The Times, The Sunday Times, The Sun*), Paul Dacre (the *Daily Mail* editor), and the Barclay brothers (*The Daily Telegraph*), wielded great power. Prime ministerial angst about what the press was saying reached fever pitch at times of general elections, with few more egregious examples of 'power without responsibility' (or indeed democratic legitimacy) than Murdoch offering support to Blair in 2005 if he promised a referendum on the EU Constitution, which he duly did.[73] Again and again, pro-EU prime ministers Blair, Brown, and Major pulled back from pro-EU actions for fear of riling the press. It is hard to believe that the referendum result, perhaps the most important decision in Britain in the last fifty years, would have gone the way it did, for better or worse, had the press for many years not been disproportionately Eurosceptic.

The arrival of television in the late 1950s ushered in new opportunities for influence from Number 10, with Macmillan and Wilson the first television prime ministers. The arrival of Sky, Channel 4, and breakfast television, and the beginning of the 24-hour news cycle, were another wave: 'The media has changed the nature of the prime minister's office', says Richards, 'from one almost totally dependent on the incumbent, with no written rules, to one that has become much more frenetic, fearful and uneasy.'[74] Social media, he believes, has only added to the pressures on Number 10: 'The sense that Number 10 is a pressure cooker has taken over from an office capable of long-term strategic thinking and other virtues of leadership.'[75] We can exaggerate its impact of course. But, around-the-clock news, first on rolling news television and then later internet sites such as Twitter, has led to what Robert Hazell characterises as a 'less deferential, more critical media'.[76]

In one of his final speeches, Blair admitted that he had erred early on in trying to influence the media too much: but then laid into it with a directness rarely seen since Baldwin, and emboldened by his imminent departure: 'It is like a feral beast, just tearing people and reputations to bits.'[77] He may have believed that the real opposition to his premiership had not come from the official opposition, but from the media. But, that said, a mature, confident PM, with a very clear agenda, can still prevail against the media.

THE CHURCH. Religion has played a declining role in British politics over the 300 years, but remains even today a restraint on the prime minister. For Walpole, the political power of the Anglican Church was considerable, not the least because in a much smaller House of Lords the bishops were a disproportionate influence. The Church of England hierarchy, for their part, did not much like Walpole, feeling him insufficiently demanding of dissenters. But Walpole made full use of patronage powers to made sure that new bishops had Whig inclinations, with Edmund Gibson, Bishop of London, a staunch ally.[78] The Church proved a block on Catholic emancipation in the early nineteenth century. When that came in 1829, and Catholics and non-conformists became widely recognised, the Church's significance diminished even though it remained 'established'.

Religion was a powerful factor in nineteenth-century politics. Even personally non-religious prime ministers like Wellington or Palmerston still believed that part of their mission was the maintenance of Christianity in general, and often the Church of England specifically. Many prime ministers were strengthened by their ability to manipulate religious feeling. Some, like Gladstone and Salisbury, were intensely serious about their faith. Numerous political issues of the nineteenth century, like Irish Home Rule, university reform, and elementary education, had an important religious dimension.[79]

Religion was a powerful factor in the abdication crisis, when Edward VIII, as the nominal head of the Church of England, was deemed unjustifiable in proposing to marry the divorced Wallis Simpson, given the Church's doctrine that divorced people should not remarry in Church if their ex-spouses were still alive. The king's position as head of the Church and Mrs Simpson's unacceptability to large parts of the British public and Empire at large made the marriage impossible. Attlee's Labour opposition backed Prime Minister Baldwin's position, signifying they would refuse to form a government should he resign.

Britain has ceased to be an avowedly Christian country during the twentieth century since the time when in 1930 75 per cent of British babies were baptised in the Church of England; 59.3 per cent were still declaring themselves 'Christian' in the 2011 census, though less than one million regularly attended a church service by 2020, with just 2 per cent of 'young adults' calling themselves Anglican. Ramsay MacDonald may have been the first prime minister to declare himself an atheist, although most British prime ministers since 1945 have avowed Christian faith.

Does this mean that religion is no longer a constraint on the prime minister? Influence continues in the House of Lords, with twenty-six 'Lords Spiritual' having a permanent berth in the Upper House. A bill in 2012 sought to cut their numbers to twelve but failed. Critics say that their voting record has been consistently pro-conservatism and Conservative positions, as on LGBT issues, though utterances by prominent clerics counter this.[80] Robert Runcie, then Archbishop of Canterbury, accused Thatcher, in 1984, of pursuing 'confrontation' politics, and her economic policies of hurting vulnerable people.[81] The following year a report, 'Faith in the City', published by the Archbishop's Commission, caused consternation when it blamed Thatcher's policies for growing economic and spiritual poverty in Britain's inner cities. In October 2020 the Anglican Church caused renewed upset in Number 10 when it warned the government that its new Brexit bill, breaking international law and going back on provisions in the Withdrawal Agreement, could set 'a disastrous precedent'. In a joint letter to *The Financial Times*, Archbishop of Canterbury Justin Welby was joined by other senior clerics to condemn the direction of government policy.[82] When in November 2020 he spoke out against the 'shameful and wrong' cut to the foreign aid budget by the Chancellor, *BBC News* led with his opposition, ahead of the criticisms from several former prime ministers.[83]

Religion may not have the same central importance in the UK that it has in the United States and much of continental Europe. But prime ministers remain personally and politically sensitive to criticisms from religious figures, which they are anxious to avoid. They are keenly aware too that non-Christian faiths are on the rise, notably Islam, the second largest in 2011 with 4.8 per cent of the population. Chief Rabbis are noticed. Elements within Christianity, including charismatic and evangelical churches, are increasing. Carrie Symonds, a practising Catholic, went to church with Johnson to have their son Wilfred baptised in 2020. The death of religion has been much exaggerated.

VARIABLE CONSTRAINTS

As if the institutional constraints on the prime minister are not weighty enough already, staking them to the ground like Gulliver, they have to contend with an altogether fresh set of constraints, which vary over time, are often unpredictable, and can be 'exogenous', originating outside their control or that of Number 10.

THE SIZE OF THE PARLIAMENTARY MAJORITY. The size of their majority in the House of Commons is perhaps the biggest constraint (or potential boon) on the prime minister. At the most basic level, it is the maintenance of that majority, or at least a workable plurality of loyal MPs, that ensures the prime minister's survival. The day that their majority disappears is the day they leave office or call an election.

As we have seen, during the eighteenth and early nineteenth centuries, party affiliations were looser, and prime ministers owed their position to their ability to command a majority amongst parliamentary groupings. There was no concept of a 'party majority' such as we have today. While some Members of Parliament were affiliated with party groupings, and could be relied upon, most MPs were 'country gentlemen' or independents, and would need to be convinced before a vote. Some Whigs and Tories served as members of the government and opposition simultaneously, so it is hard to define the size of a 'majority' for a ministry, and they didn't necessarily change hands after general elections. In fact, the government never changed hands after an election between 1722 and 1831. It was up to the prime minister to work with the parliament he had.

The period between the Reform Acts of 1832 and 1867, during which eight general elections were held, saw a new system emerging, with losing prime ministers resigning after a confidence motion following a general election defeat, and parties starting to present their achievements in office and their plans to the electorate.

The 1868 general election, the first to be fought after the 1867 Reform Act, was the first in which over a million votes were cast. It produced a clear majority for Gladstone's Liberal Party over Disraeli's Conservatives (387 versus 271 seats). It was after that election that Disraeli set a precedent when he resigned immediately, without waiting for the inevitable confidence vote defeat. From this point onwards, the winning of a large majority (or 'landslide') emboldened the prime minister and the government, and gave them enhanced opportunities in the Commons to force through their policies in the face of opposition. In 1895, Salisbury's Conservatives won 411 MPs to the Liberals' 177, while in the 'Khaki election' of 1900, fought during the Boer war, Salisbury's last, the Conservatives won 402 seats to the Liberals' 183. A more activist prime minister than Salisbury might have used that majority more. A landslide ensued in 1906 for the Liberals, who won 399 seats to the Conservatives' 156, and facilitated the busy domestic programme of the government. The 'Coupon election' of 1918, in which candidates who supported the coalition received letters of endorsement (or 'coupons') from Lloyd George, saw the combined Conservative and Liberal coalition win 529 seats to Labour's 57 and the Independent Liberals' 28. In the election of 1922, the Conservatives won 344 MPs to Labour's 142, which should have guaranteed the Conservatives five years of power had Baldwin not decided to call an election in 1923 on the issue of tariff reform, knowing he needed to gain a mandate for his policy on it after Bonar Law's pledge not to do so in 1922.

In 1945, Attlee's Labour Party won its first landslide, with 393 MPs to the Conservatives' 210, which eased considerably the government's subsequent work. Harold Wilson won his only landslide in 1966, with 364 seats to the Conservatives' 253, which gave him an authority squandered by devaluation in 1967 and by divisions between his ministers. Thatcher won three election victories, the largest in 1983, with 397 seats to Labour's 209, which paved the way for her most reformist ministry. Blair's victory in 1997, the first of his three, was comfortably his largest, with 418 MPs against just 165 for the Conservatives, while Johnson won the biggest Conservative victory for thirty-six years (since 1983) in December 2019, with 365 MPs to Labour's 202.

Prime ministers might not always have made the most of large majorities: but it gives them vast potential authority. Minority ministries with small or no majorities have proved a massive handicap for the PM: they have struggled to pass legislation and make an enduring impact. Pitt the Younger battled to obtain parliamentary majorities in the first year of his premiership (1783–4), while the Canning and Goderich ministries of 1827–8 lacked the support of all Tories, and Peel's first ministry, in 1834–5, was defeated on almost every government measure. The Derby government of 1858–9 saw another weak minority administration, which struggled to pass legislation. As he told Queen Victoria, 'Only the forbearance and support of some of his opponents ... would make it possible for him to carry on any government.'[84]

In the twentieth century, Labour's first two governments, in 1924 and 1929–31, were severely restricted by the lack of a majority. Attlee's final government from 1950–1, and Wilson's first government from 1964–6, were similarly constrained by small majorities. The minority status of Wilson's government following the February 1974 election meant he had to devote all his energy to place Labour in a position to win another general election, which he narrowly did in October. It was insufficient, though, to allow Labour to do much, bar the referendum in 1975, and Callaghan lost the majority altogether in 1977, which forced him into a pact with the Liberal Party. The failure of the Conservatives to win an overall majority in the 2010 general election produced the coalition government with the Conservatives and Liberal Democrats, while the loss of May's majority in the 2017 general election made the next two years almost impossibly difficult.

PERSONAL POPULARITY. Until the 1930s a prime minister's popularity in the country could not be assessed accurately. But the growth and sophistication of polling in the interwar years changed that, and in 1945 an offshoot of Labour correctly predicted Labour's landslide victory. Personal popularity proved insufficient, though, for Churchill to win the election for the Conservatives, although his personal standing following the war was far higher than Attlee's. From the 1950s, political parties began to scrutinise opinion polls increasingly, while from the 1980s, focus groups, to assess the popularity of leading politicians and policies, became at times all-important. Wilson had made cheerful use of opinion polls when they ran in his own favour, but then the tide turned, as Pimlott recalls: 'As the Prime Minister's ratings plummeted, anti-Wilson plotting became a parlour game . . . in the Tea Room, in Hampstead dining-rooms, and in rumour-filled newspaper offices, innumerable scenarios for the Prime Minister's forced departure were painted in vivid colours'.[85]

Consciousness of how decisions will be judged by the electorate, and the impact on a prime minister's personal approval ratings, enormously affect the thinking inside Number 10, which can worry more about the PM's ratings than the party's. When the personal ratings fall below a certain level, a premiership can become a matter of bloody endurance, as Major, Brown, and May all found. All survived in office after that point in part because of the unwillingness of any serious challenger to materialise.

THE PROXIMITY OF A GENERAL ELECTION. Prime ministers are never stronger than in the first six months after winning a general election. The honeymoon can last several years, but only if they make no bad mistakes and continue to carry their Cabinet and parliamentary party. Prime ministers who come to power between general elections know they lack authority without the personal imprimatur of their own general election victory. Callaghan from 1976, Brown from 2007, and May from 2016 all chafed at not having their own victory under their belt.

Within a few months of Eden's victory in the May 1955 general election, his authority was being questioned, even before he became embroiled in Suez, with *The Daily Telegraph* calling for 'The smack of a firm government'.[86] Conservative MP Huw Merriman revived the phrase in August 2020, just eight months after Johnson's landslide victory, when he called for 'the firm smack of government' to be shown in the face of numerous U-turns in policy that summer.[87]

Prime ministers are most at jeopardy at the midpoint between general elections. Here, as long as there is sufficient time for a leadership election to be held, and for a successor to identify themselves and make their impact, they will be under threat. This is the 'death zone', and Johnson found himself in it from mid 2020. Thatcher fell at her moment of maximum vulnerability in November 1990, but Major survived his, with it sparking the 1995 leadership challenge, and was thereafter safe to take the party into the next general election; the point was passed for Brown in late 2009 when it was deemed too late to challenge him without damaging the party's chances in the incipient general election.

ECONOMIC DOWNTURNS. Cameron encapsulated it neatly in his memoirs: 'When your GDP is on the up, your power rises with it. Your global stature increases, public confidence grows, your party's fortunes rise, and your economy's success sparks the interest of investors. Growth begets growth.'[88] The 300 years since 1721 have seen twelve recessions, all of which have damaged the prime ministers, making it harder for them to gain the confidence of their colleagues, while the impact in reducing tax yields constrained the ability of prime ministers to pursue their favoured policies.

Prime ministerial performance can be measured during these recessions, showing a negative impact in most cases. Here they are: the financial crisis in 1772; the 1812–21 adjustment caused by the prolonged Napoleonic Wars; the first global economic crisis in 1857–8, which originated in the US, and the 1867–9 economic recession precipitated by the American Civil War; the 'Great Depression' in agriculture of 1873–96; the post-World War I downturn from 1919–22; the world recession of 1929–31, beginning in Wall Street; the double-dip recession of 1973–6 with high inflation, precipitated by the Yom Kippur War and OPEC's oil price hike; the 1980–1 downturn sparked by Howe's restrictive economic policy; the post-Lawson-boom adjustment of 1990–1; the Global Financial Crisis of 2008–9; and finally the COVID depression, perhaps the biggest of all, starting in March 2020. But one truth stands: the agility with which prime ministers and chancellors respond can mitigate the negative impact.

By 1945 it had become evident that general elections fought at times of recession rebounded negatively on the government in power, and that governments prospered electorally in booms. Election timing promptly became a weapon of great importance to the prime minister. In his 'pots and pans' Budget the month before the 1955 general election, Chancellor Rab Butler cut sixpence off income tax. A large majority followed for Eden. Macmillan traded on the consumer boom to secure his 1959 election victory, while Thatcher benefited from the economic upturn in her 1983 and 1987 victories. Major's election victory in 1992 bucked the trend because he won in a recession. From the moment Blair and Brown came to power in 1997, winning a second significant general election victory (unknown in Labour history) was paramount in their minds.

The prime minister and their Chancellor may have little influence over the state of the domestic economy, for all the sophistication of economics; but the state of the economy has a great deal of influence over the prime minister and the Chancellor.

TIME IN OFFICE. While longevity in office may be no guarantee of success, brevity is a major handicap: little can be accomplished in less than three years in office. Yet twenty-two out of fifty-five prime ministers (including Johnson to date), forty per cent of the total, have served for less than this time. None of the ten shortest-serving PMs could claim to have been distinguished holders of the office: George Canning (120 days), Viscount Goderich (145 days), Bonar Law (212 days), the Duke of Devonshire (226 days), the Earl of Shelburne (267 days), the Earl of Bute (318 days), Sir Alec Douglas-Home (364 days), Lord Grenville (1 year, 43 days), the Duke of Grafton (1 year, 107 days), or the Earl of Rosebery (1 year, 110 days).

All ten of the longest-serving prime ministers in contrast left an important mark: Walpole (20 years, 315 days), Pitt the Younger (18 years, 344 days), Liverpool (14 years, 306 days), Salisbury (13 years, 253 days), Gladstone (12 years, 127 days), North (12 years, 59 days), Thatcher (11 years, 209 days), Pelham (10 years, 192 days), Blair (10 years, 57 days), and Palmerston (9 years, 142 days).[89] The most contentious figure is Lord North, criticised for his handling of the American War of Independence; but he was a successful prime minister in his first five years in power, particularly with finance.

Some prime ministers serving for short periods who might have gone on to have been considerable figures include Spencer Perceval (2 years, 222 days; assassinated), George Canning (120 days; died in office), and Bonar Law (212 days; retired through serious illness). Grey stands out as the prime minister who achieved most despite a short period in office (3 years, 230 days). Some short-serving prime ministers however achieved prominence with one singular act, including Heath (3 years, 260 days; entry into the European Community in 1973) and Brown (2 years, 319 days; handling the Global Financial Crisis in 2008–9).

LIMITED HOURS IN THE DAY. Prime ministers themselves would list the lack of time available with the pressure of non-discretionary tasks as one of the biggest constraints on their own freedom of action. We might ask, are they protesting too much? 'Prime ministers don't even pay attention to bills, whereas Gladstone drafted his own', says one commentator.[90] But much has changed since Macmillan made a long journey abroad: 'Towards the end of 1959, the Prime Minister decided to make a tour of four Commonwealth countries in Africa',[91] say the Cabinet records, leaving on 5 January 1960 and returning to the country on 15 February having visited Ghana, Nigeria, South Africa, and what was then the Federation of Rhodesia and Nyasaland. 'The Prime Minister travelled 13,360 miles by air, 5,410 by sea, and about 800 by road. He spent one night in the air and ten at sea', the minutes proudly record.[92]

Within five years, such a trip would have been considered inconceivable for a prime minister. Macmillan may have been the last prime minister to preside over the British Empire, but he could not have foreseen the explosion of think tanks pumping out ideas to be read; the rise of the 24-hour news cycle; the growth in size and complexity of government; the eruption of violence in Northern Ireland and on mainland Britain from the 1970s to 1990s; Islamic terrorism after 9/11; membership of the European Union from 1973 to 2020; enhanced expectations on the prime minister to be fundraiser in chief for their party; the proliferation of Cabinet committees and formation in 2010 of the National Security Council; the explosion of appointments to quangos and other bodies from the 1980s; attendance at the G7 from 1973 (the G8 from 1997 to 2014) and the G20; and the environment as a major concern, including hosting the COP26 UN climate change conference in Glasgow in November 2021. There are almost 200 countries in the world, double the number in Macmillan's time. The heads of state of all these countries passing through London want to spend time with the prime minister. Many can be batted off, but not all.

The tyranny of the prime minister's overnight red boxes, full of papers that demand responses by the following morning, some requiring difficult decisions, eat further into their ability to rest and sleep. Prime ministers have to be ruthless in their time management to leave space to pursue their own agenda, to see the people and make the visits they want. Time for thinking is often sacrificed. Time for contemplation, still more so. Pressure on the prime minister is particularly acute during crises and general elections. How much more effective, considered, and strategic might prime ministers be if they were allowed more space in their diaries? 'The demands of the job of prime minister naturally lead to a lack of time for reflection. The relentless pace of events as well as the 24-hour news cycle make it increasingly hard for premiers to press 'pause' and seriously consider a course of action over several days, let alone weeks', says Rhodes. 'It has had a seriously detrimental effect on the quality of political leadership. Short-termism has become a significant factor for prime ministers.'[93]

WARS AND EVENTS. These make or break prime ministers, as they should, probing their quality as leader and defender of the nation. Harold Macmillan never uttered the words for which he has become famous, in response to a question about the greatest difficulty facing a modern prime minister: 'Events, dear boy, events.' Rather he said, 'The opposition of events.'[94] But the point remains the same: life for the prime minister is unpredictable, and their response to 'events' is all-important.

The South Sea Bubble helped bring Walpole to power, while another event, the War of the Jenkins' Ear against Spain, precipitated his end. The American War of Independence broke North. The Crimean War of 1854–6 showed up Aberdeen, but it helped make Palmerston. The First World War unmade Asquith as it made Lloyd George, while the Second unmade Chamberlain but made Churchill. War in Korea in 1950–1 damaged Attlee as the nation's finances could ill afford the fight. The

Suez War sank Eden, while the Falklands War emboldened Thatcher. Wilson's steering clear of the overtures of one US president to join a war added to his stature, while Blair damaged himself by following another US president in another war. It is hard to imagine that Britain's five most successful war prime ministers, Pitt the Younger, Palmerston, Lloyd George, Churchill, and Thatcher, would have achieved that stature without their war or, in the case of Palmerston, Lloyd George, and Churchill, achieved the position of prime minister in the first place. It is equally hard to imagine that the record would appear so bleak for four of Britain's least successful prime ministers without their own failure in war: Spencer Compton (War of Jenkins' Ear), North, Portland, and Eden.

SCANDALS. Scandals, whether sex, finance, or corruption, can badly unsettle premierships, as we saw when considering resignations. For the first 200 years in the life of the prime minister, no scandals, of which there were plenty, affected the standing or perception of the prime minister. Few appear, to today's eyes at least, more overtly corrupt than Walpole, and few prime ministers had more sexual liaisons than Palmerston (there is strong competition). Corruption and extra-marital affairs were accepted as the norm until at least the late nineteenth century, when Gladstone and Salisbury, paragons of correct behaviour, helped set a new standard, with high-minded legislation, the Corrupt and Illegal Practices Prevention Act of 1883 and the Corrupt Practices Act of 1889, following suit.

Lloyd George was the first prime minister whose immoral behaviour helped to hasten the end of his premiership. Already tainted by the Marconi scandal of 1912 when he was Chancellor, when leading Liberal ministers were accused of insider trading, he was later embroiled in the honours scandal of 1922, which played a part in his downfall, even though some historians like John Campbell observe that the practice of selling honours was time-honoured.[95] It was this, particularly as the money went into Lloyd George's personal fund rather than a party one, rather than his legendary sexual exploits, that achieved notoriety and damaged his authority.

The tide turned very dramatically in the early 1960s. The much written-about Profumo scandal hit Macmillan hard, even if it fell far short, as writers have claimed, of ending his premiership.[96] Why did it become a major national scandal though, when earlier sordid affairs did not? In part, because Profumo lied to the House of Commons and to his prime minister, as Macmillan acknowledged: 'Of course it was my responsibility. But we failed, because we were deceived.'[97] The incident involved espionage, with Captain Eugene Ivanov, a naval attaché at the Soviet Embassy in London, also having an affair with Christine Keeler. The involvement of high society, including osteopath Stephen Ward, contributed. But it was mostly because of the newly intrusive media. In the early 1960s in the United States, President John Kennedy's serial philandering was not a source of widespread condemnation or even press comment: subsequent US presidents did not escape. Nor did the Royal Family with its dalliances. From this point on, prime ministers were to be regularly disturbed by scandals, probed, whipped up, and sustained by the media, creating a constant dilemma: do they sack early or hold on to the troubled minister?

Have ministers and politicians become more corrupt over the 300 years? Probably not. But their actions have become far more open to media investigation, especially in the last sixty years. It has meant an additional, and very unwelcome, distraction for prime ministers.

AGE AND HEALTH. Prime ministers can do nothing to affect their age and little their health, yet these impact significantly on how they perform. Youngest to become prime minister was Pitt at twenty-four, followed by Grafton aged thirty-three, Rockingham aged thirty-five, Devonshire thirty-six, and North thirty-seven. While Wilson could quip that he was retiring in 1976 to make way for an older man, Callaghan (by four years), prime ministers since then, notably Blair and Cameron, both aged forty-three, have been younger. The latter indeed was the youngest for 198 years since Pitt, who had more political maturity in government than either, not least as Chancellor of the Exchequer. Some become prime ministers too early in their careers with insufficient experience or personal judgment, while others move up to the top too late. The latter group includes Disraeli (63), Bonar Law (64), Chamberlain (68), and Campbell-Bannerman (69), all of whom died on or soon after leaving office. Some turned age to their advantage though: Palmerston was 74,

Churchill 76, and Gladstone 82, when becoming prime minister for their final times, their experience and authority, especially in Churchill's case, compensating for any loss of energy.

The average age of prime ministers rose mid nineteenth century and remained high until the mid twentieth century. Coleman puts this down to the decline of royal patronage, monarchs having promoted young favourites, as well as the importance of accumulated prestige, notably in the House of Lords, as political parties became the principal engines for promotion to the top job. The tradition too of families and individuals serving in politics over many decades helps explain the rising age, with long service from figures like Liverpool, Wellington, Grey, Derby, Palmerston, Disraeli, Gladstone, and Salisbury and, into the twentieth century, Balfour, the Chamberlain family, Curzon, Churchill, Eden, Douglas-Home, and Macmillan, with Kenneth Clarke an outlier almost to the present day (his first ministerial post was in 1974, his last 2014). Coleman ascribes the decline in the average age of prime ministers since the 1960s principally to the advent of probing photography, the rise of television, and the increasing rigours of the job.[98]

Poor health dogged many more prime ministers than the public and even parliamentarians were aware of at the time. In 1766, Chatham wrote to Grafton, his successor as prime minister: 'My lord – my extremely weak & broken state of health continuing to render Me entirely useless to the King's service ... His Majesty will be Graciously pleased to grant Me His Royal Permission to resign the Privy Seal.'[99] Concerns continued all the way down to Johnson nearly dying of COVID in April 2020, an illness that would have seen off his predecessors. Poor public health and unsanitary conditions took their toll on PMs until medicine improved last century. In the eighteenth century, Spencer Compton, Pelham, and Rockingham died in office, Portland survived less than a month after resigning, and Pitt the Younger expired in office in 1806. Illness afflicted several nineteenth-century prime ministers, not least Canning, Palmerston, Disraeli, and Rosebery, and diminished the performance of countless others. Depression, accompanied by a stigma that persists today against acknowledging it, assaulted an unknown number of past prime ministers, likely including Pitt the Elder, Gladstone, and Rosebery, before the condition became better understood. Bonar Law was already ailing when he became prime minister in 1922: 'Had Bonar Law at one time wished to be premier, he most certainly did not wish to be so in 1922', writes biographer R. J. Q. Adams.[100] MacDonald's performance was diminished in his final years in office: 'His health was already far from robust when he re-entered Number 10 in 1929', writes David Dilks. 'He ought to have resigned by 1933, or 1934 at the very latest, on account of his failing eyesight and general health.'[101]

It's impossible to know how far cancer affected Neville Chamberlain's judgement in his final months: he died from it six months after stepping down. Nor can we know how far his repeated ill health affected Churchill during the war, and in the early 1950s, or how far it was responsible for Eden's erratic conduct during the Suez crisis. He had almost died in the summer of 1953, when a routine operation had gone badly wrong, and was flown to Boston, Massachusetts for treatment. As prime minister from 1955, he was taking Benzedrine, an amphetamine brain stimulant, which his physician, Horace Evans, warned him about, and at the height of the Suez crisis was running a temperature of 106 degrees, while vital Joint Intelligence Committee assessments remained unread. David Owen, a physician as well as a Foreign Secretary, believes there is 'little doubt that Eden's intemperate handling of the situation was influenced both by his health and by the amphetamines he was taking'. It was certainly one of many factors behind the Suez debacle.[102]

Harold Wilson's performance was clearly affected by his ill health from the moment he returned to Number 10 in March 1974, and was finding it difficult to remember detail, which had been one of his greatest gifts. His Principal Private Secretary, Ken Stowe, later said that it could be pointless presenting fresh material to him after 5 or 6 p.m. in the evening because of alcohol and his state of mind. Robin Butler, then a junior No. 10 official, later said that he thought Wilson was displaying early signs of dementia during 1974–76.[103] Major, Blair, and Cameron were largely free of illness. Theresa May coped with type 1 diabetes. Johnson left hospital after two days in intensive care on 12 April 2020; it is a moot point whether his work rate and judgement have been affected by the illness.

PREVIOUS EXPERIENCE. A deep understanding of Westminster and Whitehall, the processes and people, matters everything to incoming prime ministers. Younger incumbents in the eighteenth century, Bute, Grafton, and Shelburne, clearly lacked it. But so too have the five holders of the office up to 2021, who had worked in just three Whitehall departments between them, Treasury (Brown), Home Office (May), and Foreign Office (Johnson), albeit covering the three great offices of state. In contrast, their five predecessors, from Heath to Major, had served in twenty-three roles, and the five before them, from Churchill to Douglas-Home, in thirty-nine. This is an astonishing change. A lack of understanding of the way Whitehall works, of experience running large departments, or indeed of running anything at all apart from their own political parties in Blair's and Cameron's cases, has given them a very different and far more limited experience. They all made mistakes and took time learning the job. Previous experience is important, vital indeed, Walpole having been Chancellor of the Exchequer, Gladstone having sixteen years as a minister before he became prime minister, Palmerston thirty-five years as War, Home, or Foreign Secretary, and Churchill also eighteen years across nine different roles.

NEW CONSTRAINTS. As if the constraints are not already daunting, prime ministers are hemmed in by a further range of factors, many new. These include the Electoral Commission, responsible for overseeing electoral process and political party spending,[104] and the House of Lords Appointments Commission[105] which rejected Boris Johnson's proposed peerages for two Tory donors in 2020.[106] A series of new bodies have emerged in the last twenty years, including the Commissioner of Public Appointments,[107] with a commitment to diversity and fair competition, and the Judicial Appointments Commission,[108] which has joined the Civil Service Commission[109] to restrict patronage power. 'Previously, without these appointment bodies, a prime minister had freedom of manoeuvre when they were making an appointment, or giving a peerage, or appointing someone to be head of a public body like the Chairman of the BBC, or a senior judge', said Hazell.[110]

The codification of the prime minister's powers, and those of ministers and special advisors, can also lead to trouble. Johnson's advisor Dominic Cummings thus came under the cosh, following his May 2020 trip to Barnard Castle, from the media and the Commons Liaison

Committee, for alleged breaches of the Special Advisors Code drawn up in 2010.[111] The Freedom of Information Act 2000 which came into full force in 2005, granting individuals the right to request information from public authorities, has been a further potential restraint,[112] and has been the cause of regular irritation in Number 10 because of the time taken dealing with requests.[113] Concerns spread that the candour of advice the PM received would suffer for fear that it could become public through an FOI request. But a recent study of its impact concludes 'the chilling effect [of FOI] to be a myth'; there was 'no evidence of any decline in the quality of official advice', with the converse being found: 'The majority of central and local government officials were more fearful of the consequences of not having a record rather than of a record being released.'[114]

So here at the end of a chapter on the constraints on the PM is a piece of good news for them: the dog that didn't bark.

CONCLUSION

The constraints, which have grown considerably since the Second World War, point inevitably to the conclusion that the power of the prime minister has become significantly restricted. Depressions, wars, the weather, harvests, and economic cycles have all buffeted prime ministers over the 300 years. Many incumbents would agree with the observation from Treasury minister Douglas Jay (1947–51), who observed that Attlee, at least in his first few months in office, was far from being a 'great man, sitting down in his office pulling great levers, issuing edicts and shaping events'. Rather, he was

> hemmed in by relentless economic or physical forces, and faced with problems which had to be solved, which could not be solved ... the position of the PM [was] more that of a cornered animal, or a climber on a rockface, unable to go up or down, than that of a general ordering his troops whenever he wished around the landscape.[115]

The prime minister seems to the outside world to be an all-powerful office. It does not often appear that way to the prime ministers themselves. Number 10 seems the epitome of a powerhouse to those who view the famous black door on their screens. Not to those who work on the other side of it. We are regularly told that the position is becoming presidential; and yet many of the most dominating prime ministers are in the distant past.

The most successful prime ministers are nevertheless able to navigate these potential pitfalls and traps, recognising dangers, and even turning a hazard into an opportunity. Power has ebbed and flowed depending on political circumstance and the quality of the PM. One thing, however, has been a constant in our story since 1721: the monarchy, and that is the topic of the next chapter.

CHAPTER 7

The Eclipse of the Monarchy, 1660–2021

THE HISTORY OF THE PRIME MINISTER AND OF THE MON-
archy are indissolubly linked. The monarchy continued to exercise
real authority for the first 200 years of the prime minister's existence. The
transfer of power was painful, faltering, and contested. The continued
existence of the monarchy was never a given. It had been abolished in
Britain in 1649, as it was in France in 1792 (and 1848 and 1870), Germany
in 1918, and Italy in 1946. Aside from the queen, and the British
Commonwealth, only twenty-eight countries still retain a monarchy,
just 15 per cent of the total. Belgium, Denmark, the Netherlands,
Norway, Spain, and Sweden retain monarchies with ceremonial duties,
but beyond Europe, they tend to be found in the Muslim world, and
include some with absolute power, Brunei, Oman, Qatar, and Saudi
Arabia.

No other country in the world has a monarch who reigns over so many
countries abroad. No other country has a monarchy as celebrated, and an
incumbent as beloved. Indeed, the history and renown of the British
monarchy militated against the earlier evolution of an independently
powered prime minister in Britain, and significantly shaped the way the
office evolved.

In this chapter, we explore how the transfer of power between the
monarch and the prime minister occurred, when it happened, how the
monarchy survived, the importance it still has in Britain, and how far the
prime minister has effectively become the head of state as well as head of
executive.

THE DIMINISHED MONARCHY, 1649–1721

The execution of Charles I on 30 January 1649 in the very heart of English power, Whitehall Palace, sent reverberations across the nation. Three days before, Charles had been sentenced to death by the Parliamentarian High Court of Justice, declaring him guilty of attempting to 'uphold in himself an unlimited and tyrannical power to rule according to his Will, and to overthrow the Rights and Liberties of the People'.[1] For eleven years following, Britain had a republic, eventually governed by Oliver Cromwell. When Charles II was restored in April 1660, he issued the Declaration of Breda which made promises in relation to the reclamation of the Crown, above all that there would be no vengeance against those who had sided with Parliament during the Civil War (except for a few dedicated regicides). He entered London on 29 May 1660, his thirtieth birthday, and was crowned in Westminster Abbey in April 1661. A royalist Parliament sat until 1679, and on the surface, normality had returned.

But the monarchy was not the same. Charles II, and James II from 1685, could never forget the fate that had befallen their father. They continued to live in Whitehall Palace only a short distance from where he had been executed. His ghostly presence hovered over them.

James II's reign hit trouble early on. He was a Roman Catholic, and many were deeply suspicious. Even before his accession, several bills had been proposed to Parliament excluding him from the throne. After he became king, three rebellions, in the south of England, in the north, and in Scotland, led to his decision to enlarge the standing army, which aroused further concerns, as did his advancement of Catholics. In November 1685, he prorogued Parliament, never to meet again in his reign. His attempts to pack Parliament with his supporters, so they would pass laws in favour of Catholics, were the last straw. In April 1688, seven bishops, including the Archbishop of Canterbury, were arrested by him and tried for seditious libel for resisting the Catholic measures. Alarm reached fever pitch when James II's wife gave birth in June 1688 to a son and heir who would be raised Roman Catholic, James Francis Edward.

That same month, a number of Whig and Tory nobles sent the famous 'Invitation' to William and Mary, inviting them to come to England with an army. Written by politician and soldier Henry Sydney, the document stated:

> The people are so generally dissatisfied with the present conduct of the government in relation to their religion, liberties and properties (all which have been greatly invaded), and they are in such expectation of their prospects being daily worse, that Your Highness may be assured there are nineteen parts of twenty of the people throughout the kingdom who are desirous of a change ... [2]

William landed with a considerable invasion fleet at Brixham, in Devon, in November 1688. As his courtiers and allies deserted to William, James II's reign disintegrated. After contemplating fighting, he gave up, threw the Great Seal of the Realm into the Thames, and William allowed him to escape. Parliament decided that, as James had dispensed with the Great Seal and fled to France, he had in effect abdicated, and they invited his daughter, and William's wife, Mary, to become queen, with William becoming king.

The prominence of Parliament was underlined when in 1689, William and Mary accepted the Bill of Rights which laid out 'the rights and liberties of the subject', thereby creating a constitutional monarchy. It listed James's crimes, above all 'assuming and exercising a power of dispensing with and suspending of laws, and the execution of laws, without consent of Parliament'. It clarified that the making of laws, and the suspending of them, 'without the consent of Parliament' was illegal. It decreed that 'the levying of money ... without grant of Parliament ... is illegal'. It made provision for 'freedom of speech' in Parliament and free elections outside of it. The raising and keeping of a standing army was made contingent on parliamentary approval, and the right of subjects to petition the king was acknowledged.[3] The departure of James II, though not recognised at the time, put to an end the strife between the monarch and Parliament that had characterised the years of the Stuart dynasty to that time, resolving the matter in favour of Parliament. Sovereignty or supremacy was firmly established, not in the monarch alone but in a Parliament consisting of Crown, Lords, and Commons.

A number of seminal Acts of Parliament followed, further entrenching its power, and restricting that of the monarchy. The Mutiny Act (1689) ensured the army had to be given annual consent by Parliament.

The Toleration Act (1689) extended religious freedoms to Protestant non-conformists. The Bank of England Act (1694) gave near total possession of the government's balances to the Bank of England. The Triennial Act (1694) ensured that Parliament would meet annually and general elections be held every three years. The Act of Settlement (1701) further ensured Parliament's oversight of the monarchy, by settling the succession to the Crown on Protestants only, thus disinheriting any descendants of Charles I other than his Protestant granddaughter Princess Anne, who became queen (1702–14). The next Protestant successor was to be the Electress Sophia of Hanover, who died in June 1714 two months before she would have become queen, and it was thus her son, George I, who suddenly found himself king, succeeding when Anne died in August 1714. Finally, the Septennial Act (1716) amended the 1694 Act and allowed Parliament to sit for up to seven years. Britain had never seen such a formidable body of legislation affecting its constitution. Historian Robert Tombs describes how

> the Crown was made subject to law, and its powers, still extensive, were defined by agreement with the nation. This time, there was no going back on the deal, which sketched out a constitution for England. Parliament had placed itself at the centre of the state. But what made these changes effective was Parliament's ancient control of taxation. The pressing need created by war to have a Parliament that would sanction ever-increasing taxation and debt changed it from a periodic event, called when the King needed it, to a permanent institution, which has met every year since 1689.[4]

William III and Queen Anne nevertheless had very clear ideas about what they wanted from Parliament. Anne was the last monarch to veto legislation, when she vetoed the Scottish Militia Bill in 1708, and she ennobled twelve Tory peers to ensure the House of Lords would assent to the Peace of Utrecht in 1711. She personally presided over some Cabinet meetings, attended debates in Parliament, and discussed business daily with her ministers, advocating and promoting policies, including the Act of Union, described as her 'personal triumph'.[5]

William had tried to be above party, working with both the Whigs and the Tories, but owned by neither. Anne too attempted to run a mixed ministry, with moderate Tories (like Marlborough and

Godolphin) and leading Whigs (like Halifax and Somers) to support the War of the Spanish Succession. It worked for the ministry of 1702–4, but, from 1704, High Tories who would not make concessions on religion and other topics were purged.

SEE-SAW DIARCHY: MUTUAL DEPENDENCY, 1721–60

During the Georgian era, the prime minister and monarchy were closely entwined. One cannot be understood without the other. The early part of this period is covered in detail in Chapters 1 and 3, with just a summary needed here. Robert Walpole and George I were an unlikely alliance, born out of mutual necessity and circumstance. George's sudden accession in 1714, his lack of English fluency, widespread unpopularity (his coronation saw rioting in some twenty towns), and his desperate requirement for a controlling figure in Westminster created just the job description for a man like Walpole to fill.[6]

The PM was often powerful, but the fundamental rules of politics during this Georgian period were, however, set by the king. George I and George II involved themselves closely in military, religious, legal, and foreign appointments. The monarch continued to set wider policy, especially on foreign affairs. Prime ministers were chosen by the king, though as the century passed, their choices became more restricted, for a series of parliamentary reasons. We first see this process developing in 1727, when George II indicated his preference for Spencer Compton over Walpole, but Compton's inability to command Parliament ultimately meant Walpole continued as First Lord. This was a pivotal moment. Later, other figures also had the monarch's support, but did not have the confidence of the House of Commons and therefore did not become prime minister.

This period saw the historical anomalies of Lord Bath in 1746 and Lord Waldegrave in 1757 being appointed First Lord but being unable to form governments and having to return the seals of office within a few days. Both had the support of George II, but neither had the political clout to form a ministry because so few heavyweight politicians were prepared to accept positions in a Cabinet under them. Of Bath's desperate attempts to form a government, diplomat James Gray wrote that a 'joker observed, that it was not safe to walk the streets at night, for fear of being pressed [to become] a cabinet counsellor'.[7] Waldegrave told George that his ministry 'would be routed at the opening of the next session of Parliament' and that it was time for the king, however reluctantly, to return to the Duke of Newcastle and William Pitt the Elder.

By George II's death in October 1760, after some uneasy times in this period of mutual dependency, the relationship had become more settled. The resounding defeat of the last Jacobite rebellion at Culloden in 1746 made the Hanoverian dynasty far more secure, and its continuation no longer a political issue. The Georges might have grumbled, but they accepted their position in the 'mixed constitution'. Not for Britain what Gustav III did in Sweden, when in 1772 he seized power from the nobles and restored royal prerogatives, and, in 1789, took powers away from the Swedish Parliament, the *Riksdag*. Indeed, the revolutions against monarchies in Europe towards the end of the century were a reminder of quite how far Britain had travelled down the path of establishing a constitutional monarchy.

MONARCHICAL REASSERTION, 1760–90

George III was a very different figure, however, to the first two Hanoverian monarchs. Born in England, he spoke English perfectly, unlike them. He was also a British patriot. Gone forever were rumblings about Hanoverian implants on the British throne. As he famously said in his accession speech: 'Born and educated in this country, I glory in the name of Britain; and the peculiar happiness of my life will ever consist in promoting the welfare of a people whose loyalty and warm affection to me I consider as the greatest and most permanent security of my throne.'[8] The young George was very bright too and from his earliest days had taken an active interest in political events. He was the first British monarch to study science systematically, with lessons in astronomy and mathematics, as well as chemistry and physics, and he learned French, Latin, history, music, geography, and law, alongside his sporting and social interests.[9] Raised as an Anglican, George absorbed a strong sense of duty and service, taking his 'piety into his politics'.[10]

We have seen earlier how George had his own ideas about the role of the Crown in politics. He believed that the king should be the decision-maker, and that far too much power had been given away to ministers by George I and George II. His model was King William III, and he wanted to reset the political environment to where it had been after the 1688 revolution. 'My political creed is formed on the system of King William', he wrote in 1771.[11] He understood far better than the first Hanoverians the political temperature and public mood. 'George III had an uncanny knack of reflecting what most people in the upper and middle classes actually felt', said historian John Clarke.[12] Clarke ascribes George III's later resistance to Catholic emancipation in 1801 to caution about public opinion at the time.

George III was the last king to try to act as his own prime minister: Indeed, in June 1779, he wrote, 'If others will not be active, I must drive.'[13] George made more use of the monarch's power of patronage than his two predecessors, happily selecting people without consulting the prime minister, and liberally appointing bishops and army officers he liked personally.[14] Andrew Roberts, his biographer, argues that far too much has been made by earlier historians, still more plays and films, of George III's 'madness': 'when George wasn't mad, he was on very good form. He wasn't half-mad. He was either completely mad or not at all.'[15]

George III also very significantly moved back towards Westminster and Whitehall from more distant Kensington Palace. In 1761, he bought 'Buckingham House' as a residence for his wife Queen Charlotte. Fourteen out of her fifteen children were born there. 'Buckingham Palace' was how it was increasingly referred to from 1791 onwards,[16] with George dividing his time between it, St James's Palace, and Kew, preferring the more rural setting of the latter.[17]

The central issue in George III's reign in relation to the prime minister was the extent to which he could choose his own ministers, and dismiss those with whom he fell out. In the first half of his long reign, his use of this power moved up and down, though it clearly fell from 1790 onwards.

George was a proud man and from his accession, aged twenty-two, he felt patronised by the old Whigs who had learned their politics under Walpole and the Pelhams. Early on, he installed his former teacher, Tory John Stuart, Earl of Bute, as prime minister. When he resigned within a year, because of his own evident unpopularity and unsuitability for the post, George was phlegmatic. He worked hard to establish good relations with Whigs as his prime ministers, but found it difficult with Grenville (1763–5), who tended to lecture him, and after Grenville dismissed some of his favourites, George dismissed him in July 1765. But he soon grew equally tired of Grenville's successor Rockingham, who lasted just little more than a year (1765–6). George found Pitt the Elder (1766–8) little better: 'He was younger than him and felt that he was being talked down to and addressed as if he was still a young man.'[18]

After the unhappy experience of Grafton, who followed for just over a year from 1768–70, George turned to Tory Lord North. Here at last, after six prime ministers in his first decade, the quickest turnover in history, he found some stability. For his first five years, he thought North a successful leader. Despite North's regular requests from 1775 that he resign, George clung onto him because he did not see any alternative to followers of Rockingham, Charles James Fox, and Edmund Burke, who he worried would turn him into a cipher king if given half a chance.[19]

During the war years, it was George III who was, according to Andrew O'Shaughnessy, 'the chief driving force in the war for America'.[20] George believed that Britain could only survive as a great power if the rebellion in the colonies was crushed, particularly after France and Spain became involved in the war. He 'exhorted, goaded and bullied' North throughout the conflict, urging the continuation of the war, keeping the government together, refusing to let the anti-war opposition near power, and ultimately prolonged the war into 1780–1, long after the possibility of decisively defeating the American forces had evaporated.[21]

Eventually, after the defeat of British forces at Yorktown under Cornwallis to George Washington in October 1781, the last major land battle of the war, and with the subsequent fall of North, George was finally forced to accept defeat. As he later told the incoming United States ambassador John Adams (later the second US president): 'I will be very frank with you. I was the last to consent to the Separation.'[22] So strong was George's belief in the war, that he even considered abdicating himself. A copy of the draft letter is in the Royal Archives at Windsor which states:

A long Experience and a serious attention to the Strange Events that have successively arisen, has gradually prepared My mind to expect the time when I should be no longer of Utility to this Empire; that hour is now come; I am therefore resolved to resign My Crown and all the Dominions appertaining to it to the Prince of Wales my Eldest Son and Lawful Successor.[23]

The impact of the loss of the colonies was the biggest shock to the system since 1688, with reverberations that echoed down the centuries even as far as Cameron in 2014 being haunted by the prospect of repeating North's ignominy if he had lost Scotland in the referendum. 'Failure in America ... was to plunge the political system into crisis', writes Black. 'George was greatly affected, not only because he was a key figure in the conduct of government and politics, but also because he was the pillar of last resort.'[24] His political role continued, but the American disaster affected his influence. Rockingham was back, and heading a ministry explicitly committed to a policy that George had opposed: ending the war, as Parliament clearly desired.

Rockingham died after fourteen weeks, and having negotiated much of the peace, his successor Shelburne's ministry fell and George appointed the Fox–North coalition with Charles James Fox, whom George loathed, overseeing foreign policy and North domestic policy, with Portland as the nominal prime minister. George had soon had enough, and after he dismissed the coalition, invited Pitt the Younger to become prime minister. At last George had the stability he hoped for, especially after Pitt's triumph in the 1784 election. The next four years saw Pitt cement his power and the office of prime minister, so much so that when George suffered his first bout of 'madness' in 1788, he was strong enough to fend off a challenge from Fox, and with the restoration of George's mental health and the ripple effect of the French Revolution in 1789, a new era began.

THE YEARS OF TRANSITION, 1790–1837

George III still had some authority after 1790. In 1801, he forced out Pitt over Catholic emancipation. Then, after Pitt's death in 1806, he dispensed with the 'Ministry of All Talents' under Grenville, a ministry incorporating both leading Whigs and Tories which broke up over

Catholic emancipation in 1807. After that, George invited Portland to form a second government. But, although he still had his commanding moments, he was swimming against the tide in the second half of his long reign. No more than the first two Hanoverians did he want to establish an absolute monarchy: 'he recognised that his dynasty depended on the Act of Succession which was a parliamentary monarchy', says Clarke. 'What he wanted to do was choose his own prime ministers and other ministers, and if he didn't like them he thought he was entitled to try someone else. But that power was waning.'[25] His patronage powers, which he had deployed so effectively earlier on, were reduced during the second half of his reign. The expense of the Napoleonic Wars and the escalating national debt forced government to cut back on appointments, pensions, and sinecures, 'which reduced the size and solidity of the King's Friends'.[26]

This attacked the very basis of the traditional Whig and Tory factions, and encouraged them to form larger and more permanent groupings. The Rockingham Whigs, the Bedford Whigs, and other family-based groups thus merged into a wider 'Whiggish' alliance, while the followers of Grenville and other groupings merged into a pro-government or Tory side. 'This meant that by 1820 monarchs found it much harder to control, or even influence, what went on in the House of Commons.'[27] Monarchs became no longer able, as in the eighteenth century, to rely on the 'King's Friends' to form majorities in the Commons. Power shifted to these new political groupings, which merged into the Conservative Party, as it began to be called from the 1830s, and the new-style Whig Party, which morphed into the Liberals in the 1850s. Both increasingly wanted their own leaders rather than the monarch's choice.

Under Pitt, Cabinet emerged as a more regular, coherent, and effective body, with the doctrine of 'collective responsibility' as a governing convention. George became increasingly willing to leave matters to be decided by it. The coincidence of having two very long-serving and proficient prime ministers almost following each other, Pitt the Younger and Lord Liverpool, covering almost thirty-four years between them, was highly significant. They both understood much more about the intricacies of politics, finance, and government than the monarch; history might have been very different had there been a succession of short-term leaders as in the 1760s. The outbreak of war with France in

1792 dominated the following twenty-two years, focusing power on Whitehall and Downing Street and not on the royal palaces. George was far more detached from the French Revolutionary (1792–1802) and Napoleonic Wars (1803–15) than he had been from the American War of Independence.

'Madness' returned to George III in late 1810, caused, he believed, by his anguish at the death of his youngest child, Amelia.[28] The Regency Act of 1811 saw the Prince of Wales rule as Regent for the rest of George's life. George moved to Windsor Castle for the last nine years of his reign, becoming increasingly frail and isolated, also developing dementia, blindness, and deafness.[29]

The Prince Regent, the future George IV (1820–30), was a much less capable, principled, and ambitious figure than his father, and was willing to let the prime minister, initially Spencer Perceval, and Cabinet decide how to run the government and prosecute the war in Europe. He had been expected to bring Grenville and the Whigs back into power, but resisted because of the effect it might have on the fragility of his father, as a keen Tory supporter. But when in 1812 it became clear that his father would be unlikely to recover, he tried and failed to appoint a Whig administration. They refused to join a ministry under Perceval, a Tory. Following Perceval's assassination in May 1812, the Regent offered the leadership of the government to Richard, Marquess Wellesley, and then to Lord Moira, encouraging both to form a cross-party ministry, but both refused, showing the diminished power of the monarchy. He then invited Liverpool to continue from where Perceval had left off.

He showed no more resolve when he succeeded his father as King George IV in 1820. He had become hard-up because of his profligate spending and dissolute lifestyle, and needed Parliament to pay off his debts. They agreed to do so on the understanding that he would maintain the status quo that they had grown used to.[30] George IV had little option but to consent: he always insisted on his right to exercise a veto, but he never refused to sign an Act of Parliament. He faced too a near-united Cabinet under Liverpool, and it was clear that he carried little weight or credibility with them.

In fact, George IV's biggest impact on political life came when, upon accession, he sought a divorce from Queen Caroline, which rapidly became a political issue. He had long been estranged from his wife, who had suddenly arrived in England from Brunswick when he became king, claiming her right to be queen. They had become engaged in 1794, despite never having met. George pressured Cabinet to introduce a bill to Parliament to annul the marriage of 1795, after which they had separated. But Cabinet refused, believing that to do so might cast further and unwelcome light on his hedonism. To get his way, George even considered changing the government entirely and placing it under a new prime minister. Reluctantly Liverpool's Cabinet agreed to the bill being introduced. But, when it came before Parliament, it generated intense public sympathy for Caroline, who was perceived to have been wronged. There were fears that Liverpool's government might collapse entirely. The debates became a sensation, with Caroline playing her full part, watching proceedings in the Lords from the gallery above. Eventually, despite the bill's passage through the Lords, Liverpool realised that it did not have political support after a third reading in the Commons and withdrew it. He argued that he 'could not be ignorant of the state of public feeling' on the matter.[31] Caroline never did take up her role as queen, was barred from George's coronation in July 1821, and died three weeks later.[32] The undignified and grubby issue showed that the monarch could still force an issue to the forefront of politics, but with the divorce eluding him, not necessarily get his way.

George's heavy drinking, sexual profligacy, and indulgent lifestyle made him a sorry figure by the late 1820s; severely obese, suffering from gout, and almost blind from cataracts.[33] He was no match for veteran military hero Wellington, who brushed aside George's threats of abdication to force through Catholic emancipation, even though his own Tory ranks were divided.

William IV succeeded his older brother in 1830. It was now, A. N. Wilson believes, that the monarchy finally lost its way, and he was only saved by his talented wife, Queen Adelaide.[34] The haemorrhaging of royal authority continued with the passing of the 1832 Reform Act which removed any residual power to which the King's Friends still clung. The Act revamped the constituency system, removing most rotten boroughs and giving seats to new towns whilst ensuring a division between politicians, who could sit in the Commons, and civil servants who could not.

William had tried to remove the Grey ministry earlier in the spring of 1832, despite their winning an election victory in 1831 on the promise of parliamentary reform, and to put back in the Tory Wellington. But Wellington and Peel (his Leader in the Commons) refused to take up his invitation, believing they could control neither the Commons nor the country if they did so. William was forced into sticking with Grey and the Whigs, and to promise them he would create enough peers to pass the Reform Bill in the Lords if required.

The final humiliation for William IV came in the botched events of 1834. William used the resignation of a group of four dissident Whigs (known as the 'Derby Dilly') from Grey's Cabinet in 1834 over the reorganisation of the Church of Ireland as pretext to force the resignation of the government, and to have the Tories return to power. Wellington again became prime minister, making way for Peel once he returned from Italy. Wellington was clear that following 1832, the House of Commons was now the principal political house, and that a general election would have to be held as soon as possible. At the ensuing 1835 contest, Peel and the Conservatives (as they were now beginning to be called to appeal to the Derbyites) gained seats, but not enough to form a majority. When the House re-met, Peel suffered a number of defeats and resigned after a confidence motion went against him. The Whigs duly returned, now led by an emboldened Melbourne, who insisted on humiliating terms for William, in effect making the king promise not to do anything to oppose or undermine his government.[35]

William spent the last three years of his life anxious about the Whigs' reforming tendencies, but not interfering. He had learnt his lesson. He died in June 1837 at Windsor Castle where he is buried, with Queen Adelaide reportedly staying up for his final ten nights to comfort him.[36] The monarchy was incomparably weaker when Victoria inherited the Crown in 1837 than it had been in 1790. But it was to be another hundred years and more before any remaining political power drained away.

THE DYING OF THE LIGHT: QUEEN VICTORIA, 1837–1901

No monarch saw a greater diminution of the power of the Crown than Victoria. Historian Jane Ridley thinks that Victoria 'didn't realise fully, or pretended not to see, the very important shift that took place in her reign with the widening of the electorate. She thought that she could still appoint, until the end of her reign, who she liked as prime minister.'[37] Her sixty-four-year reign saw her working with ten prime ministers. Some she liked initially but came to hate, like Gladstone; others she disliked initially but grew fond of, like Peel. Palmerston she disliked from the start and had a poor relationship with, while Melbourne, Disraeli, and latterly Salisbury knew her mind, and how to get what they wanted from her. Given to strong feelings, she was assiduous rather than bright, in stark contrast to her husband Prince Albert, whom she married in 1840 when only twenty. He had been led to believe in tiny Saxe-Coburg and Gotha that he would be acting as almost an imperial leader upon arriving in Britain. He subscribed to the doctrine of activism in government, meritocracy, public intervention, and a belief in science and technology, the Great Exhibition of 1851 a celebration of how he saw life.

An episode where she tried to exercise her influence, the 'Bedchamber Crisis' in May 1839, was the first and only time she successfully prevented a new administration being formed. The Whig majority in the Commons, diminished by the general election that followed William IV's death, was disintegrating. But when her beloved Melbourne resigned, she refused to accept the Conservative Peel and to exchange her three Whig Ladies in the Royal Household for Tories. Melbourne was persuaded not to resign and continued for another two years until the 1841 general election. Victoria used royal money to support Melbourne, the last occasion the monarch involved themselves actively in a general election as a blatant partisan. It was to be the first time a general election returned an opposition party majority since 1831 and replaced the monarch's favoured ministry. In a major humiliation, Victoria had to accept Peel as prime minister at the head of a Conservative government. Never again would the monarch be able to choose a prime minister from the Commons because the Crown could no longer dictate the balance of MPs. Traditionalists feared that, as the Crown no longer had the capability to dominate the Lower House, political instability would ensue. For a while, the monarchy withdrew from public politics, and when the years that followed saw stable transfers of power between governments of different parties without it producing instability, this further eroded the power of the Crown.

Victoria and Albert may have been bruised by the bitter rebuff of 1841 and the public reaction, but they refused to believe that the royal prerogative had shrunk fundamentally, and continued to interfere regularly, if more covertly, in political matters.[38] In December 1851, they conspired with Russell to remove Palmerston from the Foreign Office, whose foreign policy was insufficiently pro-German for them. As Coleman says, 'Albert and Palmerston were regularly at loggerheads.' Victoria's pro-German sentiment ran deep: 'The Hanoverians and Saxe-Coburgs were enmeshed with dynastic marriages with Protestant (mainly German) ruling houses ... In the 1880s Victoria's eldest child, also named Victoria, was briefly Empress of Germany' due to her marriage to Emperor Frederick III.[39]

Victoria and Albert tried to keep Derby out of office, accepting his protectionist ministry with ill grace for ten months in 1852, and then helped to induct Aberdeen as prime minister of a Whig–Peelite Coalition in 1852, in the hope the Peelite grouping would control the Whigs. The Crimean War (1853–6), in which Victoria took less interest than any earlier monarch in a major war, overwhelmed Aberdeen, and she had no option but to accept a ministry headed by Palmerston in February 1855. After it fell in February 1858, a minority Derby ministry returned but she then tried to implant Granville, who had played a prominent part in the Great Exhibition of 1851 and who led the Liberals in the House of Lords.[40] But Palmerston and Russell resisted, and Palmerston became prime minister again in 1859 until his death in 1865 with Russell as Foreign Secretary. Given the great importance Albert had to her official duties, there was much speculation that she would withdraw fully from political life after his death in 1861. But after the final Derby minority ministry (which passed the Second Reform Act in 1867), Victoria made one of her strongest interventions, preferring Gladstone to the senior figure of Russell after the Liberals had won the 1868 general election.

The 1867 Second Reform Act, promoting the spread of mass political parties, further limited the powers of the Crown. Plainly, it meant that 'the Head of State would not in future dismiss Parliament, the electorate would', as Philip Norton puts it.[41] Public criticism of Victoria rose following her withdrawal from public life after Albert's death.

Gladstone tried to encourage her out into the open, including for the opening of the new Blackfriars Bridge in 1869: 'He went to enormous lengths to rehabilitate her, and she threw it back in his face, and was insulting about him in her private correspondence', says Simon Heffer.[42] The publication of a celebrated pamphlet *What Does She Do With It?*, which explored Victoria's finances, a speech by Charles Dilke advocating a republican alternative, and pro-French sentiment during the Franco-Prussian War saw anti-monarch feeling reach a high point. But the recovery from typhoid of the Prince of Wales (the future Edward VII), a thanksgiving service at St Paul's in 1872 engineered by Gladstone, and the thwarting of an assassination attempt on her life two days later, one of seven attempts during her reign, all contributed to the decline of republicanism and the recovery of her own standing.[43] Gladstone thought he enjoyed a good relationship with her in his first 1868–74 ministry: but Anne Somerset, who is writing on her relationships with her prime ministers, says he never realised how much she hated him.[44]

In 1870, Henry Ponsonby became Victoria's Private Secretary (1870–95). He became an increasingly powerful figure in tempering her desire to meddle. A Whig/Liberal, he understood the shift in power that followed the Reform Acts, and was, as Ridley says, 'brilliant at manoeuvring her into accepting the new realities, by never arguing directly with her but making her think she had reached the conclusions herself'.[45] She also contends that because Victoria was a woman, and politics was still a male-only monopoly, it was easier for politicians to ignore her wishes.[46] Disraeli's genius, in her happiest and most unctuous relationship of her ten prime ministers, was to make her feel she was a serious figure. Somerset believes, though, that Salisbury handled her the best: 'He could say "no" to her and because she loved him, she could take it from him.'[47] After Gladstone's advocacy of Home Rule in 1886, Salisbury's and Victoria's deeply unionist sympathies strengthened their political bond, and further distanced the queen from Gladstone.

Victoria did much to create the modern idea of the monarchy. She became the symbol of Empire, with two major Jubilees, at which the prime ministers of the self-governing colonies met together in London, to partake in the celebrations. A number of initiatives derived from her reign. The modern version of the ceremony around the State Opening of

Parliament began in 1852, during her reign.[48] The convention of frequent meetings with the prime minister was regularised by her. The post of Private Secretary to the monarch, of such importance after her reign, became consolidated under her, with Ponsonby the first 'modern' figure to hold it. Hitherto, Melbourne had fulfilled it while PM (1837–41), then Albert informally (1840–61), followed by two short-term figures. Ponsonby paved the way for the all-dominant Private Secretaries in the twentieth century, including Lord Stamfordham and Alan Lascelles. No monarch after her tried to repeat her frequent interference in politics. At the end of her reign, for all her persistent active involvement, the prerogative powers of the monarch were considerably weaker in 1901 than they had been in 1837.

THE LAST HURRAH OF POLITICAL INFLUENCE, 1901–52

Edward VII, eldest son of Victoria and Albert, had been Prince of Wales and heir apparent for almost sixty years when he became king in January 1901. Deliberately excluded from active involvement under Victoria, few expected much from him when he became monarch, but he proved a better king than he had a Prince of Wales. 'We grovel before fat Edward – Edward the Caresser as he is privately named', wrote Henry James, while Rudyard Kipling referred to him as a 'corpulent voluptuary'.[49] But his biographer Jane Ridley thinks quite highly of him as monarch. 'He understood that the role of the monarch was not to resist the verdict of the electorate. He knew that he should not meddle in domestic politics like his mother', she says. 'He was thus the first monarch to be fully aware of and accept that he was *only* a constitutional monarch.'[50] Lazy and lethargic, he was far less disposed for intervention. He too was very influenced by his Private Secretary, Lord Knollys (1901–13), who gave him most of his advice and helped ensure that he performed his duties well and responsibly, especially given his reputation before 1901 of being a bon viveur and womaniser.

Edward played no hand in Balfour's decision in 1905 to cede power to Campbell-Bannerman and the Liberals, and nor did he become involved when Campbell-Bannerman retired in April 1908 shortly before his death. Asquith was accepted in political circles as his successor and affirmed by a party meeting of Liberals shortly after. But, as Edward VII was on holiday in Biarritz, he sent for Asquith who meekly made the long journey by boat and then train down to the south of France where he 'kissed hands' with the king in the Hôtel du Palais in Biarritz.[51] Edward preferred Asquith to Lloyd George, disapproving of the latter's speeches and attacks on the aristocracy, and made his views clear. But he did not seek to become involved in domestic politics in the constitutional crisis from 1909, which was in full rage when he died in May 1910.

Edward VII in contrast was more involved in foreign policy and signalled his strong views early on when Salisbury was still prime minister, when he made his disgust clear about the award of the Order of the Garter to the Shah of Persia on the State Visit in August 1902. 'Edward VII thought he was a barbarian, a savage and a brute, and didn't want to give him a Christian order of chivalry as he wasn't even a Christian', says Heffer.[52] Edward was so disgusted that he threw the designs for the star out of the porthole of the new yacht, HMY *Victoria and Albert*. Indicatively, and after weeks of argument, it was Edward who had to relent, and the Shah received the honour the following year in 1903.[53] A keen supporter of the Entente Cordiale with France, Edward travelled to Paris in 1903 without ministerial approval, and indeed 'without even telling his government that he intended to go', says Brazier.[54] Edward was related to royal families across Europe, becoming known as the 'Uncle of Europe' which gave him enhanced ability, he thought, to exercise influence in foreign policy. In 1908, he met Tsar Nicholas II in the Baltic shortly after the 'Triple Entente' had been signed with Russia and France, and the following year, he went to Berlin to try and improve relations with his nephew, Kaiser Wilhelm II.[55] But their relationship was poor, and was not helped by Edward's evident enthusiasm for modernising the British home fleet, reorganising the British army. and, indeed, for encircling Germany.[56] While Edward might have believed he was shaping foreign diplomacy, Coleman argues he was still following government policy and was essentially 'a poster boy' for promoting goodwill on his trips abroad.[57]

If Edward VII stabilised the monarch's position in political life after his politically demanding mother, his son George V (1910–36) was to be the last British monarch to exercise any real political power. The new king did not actively look for opportunities for political influence but he had a number of occasions thrust upon him, and he was not shy about exercising his influence in them. We again see another highly influential Private Secretary, Stamfordham: it is perhaps unsurprising that, as monarchs lose power, they come to rely increasingly upon their Private Secretaries for advice, who in turn possess a subtler understanding of their diminished authority in the modern world. If ever there was a political crisis, Stamfordham swung into action, talked to the key figures, including the Chief Whip and senior politicians, the editor of *The Times* (Geoffrey Dawson), and elder statesmen, and prepared long memoranda for George to digest. For historians to discern how far the decisions were the king's or the Private Secretary's is almost impossible, for the records in the Royal Archives reveal just an occasional 'I agree' from George on the corner of a piece of paper. They trusted each other implicitly, and Ridley is unaware of any occasion on which they disagreed.[58] At one point during the constitutional crisis of 1909–11, George had considered removing Asquith and the Liberal government, but Stamfordham omitted to inform him that Conservative leader Balfour might be willing to head a minority ministry in its place, and the moment passed.[59]

George was thrust into the fray immediately in May 1910. Asquith made it clear that he wasn't going to deviate from taking on the Lords because of the king's reservations. Having secured a parliamentary majority in January, he told the king that if the House of Lords continued to prevent their powers being reduced, he would ask him to create sufficient peers to force it through, as Grey had asked William IV to do when facing his own battle with the Lords over the First Reform Act. Asquith sent George a most significant minute in December 1910 making brutally clear the position of the monarch by the early twentieth century:

> The part to be played by the Crown ... has happily been settled by the accumulated traditions and the unbroken practice of more than seventy years. It is to act upon the advice of Ministers who for the time being possess the confidence of the House of Commons, whether that advice does or does not conform to the private and personal judgement of the sovereign.[60]

The Lords backed down, allowing the Parliament Act of 1911 to pass. His efforts in 1914 to reach a settlement over Irish Home Rule, by bringing together government and opposition leaders at the Buckingham Palace constitutional conference, failed. If George had any doubt when he came to the throne where political power lay, he had no doubt now.

Neither was he left in any doubt that the run-up to, and the conduct of, the Great War were matters exclusively for politicians. But he and Queen Mary busied themselves by visiting munitions factories and seeing the wounded in hospital and touring the East End of London in the food shortages of 1917. A new tradition, the morale-lifting monarchy, was born. That year too, George instituted an important change which would have reflected badly upon the monarchy if not made, changing the name of the dynasty from the Germanic-sounding 'House of Saxe-Coburg and Gotha' to the more British-sounding 'House of Windsor'.[61]

This decisive action expunged any lingering suspicion of George's patriotism, which had been heightened by his being first cousin of the hated Kaiser Wilhelm II. Another first cousin was Tsar Nicholas II of Russia: the fraught story of why George did not offer him and his family asylum after the 1917 Bolshevik Revolution is discussed in the next chapter.

The first meaningful intervention by George postwar came in May 1923, when Andrew Bonar Law retired upon his diagnosis of terminal cancer. The two clear candidates to succeed presented themselves: Lord Curzon, the vastly experienced Tory grandee and foreign policy expert, and Stanley Baldwin, the Chancellor of the Exchequer, but new in the post and inexperienced. The decision was George's: on the advice of Balfour and Stamfordham, who both argued that the prime minister now needed to be in the House of Commons, he went for Baldwin. Later that year, Baldwin decided to call an election in December 1923 to seek a mandate to introduce protectionist tariffs, hoping to unite his divided party. The result was inconclusive, with Ramsay MacDonald's Labour achieving 191 MPs, the second largest number. Baldwin continued in office until January 1924 when his government was defeated on its programme as set out in the King's Speech, and he immediately offered his resignation.

George V was significant in the decision to invite MacDonald to form a minority Labour government. Doing so ensured that Labour could become a party of power, bound into the British constitution and parliamentary democracy, rather than a party of protest and direct action. Whilst some in the Labour movement remained wedded to republicanism, the sentiment largely diffused away from the Labour Party and into communist elements in trade unions. Stamfordham had his own clear views on the proper functioning of a constitutional monarchy with relations to the working classes:

> We must, however, endeavour to induce the thinking working classes, Socialists and other, to regard the Crown not as a mere figurehead and as an institution which, as they put it, 'don't count', but as a living power for good, with receptive faculties welcoming information affecting the interests and social well-being of all classes ...[62]

MacDonald grew to admire George V, and how far he went out of his way to accommodate Labour, even to the extent of relaxing rules on dress at Court which for George V, as for his father, was sacred.

When Baldwin returned to power in 1924, the king exercised his influence again, intimating that he would be glad if Austen Chamberlain could be appointed Foreign Secretary. His major intervention though came when the second Labour government broke up in 1931 and a National government was formed with a very small Labour contingent. George pressured MacDonald to stay on as prime minister, despite his repeated protestations, and was decisive in him accepting. This meant that MacDonald, who had played such a crucial role in building up and habilitating Labour, was now instrumental in its divisions, which resulted in it being unable to form a government on its own for another fourteen years.

The monarchy retained a slender measure of political power right up to George V's death in January 1936. The king believed, as Brazier has argued, that 'if circumstances required it, he could use the sovereign's legal power to withhold royal assent to legislation, and could make his own choice of Prime Minister'.[63] The abdication in 1936 changed the monarchy and its residual power forever. Baldwin, in his final year as prime minister, made it clear to Edward VIII that his marriage was not acceptable to the British people, blocked Edward's attempts to announce a morganatic marriage, and forced him to choose between Wallis

Simpson and the Crown. Baldwin had concluded that Edward was not up to the office, and more than any other single person forced the issue. With necessary deference to the king, he suggested he could have Wallis as his *mistress*, but absolutely not marry her. Edward maintained he found this deeply offensive, responding that 'Mrs Simpson is a lady'.[64] Anne Sebba, biographer of Wallis, argues that 'it was the King not Baldwin who made the decision. My view is that Edward really did not want the Crown enough to fight for it, although he would have gone through with it if he could have had Wallis by his side.'[65]

The abdication rocked the monarchy more than any event since 1688. For the first three years, the new King George VI was timid, changing his name from Edward to George, deliberately like his father, and wanting to show himself as the 'continuity' monarch. His political interventions were minor, as when he asked to be sent details of political disagreements before they blew up, because he hadn't been informed of Eden's resignation as Foreign Secretary in February 1938 and he believed he might have had some influence in preventing it.[66] Despite that, he got on well with Neville Chamberlain, effectively his first prime minister, and twenty-six years his senior. 'Both the King and Queen liked Chamberlain very much, as he did them. They were on extremely confidential terms, with Chamberlain dealing with many complicated and potentially embarrassing financial matters relating to the Duke of Windsor', says Dilks.[67] Assessing the extent of Chamberlain's influence on George, and vice versa, is difficult, because Chamberlain only recorded actionable points from their meetings. Chamberlain was even invited onto the balcony of Buckingham Palace, to share the platform with the royal couple, after the Munich Agreement of 1938 – with hindsight, an awkward moment that some saw as demonstrating sympathy for appeasement, but nevertheless a rare honour that has been afforded only once since, to Churchill in 1945. The fact that no prime minister has been invited onto the Buckingham Palace balcony since suggests a deliberate distancing between the Palace and Whitehall.[68]

When Chamberlain fell in May 1940, George preferred Halifax as the successor, but quickly formed a close bond with Churchill, who himself was twenty years his senior. Churchill advised George in writing in the hope that, should he die, Anthony Eden rather than Halifax would succeed.[69] They went on to form what historian Robert Rhodes James has described, not entirely fairly, as 'the closest personal relationship in modern British history between a monarch and Prime Minister'.[70] The reason for doubting his assertion is that so little is known, in the absence of records, about how close each new relationship between prime minister and monarch truly is.

George and Churchill began a pattern of regular lunches on Tuesdays which, after the war, morphed into the weekly Audience which continues up to the present day, usually on Wednesdays when Parliament is sitting and both principals are in London.[71] George V, as his diaries reveal, saw his five prime ministers far less regularly than George VI his three or Elizabeth II her fourteen, and counting.[72] George VI is believed to have given just three 'warnings' (in the terminology of Bagehot) on ministerial appointments: advising Churchill against appointing Beaverbrook to the new post of Aircraft Production in May 1940, not heeded, against making Brendan Bracken a Privy Councillor, not heeded, and advice to Clement Attlee in 1945 not to make Hugh Dalton Foreign Secretary. Bevin was appointed but it is uncertain how significant the king's advice was.[73] George's official biographer John Wheeler-Bennett was deliberately vague on the king's personal views on the Attlee ministry, but it is clear he was more uncomfortable around 'socialists' than his father, showing great discretion with his lack of commentary on the NHS reforms, and managing only to say that he liked Nye Bevan's 'effervescent personality'.[74] By the end of his reign in February 1952, when he was delighted to see Churchill returned to power the previous October, the effective personal prerogative powers were all but dead.

Alan 'Tommy' Lascelles, the magisterial Private Secretary (1943–53), felt the need in February 1950 to write an anonymous letter to *The Times* under the pseudonym 'Senex' (Latin for 'old man') setting out the remaining three conditions under which a monarch could refuse a prime minister's request to dissolve Parliament:

(1) if the existing Parliament was still 'vital, viable, and capable of doing its job';

(2) if a general election would be 'detrimental to the national economy';

(3) if the sovereign could 'rely on finding another prime minister who could govern for a reasonable period with a working majority in the House of Commons'.[75]

Senex's constitutional convention that a monarch might choose *not* to use their prerogative power to dissolve Parliament was accepted until 2011 when the Fixed-Term Parliaments Act removed this remaining prerogative power. The other remaining prerogative power by the end of George VI's reign was an element of discretion over the appointment of a prime minister (albeit by the twentieth century the monarch was confined to a choice within a single party possessing a Commons majority). This was to be tested just twice in the reign of Elizabeth II (1957 and 1963), before the method of parties choosing their own leader became entrenched. A Palace insider could write in 2021, in the tradition of Senex:

> I would say the royal prerogative has been essentially taken over by the government. Within that, there have been certain powers involving the beginning and end of a ministry where monarchs felt they had discretion because it wasn't absolutely clear on whose advice they might act. Hence the Lascelles letter saying a monarch could, in certain circumstances, refuse a dissolution. I would say that these residual personal prerogatives shifted in the course of the Queen's reign, into not exercising personal prerogative power and not being *seen* to exercise it. That's why I would say a Private Secretary today would want to think very carefully before writing as Alan Lascelles did.[76]

FROM PREROGATIVE POWERS TO NATIONAL LEADER: QUEEN ELIZABETH II, 1952–2021

We have already seen that Queen Victoria thought the essayist Walter Bagehot far too restrictive when he wrote that the constitutional monarchy has only three rights, these being 'the right to consult, the right to encourage, [and] the right to warn'.[77] She fought vainly against the dying of the light. Today, however, Bagehot's words have come home, accurately describing the relationship between monarch and prime minister. But what have they meant under Elizabeth II?

Barring a few areas of patronage and the conferring of titles within the royal family itself, the prerogative powers are exercised very clearly and obviously today by the prime minister. The events of August 2019, when Parliament was ordered to be prorogued by the queen on the 'advice' of Boris Johnson, advice that was later ruled by the Supreme Court in September 2019 to be unlawful, shows the complete dominance of even a very new prime minister over the longest-serving and arguably most experienced monarch in British history. Every one of the significant royal prerogative powers are now firmly and squarely in the hands of the prime minister or Parliament. The last of these to go was the power to refuse a dissolution in 2011, with the choice of prime minister already effectively lost in the 1960s. The queen, advised by the 'magic circle' of senior Tories and the Cabinet, had chosen Alec Douglas-Home over Rab Butler and others in succession to Macmillan in 1963. It proved the last moment the queen was drawn into the selection of the PM. Rule changes in the Conservative Party, which came into effect when Heath was elected Douglas-Home's successor in 1965, meant that Britain no longer had a political party without mechanisms for selection of their leader and hence potentially needing to resort to the monarch.

What might happen in the event of a coalition or hung parliament, was another prerogative power to fall, with *The Cabinet Manual* establishing procedure for what to do after a hung parliament. Indecisive elections in 2010 and 2017 were resolved fairly quickly by party leaders. 'The experience of the last few years with hung parliaments has reinforced that the queen actually is not involved', admitted a Palace insider. 'The prerogative might be there, but it will not be exercised. The queen deliberately went to Windsor in 2010 to be *seen* not to be exercising prerogative power, but to be kept informed, while leaving it to politicians to sort it out.'[78]

One final prerogative power – the ability to dissolve Parliament – will be returned to the queen after the repeal of the Fixed-Term Parliaments Act in 2021, though it is almost impossible to think of circumstances where it would be used without the prime minister's approval. So while the legislation formally returns the prerogative power to the monarch, in practice it returns it to the prime minister.

The continuing importance of the monarch has changed in the nearly seventy years of the reign of Queen Elizabeth II. Under her, the monarchy's role has clearly become 'National Leader'. She is the figurehead, more than the transitory and party political prime minister, to whom many in the nation look, not least at times of national reflection, anniversaries, and emergencies. As George VI modelled himself on his father, so too has she on hers. George VI cemented his initially uncertain relationship with the British public by his visibility during the Second World War, visiting sites in cities that had been bombed.

The first 'special address' delivered by radio was Edward VIII's speech to the Empire after the death of George V, a formula he repeated after his abdication. George VI made six such broadcasts, including one on 3 September 1939 upon the outbreak of war, and two at the end. Elizabeth has made seven 'special addresses', waiting forty years to make her first at the time of the Gulf War in February 1991 and second on 5 September 1997 after the death of Diana, Princess of Wales. The others came after the death of the Queen Mother in 2002, at the Diamond Jubilee in June 2012, and three speeches during 2020, one in April at the start of the COVID-19 pandemic, the second an Easter message, and the third on the seventy-fifth anniversary of VE Day in May. These occasions underline her increasing importance as a focal point at times of national crisis. They come on top of her annual Christmas broadcast, a tradition started by George V in 1932, one of the rare occasions where she can speak personally, albeit within tight conventions, about her own values and hopes.

The queen is the figure who symbolically, more than any other, holds the United Kingdom together. On her Silver Jubilee in May 1977, she gave an address to Parliament in which she said, 'I cannot forget that I was crowned Queen of the *United* Kingdom and Northern Ireland.'[79] This was a response to mounting pressure for devolution to Scotland and Wales. Hennessy has described it as 'the most political comment she ever made'.[80] Her comment made to a well-wisher the Sunday before the Scottish referendum on independence on 18 September 2014, as she left church at Balmoral, that 'I hope people will think very carefully about the future', was interpreted widely as an encouragement to voters to keep Scotland in the Union.[81] Cameron's indiscretion when he said, after the result, that the queen 'purred' when told about Scotland's rejection of independence probably revealed her deep instincts.[82] Her State Visit to Dublin in May 2011, the first visit to the Free State/Republic of Ireland for 100 years since George V's visit in 1911, was inspired by her desire to heal divisions and normalise relationships between the Republic and Northern Ireland. Rarely was she more influential.

The queen is a voice of wisdom and experience. Her fourteen prime ministers over sixty-nine years to 2021 have come at an average of four years and ten months each, in contrast to Victoria's ten prime ministers over her sixty-four years, an average of six years and four months. In place of Victoria's ceaseless open interventions, Elizabeth has given her counsel in total confidence, and until records appear, it will be impossible, as Bogdanor reminds us, to understand quite how influential her advice has been: 'We won't know until long after she's gone', he said.[83] Victoria made no secret of her favourites; Elizabeth has scrupulously kept her opinions to herself despite attempts by writers and filmmakers to tell us what her feelings were.[84] Apart from the principals themselves, the only figures that know what passes between the monarch and the prime minister are the queen's Private Secretary and the prime minister's Principal Private Secretary, and they have remained completely discreet. 'I can't possibly imagine anything like a sense of favouritism affecting the queen's behaviour', says one Palace insider. 'She sees galleries of people, some probably more charming than others, but she would certainly not differentiate in her exchanges with her prime ministers.'[85]

Elizabeth, like Victoria, began with a prime minister who was like a grandfather to her, Churchill (and Melbourne for Victoria). Victoria finished with a prime minister akin to a knowing younger sibling, Salisbury; Elizabeth's current prime minister is much like an errant grandson, Johnson. Prime ministers testify in their memoirs to the value of their meetings. So what might the queen add to prime ministers awash with advice, much of it unsolicited? Another Palace insider:

> I think the Queen has developed an extraordinary degree of confidence in herself that places no value on excessive degrees of formality. Indeed those prime ministers who have seen her – certainly in my time and a little bit before about whom I can speak with some authority – would say that they

were astonished at the degree of almost immediate ease and informality that they experienced in their exchanges with the queen despite I daresay some moments of trepidation as they drove down the Mall. The reality was one of highly useful informality.[86]

The queen epitomises the concept of national service, military and voluntary, constituting what Frank Prochaska has titled the 'Welfare Monarchy'.[87] His book describes the evolution of the monarchy from George III to the end of the twentieth century, his writing both reflecting but also helping to shape a remodelling of the monarchy from the late twentieth century.[88] As one insider said, 'I spent more time thinking about the soft power of the monarchy rather than the constitutional and prerogative powers. It's as Head of the Nation rather than Head of State which I think has become so important, and describes the way this reign has evolved.'[89] The direction was set early on by the Duke of Edinburgh's award scheme, established in 1956 to encourage the young into service activities, a tradition Prince Charles and his three siblings have actively encouraged. The system of awards and recognition in the Queen's Birthday and New Year's Honours Lists, albeit largely compiled outside the Palace, helps underline and reward behaviours that the monarchy values. Those who serve in Her Majesty's Armed Forces look to the queen and other members of the royal family who have honorary military positions in shaping their *national* understanding of the role of the armed services. They see themselves as fighting and even dying for the country represented by the Monarch, rather than the Prime Minister The Church of England looks to the queen at its head. The continuation of the name *Her Majesty's* Government helps underline a sense of national rather than purely party political responsibility that ministers assume once they take office. It can jolt incoming ministers into a new sense of responsibility.

The queen more than the prime minister is a major international figure. She is the most photographed figure in world history,[90] and is the most travelled head of state, having made, up to the time of her Diamond Jubilee in 2012, 96 State Visits to 116 countries and 261 overseas visits overall.[91] Few State Visits had taken place before Elizabeth became the queen but they included Napoleon III's visit to Windsor Castle in 1855, and Kaiser Wilhelm II's trip to see Edward VII in 1907. Since 1952, the queen has hosted 152 State Visits, including three from the United States, George W. Bush in 2003, Barack Obama in 2011, and Donald Trump in 2019;[92] many of the most powerful leaders in the world are very anxious and proud to achieve one. The monarchy significantly shapes their understanding of Britain. Foreign ambassadors are formally received by the Court of St James's, and British ambassadors working abroad are accredited by the queen.

The influence of the queen goes far beyond the ceremony and prestige. She played a small part in encouraging the end of apartheid and welcoming South Africa back into the Commonwealth after Nelson Mandela became president in 1994. Charles Moore sees the row over South African sanctions in 1985–86 as the biggest difference between Thatcher and the queen in a generally strong relationship: 'I think the way it was portrayed, with Thatcher lecturing the queen, in programmes like *The Crown* is fundamentally wrong. The problem was that Margaret Thatcher, as a lower-middle class grocer's daughter and also as a woman with a woman, was far too deferential to her. She also struggled over who was the biggest star in the room.'[93]

Very demonstrably, the monarch is a far more significant figure in the Commonwealth, which currently constitutes fifty-four members, than the prime minister. This fact may account for the continuing tension between the Palace and Number 10, with a very palpable frustration from the former that the prime minister has not done enough over the years: 'If I were to identify a weakness, it is the inability of Her Majesty's Government to exploit better the potential of the Commonwealth which enjoys the queen at its head to more purposeful effect', says one insider. And another: 'The queen's role has been at its most powerful in holding together the sentiment of a very, very diverse group of member nations in the Commonwealth in a way that I would struggle to imagine any other figure carrying off.'[94]

It wasn't always thus. In Number 10 there are the faces of beaming prime ministers often in the principal seat, like the captain of a football team, at the Imperial conferences of 1911, 1923, 1926, and 1937; and photographs of the Imperial War Cabinet in May 1917 and Imperial War Council in June 1918 testify to the importance of the Empire in the Great War. Eight photographs were taken during meetings of Commonwealth prime ministers with, again, the British prime minister in pole position, from 1944 to 1979, with a final one in 1991. But visitors to Downing Street never see these pictures, because unlike the photographs of the prime ministers, instigated by Campbell-Bannerman, which are prominent on the central staircase which visitors see on the journey to and from the state rooms, these Imperial and Commonwealth photographs are 'below stairs', on the way down to the basement – an indication no doubt of the Commonwealth's place in prime ministers' priorities, not helped by a folklore in Number 10 that disasters often happen when prime ministers are away for Commonwealth heads-of-government meetings every two years, which few prime ministers have relished attending.

In 2021, the monarchy is not a diminished, irrelevant institution, in contrast to an all-powerful prime minister. Rather we have a monarch who, in terms of public popularity and influence, is, by a very considerable margin, ahead of the prime minister as a symbol of national influence and identity. But is that just a reflection of the queen's continuity and endurance? What will happen with the accession of the Prince of Wales? Will Brexit revive the Commonwealth? To understand this last question at least, we turn to look at how the prime minister took over from the monarch as the principal determiner of the country's foreign policy.

CHAPTER 8

The Rise and Fall of the Foreign Secretary, 1782–2021

BY 2021, the prime minister had emerged in largely undisputed control of foreign policy, taking over the powers initially from the monarch, then Parliament, then the Foreign Secretary. The prime minister decides British foreign relations, whether the country goes to war, and how it is fought. This chapter will examine how and why this transition occurred, and why the prime minister today can afford to be more preoccupied with foreign rather than domestic policy, and what this has meant to the office and powers of the prime minister.

THE ECLIPSE OF THE MONARCHY, 1660–1812

Two powerful offices were created at the Restoration in 1660, the 'Northern Department' which conducted diplomacy with Russia, Prussia, Sweden, and other northern states, and a 'Southern Department' which oversaw relations with France, Spain, Italy, and increasingly concerned itself with colonial policy. The Secretaries of State in charge of these departments had domestic responsibilities as well: the Northern Secretary thus oversaw Scotland (in the absence of a Scottish Secretary).[1] The two Secretaries wielded great power and autonomy, seeing the first or prime minister at first as of no great consequence, but heeding carefully and with discrimination the views of the monarch. In the words of Peter Jupp, they 'were regarded, and regarded themselves, as the monarch's representatives', and with additional nominal authority 'over the Treasury, the Admiralty, the Ordnance and the Victualling Departments'.[2]

Their power was all the greater because Britain was so often at war in the period between 1688 and 1815: the Williamite War (1689–91), the

War of the Spanish Succession (1701–14), the War of the Austrian Succession (1740–8), the Seven Years' War (1756–63), the American War of Independence (1775–83), the French Revolutionary War (1793–1802), and the Napoleonic Wars (1803–15). If we include 'smaller' wars, including Jenkins' Ear (1739–48) and the wars in India between 1746 and 1792, Britain was almost continuously fighting. William III had been responsible for initially repivoting the thrust of foreign policy away from France, but other factors, including the boundaries of the American colonies, would repeatedly create tensions in the century that followed, ushering in a series of wars between France and Britain that were, according to Robert Tombs, 'five of the eight bloodiest wars in world history'.[3]

It would be wrong to see the monarch as all-powerful over foreign policy from 1688. Memories of the Civil War, and James II's use of the military to suppress unrest, emboldened Parliament to pass the Mutiny Acts (from 1689) which required the existence of the army to be ratified annually, while the doctrine of parliamentary supremacy ensured that in the future, before taking the country to war, monarchs would be required to seek tacit parliamentary approval, for without Parliament there would be no funds to finance the war.[4] Fears of an out-of-control army explain, too, Parliament's reluctance to fund it compared to the navy, which became a standing force under Henry VIII, ahead of the army, hence its moniker the 'senior service'. For years after 1688, the army was weak and inadequate in contrast to the Royal Navy which protected trade and prevented the country from being invaded. The navy was already heavily institutionalised, with a First Lord of the Admiralty, an Admiralty Office, Admiralty Board, and Navy Board.

William III was not going to let his wings be clipped, and employed his own superior Dutch forces for combat in the war in Ireland, deploying the inferior English army for less important tasks. But his taking the country into war on the mainland of Europe for the sake of the Netherlands prompted the section in the Act of Settlement of 1701 which decreed that 'this nation be not obliged to engage in any war for the defence of any dominions or territories which do not belong to the crown of England, *without the consent of Parliament*'.[5]

Queen Anne was her own person in the conduct of foreign policy and war, issuing orders, conducting diplomacy, and appointing military commanders. The surviving correspondence is full of examples of her engagement, as in October 1704, when she wrote to the Habsburg claimant to the Spanish throne: 'The capture of the town of Gibraltar upon which you congratulate me is the more pleasing since it will open a passage into Your Kingdom of Spain.'[6]

George I's accession in 1714 marked a significant easing of monarchical control. The king was keenly interested in foreign policy, though his fondness for the principality of Hanover caused concern in Westminster. But his lack of detailed grip showed in the 1720s, when Townshend dominated foreign policy as Northern Secretary, and for much of the 1730s, when Walpole held sway, keeping Britain out of the War of the Polish Succession (1733–5), boasting that 'there are 50,000 men slain in Europe this year, and not one Englishman'.[7]

George II was a more determined figure, and famously was the last monarch to lead British soldiers on the field in battle, at the victorious, though strategically indecisive, Battle of Dettingen during the War of the Austrian Succession. But he was no 'warrior king' like Richard the Lionheart (r. 1189–99) or Henry V (1413–22), or even a William III (r. 1689–1702), who was a veteran of many battles on the Continent against Louis XIV and was a great strategist. No, rather George II was an 'armchair general' whose presence at Dettingen was more a concern and liability to his generals than an asset. They were right to be worried; in 1485 Richard III had been slain at the Battle of Bosworth, and less than four decades later King James IV of Scotland was killed, along with much of the Scottish nobility, at the Battle of Flodden in 1513. Further afield, in 1718 Charles XII of Sweden had been killed while inspecting his army's positions during a siege. Such fear trickled all the way down to the twentieth century, explaining the grave concerns about Lloyd George and Churchill in two later wars being exposed on the field of battle. After George II, no British monarch would take their forces into the field, in contrast to French, Russian, Prussian, and Austrian rulers who regularly commanded their forces in battle for the rest of the century and beyond. Napoleon III, copying his famous uncle, faced Austrian Emperor Franz Joseph at Solferino in 1856 and was subsequently captured while commanding the French army at the Battle of Sedan in 1870 in the Franco-Prussian War.

Two notable figures in particular under George II anticipated the preeminent position the Foreign Secretary was to achieve in the next century. Carteret, the Northern Secretary, was a dominant figure in the War of the Austrian Succession in the 1740s, declaring at one point: 'What is it to me who is a Judge and who is a Bishop? It is my business to make Kings and Emperors, and to maintain the balance of Europe.'[8] More significant still was Pitt the Elder in his capacity as Southern Secretary from 1756–61 during the Seven Years' War. Here was a supremely confident and magisterial figure, bringing insight and sharpness to Britain's efforts during the war. He authored the strategy of tying French forces down in Europe, where they were fighting Prussia, while using Britain's naval strength and expeditionary forces to seize the French Empire overseas: 'America has been conquered in Germany', he boasted to the House of Commons in 1761.[9] But Pitt was not all-powerful. He depended totally on Newcastle's ability to provide the money to fight the war, against an uncooperative Bank of England and City, fearful of paper money, the rise of interest rates, and the lack of control over government spending: 'No essential services or operations failed for want of money, as those of France had on occasion', says Richard Middleton of Newcastle's contribution.[10]

Conducting a war at such a distance meant that Pitt's control of operations was blunt at least. Field commanders had wide discretion in how they would accomplish objectives. 'From emergent circumstances not to be known here', Pitt wrote to Jeffrey Amherst, the Commander-in-Chief in North America in early 1760, that he 'proceed to the vigorous attack of Montreal, and exert your utmost efforts to reduce that place, as well as all other posts belonging to the French in those parts'.[11] Every other decision was left in Amherst's hands. Oversight from London had, in the eighteenth century, as in the nineteenth, a very different meaning to what it became.

Moreover, Pitt's political control was not absolute. Pitt had to take Cabinet with him, and when he failed to do so for a pre-emptive attack on Spain, he chose to resign as Southern Secretary in October 1761.[12] When Spain finally did attack, Britain swiftly seized Havana in 1762, which convinced Madrid to make peace. It showed that while Pitt had been vital to Britain's effort during the early part of the conflict, he was not indispensable, and success could be obtained without his guiding hand. British victories in this stage of the war though, and during the Seven Years' War more generally, illustrated how far the British army had come since 1688.

The slow decline in monarchical control of war and foreign policy can be vividly illustrated by its role in the two major conflicts during the reign of George III (r. 1760–1820): the American War of Independence (1775–83) and the wars against France from 1793–1815. In the first, George was preeminent. He personally rejected the 'olive branch petition' adopted by the Continental Congress in July 1775 which affirmed American loyalty to Britain and beseeched him to prevent further conflict. He refused to read it before rejecting the document and declaring the colonists traitors.[13] He negotiated with foreign powers to secure mercenaries to fight the war,[14] and personally selected the commanders, including Generals Burgoyne, Clinton, and Howe.[15]

As we saw in Chapter 7, George's determination that 'this country must never submit'[16] was a crucial factor in the conduct and prolonging of the American War. But even early on, Cabinet could and did overrule his wishes on several occasions. Much of the detailed conduct and financing of the war was in the hands of Lord North himself, and strategy was conducted by Colonial Secretary Lord George Germain. 'From the siege of Boston until after the defeat at Georgetown, Germain presided over the war in America', says O'Shaughnessy.[17]

The British effort again suffered from the tyranny of distance and communication. Strategy was regularly guided by overoptimism from commanders and governors in the field which exaggerated support for the Crown in the Thirteen Colonies, and discounted the depth of popular (and growing) support for independence. George took the series of defeats very personally, as well he might, and after the final defeat the monarch never again assumed such personal authority in the conduct of any war.

The Foreign Office was created in 1782 from the Southern and Northern Departments in the space between the American and French wars. Historians have struggled to identify the exact reason for this change: 'everyone who has written on the subject has come to the same problem', writes the Foreign Office chief historian, Patrick Salmon, 'because there is hardly any record left of why the decision was taken'.[18] But in all likelihood the need to regroup after the American War, the ministerial politics, with a desire to split up Fox and Shelburne, the desire to find a new berth for the post of 'Secretaryship for America' (formally, the Secretary for the Colonies) which George wanted abolished, and 'the absurdity', in the words of Hennessy,[19] of having two departments that dealt with foreign *and* domestic matters, all pointed to the need for the change.[20] Not that it led to any improvement in facilities. The new Foreign Office received no immediate institutional upgrade; it remained based in the same rickety buildings, which spread from Number 14 Downing Street into adjacent buildings facing Number 10.[21] Not for another eighty years would the Foreign Office move into its magnificent new edifice. The uneven quality of the Foreign Secretaries, and the presence of Pitt the Younger anyway, dictated that for its first twenty-five years in existence the Foreign Office 'was overshadowed by that of the Prime Minister'.[22]

Though chastened by America, George was still capable of interventions on foreign policy afterwards: he intervened decisively against the India Bill in 1783, and played a key role in the formation of the League of German Princes, the *Fürstenbund*, in 1785 which hastened the controversial alliance with Prussia.[23] He opposed an alliance with Austria during the 1780s proposed by Foreign Secretary, Marquess of Carmarthen (1783–91).[24]

But once the wars with France started, George took a backseat. The French Revolutionary War (1793–1802) and Napoleonic Wars (1803–15) demonstrated the decline in monarchical ambition and reach. Significantly, George trusted Pitt the Younger much more than he had done North.[25] As we have seen, George's health began to decline from 1788–9 and from then onwards he opted for more of what he called a 'superintending eye'.[26] In the later phases of the war, he suffered a rapid physical and mental deterioration and was no longer a meaningful force on the conduct of the last five years of the war leading up to Napoleon's final defeat at Waterloo (1815).

Pitt became increasingly confident too in his own judgement. His biographer William Hague records how his early distrust in his own ideas on military subjects dissipated after sending Nelson with a large part of the navy to the Mediterranean in 1798. Although Britain was under threat of invasion, the decision was vindicated by the Battle of the Nile that August which left Napoleon's army stranded in Egypt.[27] Before hostilities broke out, Pitt worked hard to rebuild the navy in the 1780s after the humiliations of the American War, ensuring that the military secured the finances that it needed. John Kerr sees Pitt as the first key figure in British history, apart from a monarch or Cromwell, who was decisive over war and foreign policy: 'Pitt was fascinated by everything, worked day and night, and was forced by events to take a keen interest in foreign affairs.'[28] Pitt drew on the experience of the Seven Years' War, which in folk memory was seen as a success with his father the heroic figure, in contrast to the American War of Independence, where ministers had been divided and the result a disaster.[29]

When Liverpool became prime minister for the final three years of the war, Wellington, who had come to prominence commanding British forces in the Peninsula campaign from 1808, and was promoted to Field Marshal after his victory in the Battle of Vitoria in 1813, was the undisputed master of the field of battle. 'Liverpool recognised that what Wellington needed was political support at home, resources and discretion to act as events demanded. It was difficult if not impossible to closely manage operations from London, given the nature of communication', says Hay.[30] As further evidence of the decline in monarchical authority over the war, the decision to appoint Wellington to command British forces during the peninsula campaign had been War Secretary Castlereagh's, says his biographer Bew: 'Taken against the advice of George III, who wanted to appoint a more experienced general'.[31] Castlereagh, not George, nor the Prince Regent, was the principal British diplomat at the Congress of Vienna (1814–15) which reshaped Europe after the war.

THE GOLDEN AGE OF THE FOREIGN SECRETARY, 1812–1914

For the next one hundred years, the Foreign Secretary, not the monarch nor often the prime minister, was dominant in guiding and shaping Britain's foreign policy. Four in particular stand out, and one Colonial Secretary. At the time, the office acquired a status almost above politics.

The same sense of being above it can be found in the position of the US Secretary of State today, a job and department also founded in the 1780s. The position of being able to speak for the whole nation enhanced the authority of the position considerably. This 'speaking for the country' element helps explain also why an unusually large number of Foreign Secretaries were in the House of Lords: between 1812 and 1914, fourteen out of the seventeen Foreign Secretaries served in the Lords, accounting for 64 out of the 102 years. Indeed, all of Gladstone's Foreign Secretaries were in the House of Lords. 'I think it partly insulated the Foreign Secretaryship from the normal rough and tumble of parliamentary and Cabinet debate, highlighting the quasi-independent status of the Foreign Secretary', says Adonis.[32]

In stark contrast to our first period (1660–1812), when Britain was regularly at war, these 102 years till 1914 mark a period of great-power tranquillity. The Crimean War (1854–6), fought to contain the ambitions of Russia over the declining Ottoman Empire, exposed how far Britain's army had fallen behind again since the end of the Napoleonic Wars forty years before. After the inconclusive battle at Balaclava and a narrow victory at Inkerman in 1854, the tide turned in 1855 as the French and British took Sevastopol, their objective, and the war was concluded in 1856.

Britain's other wars in this period saw victories against three countries that became the superpowers of the twenty-first century. The War of 1812 saw British troops fight off American invasions of Canada and briefly occupy Washington DC in 1814, where they set fire to the White House and government buildings on Capitol Hill. In the Opium Wars (1839–42, 1856–60), a Franco-British alliance successfully defeated the Qing Dynasty in China to keep the opium markets open. The Indian rebellion of 1857 saw a wide-scale uprising against the East India Company's rule, until British and British-aligned forces eventually brought India back under control, and it remained subdued until the 1920s. Consequently, the East India Company's rule was ended and an Act in 1858 set up an India Office in Whitehall overseen by the India Secretary with a Viceroy in India itself. The Second Boer War (1899–1902) was the final conflict in this period, which, as with the Crimean War, exposed the British military early on, until the army recovered, and, by using repressive measures against civilians, eventually crushed the independence of the Boer Republics, with the war ending in 1902.

In this second period, the Foreign Secretary emerged as very clearly the second most senior member of the Cabinet behind the prime minister, although, as historian Michael Hughes says, 'in a fluid system of collective government, such a notional rank did not automatically translate into real power', above all in domestic politics. The Foreign Secretary was a situational player, and had to share authority when there was a particularly influential Colonial, India, or War Secretary.[33] But, even as late as 1927, historian of the Foreign Secretary Algernon Cecil could write: 'The Foreign Office must, in short, be reckoned the most anxious appointment that a Prime Minister has to make', on account of its seniority and importance in world affairs.[34]

With that said, for all the pomp of the Foreign Secretary, the grandeur of his position contrasted sharply with the shabbiness and small size of the office itself. The Foreign Office remained a minuscule operation 'seldom employing more than 50 diplomatic clerks, many of whom spent their day engaged in the routine work of copying dispatches and making up the diplomatic bag'.[35] By the 1830s, Palmerston decided something better was required, and that new offices should be constructed, a sensible initiative, not least after the similarly elderly Palace of Westminster was largely destroyed by fire in October 1834. After prolonged parliamentary wrangling, George Gilbert Scott was selected as the architect and the new building was erected in 1861–8 in between Downing Street and King Charles Street, pulling down the hundreds of historic buildings in the streets between to construct the classical edifice that stands today. The new block was built to house the Home Office, the India and Colonial Offices, as well as the Foreign Office; indicatively the Foreign Secretary was given the largest room, overlooking St James's Park, and retains it to this day.[36]

It is not a coincidence that the Foreign Secretary was at his most powerful at the time when Britain was at its most powerful on the world stage. The nineteenth century was the era of the 'Pax Britannica', with Britain the paramount military, economic, and political power. As a result, British politicians and Foreign Secretaries had considerable freedom over how they chose to wield that power. During this era,

British foreign policy was generally successful in meeting its shifting aims. After leaving the great-power Congress system in 1818, Britain pursued a policy of isolationism, avoiding alliances with continental powers and aiming to create a 'balance of power' on the Continent. Geographically, the stretch of coast alongside the Channel, closest to Britain, had to be kept out of potentially hostile hands, and Britain played a key role in the creation of Belgium in 1830, with the 1839 Treaty of London ensuring its neutrality, to this end.

Protecting and advancing the British Empire and its dominions, promoting free trade, and maintaining the power of the Royal Navy as the symbol of British military pride also remained objectives throughout. Within this framework, some of the key figures, like the Tory prime ministers Wellington, Disraeli, and Salisbury, preferred a more pragmatic and conservative policy. Some, like Canning and Gladstone, were guided more by liberal and moral objectives, while others like Castlereagh and Palmerston preferred a blend of both approaches. Castlereagh, acting semi-autonomously, played a principal role in designing Europe's reactionary post-Napoleonic order and creating a 'balance of power'. Palmerston, also acting largely as his own agent, could use hard British power in cases like the Don Pacifico Affair in 1850, when he sent the Royal Navy to blockade Greece until they compensated a wronged British merchant (seen as a classic example of 'gunboat diplomacy'). Equally, Palmerston lent rhetorical support to the liberal revolutions of the 1840s.

British prime ministers had an uncertain relationship with the growth of empire which helped Britain climb to perhaps the apex of its power internationally in the 1860s, with America divided, Germany still disunited, and Napoleon III proving an inconsistent leader in France. Foreign Secretaries were very conscious of a Britain at the cutting edge of a new morality of anti-slavery and free trade, spreading liberty in the form of liberalism and progress, much as the United States was to do in claiming the moral beacon in the next century.

The British Empire, however, gave the monarchy and the military more prestige than it did the office of prime minister, for whom it proved a frequent headache: 'the Empire, even at its peak and extent of prestige, did not leave much mark on the premiership', writes Coleman. 'Perhaps Disraeli in his last few years and then Salisbury gained some extra gloss from it, before things went wrong for them.'[37] Colonial wars fought far away were expensive, and were not always welcome to an increasingly engaged domestic opinion, especially when they went wrong. Reversals, like the Indian Rebellion of 1857, the complete destruction of British forces at the hands of the Zulus at Isandlwana in 1879, the killing of General Gordon in Khartoum in 1885, or defeats in the first year of the Second Boer War in 1899–1900, produced backlashes from which it was the prime ministers primarily who suffered. Growing criticism of Empire from non-conformists, the progressive left, and Irish Home Rulers also created a more difficult domestic background.

Prime ministers found themselves regularly frustrated that they could not exercise more direct control over the Empire even after the telegraph arrived, with the practice remaining that the local governors and military commanders had the last say. No prime minister ever visited India, nor monarch, in the nineteenth century: but neither did they visit any other part of the Empire that century.[38] It took two years for Disraeli to replace the Whig Northbrook as Viceroy of India and install his own man, Lord Lytton, while Evelyn Baring (later Earl of Cromer) was virtually irreplaceable as Consul-General of Egypt (1883–1907).[39] From the 1860s onwards, many of the settler colonies like Canada and Australia were effectively self-governing, contributing troops to Britain's wars but considering themselves increasingly autonomous.

Lord Castlereagh was the twelfth Foreign Secretary since the office was created in 1782, but he was the first to stand out and show just how much authority the officeholder could wield. There had been great figures as Foreign Secretary before, including Charles James Fox on three occasions, and one landmark Foreign Secretary, George Canning (1807–9), who returned to the position after Castlereagh's death. But Castlereagh was unique. He had come to prominence as Pitt's Chief Secretary for Ireland (1798–1801), but it was as War and Colonial Secretary (1805–6 and 1807–9), then Foreign Secretary (1812–22), that he excelled. 'He remained at the heart of the war effort from the Battle of Trafalgar [1805] to the Battle of Waterloo [1815], and oversaw the European peace which followed it', writes John Bew.[40] War put foreign policy at the fore, particularly given Britain's role as the banker and organiser of repeated anti-Napoleon coalitions. Castlereagh spent many long hours negotiating with monarchs in Austria, Prussia, and Russia over how many soldiers in their combined armies Britain would itself fund.[41]

At the Congress of Vienna in 1814–15, he stood out for his brilliance alongside the Austrian foreign minister Klemens von Metternich. 'One reason why Castlereagh was British plenipotentiary [a diplomat who is given full powers] was that, even though he referred back and forth to London, to do business from Vienna required him being given extraordinary authority', says Hay.[42] Although careful to keep Liverpool and Cabinet informed, on occasion he 'far exceeded his brief', according to Bew.[43] The Treaty of Ghent (1814), which concluded the 1812 war with America, had earlier seen Liverpool and the Cabinet kept far better informed. But Ghent was only 170 miles from London: Vienna in contrast was 770 miles.[44] Castlereagh was not sorry about the distance.

Castlereagh has been widely admired, and vilified, down the ages, as he was by contemporaries. For critics he was an unfeeling reactionary who was so mesmerised by great-power concerns that he created a European order that crushed legitimate national aspirations and, in doing so, helped to set the scene for the horrors of the twentieth century. By contrast, admirers include former US Secretary of State Henry Kissinger, a connoisseur of the period, who credits Castlereagh with helping to create the notion of collective security: 'Castlereagh thought that the best way to defend that interest was to have a hand in shaping the decisions afflicting international order and in organising resistance to violations of peace.'[45] But the doors were closing on Castlereagh. Cabinet refused to let him attend any further European congresses after Britain left the congress system at Aix-la-Chapelle in 1818. Political reversal and depression probably played their part in his suicide, in August 1822.

Canning proved another powerful, semi-autonomous Foreign Secretary. He was more a liberal than Castlereagh. He helped guarantee the recently won independence of the new South American republics like Argentina and Mexico, not only stymying French ambitions in the area but opening up lucrative new markets for British financial and mercantile interests.[46] After Castlereagh's long tenure as Foreign Secretary, Canning redirected the gaze of the Foreign Office away from Europe towards other corners of the world.

Palmerston was the single most influential figure in the foreign policy of the 1812–1914 period, having been Foreign Secretary (1830–4, 1835–41, and 1846–51) for a total of fifteen years and dominating it as prime minister (1855–8 and 1859–65), albeit with diminishing success. A pragmatist in his pursuit of British interest, he said in 1848: 'We have no eternal allies, and we have no perpetual enemies. Our interests are eternal and perpetual, and those interests it is our duty to follow.'[47]

Palmerston could be imperious as Foreign Secretary, ignoring the prime minister on occasion, as when in 1848 he sent dispatches to Spain and Portugal that had not been approved.[48] He thought nothing of defying Queen Victoria's 'strongly worded suggestions and emendations' or the advice offered by Albert. He caused great offence at the Palace when clerks at the Foreign Office opened and read the letters she sent to her relatives, and the impertinence was one of the factors leading to his forced resignation in 1851,[49] as was his sending dispatches without awaiting her approval.[50] Too much can be made though of his overruling Prime Minister Russell: 'Lord John [Russell] and Palmerston worked well together on foreign policy. Contrary to widespread belief, both then and now, Palmerston did not dominate the partnership', writes Russell's biographer.[51]

As prime minister, too much can again be made of his unilateralism. From his perch as Home Secretary, he helped winkle out Aberdeen as prime minister in 1855, making free with the assumption that, if only he were to be prime minister, he would conduct the faltering war in Crimea far better. 'People thought when Palmerston took over from Aberdeen that he would be a much better war minister. But Palmerston was not a strategist. The great thing about war leaders like Pitt the Elder and Churchill is that they were proper strategists who were *interested* in war', says Andrew Roberts.[52] The detailed work was left to Foreign Secretary Clarendon and Russell, who in a reversal of roles, was Colonial Secretary for a while in between stints as Foreign Secretary himself. 'Palmerston never really reconciled the tensions within government over conduct of the Crimean War, over whether to be forward or defensive: to many, he is starting to look a little disappointing by 1856', concludes David Brown.[53] By the time news of the Indian Rebellion of 1857–8 reached

London, Palmerston publicly 'played down the gravity of the situation'[54] and it failed to engage his full attention: 'he's not really that interested'.[55]

During the American Civil War (1861–5) Russell, in his second stint as Foreign Secretary, and Gladstone, as Chancellor, pressed hard for mediation: Palmerston, however, by now well into his seventies, was indecisive, allowing Cabinet to argue it out, and on occasion absenting himself as a way of avoiding a decision,[56] before concluding, 'I am very much come back to our original view of the matter, that we must continue merely to be lookers-on till the war shall have taken a more decided turn.'[57]

Salisbury, our third dominant Foreign Secretary, served initially under Disraeli from 1878–80, and then as prime minister until prevailed upon to give up the Foreign Secretaryship in November 1900, twenty months before he ceased to be prime minister. The only other prime ministers to combine the post with that of Foreign Secretary were Wellington, very briefly in 1834, and Ramsay MacDonald in his first government in 1924. First elected to the Commons as Lord Robert Cecil in 1854, before being elevated to the Lords in 1868, Salisbury served as India Secretary under Derby and under Disraeli from 1874 until appointed Foreign Secretary shortly before the 1878 Berlin Congress. He prevailed upon Disraeli to let him attend, arguing that 'you must have men from the Cabinet who knew all the ins and outs of the recent negotiations'.[58] As Salisbury's notes held in Oxford's Bodleian Library show, much of the detailed negotiations were conducted by Salisbury himself. The papers show his mastery of French, the diplomatic language of the time, and his ease in switching between languages.[59]

Salisbury was at the height of his power over foreign policy from 1887–92. Against his better judgement, he appointed Stafford Northcote – Earl of Iddesleigh – Foreign Secretary in 1886. But when the luckless Iddesleigh died in January 1887, at Number 10 no less, Salisbury became Foreign Secretary again, revealingly 'because he felt he lacked the power of the prime minister not being in charge of foreign affairs in part because he was in the House of Lords', says Adonis.[60] During Salisbury's time, the Empire expanded by 6 million square miles and by perhaps 100 million people.[61] He reshaped history by acquiring for Britain the majority of new territory in the so-called 'Scramble for Africa', while avoiding a major war or serious confrontation with other European powers.

His policy was to keep the peace in Europe, exploiting the position Britain possessed at the peak, he believed, of its power and global influence. A war would, he calculated, likely ruin that. His method was to keep Britain unencumbered by military alliances – a policy which became known as 'Splendid Isolation'. He shared the peace policy with German Chancellor Otto von Bismarck, who was then constructing a network of alliances to keep Germany safe. They 'appreciated the dangers of war', wrote Roberts. 'It was only when both men had quitted the scene that the Great European Peace of 1871–1914 came to an end.'[62] Salisbury reluctantly took Britain into the Second Boer War in 1899, replacing General Redvers Buller with Lord Roberts after the disastrous 'Black Week' of defeats in 1899, but was content to leave the conduct of the war to those in the field.[63]

Salisbury was losing his command in his final ministry and from 1895 delegated much colonial policy to his energetic Colonial Secretary, Joseph Chamberlain (1895–1903), including in South Africa where Chamberlain had helped precipitate the Boer War and then oversaw its conduct in Cabinet. Chamberlain became increasingly obsessed by the idea of Empire, resigning from Cabinet in 1903 to campaign for imperial preference, a protectionist measure prioritising the Empire, as opposed to free trade. This issue split the Conservative Party, as it is wont to do to Tory cabinets every seventy years or so, and played an important role in their defeat in the 1906 election.

Edward Grey, our final Foreign Secretary of the period, and the longest continually serving in history (1905–16), was well schooled in foreign policy, having served as a junior minister at the Foreign Office under Gladstone and Rosebery as prime ministers. His time came at a period of change in British foreign affairs. Increasingly, British politicians had become concerned with the rise of Germany, especially after the fall of the conservative and cautious Bismarck in 1890, and feared that German power might become a threat. Britain slowly abandoned isolationism, with a formal agreement with Japan (due to concerns over Russia) in 1902. Grey's predecessor, Lord Lansdowne (1900–5), was instrumental in this process, negotiating the Anglo-Russian agreement with little interference from his Cabinet colleagues.[64] Far more significant, however, was a series of agreements with France in 1904, the

'Entente Cordiale'. An expensive Anglo-German naval race from 1906 seemed to justify the fear. For their part, the Germans were envious and frustrated by what they saw as swaggering British power.

Grey played a key role in designing this new environment. He negotiated another entente, with Russia in 1907, and chose to support France in the Agadir Crisis of 1911. Critically, he and Asquith authorised secret staff talks between British and French generals in 1906 without informing Cabinet.[65] He also negotiated the secret 1912 Anglo-French naval agreement with the ambassador, whereby the Royal Navy would protect the Channel, and the French navy the Mediterranean.[66] This all played a part in preparing the ground for the first major war in Europe for a hundred years.[67]

Grey relished his exceptionally cordial and close relationship with Prime Minister Asquith, who wrote of it: 'Between him and myself there was daily intimacy and unbroken confidence. I can hardly recall any occasion on which we had a difference of opinion which lasted for more than half an hour.'[68] For his part, Asquith was preoccupied elsewhere and was more than happy to leave foreign policy largely in Grey's hands. Asquith biographer Markham Lester notes how, in Asquith's two-volume book *Fifty Years of Parliament*, published in 1926, the index lists only one reference to France, and none to Germany.[69] Those fateful years in the build-up to the First World War we now see as the peak of the Foreign Office's influence over policy. 'The Foreign Office was more often than not the primary location for initiating important proposals about foreign policy', writes historian Michael Hughes.[70]

The height, and the limits, of Grey's influence would be shown in the fraught weeks leading immediately up to the outbreak of war in August 1914. As the crisis escalated, he, not Asquith, negotiated with foreign leaders via their ambassadors, and can be criticised for failing to establish a clearer and more consistent policy which might have restrained allies or sufficiently deterred Germany.[71] Ultimately, it was Grey who came out as the principal advocate for war, threatening resignation when a policy of non-intervention was discussed in Cabinet. Instead, two Liberal-supporting stalwarts, John Burns and Lord Morley, resigned rather than endorse the war.

It was Grey, not Asquith, who gave the seminal speech in Parliament on 3 August, laying out the reasons for the government's ultimatum to Berlin to withdraw their forces from Belgium, after the invasion had broken the 1839 Treaty of London. 'That afternoon Grey stood up in the House of Commons to make the most important speech of his life. The task fell personally to Grey, to an extent inconceivable today', wrote Hurd, himself a Foreign Secretary (1989–1995). 'As Prime Minister, Asquith fully supported his Foreign Secretary but totally neglected what would normally be regarded as the Prime Minister's task, namely explaining to the public the new crisis which was about to engulf them.'[72]

But Grey did not go into the crisis frivolously. Famously, on the evening of 3 August, looking out at the fading light over St James's Park from the windows of his magnificent room in the Foreign Office, Grey said that 'The lamps are going out all over Europe, we shall not see them lit again in our lifetime.'[73] For him, it was also a personal comment; he knew that he was losing his sight, and he would suffer from increasing blindness for the rest of his life.

Grey largely withdrew once war broke out, recognising 'that diplomats had to take second place to soldiers at times of war, and became less inclined to assert the right of his department to act as the principal location for decisions about foreign policy'.[74]

The golden age of the Foreign Secretary from 1812–1914 had only been made possible by the unexpectedly quick withdrawal of monarchs from a wish to be the arbiter on foreign policy. As we have seen, George III contributed little in his final years before his death in 1820, and while George IV, according to Aspinall who chronicled his correspondence, had 'very definite views on British policy', he did not make much of a mark.[75] Victoria had pronounced views on foreign policy, as she did on many topics. At times she could be interfering, prompting a clearly exasperated Russell to write to Palmerston in 1848, after prolonged wrangling between the Palace and Downing Street, asking him to 'save the Queen anxiety, & me some trouble by giving your reasons before, & not after an important dispatch is sent'.[76] Two years later during the Don Pacifico Affair, Albert wrote to Russell in an uncustomary humble tone, 'when overruled by the Cabinet, or convinced that it would from political reasons be more prudent to waive her objections, she [the queen] knew

her constitutional position too well not to give her full support to whatever was done on the part of the government'.[77]

Divisions between the strongly pro-Prussian and pro-German Court
and often more neutral politicians were a theme in the second half of
this period. The 1860s saw the first reaction against a more assertive
Prussia in the years leading up to the Franco-Prussian War (1870–1)
and the unification of Germany in 1871. Victoria intrigued with
Cabinet, including Gladstone, to check Palmerston's anti-Prussian
inclinations, but gradually German ambition under Wilhelm II began
to alienate Victoria, and she agreed with Salisbury and Chamberlain
that the Diamond Jubilee of 1897 should be very clearly an *imperial*
celebration, unlike her Golden Jubilee of 1887 which had seen the
European ruling houses invited.[78] Victoria accepted Salisbury's views
in her last years, and while Edward VII from 1901 had more ambition
on the foreign stage, his Francophile and anti-German stance chimed
with government policy, avoiding difficulties. From the 1870s, the royal
family shifted its identity away from Germany and Europe towards an
imperial role, and in the Empire and Commonwealth the monarchy
found much more purpose and a clearer identity than in foreign
affairs.

During the First World War, while the monarchy's shedding of its
German names soothed popular feeling, its principal foreign involvement concerned whether George V would allow his cousin Tsar
Nicholas II of Russia and his family to have refuge in Britain. It is
debatable whether the Bolsheviks would have released them, but
Lloyd George made plans for a destroyer to go to the Black Sea to
bring them back. George V's Private Secretary, Stamfordham was
decisive, fearing that, in the volatile domestic climate, the arrival of
the Romanovs might spark a working-class revolt. So he collected a
scrapbook of articles showing how the radical Left was saying it might
react, showed it to the king, and told him, in the words of Heffer: 'If the
Tsar comes here we are all in trouble because everyone will know that he
wouldn't come without your approval because you are his cousin!'[79]
George eventually refused to allow the Tsar refuge. It was to be the last
significant intervention by the monarchy on what would have been
a very major policy decision.

THE ECLIPSE OF THE FOREIGN SECRETARY, 1914-79

These years see the final disappearance of the monarch's influence over the conduct of foreign policy, a steady waning of the authority of the Foreign Secretary, and by the end, the emergence of the prime minister as the decisive figure in diplomacy and war, as in peace. Twenty-three Foreign Secretaries served in these years compared to fourteen prime ministers: as only eighteen served between 1812 and 1914 compared to eighteen prime ministers, it suggests brevity of tenure was a factor in the eclipse after 1914. A measure of the continued stature of the Foreign Secretary, though, is that it is the only position that former prime ministers have occupied on returning to serve in government, with Balfour (1916–19) and Alec Douglas-Home (1970–4) bookending the period. Douglas-Home was 'left to conduct foreign affairs as he thought best', as biographer Philip Ziegler put it, after the prime minister, Heath, had taken the major chunks of it, namely Europe and the relationship with the United States, for himself.[80] Ramsay MacDonald, the last figure to serve as both prime minister and Foreign Secretary, told Parliament that he wanted to use 'the weight of his office' to resolve the country's 'unsatisfactory' relationships with European governments, (déjà vu) although other potential candidates had been ruled out for internal Labour Party reasons.[81]

Four former Foreign Secretaries went on to become prime minister in this period (Eden, Macmillan, Douglas-Home, and Callaghan) compared to eight former Chancellors of the Exchequer (Asquith, Lloyd George, Bonar Law, Baldwin, Chamberlain, Churchill, Macmillan, and Callaghan). One dog that didn't bark to challenge the Foreign Secretary was the Home Secretary, ranked technically as senior.[82] The Home Office began to lose ground from the 1820s, after the exceptional Home Secretaryships of Addington (1812–22), after he had been prime minister, and Robert Peel (1822–7, 1828–30) *before* he became prime minister. The Home Office 'fell down the pecking order and found itself increasingly confined to matters of criminal justice, policing and domestic security', writes Coleman, 'all of which lost prominence as Britain became stabler after the 1840s'.[83] As social and economic policy loomed larger, the Home Office was steadily divested of responsibilities, with the creation of the Board of Local Government (1871) and subsequent ministries, including Labour (1916) and Health (1919). A symbolic moment was when the new Gilbert Scott building was opened in 1868, when, despite it containing the Home Office as well as the Foreign Office, it was named after the latter. Subsequently, although some former Home Secretaries like Asquith, Churchill, and Callaghan went on to become prime minister, they occupied more senior roles in the interim, and many Home Secretaries have been minor political figures. No one between Robert Peel and Theresa May won the top job *because* they had been Home Secretary.

The First World War itself was one of a series of events that tilted the foreign policy balance firmly in the direction of the prime minister. Technological advancements, as discussed, and the increasing prevalence of international meetings, starting with the postwar Versailles Peace Conference attended by the prime minister, helped in that direction. At that very moment, Britain's predominance in the world came under greater challenge during the 1920s, not least by the potential of America and the new Soviet Union. Britain had ended the war deeply in debt, and its military power had been damaged. In 1922, Britain signed the Washington Treaty with the US and other powers, placing limits for the first time on the size of the Royal Navy.[84] Foreign policy debates often took on an unwelcome economic edge as Britain negotiated with countries like the US, which held Britain's loans. On matters like German war reparations, it was not the Foreign Secretary, but often the Chancellor who came to the fore. The Empire, once a source of potential strength, started to seem more vulnerable as rumbles of discontent from India and the new 'Mandates' in the Middle East grew louder. On top of all this, there was now more public scrutiny in foreign policy, and popular suspicion of the sort of secret diplomacy that many blamed for the First World War. No longer did Britain's politicians seem to be the masters of their country's fate.[85]

Given Lloyd George's character and the circumstances of his coming to power, it was inevitable that his fingerprints would be on many of the key decisions of the final twenty-three months of the war, from December 1916. In Maurice Hankey, the head of the Cabinet Secretariat, the PM had an advisor at his right hand in Downing Street, for the first time, who was an authority on war and diplomacy.[86] The peace settlement that followed the war was the first in the history of the prime minister where the incumbent could be regularly present in the discussions, as were Georges Clémenceau, prime minister of France, and US president Woodrow Wilson, as was Vittorio Orlando, prime minister of Italy. From 1919–21, Lloyd George was almost constantly travelling or engaged in foreign business. He revelled in foreign policy, as prime ministers do the longer their premiership lasts, driving forward British policy in discussions that led to the Treaty of Versailles and pushing through a trade agreement with the new Soviet Russia in 1921, 'despite the strong opposition from [Foreign Secretary] Curzon and a number of other senior ministers'.[87] Curzon, who succeeded Balfour as Foreign Secretary in 1919, had been Viceroy of India (1898–1905) and had hoped to be an independent Foreign Secretary in the mould of a Palmerston or Salisbury. But the world had moved on. By 1922, he had become so frustrated that he drafted a letter of resignation to Lloyd George, a letter which could have been written by a number of his successors as Foreign Secretary:

> A system under which there are two Foreign Offices, the one for which I am for the time being responsible, and the other at No. 10 – with the essential difference between them that, whereas I report not only to you but to all my colleagues everything that I say or do, every telegram that I receive or send, every communication of importance that reaches me, it is often only by accident that I hear what is being done by the other Foreign Office.[88]

Closer to home, Lloyd George seized control of policy on Ireland too as it became ever clearer that Britain would be forced to recognise some kind of autonomous Dublin government. He communicated regularly with Éamon de Valera, one of the leading Republican figures in the Irish War of Independence, and presented personally the ultimatum to the Irish leaders in December 1921, announcing that one telegram would renew the war while the other would end it: 'We must know your answer by ten tonight.'[89] 'You couldn't imagine two more distinct characters than Lloyd George and de Valera who didn't like each other, but felt they had to reach an agreement: it was the first classic example of the British government being forced, as later in India, to come to terms with its political enemies and reach a solution', says Kenneth Morgan.[90]

With Lloyd George gone by October 1922, the Foreign Office recovered some lost ground in the mid to late decade with some spirited Foreign Secretaries, including Austen Chamberlain (1924–9) and Arthur Henderson (1929–31). But they were followed, over the 1930s, by a succession of weaker, younger, or more detached Foreign Secretaries in the form of the Marquess of Reading (1931), John Simon (1931–5), and Samuel Hoare (1935). The Permanent Under-Secretary (PUS), notably Robert Vansittart (1930–38), filled some of the void. While Eden was just thirty-eight when he took over in December 1935, and a comparative light-weight as Foreign Secretary, he went on to serve in the position for over eleven out of the next twenty years. Lord Halifax, Foreign Secretary from 1938–40, like Curzon a former Viceroy of India (1926–31), was clearly subordinate to Chamberlain in the key stages that led to the Second World War. Whereas it was Grey who made the case for war in the House of Commons in 1914, it was Chamberlain who took to the Despatch Box in 1939.

When Churchill became prime minister in May 1940, Eden returned as Foreign Secretary that December when Churchill appointed Halifax the ambassador to the USA, but found himself under the shadow of a still more domineering prime minister. Churchill's decision to become Britain's first Minister of Defence, Packwood argues, was 'his first real decision as war leader', and by doing so 'Churchill had deliberately put himself at the heart of the British war machine'.[91] The most important decisions during the war were taken by Churchill, including the initial decision to fight on in May 1940 with Cabinet deeply divided on the issue. He was responsible too for the destruction of the French fleet at Mers-el-Kebir by the Royal Navy in July 1940; the decision to prioritise fighting the Axis powers in the Middle East, Mediterranean, and then Italy; and the decision at the Casablanca conference in 1943, after consultation with the War Cabinet, to embrace 'unconditional surrender' as the Allied policy towards Germany and Japan. Like Lloyd George, Churchill used the new opportunities for travel, making twenty-five trips, more than any other wartime leader. They included 'hazardous trips' across the Channel in 1940, 1944, and 1945, meeting Roosevelt on eleven occasions and Stalin on three. Roosevelt and Stalin indeed never met except when Churchill was present, as at Tehran in 1943 and Yalta in 1945. 'Churchill's travels during the Second World War provided the glue that held the Big Three together', concludes Roberts. When he traveled, as Peter Ricketts reminds us, he took the Foreign Office's PUS, Alexander Cadogan (1938–46), 'while Eden stayed at home to mind the shop'. Churchill trusted Cadogan's judgment implicitly, as later prime ministers did with certain pet diplomats.[92]

Independent Foreign Secretaries could still be found after 1945 but they were operating in a different world, one even more constrained by circumstances. Bevin (1945–51) was the architect of Labour's foreign policy. His greatest achievement was the establishment of a collective security ideal once dreamt by Castlereagh, and all the more impressive given Britain's straitened economic situation during the late 1940s. Bevin established the Treaty of Dunkirk in 1947, a defence treaty with France, extending it to the Brussels Treaty in 1948 to include the Netherlands and Belgium, and then played a prominent role in the establishment of NATO in 1949. He was responsible for cementing the 'special relationship' with the United States: Attlee and President Truman didn't meet for five years after 1945, and much of the weight of the relationship was taken by Bevin himself.[93] 'Some of the relationships Bevin had with Stalin and other leaders were remarkable for a British Foreign Secretary, the legacy of Britain having won the war and lost its imperial power', says Michael Jay.[94] Eden returned as Foreign Secretary under Churchill from 1951–5, his most effective period. Churchill took over the running of relationships with American presidents Truman and Eisenhower, and attempted to create a thaw in the Cold War.[95]

Eden busied himself after 1951 with 'second order' issues like Egypt, European defence, Yugoslavia, and the Far East, where he brokered an agreement over Indochina at the Geneva conference of 1954 creating North and South Vietnam, albeit a solution that did not endure. He had more success with the Austrian State Treaty the same year, which guaranteed Austrian neutrality, ended the Allied occupation, and re-established an independent Austria. This was likely the last time that the architecture of a major treaty could be attributed to a Foreign Secretary.[96] After Eden became prime minister in April 1955, he continued to try to be his own Foreign Secretary. Henceforth, strong and independent Foreign Secretaries began to wane – Macmillan might have been one but he lasted just eight months in post in 1955 before being moved, tellingly, to the Treasury. His successor Selwyn Lloyd (1955–60) was totally overshadowed by Eden, then Macmillan when he became prime minister. George Brown (1966–8) suffered by having a deplorable relationship with his prime minister, Wilson, and the only Foreign Secretaries with real authority in this period were Douglas-Home (1960–3, 1970–4), Callaghan (1974–6) in Wilson's last government, David Owen his successor (1977–9), Lord Carrington (1979–82), and Douglas Hurd (1989–95). Big figures who might have emerged as powerful Foreign Secretaries were there for too short a time, including Anthony Crossland from 1976–7 and John Major for three months in 1989. Others, who had longer in office and political clout, such as Geoffrey Howe from 1983–9, suffered from a prime minister with their own foreign agenda.

HOW DID THE PRIME MINISTER TAKE CONTROL?

The tide of history from 1945 was running strongly in favour of the prime minister and Number 10 winning out against the Foreign Secretary and the Foreign Office. In this struggle of little David in the cramped Number 10 and the mighty Goliath on the other side of Downing Street, there was ultimately no competition.

The trends that we saw after the First World War were even more strongly in evidence after the Second, and the Foreign Secretary was no match for them. The first two decades after the war saw extensive decolonisation and a retreat from empire. The Suez fiasco of 1956 demonstrated that Britain could no longer act as a great power ignoring what the US and UN said. The realities of the Cold War further constrained British independence. Membership of the NATO alliance curtailed the requirement to build new alliances and reduced the initiative to act at will. The relationship with the United States, the world's paramount capitalist, democratic, and military power, became the most important strand of British foreign policy. Debates about national issues were expected to be solved at the UN, even if that did not often happen quite as intended. From 1973, the UK entered into a new dynamic of political cooperation with the European Community, giving a new role to officials and the Foreign Secretary themselves at the Foreign Affairs Council. 'EC membership became a multiplier of UK diplomatic influence, largely because we were thought to have some influence in Washington', says one former official.[97] Whether this increased the Foreign Secretary's power is arguable. 'Ever closer union' with Europe took away the need to enter into trade deals or negotiate with other countries, while placing the PM centre stage in key talks.

Britain's reduced economic condition also dictated a smaller military. The once mighty Royal Navy ceased to have the global dominance and reach of earlier eras, and in 1968 Harold Wilson announced that British forces would withdraw from bases 'East of Suez', which was more than just a symbolic retreat from a global military role. During the Cold War, it was increasingly the United States armed forces that could project power all over the world, and which took the lead on fighting communism (and later Islamic fundamentalism) and providing economic support to allies at times of war, once the role of Britain. Indeed, it was now the US Secretary of State who basked in the prestige and limelight hitherto shone on scions of the Foreign Office, with figures like General Marshall, Dean Acheson, John Foster Dulles, Henry Kissinger, and Colin Powell playing some of the role of Castlereagh, Palmerston, and Grey in our earlier period.

Personal factors, as always in our story, played their part. After 1945, Britain had a stream of commanding prime ministers who dedicated much of their premierships to global affairs – Churchill, Macmillan, Heath, Thatcher, Blair, and Cameron – leaving little space for the Foreign Secretary. A succession of Chancellors largely outshone, outgunned, and outmanoeuvred their opposite number in the Foreign Office, including Rab Butler (1951–5), Roy Jenkins (1967–70), Denis Healey (1974–6), and Gordon Brown (1997–2007). The prime minister meanwhile, who, remember, is the one without a Whitehall department of their own, found that they did not *need* one to be dominant in foreign policy. Just a handful of very bright diplomats in Number 10, or one in Thatcher's case, provided all they needed to know.

Technology, as we have seen throughout the book, changed the nature of communication and boosted the capability of the prime minister. Lloyd George was the first prime minister to be in regular contact with what was happening on the battlefields. Chamberlain's visits to Germany, and Churchill's flights during the Second World War, set the direction for the postwar international premiership. Hotlines to Moscow and Washington, and secure lines through the telephone sitting on the prime minister's desk in Number 10, bypassed their need to work through the Foreign Office's network of ambassadors and plenipoten-tiaries. 'The consequence of this the technology is that foreign affairs became much more personalised with the prime minister in Downing Street', says former Cabinet Secretary Robin Butler. 'Blair spoke to Bush regularly while Foreign Secretary Jack Straw was often kept in the dark', having to be informed privately through indirect channels.[98] Ease of travel means that foreign leaders pass far more easily through London, and when they do, 'it is not good enough for them to see the Foreign Secretary, they all want to see the prime minister'.[99]

The increasing sophistication of intelligence and paramount need for secrecy equally further focused power in the prime minister, a process begun under Salisbury with the Official Secrets Act 1889 and continued by Asquith with the Secret Service Bureau in 1909 and Official Secrets Act 1911.[100] MI5, which oversees homeland security, and MI6, or the Secret Intelligence Service, were both originally established by him in 1909. The Government Code and Cipher School was created in 1919 out of separate intelligence-gathering offices run by the services, and it adopted its name, GCHQ, in 1946. Churchill was intrigued by their world and understood the value of intelligence during the Second World War, building up the Joint Intelligence Committee (JIC) under him as the central machine of intelligence-gathering: 'Above all, he understood the importance of intelligence at the top and was the first Prime Minister to have a special assistant dealing only with intelligence', write Richard Aldrich and Rory Cormac.[101] In 1957, the JIC was removed from the Chiefs of Staff and brought directly under the prime minister in the Cabinet Office: 'the Prime Minister is the only minister who can lead the entire UK intelligence and security effort. Only he or she is in a position to take a complete overview', says Hennessy, who adds wryly, 'most premiers love this side of their work – so much more exciting than dealing with local government finance'.[102]

Britain became a nuclear power in 1952 when it detonated its first atomic bomb on the Montebello Islands near Australia, which was followed in 1957 by its first hydrogen bomb test. A desire to reduce overall defence expenditure meant that in 1963 Macmillan secured US agreement to supply Britain with Polaris missiles and the submarine technology to deliver them. Since 1994 Britain has used the Trident missile system, based on four submarines, at least one of which is constantly on patrol carrying up to sixteen Trident II nuclear missiles. It further increased the power of the prime minister by placing the authorisation for a nuclear strike in their hand, not that of the Foreign Secretary.

Nuclear, security, and intelligence cooperation, which has underpinned the special relationship between the United States and Britain since 1945, again played to the prime minister, whose relationship with a succession of US presidents, reaching a high point with Churchill and Truman (1951–2), Macmillan and Eisenhower (1957–61), Macmillan and Kennedy (1961–3), Thatcher and Reagan (1981–9), and Blair and Bush (2001–7), focused attention again on Number 10. In this big league, there is less space for the Foreign Secretary, except as an interlocuter for less critical issues. The ambassadorship to the US though has survived as a relatively important position, not least because of the need to cultivate friendships with the presidential administration.

The explosion of multinational gatherings since 1945 has further played to the strengths of the prime minister and to the detriment of the Foreign Secretary. It is the prime minister who is expected to travel to gatherings of world leaders, including the UN General Assembly from 1946, NATO summits from 1974, G7 meetings from 1975, EU Councils from 1975, and G20 from 2008.[103] 'Travel, summits, meetings, became much more common, particularly after Britain joined the European Union', says Michael Jay. 'Prime ministers became much more involved, they travelled more, and the Foreign Office would have to brief them. I think the shift came in the 1960s and 70s with Number 10 having more influence.'[104]

Gordon Brown wrote about this personal aspect of modern diplomacy in his memoirs:

Now prime ministers regularly meet their counterparts at annual gatherings ... and on any day you can talk by phone or video. It is yet another instance in which the direct involvement of the prime minister has so markedly expanded. Communications ... now rely on constant personal contact at the top. This means that for a prime minister today, foreign affairs involve not only the calculation of national interests and ideas but the cultivation of a wide range of different individual relationships.[105]

Brown was enormously helped in his foreign policy dealings, not an area where he had much previous experience outside international finance, by the young diplomat Tom Fletcher, who throughout his time as PM guided him in his capacity as Foreign Affairs Private Secretary at Number 10.[106] This shift would not have been possible had the prime minister not been able to rely on diplomats seconded to Number 10 to help them develop their own foreign policy ideas and briefings.[107] Jock Colville, the Principal Private Secretary to Churchill (1951–5), was the first figure postwar to provide this service for the prime minister, a tradition continued with the development of the position of Foreign Affairs Private Secretary within the prime minister's Private Office team. Philip de Zulueta served Eden and then Macmillan in this capacity, his loyalty soon firmly with the PM rather than the Foreign Office from whence he came. Michael Palliser continued the tradition of fiercely independent-minded diplomats advising the prime minister. George Brown blamed Palliser for turning Harold Wilson's mind against his and the Foreign Office's advice: 'We thought we had sent the prime minister a Father Confessor, it turns out we sent him a Cardinal Secretary of State', John Kerr recalls Brown saying.[108] The absolutely pivotal figure in this process was Charles Powell, Foreign Affairs Private Secretary to Margaret Thatcher from 1983–90. He became, with her Press Secretary Bernard Ingham, one of her two most influential advisors in Downing Street. Thatcher had strong pro-US and increasingly anti-EU instincts which Powell helped her articulate, to the fury of the Foreign Office who repeatedly tried to move him to an ambassadorial post, all of which he flatly refused.

From Powell onwards there was no going back, and the prime minister's ability to dominate and control foreign policy was enshrined in a series of administrative enhancements culminating in the formation of the National Security Council, chaired by the prime minister, in 2010. David Cameron explained in his memoirs:

> The rationale was simple. It no longer made sense to consider foreign policy on its own. The challenges we faced required a response from across government, not just the Foreign Office. Particularly with the rise of threats from what the experts called 'non-state actors' – basically terrorists . . .[109]

The National Security Council brought together the Foreign Office, Ministry of Defence, Home Office, and Department for International Development, along with the intelligence services and any other relevant actors. Hague described it as a 'means of pooling and bringing together foreign and security decisions for collective consideration with the Foreign Secretary and the prime minister always there together.'[110] The Foreign Secretary might well have been present: but it was the prime minister in the chair, and the meetings took place in his parish, not at the Foreign Office.

PRIME MINISTERIAL ASCENDANCY, 1979–2021

In the last forty years, almost all the major foreign policy initiatives have been initiated by the prime minister. Thatcher came to power with as little experience of foreign policy as any prime minister since 1945 but quickly made the subject her own. The Falklands War of 1982 was decisive. 'I think she lived in those hours more fully than at any other time in her premiership', recalled her Cabinet Secretary Robert Armstrong. 'She was conscious that this was her hour, and of the responsibility that fell on her to rise to it.'[111] It was Thatcher herself who authorised some of the direct operational decisions, including authorising a British submarine to sink the Argentinian cruiser, the ARA *General Belgrano*.[112]

She also set the foreign policy direction when she decided to align Britain strongly with Ronald Reagan after he became US president in 1981, forging one of the most significant relationships in postwar international politics. She took the initiative in meeting General Secretary of the Soviet Union Mikhail Gorbachev in 1985, which helped thaw the Cold War. Her premiership encapsulated in a nutshell the trajectory of the Foreign Secretary in the twentieth century: Lord Carrington, her first, had considerable authority, but by her end, she had eclipsed even Douglas Hurd, despite his experience as a former Foreign Office diplomat. On her trip to Moscow in late March/early April 1987, observers noted that she was clearly the figure who counted: 'A plenary meeting involving him was cancelled and no one cared', says Peter Riddell who was on the trip with the press. 'It was clear to us that the Foreign Secretary was doing the second-tier visits, and not the first.'[113] On the day the Berlin Wall fell, 9 November 1989, Thatcher was on her third Foreign Secretary in less than four months, the most recent, Douglas Hurd, having been in post for only two weeks.

Thatcher's increasing outspokenness on foreign policy played a role in her downfall. She followed up her Bruges speech of 1988, which upset many pro-Europeans in her party, by vocal opposition to a reunited Germany in 1989–90, which left her diplomatically isolated, with neither George Bush nor Francois Mitterrand prepared to join her in opposing the process.[114] Foreign policy resolve over the Falklands had helped to make her premiership; it would be her foreign policy resolve on Europe that helped to isolate her and bring it to an end.

The most important decisions under John Major, to take Britain into the Maastricht Treaty, and secure the opt-outs, and British involvement in the former Yugoslavia's wars, were his. Blair chose military intervention in Kosovo and to align with President George W. Bush after 9/11 in the wars in Afghanistan and Iraq. His three foreign secretaries (Robin Cook, Jack Straw, and Margaret Beckett) were all marginalised. Cameron's principal foreign policy decisions, to foster relations with China and India, to participate in military action against Gaddafi's Libya in 2011, and to offer a referendum on continuing membership of the EU, were taken by him, closely consulting William Hague (2010–14), who, as a former party leader and Conservative grandee, had more political experience than either him or Osborne. Theresa May's policy on securing Britain's exit from the EU and her coordination of the international response against Putin's Russia in the wake of the Salisbury poisonings by Novichok in March 2018 were equally her own, as have been the principal foreign policy decisions under Boris Johnson, above all in his hardline stance against the EU. Not, as we have seen, that the PM is unchecked in their foreign ambitions.

Need it have ended up like this? After Carrington, Thatcher appointed Francis Pym her Foreign Secretary, later writing in her memoirs witheringly that she disagreed with him on 'policy ... approach to government and indeed about life in general'.[115] Consider Blair's curt words to Cook when he replaced him in 2001. 'I want you to move. I know this is not fair. You have not done anything wrong, but I do need to make changes.'[116] The change he most wanted to make was to move Gordon Brown into the job, but Brown thought the position insufficiently important and would not even consider it. In 2016, the appointment of Boris Johnson as Foreign Secretary was a shock to most, but not as big a shock as it was to Johnson himself when he realised how little power he wielded: he became frustrated and eventually resigned.[117]

The Foreign Secretary's main task by 2021 had become to support the overall policies set by the prime minister, by meeting foreign counterparts, attending summits and negotiations on their behalf, and crunching the detail. Hague puts it thus:

> A Foreign Secretary and their prime minister need to be absolutely agreed on what are their overall objectives. But the great majority of the diplomatic work and a lot of decisions about 'how are we going to get that UN Security Council vote and what is it exactly we are putting to the United Nations?' are still done by the Foreign Secretary.[118]

Could this relationship change again? With the Foreign Office absorbing the Department for International Development in 2020, and some restructuring of the budget for foreign policy, the Foreign Secretary may well grow again in power. But the direction of travel, evident in most other countries, so clearly favours the head of government over the Foreign Secretary, that significant change is unlikely. Rather, as we suggest in the final chapter, other steps are needed to bolster the Foreign Secretary.

Some of the same forces that militated against the Foreign Secretary have benefited another great office holder, the Chancellor of the Exchequer, which is now the biggest challenge and threat to the authority of the prime minister, as we see in the next chapter.

CHAPTER 9

The Rise, and Rise, of the Chancellor
of the Exchequer, 1660–2021

BY THE EARLY TWENTIETH CENTURY THE PRIME MINISTER had reached the status of being the preeminent figure in British politics. The monarchy and the royal court had steadily declined in influence, as seen in Chapter 7. The Foreign Secretary and the Foreign Office rose, but then fell in power, as described in Chapter 8. But the Chancellor of the Exchequer and the Treasury rose, and then rose again, to become, by the end of the twentieth century, the biggest single potential challenge to the power of the prime minister. No longer subordinate at all. Naked political power, ambition, the knowledge that some were virtually unsackable, and the backing of the mighty resource of the Treasury, ensured that Chancellors could be a power to themselves, strutting around Westminster and Whitehall like an almighty baron in medieval England.

The Treasury over the last century has accumulated more powers than almost any of its equivalents abroad. The United States, in addition to its Treasury, has the Office of Management and Budget at the White House, the Federal Reserve Board for monetary policy, and the Council of Economic Advisors providing economic counsel. The British Treasury is far more powerful, and saw off the Foreign Office and the Home Office. It accommodated itself to the rise of the Cabinet Office, and it repelled a series of attacks on its power and independence by Number 10. Routinely, each new PM and team arrive in Number 10 determined to seize control of the major financial events: routinely, the Treasury sees them off. It is the great survivor. No one has summed up its power more succinctly than J. M. Keynes: a 'very clever, very dry and in a certain sense very cynical [place]; intellectually self-confident'.[1] Reaching this elevated position was not preordained, as we shall see in this chapter, and it occurred through seven successive phases, often associated with a commanding figure, usually the Chancellor, who has shaped the office, much as our landmark prime ministers have done.

THE DOWNING TREASURY, 1660–1782

George Downing, Teller of the Exchequer (1660–84), the office that collected taxes and revenues, was much more than the property speculator who built the houses on either side of Downing Street. He was a seminal figure in the evolution of financial and commercial policy, especially after he became Secretary of the Commissioners of the Treasury in 1667. Many other figures were to shape the Treasury over the following 120 years, but none as important as him, in a way still largely recognisable when Pitt became First Lord and Chancellor in 1783.

Charles II was more business-like than many Stuart monarchs. He realised the Second Anglo-Dutch War (1665–7) had been a military and financial disaster, and determined to overhaul the government's financial system to ensure it didn't happen again. The upshot was a new Treasury Commission, drawing on the experience of government finances in the Netherlands and also France, where the brilliant Colbert had taken over control of government finances in 1661. The Treasury henceforth demanded that all requests for money from the navy, the army, and the Royal Household be countersigned by a Treasury Lord.

Downing was responsible for the introduction of the principle of 'appropriation of supply' which ensured that the monarch would no longer be at liberty to spend revenue agreed by Parliament at will, but only in ways it had specifically designated. Parliament's oversight of royal spending was enhanced further when the Civil List, which the monarch used to spend at pleasure, was brought under its remit, with annual votes 'steadily chipping away' at the royal prerogative. By the time William IV became king in 1830, the Civil List was restricted only to the expenses of the Royal Household.[2]

The Treasury's influence over the House of Commons was critical to its ascendancy, Treasury official Nick Macpherson argues, as was its ability to raise money for war and to outwit other departments in Whitehall. Its tight grip ensured that the War of the Spanish Succession (1701–14) could be comfortably financed. The setting up of the Bank of England in 1694 and the rapid development of the City of London helped the funding environment, while vital resolutions of the House of Commons in 1706 and 1713 conceded the right of financial initiative, i.e. proposing taxation and spending, to representatives of 'the Crown', i.e. to Treasury ministers.[3]

When Walpole became Chancellor of the Exchequer in 1716, he introduced the 'Sinking Fund' to reduce the national debt (albeit only in operation after he left office in 1717). In an effort to reduce national debt further, the Treasury tried to convert floating debt into stock in the South Sea Company, a calamitous decision. The fiasco precipitated Walpole's appointment as First Lord of the Treasury in 1721, a position combined with the Chancellor, if a member of the House of Commons, until 1841 (except for a brief period in 1743 when Samuel Sandys was Chancellor and Pelham First Lord whilst both were in the Commons). When both roles were not occupied by the same person, it became the custom for the Chancellor to occupy the second place to the First Lord in the Treasury Commission.[4]

Britain's first annual Budget, another historic innovation, outlining fiscal measures to help restore confidence after the 'South Sea Bubble', was delivered by Walpole in the early 1720s.[5] In 1733, he attempted to introduce an excise tax on wine and tobacco, which led to an outcry. By the 1760s, the annual Budget had become firmly established: in 1764, Grenville introduced a sugar tax and stamp duty to collect extra revenue from the American Colonies. Applauded by the 'whole House' at the time, these measures caused outrage in the colonies and escalated the burgeoning American crisis.[6]

The Treasury's move in the 1730s into its new Kent-designed offices at the end of Downing Street further strengthened its relationship with Walpole, with the Treasury's sheer proximity further boosting his power. This gave him the unofficial power of a 'parliamentary' or 'patronage Secretary' – later to become the job of Chief Whip – and helped him ensure the distribution of posts that he needed to secure the passage of legislation. The junior Lords of the Treasury were crucial supporters in Parliament, and have become 'junior whips' today, thereby consolidating the Treasury's control: 'With every extension of the financial basis of government, the Treasury's access to the roots of power grew more secure', writes Henry Roseveare.[7] J. H. Plumb summarises Walpole's two particular uses for the Treasury thus: patronage, i.e. the trading of money for parliamentary support, and using its financial role to justify his interventions in the departmental affairs of other ministers.[8]

The twelve prime ministers following Walpole until Pitt the Younger all, with the exception of Rockingham and Pitt the Elder, saw their core task in office as the oversight of financial matters. None managed it better than North, particularly in the first years after his appointment in 1770 before the American War diverted him. North introduced a new system, anticipating some of the recommendations of the Northcote-Trevelyan Report of 1854, which ensured that each Treasury official should 'personally transact the business assigned to them', thereby challenging the culture of absenteeism, as well as introducing training and the principle of merit as justification for promotion. A Treasury minute cited by Macpherson puts it thus: 'ability, attention, care and diligence of the respective clerks, and not their seniority' were now valued within the Treasury.[9] Another edge over rival departments of state, brainpower, was thus handed to it.

THE PITT TREASURY, 1782–1852

Like Walpole, Pitt the Younger became Chancellor before becoming prime minister, appointed in July 1782 at the age of just twenty-three, nine months before George III moved him up to the premiership. As historian Patrick O'Brien neatly puts it: 'To the disdain of his aristocratic colleagues and his Whig opponents, Pitt gave more attention to public finance than to any other area of statecraft . . . in an age when most [MPs] could hardly count or be bothered with matters that Wilberforce referred to as of "a low and vulgarising quality".'[10] He recognised that financial mastery was sine qua non to his dominating the House of Commons and retaining the confidence of the monarch.

Pitt came to power as the wars in North America were winding down. By 1783, the national debt had risen to £243 million in government loan stock, with interest alone consuming over half the government's annual revenue. Yet he managed within three years to increase revenue sufficiently to cover expenditure by persuading Parliament to increase duties on luxuries and other items. In the 1780s, an estimated one-fifth of potential tax revenue was being lost because of smuggling activities. So he sought to reduce the tariffs on goods that were easily smuggled, including tea, wine, spirits, and tobacco, which led to customs and excise rising by almost £2 million a year as the activity became less profitable. His methods were successful in pecuniary terms, and saw him also engage in strong-arm tactics, as in Deal in Kent, a notorious hive of smuggling, where in January 1784 he dispatched troops to set fire to all the boats in the town.[11]

In 1786, as Walpole had done before him, Pitt introduced a 'sinking fund'. The wars against France from 1793 posed an even bigger headache, with public spending rising from 12 to 23 per cent of national income. By 1815, national debt had risen from £2 million, or about 5 per cent of GDP, in 1688 to £834 million, twice the national income.[12] A financial crisis in 1797 saw him ordering the Bank of England to suspend the convertibility of its notes and cash, effectively taking Britain off the gold standard.[13] Through a mixture of borrowing and tax innovation, including the introduction of the temporary 'income tax' of 1799, Pitt was able to finance the war, the longest and most expensive of the modern era (from 1793–1815), ensuring the navy and the army had the money that they needed to fight. He provided the Chancellor with the tools for the management of the economy, which were to prepare the ground for more activist social and economic policies to come.

The years that followed Pitt's death in 1806 were important in the post of Chancellor establishing its own identity, notably under Liverpool (1812–27); with the PM a Lord, the Chancellor necessarily sat in the Commons. Nicholas Vansittart (1812–23), as the longest incumbent since 1721, provided stability, not least through longevity, though he is best-known as the Chancellor who lost income tax to a Commons rebellion in 1816. Frederick Robinson (1823–7) was a much happier and more competent Chancellor than he was prime minister (known then as the Viscount Goderich), who 'gave with Vansittart an identity of its own to the Chancellor position, not just as the First Lord's subordinate', as Coleman puts it.[14] Lord Althorp, Grey's Chancellor (1830–4) then built on their work, acting as the clear second, or more, in the ministry. After his elevation to the Lords as Earl Spencer in 1834, the ministry crumbled.[15]

Major change came in 1841 when Peel separated the jobs of prime minister and Chancellor of the Exchequer, even when, like him, the PM sat in the Commons (only Gladstone in 1873–4 and 1880–2 and Baldwin in 1923 briefly combined both offices thereafter). Peel nevertheless, shorn of the Chancellorship, continued to present Budgets after 1841 (a recognition of the importance of seizing the bold major financial event of his day). But he sought to free himself of the detailed financial oversight of the Chancellor to range more easily across all government policy: 'The office of prime minister had become a full-time job by 1841, hence his decision to release himself from the day-to-day running of the Treasury', says Hawkins.[16] Peel's Chancellor from 1841, Henry Goulburn, who had been Chancellor under Wellington from 1828–30, was not prominent, acting almost as a Chief Secretary to the Treasury for Peel. The Whig Lord John Russell, who succeeded Peel in 1846, pointedly did not take back the Chancellorship of the Exchequer. Derby, who followed briefly in 1852, was in the Lords, and made the voluble Benjamin Disraeli his Chancellor, who in turn was succeeded in the Aberdeen coalition by the forty-two-year-old Peelite William Gladstone. A pattern had been set.

THE GLADSTONE TREASURY, 1852–1908

No Chancellor of the Exchequer in history has made more impact on the office than William Gladstone, four times Chancellor (1852–5, 1859–66, 1873–4, and 1880–2), the last two whilst also prime minister. No Chancellor of the Exchequer before, who was not also prime minister, wielded so much broad authority. 'The Treasury was asserting its right to control the activities and personnel of the Civil Service as a whole', writes Colin Matthew. 'Gladstone asserted the political position of the Chancellor in the Cabinet, in Parliament and hence in the country.'[17] Gladstone's presence still looms large over the Treasury, as it does Number 11, where his image is ubiquitous. His shadow can still be seen on Budget Day: until 2010, the red despatch box used by Chancellors was almost always his own, and the current replacement is modelled upon it.[18] It is his principles which still inform the Treasury 170 years later: free trade, sound money, and a passion for efficiency, accountability, and the avoidance of waste. As he said in 1879: 'No Chancellor of the Exchequer is worth his salt who is not ready to save what are meant by candle-ends and cheese-parings', referring to the requirement that every drop of taxpayers' money be wisely spent.[19] As Toye argues: 'He was not content merely to balance the books on a year-by-year basis but had a political programme and a vision of how to create prosperity, which put the Exchequer at the heart of domestic politics.' As Gladstone himself said in 1858: 'Finance is, as it were, the stomach of the country, from which all the other organs take their tone.'[20]

Aberdeen first appointed him Chancellor in his mixed Whig and Peelite coalition. His first Budget in April 1853 lasted nearly five hours, was widely praised by contemporaries, and established him as a figure with absolute mastery over finance. This first Gladstonian Budget almost completed the work of Peel in his 1842 Budget, simplifying duties and customs, with 123 duties abolished and 135 reduced. He announced that he wanted to abolish income tax but proposed to extend it for seven years before doing so. His second Budget in March 1854 came five months after the outbreak of the Crimean War. To pay for it, he now proposed raising income tax, as well duties on spirits, malt, and sugar: 'The expenses of a war are the moral check which it has pleased the Almighty to impose upon the ambition and lust of conquest', he proclaimed in a speech bristling with religious and moral fervour.[21]

The Northcote-Trevelyan Report of 1854 (the first to become a Chancellor, the latter Treasury Permanent Secretary) was commissioned by Gladstone when Chancellor and signalled his belief that promotion should be based on merit and open competition rather than familial connections. Building on the earlier initiatives of North, it stands as the landmark in the evolution of the British Civil Service, that was later much copied across the dominions and nations beyond. Unimpressed by the progress in the intervening fourteen years, however, it was only when he became prime minister in 1868 that he asked his own Chancellor, Robert Lowe, to act on the Report. The Foreign Office and Home Office resisted on the grounds that 'character' and not intellect were important in promotion, leaving the Treasury to benefit from the open competition that the Report had advocated, further entrenching its aim to recruit the ablest; a characteristic that has helped it to keep ahead of its departmental rivals in Whitehall over the intervening 150 years.[22]

Gladstone's pioneering reforms came mostly in his second period at the Treasury under Palmerston and Russell from 1859–66, when he clashed frequently with the former. Prevailing economic thought, as far as the Treasury was ever affected by it, was dictated by the writings of Adam Smith, Thomas Malthus, David Ricardo, and John Stuart Mill. They believed that prosperity and 'liberty' were promoted more by the actions of private individuals and companies rather than government spending: 'It [is] clear that that money, if left to fructify in the pockets of the people, would be productive of infinitely more benefit to the country', as an earlier parliamentarian, Lord Milton, memorably said.[23] The Crimean War had finished three years before, but Gladstone still inherited a deficit of nearly £5 million in 1859. His Budget in February 1860 showed his commitment to free trade, with a reduction of the 419 duties in 1859 down to merely 48. To finance it, he was forced to increase income tax, but when conditions allowed, smartly reduced it in stages from 1861–5.

He found himself at odds with Palmerston over the abolition of duty on paper, recording in his diary that in one Cabinet meeting 'Lord P spoke 3/4 hour [against] Paper Duties Bill!' Palmerston went over his head to write to Victoria that the House of Lords would perform a 'good public service' if they were to vote down the bill, which they duly proceeded to do.[24] Gladstone emerged the winner though when, in his Budget of 1860 the following year, the abolition of paper duties was included in the legislative package. In so doing, he produced the first consolidated financial bill, establishing a precedent of there being only one financial bill per parliamentary session, which endured thereafter. As Matthew writes, 'Gladstone believed that big bills and budgets were a necessary feature not merely of executive government but of post-1832 politics.'[25] By the very act of consolidation, he made it much harder for Parliament to vote it down, a big increase in the Chancellor's power. His outflanking of the Lords was a significant personal success too, the repeal of the paper duties paving the way for a mass, cheap, and popular press which dutifully rewarded Gladstone with favourable coverage and column inches.

In 1861, he set up the House of Commons' Public Accounts Committee (PAC) which ever since has helped ensure that public money is spent with strict parliamentary oversight. His Exchequer and Audit Departments Act in his final year as only Chancellor in 1866 then brought together estimates, appropriation, expenditure, and audit into one system, ensuring that in future 'Treasury control' was further embedded. The House of Commons would now require prior approval, for amount and purpose, year by year, of all government expenditure. Henceforth, 'no department could ensure new expenditure, or add to its establishment of civil servants, or their salaries, without Treasury assent', wrote Peden.[26] The Office of Comptroller and Auditor General was created by the Act, combining the Comptroller General's responsibility for authorising the issue of public monies with the Commissioners of Audit's responsibility for presenting the government accounts to the Treasury. In 1872, after Gladstone had become prime minister, the Treasury introduced a new system whereby permanent secretaries of Whitehall departments (i.e. their top civil servant) would be nominated the 'accounting officers' for signing off the accounts to the Comptroller, taking the responsibility themselves for spending within their departments. Macpherson cites Warren Fisher, the long-serving Permanent Secretary at the Treasury (1919–39), telling the PAC in 1921: 'It should not be open to any permanent head ... to say "please, sir, it wasn't me" ... Pin it on him in the last resort and you have got him as an ally for economy.'[27]

None of the Chancellors who followed Peel had been especially prominent figures: Henry Goulburn, Charles Wood, and Cornewall Lewis; even Disraeli failed to sparkle. When Disraeli was first asked in 1852 by Derby to become Chancellor, he pleaded ignorance: Derby tried to reassure him, saying he shouldn't worry because 'anyway they [the Treasury officials] give you the figures'.[28] Gladstone almost alone created the modern and independent Chancellor of the Exchequer as one of the major posts in government apart from the prime minister. After him, the office took a dip before another Chancellor in the early twentieth century rewrote the rulebook again, changing the stature and scope of the office forever.

When Salisbury appointed Randolph Churchill Chancellor (and Leader of the Commons) in August 1886 on his return as prime minister, 'the implication now seemed to be that the Chancellor was the senior domestic post in the Commons when the PM was in the Lords', writes Coleman.[29] But the battle that autumn over army estimates, which Churchill wanted to be cut, saw him offering a high-risk resignation, Salisbury calling his bluff, and Churchill's fiery departure that December. It caused Salisbury to rethink his statecraft. Like some later prime ministers, Winston Churchill in the war and Macmillan, he now went for biddable Chancellors, George Goschen (1887–92) and Michael Hicks Beach (1895–1902), neither lightweights, but neither domineering presences. Further, he removed the Commons leadership from them, giving it instead to the easy-going W. H. Smith (1887–91), then to his nephew Arthur Balfour (1891–2 and 1895–1905), both of whom combined the position with First Lord of the Treasury (the first non-PMs to do so since 1768), clearly denoting that they, not the Chancellor, were the senior domestic figure below the prime minister.

LLOYD GEORGE'S TREASURY, 1908–47

Lloyd George was the first Chancellor to clamber out above the roof of the Treasury, and to drive and dictate government policy on subjects that went far beyond its usual lot of financial policy. Not only did he drive social and economic policy, but he extended his reach into major foreign policy concerns, to the consternation of the Foreign Secretary. The job of Chancellor and the position of the Treasury were never the same again after him, and the impression that he left lasted for forty years until Stafford Cripps gave the Chancellor's job a new twist from 1947. Gladstone's Chancellorship had seen the office establish itself as a very senior post in government, second only to the Foreign Secretary, and clearly above the Home Secretary. After Lloyd George's Chancellorship, depending on the incumbent, the position became more prominent even than the Foreign Secretary, despite the Treasury remaining for the next three decades primarily a *finance* department.

The Treasury in 1900 was still not the all-powerful body it was to become by mid century. Salisbury said that year that 'by exercising the power of the purse it [the Treasury] claims a voice in all decisions of administrative authority and policy'.[30] Other Whitehall departments, however, had powers and means to circumvent the Treasury's wishes: 'It had to contend with the fact that there are always people who can think of new ways in which to spend public money', wrote Peden.[31] The Reform Acts of 1867 and 1884 saw mounting demands from parliamentary elites for expenditure on social needs, including schooling and sanitary reform. But the financial regime to deliver them had very limited involvement from central government, and ensured local government was left to do the heavy lifting, which was largely self-supporting through local rates (many more paid them than income tax). It gave local government a particular utility and purpose. The expansion in central government spending that came in the last quarter of the nineteenth century was thus predominantly directed at the navy and army: in 1880, 33 per cent of central government spending went on defence, and this had risen to 41 per cent by 1905.[32]

Lloyd George, appointed Chancellor in April 1908 by Asquith, was quick off the mark, introducing the Old-Age Pensions Act only a month later. In his first few months, he fell out with suffragettes, who felt that he was not doing enough to promote their cause in Parliament, and was outvoted in Cabinet on navy spending, on which he had stuck to the line in the Liberal Party manifesto, arguing it should be cut. He sought to build upon the seminal creation of old-age pensions by finding money for state financial support for the sick and infirm (once known as 'going on the Lloyd George'). This impetus eventually became the transformative National Insurance Act of 1911 with benefits based on contributions from government, employers, and the workers themselves. As Kenneth Morgan explains, Lloyd George 'was determined that his new social venture should appear financially sound, while the familiar principle of insurance provision gave it a broad popular credibility'.[33] The proposals were developed largely independently of Asquith, even though he himself had been Lloyd George's predecessor as Chancellor.

In his 1909 Budget, described by Roy Jenkins as the 'most reverberating' since Gladstone's in 1860,[34] Lloyd George imposed a 20 per cent tax on the unearned increase in the value of land, an increase in death duties, a rise in income tax, and the introduction of 'super tax' on annual income over £3,000 p.a. Indirect taxes on luxuries and alcohol were also introduced. Landowners in and outside the House of Lords were incensed. Rosebery broke from the Liberal Party he had led until 1896, while Conservative leader Balfour denounced the measures as 'vindictive, inequitable, based on no principle, and injurious to the productive capacity of the country'.[35] During the protracted battles with the House of Lords that followed, Asquith distanced himself at times from Lloyd George's 'wilder rhetorical excesses'.[36] Indeed, concern was expressed across the political spectrum, not least at the Liberals' reliance on Irish votes in Westminster.

The passage of the Parliament Act of 1911, following the two close general elections of 1910, did little to assuage wide sections of opinion, but was a moral vindication for Lloyd George. A newly emboldened figure, he gave the Chancellor's speech at Mansion House in July 1911 after consultation with Asquith and Foreign Secretary Grey, during mounting tensions in Morocco, known as the Agadir Crisis. Despite being himself pro-German, a minority view in Cabinet, and his earlier resistance to military spending, Lloyd George came out as a patriotic warrior proclaiming that German aggression should be tamed: 'If a situation were to be forced upon us in which peace could only be preserved by the surrender of the great and beneficent position Britain has won by centuries of heroism and achievement . . . then I say emphatically that peace at that price would be a humiliation intolerable for a great country like ours to endure.'[37] Germany was incensed, saying that the speech had done 'untold harm to relations'. In his memoirs, Foreign Secretary Grey cited the German response in remarking that 'Mr Lloyd George's speech came upon us like a thunderbolt'.[38] Never before had a Chancellor of the Exchequer strode so boldly onto the Foreign Secretary's turf at such a sensitive time on an issue of such major national importance.

Lloyd George had not expected relations with Germany to break down quite so quickly, and was one of those reluctant in Cabinet in late July 1914 to see the country become involved in a war. But at the critical Cabinet on 3 August, he changed his position based on liberal principles concerning the rights of small nations, and argued that the invasion of Belgium now legitimised British intervention. His shift proved influential in persuading other members of the Cabinet to commit to war on 4 August. Asquith's biographer, Roy Jenkins, believes it was 'crucial'.[39] Such a monumental decision required the support of all of Cabinet. Like Pitt and Gladstone before him, he now had to find the money for war, doing so by debt-financing £321 million, large (but deferred) increases in income tax, and increases in excise duties.[40] He gave up the Treasury in May 1915 to become Minister of Munitions, but the office of Chancellor was changed forever.

The First World War brought the Treasury closer to the Bank of England. From Pitt and before, with rare exceptions such as Walpole's sinking fund, the latter operated largely separately, responsible for the bank rate, in effect the rate at which it lent to other banks. The Governor was rarely seen at the Treasury or the Chancellor at the Bank. But they now became frequent visitors, as both institutions grappled with financing the conflict.[41] The Great War also precipitated a global banking crisis, with banks calling in their loans to stockbrokers and the London Stock Exchange being forced to close on 31 July 1914. Keynes and Lloyd George averted disaster with their emergency treasury team: markets reopened on 7 August, interest rates were reduced from 10 to 5 per cent on 8 August, and the printing of £1 banknotes was announced by the Treasury. Their quick action helped to restore calm amid growing financial panic.[42]

The Treasury under Lloyd George, and for his successors until the 1940s, remained fundamentally the finance ministry it had been since Downing. Its three principal tasks were to raise revenue to match central government spending and ensure through Parliament that spending was kept at a level compatible with tax revenues; to oversee the gold standard, which fixed the value of sterling in terms of gold and against other currencies also on the gold standard, giving the Bank of England a target free of political pressure in its management of the monetary system; and finally, to encourage free trade, to ensure that no one producer group would exert undue pressure for its own objectives. But fresh demands were being made of the Treasury. Involvement of central government in social policy from the start of the century increased the demand for revenue, and financing the First World War placed further burdens, damaging the gold standard's supposedly automatic ability to ensure the soundness of sterling, while high unemployment levels after the war placed further pressures on it to find the money.[43]

Just as well that the Treasury was strengthened by a series of powerful Chancellors of the Exchequer in the interwar years, including Austen Chamberlain (1921–2), Stanley Baldwin (1922–3), Philip Snowden (1924, 1929–31), and Neville Chamberlain (1923–4, 1931–7). All held their own against their prime ministers, and some, including Chamberlain with MacDonald, were the more dominant political figure. Chamberlain, who had turned down the offer of Chancellor in 1924 in preference to Minister of Health (1924–9), said of his period as Chancellor in the 1930s: 'I am more and more carrying this government on my back.'[44] Few achieved more as Chancellor – the Ottawa agreements in 1932 (a form of imperial preference), alleviating some of the hardship caused by the Great Depression through the creation of the Unemployment Assistance Board, and greater state involvement in the economy: off the back of his record 'he was one of only two Chancellors after 1918, Brown being the other, to win the premiership *because of* it'.[45] Since 1918, only five of the twenty prime ministers have moved directly from the Treasury to Number 10 (Baldwin, Chamberlain, Macmillan, Major, and Brown).

A new type of Chancellor had been born. Before Lloyd George, many, whether they were aware of it and complicit or not, were swept up in the overall Treasury view, so pervasive was it, and so intellectually brilliant were the officials in contrast to their ministers. Lloyd George broke this rule, and was still being described in the late 1920s as the only Chancellor 'who had made the Treasury do what it had not wanted to do'.[46]

Underpinning these interwar Chancellors and the evolution of the Treasury was Warren Fisher, Permanent Secretary, who combined the job with the new position of Head of the Home Civil Service (1919–39). This allowed him, and the Treasury, even more licence and means to range more over the whole of Whitehall. The Treasury was far from pleased when Lloyd George created the Cabinet Office in December 1916. It tried and failed to smother or absorb it at the end of the war, and the interwar years would see regular turf wars between Fisher and first Cabinet Secretary, Maurice Hankey (1916–38).[47] But, with Lloyd George gone, and none of the rapid succession of prime ministers in the next two years, Bonar Law, Baldwin, and MacDonald, having the same interest in the new secretariat, Fisher steadily outgunned Hankey. By the mid 1920s, the Treasury had re-established itself as the core home department in Whitehall.

Fisher had to see off another challenge to Treasury primacy from the Home Office, which had the formidable John Anderson as its Permanent Secretary from 1922; a potential threat alleviated when Anderson was appointed Governor of Bengal in 1932. Anderson later 'swapped sides', becoming an MP in 1938, and Home Secretary and then Chancellor of the Exchequer in the War Cabinet (1943–45). Permanent Secretary at the Foreign Office was another powerful adversary, particularly when in 1930 Robert Vansittart moved into the position from Number 10, where he had been Principal Private Secretary. Fisher even sought authority over Foreign Office appointments. His influence was feared across Whitehall departments, it being widely understood that desire for promotion by ambitious officials in other departments involved them pleasing rather than upsetting the Treasury.[48]

Fisher was responsible for introducing City figures into Treasury discussions, including Reginald McKenna, the former Chancellor (1915–16), who had moved on to the more lucrative berth of the Midland Bank as Chair. The close proximity of the Treasury to the City of London ensured that its London bias, a feature of its outlook since its origins, continued, as reflected by officials' financial reading, 'dominated by the *Economist*, the *Financial Times*, the *Statist* and *The Times*', as Peden found in the Treasury files. To which he adds: 'It is doubtful whether advice from academic economists based in Cambridge or Oxford did much to broaden this world view.'[49] Indeed. And not just in the interwar years.

The Treasury's cause was helped by a six-fold leap in the number of its senior staff. In 1906, it had only 27 senior officials, just one more than in 1870, but by 1947, when Cripps became Chancellor of the Exchequer, this number had risen to 168.[50] It recruited too some of the most brilliant civil servants, including Richard Hopkins and Edward Bridges, both later Permanent Secretaries of the Treasury, as well as a new generation whose careers blossomed in the early postwar years.

The undergraduate degree combining Philosophy, Politics and Economics (PPE) had become established at Oxford in the 1920s as a modern alternative to 'Greats' (Classics): Economics as a discipline was taking off too at Cambridge, and at the London School of Economics. The Treasury might have remained sceptical about the subject's practical relevance, sticking to its nostrums of the 'Treasury view' which rejected the role of fiscal policy. But economics was the coming subject, and ambitious young graduates, who had long been attracted to the Treasury for its financial activity, also saw it increasingly as an intellectually stimulating place of employment.

Keynes himself had resigned from the Treasury in 1919 to return to Cambridge, and in the 1920s, dogged Treasury officials prepared briefs for Chancellors countering his thinking. Retrenchment in the form of the 'Geddes Axe' followed the recession from 1921: Treasury orthodoxy was the order of the day. But change was coming. In 1930 MacDonald established an economic advisory council, and in 1939 economists received a permanent home in Whitehall with the creation of what became the Central Statistical Office (CSO) and the Economic Section. Lionel Robbins and James Meade were among the economists who helped introduce Keynesian ideas into government thinking, notably on fiscal policy and its impact on full employment.[51] To most prime ministers, though, economics remained an alien subject: not till Wilson in 1964 did Britain have its first economically trained incumbent in Number 10.

THE CRIPPS TREASURY AND THE ERA
OF 'CO-DEPENDENCY', 1947–76

Hugh Dalton, Attlee's first Chancellor (1945–7), 'could not get his way in Cabinet, nor could he exercise comparable influence with the Prime Minister', writes Edmund Dell.[52] It was with the appointment of Stafford Cripps (1947–50), an ascetic vegetarian who had been ambassador to the USSR, and Minister of Aircraft Production during the war, that the Treasury changed from being primarily a financial department into an economic ministry as well. In its new iteration, it was to acquire responsibility for the management of the national economy. Cripps had to confront the massive debt left behind by the Second World War, and the fact that Britain didn't default, trying to pay for the war legitimately and refinancing the debt, put the chancellor, Macpherson says, in a 'totally pivotal position'.[53]

For two months before Cripps was appointed, following Dalton's shock resignation after a Budget leak, he had been 'Minister of Economic Affairs', a new post created for him that disappeared with his elevation to the Chancellorship, but which had been designed to help Attlee with countervailing advice to the Treasury. 'He was to [have had] overall responsibility for planning and exports', writes John Bew.[54] Cripps now found himself at the Treasury presiding over a much bigger job, responsible for engineering a steady improvement in the economy for three years until having to resign in October 1950 because of ill health.

The Budget of 1941 had been critical to the transition of the Treasury into an economic ministry. Under Keynes's influence, Treasury officials and Chancellor Kingsley Wood were persuaded that a detailed analysis of national income would allow government to maintain high and stable employment levels. Keynes's theory of 'aggregate demand' – as it came to be known – was more congenial to the Treasury than Labour's prewar policy of physical planning and controls, to which elements of the party remained wedded for many years afterwards.

Keynesian policies became the guiding light of policy in the postwar world until the 1980s. The Treasury's capability to execute this was boosted when the Economic Section moved into it from the Cabinet Office in 1953. Nationalisation of the Bank of England in 1946 helped too by bringing it under closer Treasury oversight (although not until 1959 did the Chancellor become fully responsible for bank rate changes, making monetary policy an additional tool at his disposal). The key role the Treasury played in the 'Bretton Woods' system of monetary management, maintaining external exchange rates within 1 per cent, further aided its task of establishing and operationalising the macroeconomic policy framework. Officials devoted to work on overseas finance exploded in number: in the interwar years, there had only been one division; by the 1950s, there were eight at the Treasury.[55] In recognition of the expansion of the Treasury's work, an Economic Secretary, a second ministerial post to that of Financial Secretary, was added in 1947 (and in

1961, a new post of 'Chief Secretary' was added, to support the Chancellor specifically on public expenditure).

The Chancellor's position with his colleagues was strengthened again when, in 1950, it was decided that he was able to withhold tax proposals from Cabinet until the morning of the Budget itself when, just ahead of the Budget, Cabinet would have a formal discussion of the economic and financial position of the country. Lloyd George's pathbreaking 1909 Budget had been preceded by fourteen meetings, and up to the mid 1930s, lengthy discussion in Cabinet had been common. But a leak of information to speculators in 1936 had made the Treasury cautious about a wider discussion amongst Cabinet ministers. The new era of secrecy, catalysed by the increasing practice of leaking after 1945, played into the Chancellor's hands, and into the bilateral exclusivity of his relationship with the prime minister.[56] In Whitehall, information is power.

'Co-dependency' best describes the relationship between the prime minister and Chancellor in this 1947–76 period. Chancellors needed to be strong when up against big spending beasts heading well-resourced departments, and they needed the political cover of the prime minister to win difficult battles in Cabinet. In contrast to the nineteenth century, when the Chancellors' battles were mostly with the Admiralty and War Office ministers, the new departments created in the twentieth century – Health, Education, Pensions, Housing, and Local Government – saw the biggest fights, and ones the Chancellor did not always win.

Many disagreements were ironed out between the Treasury and departments, but the more difficult issues came up through committee to full Cabinet itself. The authority of the Treasury was enhanced by the ability of its Permanent Secretary to retain the position of Head of the Home Civil Service throughout the war and postwar period until 1968, when the Civil Service Department head took it on until, in 1983, the Cabinet Secretary took over. While it lasted, it gave the Treasury considerable power across Whitehall, not least in the selection of top civil servants. The Treasury retained its near monopoly thereafter of the selection of the Principal Private Secretary (PPS) to the prime minister, which gave it a unique window and earpiece into Number 10, as well as educating the prime minister in the Treasury viewpoint.

Chancellors after Cripps were a mixed bag. Hugh Gaitskell (1950–1) and Rab Butler (1951–5) were both strong, with more economic understanding and energy than their respective prime ministers, and usually got their own way. Macmillan might not have wanted to give up the Foreign Secretary post in December 1955 to move to the Treasury, having only just moved to the FO eight months before, but he visibly outfoxed Prime Minister Eden on economic as well as political matters. As prime minister, he learnt his lesson when he appointed independent-minded Peter Thorneycroft as his first Chancellor, who resigned with his two junior ministers in 1958, complaining about Macmillan's munificent financial plans, a move some historians have seen as anticipating Thatcher's restraint, underlined when she brought back Thorneycroft as her first party chairman in 1975.[57] Macmillan then appointed two biddable figures in succession: Heathcoat-Amory (1958–60), well-liked but no Keynes, and Labrador-loyal Selwyn Lloyd (1960–2), whom he sacked. Nigel Birch, one of the two to resign with Thorneycroft, wrote to *The Times* on 14 July 1962 after the 'Night of the Long Knives': 'For the second time, the Prime Minister has got rid of a Chancellor of the Exchequer who tried to get expenditure under control. Once is more than enough.'[58] Macmillan, who had blithely dismissed the 1958 resignations as 'a little local difficulty', never recovered from the 1962 sacking of the Chancellor, along with six other colleagues, showing the limitation of prime ministerial power.

Wilson came to power in October 1964 absolutely determined to be the master of the Chancellor and the Treasury, and he was fired up by being the only professional economist/statistician to become prime minister. Having had a ringside seat in Attlee's Cabinet while Cripps embraced economic policy within the Treasury, he decided to separate it again by creating a 'Department of Economic Affairs' (DEA). Prioritising growth was his mission, and he believed the Treasury was altogether too laissez faire and overly obsessed not with promoting it, but with controlling expenditure. It was a reasonable enough change: many other countries have economic ministries separate from their finance ministries. To strengthen his economic advice in Downing Street too, he brought in two sympathetic economists: Thomas Balogh from Balliol College, Oxford and Nicholas Kaldor from King's College, Cambridge, along with Peter Shore as his Parliamentary Private Secretary, the author of the 1964 election manifesto (promoted to Secretary of State at the DEA in 1967). However, the DEA's National Economic Plan fell foul of the sterling crisis that battered Britain in the mid 1960s, and by 1969 it had been reabsorbed by the Treasury, a humiliating defeat for the prime minister. Douglas Allen, seconded to the DEA and later Treasury Permanent Secretary (1968–74), thought that the DEA's failure was 'connected with personalities ... with a very strong Chancellor with Jenkins from 1967 and weaker DEA ministers'.[59]

In 1967, in the wake of Wilson's forced devaluation, he replaced Callaghan with Roy Jenkins as Chancellor. But his intellectual brilliance could not find full outlet as he spent the time battling to restore the stability of sterling by achieving a balance of payments surplus, work undone substantially by a 13 per cent increase in wage rates and average earnings from 1969–70. John Campbell calls it a 'serious failure, for which Jenkins bears the responsibility, and to which he contributed by weakness and a critical misjudgment'.[60] Rarely had two more sparkling minds succeeded each other as Chancellor than at the change of government in 1970. Had he not died within four weeks of being appointed, Heath's first Chancellor, Iain Macleod, might have further consolidated the Chancellor's position. But in his place, Heath appointed the lightweight Tony Barber (1970–4), aggressively running economic policy himself over his Chancellor's head, and bringing into Number 10 to help him the biggest beast then in the Whitehall jungle, former Permanent Secretary to the Treasury, then Head of the Home Civil Service, William Armstrong. It earned Armstrong the unwelcome nickname of 'Deputy Prime Minister'. It proved no happier nor more successful than Baldwin's bringing into Number 10 of Horace Wilson thirty-five years before, and ended with Armstrong having a breakdown, and the government's economic policy in tatters, amid strikes, U-turns, and rampant inflation.[61]

On his return to Number 10, Wilson appointed Denis Healey his Chancellor (1974–9). For his first two years, Healey pursued traditional Labour policies, including full employment, but when it became clear that the country would have to appeal to the International Monetary Fund (IMF) for funds to bail it out, a new Healey emerged, and with him, a new era for the Treasury.

THE POISED CHANCELLOR–PRIME MINISTER
RELATIONSHIP, 1976–97

In this period, the Chancellor and the prime minister were often the closest of allies, with both considering the relationship their most important, but with a new element of edge. The Treasury had been at an historic height of its powers and functions in the 1960s, managing not only the whole Home Civil Service, but also directly funding the overseas aid programme, higher education, museums and art galleries, as well as being responsible for the macroeconomic framework and setting interest rates as the Chancellor saw fit. Overseeing it was a complement of five of Permanent Secretary rank and seven deputy secretaries. The Treasury also had built up its role over the supply side of the economy, reflecting the shift in economic thinking to the core role of microeconomic policy and promotion of growth.

From the 1970s, the Treasury transitioned into a new phase. A succession of minor banking crises, where the Treasury felt the Bank of England had failed to keep them informed, coupled with abolition of exchange controls in 1979, ushered in a new era in which the Treasury played an increased role in the financial sector. The 1979 and 1987 Banking Acts placed banking supervision on a statutory basis, with responsibility for securities, services, and insurance moving to the Treasury from the Department of Trade and Industry in the 1990s.[62]

These years saw the Chancellor still vying for second-place status with the Foreign Secretary. The most notable incumbent at the Foreign Office was Tory grandee Lord Carrington (1979–82), who had been Party Chairman (1972–4) and Defence Secretary (1970–4), and whose popularity in the party scared Thatcher.[63] He was clearly more influential in Cabinet than Geoffrey Howe, the Chancellor. Douglas Hurd, Foreign Secretary from 1989–95, was another imposing figure largely by dint of his effortless command of foreign policy and his personal relationship with Prime Minister Major after 1990, built in part on his long understanding of politics (he had been at Heath's right hand as an advisor in Number 10 throughout 1970–4).[64]

When Callaghan succeeded Wilson in April 1976, he retained Wilson's Policy Unit and appointed Gavyn Davies his economic advisor.

Callaghan also retained Healey as Chancellor. Although he had been Chancellor himself under Wilson (1964–7), Healey was by far the more astute economist and tactician, and it was his strategy which was largely responsible for Cabinet accepting the conditions of the IMF loan in 1976, in the face of stiff opposition.[65] Healey became increasingly confident of his own point of view and muscle, as Chancellors tend to do the longer they are in office, and grew impatient with Callaghan: 'The prime minister has said the following, and this is how we're going to fucking stop it!', he would regularly report back to his officials at the Treasury when he returned from meetings at Number 10. 'We're going to overturn it by the fucking weekend!'[66] Callaghan recognised he had to tread carefully: 'The government could not have survived his resignation as Chancellor', he wrote in his memoirs.[67] Healey looked back more kindly in tranquility, writing that Callaghan gave him 'unstinting support' once 'Jim was convinced there was no alternative to the IMF loan'.[68]

When Thatcher appointed Howe her first Chancellor in 1979, they were both relatively inexperienced, and, in a Cabinet full of those unsympathetic to her cause, they formed a close bond: they would have long talks together on Sunday evenings face-to-face, discussing the week ahead. 'Geoffrey would take her through the Budget in a long series of meetings. She would sometimes disagree and they'd bring in a third party, usually Willie Whitelaw, to adjudicate', says John Kerr, Howe's Principal Private Secretary. 'Willie would sometimes go one way, sometimes the other. But they made it work, not least over the 1981 Budget, on which they were at one.'[69]

Thatcher preferred the company of Nigel Lawson, whom she promoted as Howe's successor in 1983. He had proven himself as an economics minister since 1979, and he gave her conviction and confidence, attributes she admired. They worked together closely, not least on privatisation, and in 1986 Lawson oversaw the further deregulation of the financial markets known as 'Big Bang'. For several years, it was the most creative and productive ministerial relationship of her premiership, described as 'extraordinarily powerful' by Turnbull.[70] After her third general election victory in 1987 though, the relationship began to sour. In his memoirs, Lawson recorded how uncomfortable she became in their discussions, unwilling to offer comments of her own on his proposals, and unsure of what she thought until she had first sought the advice of the economic advisor Alan Walters she had controversially brought back.[71] Walters was known for his strong views on monetarism, but as Chief Economic Advisor from 1981–3, his presence in Downing Street had seen comparative calm. But after he moved to Washington from 1983–9, and held no official position in Number 10, Thatcher continued to turn to him.[72]

When she brought him back to Number 10 officially for five months in 1989, all hell broke loose. She worried that Lawson was departing from the tenets of monetarism, and from her convictions that sterling needed to be strong, inflation and interest rates kept low, and the economy to be steadily growing and reserves accumulating.[73] The dam broke over Lawson's desire to join the European Exchange Rate Mechanism (ERM) and his policy of shadowing the Deutschmark: 'A bizarre policy that the Treasury was following, but the government wasn't explicitly, and the prime minister most certainly disapproved of', as O'Donnell encapsulates it.[74] Their long personal and ideological affinity was suddenly at an end: 'Nigel had pursued a personal economic policy without reference to the rest of the government. How could I possibly trust him again?', she wrote in her memoirs.[75] Lawson knew he could not continue, but equally, he faced the same dilemma of every Chancellor by the second half of the twentieth century ambitious to remain in the game: there is no other job to go on to bar Number 10. Relations between the Treasury and Number 10 reached a low rarely seen in history before Lawson decided he had to resign in October 1989, saying he felt that she had undermined him repeatedly: 'A sequence of events without parallel in modern British political history', in the words of Edmund Dell.[76]

Lawson's time at the Treasury provides a pen portrait of the Chancellor's relationship with the prime minister as it had evolved by the 1980s. The relationship was mutually productive when they both worked together well, but when they didn't, it was impossible. Thatcher, fatally weakened by his departure, never recovered, as often happens to prime ministers. He was not the first Chancellor to pursue his own pet policies, but he was the first who did so while deliberately keeping the prime minister in the dark, justified by his belief that he knew better than she what was in the economic interests of the country.

It was a dangerous belief, and one that successive Chancellors were to follow. Thatcher, running out of options for Lawson's successor, snatched Major out of the Foreign Office where she had placed him only three months before. She and Major had what can only be described as an uneasy relationship for her final thirteen months as prime minister, in which he bludgeoned through entry into the ERM, 'a massive statement of Chancellor power, and the weakness of Thatcher by 1990'.[77]

Major's premiership (1990–7) saw a degree of normality return between two explosive PM–Chancellor relationships. He was no stranger to the subject, one of ten prime ministers to have been Chancellor since 1900, though the only one to have also been Chief Secretary. To increase his firepower in Number 10, he brought in financial journalist Sarah Hogg as head of the Policy Unit, who later went on to be the first woman to chair a FTSE 100 company, Judith Chaplin, who had been Special Advisor to Lawson and then to him at the Treasury, and he retained the Treasury-bred Turnbull as his Principal Private Secretary. Rarely had Number 10 had more economic know-how. As his first Chancellor, Major selected Norman Lamont, his campaign manager. 'Chancellor, you do realise you will soon be the most unpopular man in Britain?', Lamont was told by officials on his first day, later commenting wryly that it was 'the only Treasury forecast in my time that was ever correct'.[78] Initial doubts in Number 10 about the wisdom of the choice were accentuated after 'Black Wednesday' in 1992, when Britain was ejected from the ERM, described by Lionel Barber as 'a devastating intellectual blow to the Treasury' – as severe as the sterling crisis of 1976 – though he notes the Treasury 'has a record of taking humiliation on the chin and – somehow – emerging stronger'.[79] Lamont was increasingly at odds with Major, and was dismissed in May 1993. Two weeks later came his response when, in the House of Commons, he uttered the devastating words: the government 'gives the impression of being in office, but not in power'.[80] 'He had to go, but I was sad he went with such rancour', Major later lamented.[81]

Major struggled to regain the initiative after 'Black Wednesday' and Lamont's resignation, but in Ken Clarke he found an ideal partner and they experienced one of the most harmonious personal and policy relationships of the late twentieth century between two top politicians.

'Of all the prime ministers I worked with, the relationship with the Chancellor that worked best was with Ken Clarke', says O'Donnell. 'Clarke was a seriously experienced minister, a potential successor to Major, but they respected each other, and while Ken might not always have been a great listener, he listened to the prime minister'.[82] Indicatively though, in words that echo the relationship between monarch and prime minister, Clarke said that, while the job of the prime minister was to 'advise and warn ... it was the Chancellor's Budget'.[83] 'It was undoubtedly helpful to me that John Major had already sacked one Chancellor of the Exchequer – in my opinion the maximum permitted limit for any Prime Minister', wrote Clarke in his memoirs. He pinpointed in the book a core difference in outlook between both offices: the prime minister 'had to be extremely sensitive to political events, while I had to be equally sensitive to economic reality'.[84]

Jeremy Heywood, the most continuously influential civil servant of the last twenty-five years, Treasury of course, first became prominent at this time, appointed Principal Private Secretary at the age of thirty to Lamont, and remaining throughout Clarke's time, before he started at Number 10 under Blair. Lamont had been the first to recognise his talents, which included improving Number 10–Treasury relations. Aided by a benign international environment, Clarke and Major were able to rebuild the economy with a policy based on inflation targeting, but insufficiently to prevent being swept away by the Labour landslide in May 1997.

CHANCELLOR UNBOUND, 1997–2021

In this period, we see the Chancellor emerge indisputably as the second most powerful figure behind the prime minister. Two of the six Chancellors during it, Brown and Osborne, were in office for sixteen of the twenty-four years. Their success in office was much enhanced, as we see with the PM also, by their being *Shadow* Chancellors before, five years apiece. The Foreign Secretaries under Blair, Robin Cook (1997–2001), Jack Straw (2001–6), and Margaret Beckett (2006–7), were overshadowed by Brown as Chancellor, as were Hammond as Foreign Secretary by Osborne under Cameron (2014–16), and Johnson under May (2016–18). Only two of the Chancellor–prime minister relationships of these twenty-four years could be described as happy: Brown in the first few years and Osborne throughout, while three, Darling (2007–10), Hammond (2016–19), and Javid (2019–20), were toxic. Rishi Sunak has an uneasy relationship with Johnson, predicated on the fact that he is able to do largely what he wants. 'There are only so many times I can threaten to resign', he might intimate, while Johnson weighs up if he is in earnest.[85]

The distinctive feature of these 'unbound' years, and why they differ to what went before, is that Chancellors were now at times pursuing their own agendas, whether or not the prime minister agreed with them, most blatantly Brown in the mid and late stages of his chancellorship (2003–7) and Philip Hammond throughout. The historical record of the Blair, Brown, and May premierships would have been very, very different had they had compliant Chancellors willing to carry out their wishes, as opposed to blocking them at critical points.

The Treasury re-established its preeminence, having lost some of its powers from its heyday in the 1960s to the 1980s, under permanent secretaries William Armstrong (1962–8) to Peter Middleton (1983–91). A slimmer body than it was (senior officials have been halved since the 1960s), it has become more strategic and less operational. Nick Macpherson (himself Permanent Secretary 2005–16) describes its role now as follows: it sets the monetary policy target but delegates its operation to the Bank of England. It determines the regulatory framework, but delegates its operation to the Prudential Regulation Authority (PRA) at the Bank of England. It sets public expenditure totals, but it falls to the Cabinet Office and the rest of Whitehall to execute them and achieve the efficiency improvements required. It determines that there should be two fiscal forecasts a year, but leaves it to the Office for Budget Responsibility (OBR) to provide them.[86] It helps growth policy, but works with other departments including the Department for Business, Energy and Industrial Strategy (BEIS) to achieve it. It saw Brexit policy delegated after 2016 to the Department for Exiting the EU (DExEU) and the Department for International Trade (DIT), both newly created by Theresa May that year, but it moved centre stage in 2020–1 in determining and executing a policy for tackling the COVID-19 pandemic.

Brown (1997–2007) became the longest continually serving Chancellor since Vansittart served from 1812–23. None since Gladstone and Lloyd

George had come to office with so much pent-up energy and so many ideas, worked up during the years in opposition. This was a diarchy Chancellorship, but less with the prime minister than with the brilliant financial journalist Ed Balls, whom Brown had brought in as an economic advisor to assist him when Shadow Chancellor in 1994, and who continued to advise him in government after 1997. Even after Balls became an MP himself in 2005 and Economic Secretary in May 2006, he continued to advise Brown. He wanted to be Chancellor.

Brown worked happily enough with Blair in his first government from 1997–2001; they agreed on most issues, though Brown wouldn't have cared overly if they hadn't: he regarded himself as Blair's intellectual superior, the true Labourite and, since their understanding in 1994, the nature of which they differed about, the heir apparent. Brown's immediate decision to give control of interest rates to the Bank of England was a key moment: this was all Brown, not Blair. What Brown cared about was achieving high and stable levels of growth and expenditure, and he believed the Bank of England move 'would create space for us to get rid of the debilitating meetings on monetary policy', as Balls later put it.[87] Brown agreed with Blair over their initial spending plans, but the pair disagreed when the booming economy created space for money to be spent. As the months dragged on, Brown's simmering resentment that Blair had become leader rather than him exploded. He and Balls were increasingly brazen, as Cabinet divided into two rival camps, about his view that Blair was a lightweight and not in tune with Labour's historic values. 'One reason Tony Blair didn't like to take matters for discussion to Cabinet was that only some were his supporters, and the rest were Gordon's supporters', says Richard Wilson, Cabinet Secretary (1998–2002). 'I could have gone around the table and told you who was a Blairite and who was a Brownite; it was very binary. Most ministers were one or the other.'[88]

Never before had a Cabinet been so divided for so long on what fundamentally were personality issues. Thatcher's Cabinet had been divided between 'wets' and 'dries', Major's over Europhiles and Eurosceptics, and May's over a 'hard' and 'soft' Brexit. But one has to go back to the Cabinets of Lloyd George, Balfour, or Peel to see such bitterness. Blair had gone along with Brown's bolstering of the Treasury's position after 1997,

Brown effectively overseeing social policy himself, and bringing into the orbit of the Treasury parts of other departments, including Social Security. But buoyed by the success of the 2001 general election, Blair determined to rein Brown and the Treasury back in. He brought in John Birt, former Director General of the BBC, as strategy advisor to help him develop his own domestic agenda and to find ways to combat the Treasury's influence. He leant heavily for economic advice too on his close colleague Peter Mandelson. Brown predictably was riled and considered Mandelson, once his close political friend, a traitor.[89]

The stage was set for a classic confrontation, and it came in the spring of 2003 over Blair's major second-term ambition, for Britain to join the Euro, in which Brown and Balls roundly outmanoeuvred him. 'You will have to consider your position', Blair said to him at a particularly acrimonious meeting on 2 April 2003. 'I'll do just that', said Brown before storming off with his team. For some hours, the Treasury was uncertain whether the Chancellor had been sacked. But, typically, both drew back, as they did often after their shouting matches.[90] The partnership hit rock bottom in their final few years: 'Completely broken down', was John Kerr's verdict. 'I knew how bad it was when the Treasury said they were not going to tell Number 10 what was in the Budget, and that Number 10 would hear what was in it on the morning of Budget Day when Cabinet was briefed.'[91] While Brown and his supporters sought to undermine Blair's domestic agenda on foundation hospitals and academy schools, and increasingly manoeuvred to unseat him as prime minister, Blair found himself powerless to act, with insufficient political capital to sack him or to move him, even after the 2005 general election victory.[92] Had the Foreign Office packed more punch by 2005, it might have provided a way out for both of them. But Brown wasn't interested.

When Brown at long last had his wish in 2007, he considered it too big a leap to appoint Balls straight off, desperate though he was for the job, and chose instead Alistair Darling, planning to give him a lot of space. But the Global Financial Crisis intruded: 'It was tricky for Gordon because it meant that he really wanted to be prime minister and Chancellor at the same time', says Gus O'Donnell, by now Cabinet Secretary (2005–11). 'A lot of the big issues were around the economy which was what Gordon himself wanted to do. He really struggled that his beloved Treasury was no longer at his beck and call but at the beck and call of Alistair Darling instead.'[93] Brown fell back on the resort of all post-1945 prime ministers when worried about their Chancellor: he increased the firepower in Number 10: so Balls (who was always a better economist) joined him in Downing Street, along with investment banker Shriti Vadera. This only increased tensions with the Treasury, as such moves always have done. Brown, after a hesitant start, was in his element in handling the crisis, leading on a recapitalisation of the banks and coordinated stimulus for the world economy, in what Lionel Barber calls 'in retrospect his – and the Treasury's – finest hour'.[94] A nadir was reached in his relationship with his Chancellor in August 2008, when Darling gave an interview to the *Guardian* in which he said the world economy was facing 'arguably the worst' conditions in sixty years.[95] 'That fucking Darling interview!' Brown said. 'It fucked up everything!' Darling's response came in February 2010 when he accused Brown and his aides of undermining him: 'Nobody likes the sort of briefing that goes on', he told *Sky News*.[96]

Cameron's relationship with Osborne (2010–16) has been described as the closest PM–Chancellor relationship since Asquith and Lloyd George (1908–15). Cameron, a better economist than Blair, didn't see it quite that way: 'George and I would to and fro endlessly about [austerity] measures, but we never argued about the necessity of it all. Not once.'[97] Osborne was 'completely clear' from the moment he backed Cameron's candidature for leader in 2005 that he was the subordinate figure and that Cameron's wishes would prevail: that Cameron would always listen to him on any subject, but in the last analysis, they were his decisions and Osborne would accept it. 'It was a real partnership of equals with no complication about who was the senior partner', says Rupert Harrison, Osborne's Chief of Staff (2010–15).[98] 'Rarely had there been a prime minister who subscribed so much to the Treasury view', reflects O'Donnell.[99] One decision in particular was Osborne's: the choice of Mark Carney as Governor of the Bank of England in 2013, seen in part as an attempt to claw back some of the Chancellor's authority over the Bank. Some creative tension was lost by their personal and political closeness: Osborne's reluctance to stand up more to Cameron when he proposed a referendum on the EU is an example. Absence of argument is not necessarily a sign of strength.

Both had resolved to be as unlike Blair and Brown in their relationship as possible. Incoming prime minister Theresa May from 2016 was one of those who thought Cameron and Osborne had been far *too* close. She appointed as her Chancellor Philip Hammond, who she was clear from the outset would *not* be a regular part of the furniture at Number 10, as Osborne had been, and most certainly not part of the daily meetings in her room with her staff. Hammond deeply resented being shut out. He'd seen the previous regime close-up, and he wanted to be at the heart, not the margins. Jeremy Heywood said that in his career he had never seen a relationship between a prime minister and Chancellor go wrong so quickly.[100] Realising how little she knew about economics and finance, Hammond turned to explaining economic realities and simple financial truths to her: 'Theresa, that's not how it works', he would tell her regularly at their meetings. She felt she was being patronised and she hated it.[101] May had come to power with plans, created with Chief of Staff Nick Timothy, that Number 10 was going to be the powerhouse in her premiership, and the Treasury emasculated. It had been significantly damaged by its association with 'project fear' during the referendum campaign, when it unwisely over-stated the dangers, losing respect across the spectrum. The scene was set for what became three years of acrimony and dogfights, with divisions over Europe, May's plans for an industrial strategy, and expenditure plans, continuing all the way until her final days in power, when Hammond went behind her back to block her. 'The final weeks were spent in a really undignified battle over whether she should spend the financial headroom I had helped create on her legacy', he said. 'I regarded it as a matter of constitutional principle that an outgoing PM should not make significant long-term spending commitments.'[102] No prime minister and Chancellor relationship since the separation of 1841 was more constantly toxic.[103] 'Neither of them had a sense of humour. Neither of them liked each other as far as I could tell. It was really *truly* awful', said one official.[104]

The lesson Johnson absorbed from watching this horror unfold was to rein the Treasury in. But when he and Dominic Cummings tried to do so in February 2020 by telling his Chancellor Sajid Javid who should be his special advisors, Javid took the nuclear option and resigned. The brave decision by Javid has made it very hard for

Johnson to remove another Chancellor, as Sunak and his team banked on from day one.

What explains the acrimony between prime minister and Chancellor, and why has it become pronounced? Policy differences are part of the explanation: if both agree on the direction of government economic policy, then there is a much greater chance of harmony, but when they don't, prime ministers fall back on the expedient of building up their own economic resources within Number 10. The longer Chancellors are in office the more specialist knowledge they acquire and the greater their claim, as Second Lord, to be the best expresser of the country's economic and financial interest. Structural factors have exacerbated the difficulties. Number 10 is 'underpowered' in comparison to the Treasury, lacking 'analytical resources, senior staff in numbers, and direct levers of power', says Harrison.[105] Institutional tensions between the Treasury, which can possess a self-confidence and monopoly of information bordering on arrogance, and prime ministers, who often enter Number 10 with their entourage suspicious of the Treasury, are all too common. Political staff on both sides can magnify tensions, especially given the growth in special advisors since the 1960s. Emotional and political factors play their part: prime ministers normally like to spend money and Chancellors to control it. Prime ministers receive credit from largesse in the short term, Chancellors from being cautious, with dividends coming in the long term. Chancellors are jealous of the limelight and the success that the prime minister can achieve from decisions for which they believe they deserve the credit. Prime ministers can become jealous, as Wilson was with Roy Jenkins, Callaghan with Healey, Thatcher with Lawson, and Blair with Brown, if they see them taking the glory. Prime ministers can have surprisingly little leeway over the choice of their Chancellor and appoint people whom they may find personally uncongenial, as Churchill did with Butler, and May with Hammond. Personal factors feature too: a smooth personal relationship, as with Macmillan and Heathcoat-Amory (1958-60), doesn't necessarily make for a successful PM–Chancellor partnership, though the opposite most definitely spells trouble.

Many of these factors have been around for a long time. The comparatively new element is the rise in the status of the Chancellor above that of Foreign Secretary, Home Secretary, and all other positions, and a culture where Chancellors no longer fear the prime minister. A prime minister is often not able to sack a Chancellor – 'a nuclear option',[106] not least for its impact on the financial markets and their own standing in Westminster – and a Chancellor has nowhere else now to go – it is forty years since Howe accepted the Foreign Office after the Treasury – other than becoming prime minister: this double bind is the ultimate reason for the ongoing tension between the First and Second Lords of the Treasury. Not that Chancellors always have it their own way. Among the 'almost' prime ministers, no job features as regularly as Chancellor, especially if they have been restrictive on spending: Gaitskell, Butler, Jenkins, Healey, Howe, Lawson, Clarke, Darling, and Osborne. By that measure, Brown is unusual in making it to the top.

By 2021, the Chancellor has emerged nevertheless as the most power-ful figure in government and the Treasury as the most powerful depart-ment. Lionel Barber has recently questioned whether the Treasury, having been chastened by its reversals over Brexit and COVID-19, defeated on a second lockdown that led Sunak into his own 'winter of discontent' in 2020, is still the all-powerful department it once was.[107] But does he protest too much? Sunak is still a strong contender to succeed Johnson above Foreign and First Secretary Raab and de facto deputy Gove.[108] Tom Scholar, Treasury Permanent Secretary, survived the Cummings winter and has now been told he is remaining in the depart-ment in a Whitehall more denuded of big beasts than ever. James Bowler, ex-Treasury, is the new Permanent Secretary at Number 10. Dan Rosenfield, ex-Treasury, is the new Chief of Staff. Stuart Glassborow, a Treasury man, is the dominant figure in the prime minister's Private Office. Johnson knew, post-Cummings, that he had to accept the Treasury back in. The Treasury is still recruiting the brightest and best, as a prelude to, or as part of, a career in the City. The Treasury is the sponsor department for the finance industry. Its leading position will not change post-Brexit.

The continuing mastery and dominance of the Treasury over Whitehall, and the newfound independent-mindedness of the Chancellor, create real and enduring problems for the prime minister that will have to be resolved as the office enters its fourth century. The rancorous nettle has to be grasped. A way of doing so is proposed in the final chapter.

CHAPTER 10

The Impossible Office?

The Prime Minister by 2021

OUR EXPLORATION OF THREE HUNDRED YEARS OF PRIME ministers, and the experiences of the fifty-five different incumbents, is almost at an end. The country they led changed fundamentally over that three-hundred-year period, yet their job of leading the nation has in many respects remained the same. This final chapter seeks to provide answers to a number of questions that have come to the fore in the book.

WHO COMES TOP?

Ranking the fifty-five prime ministers from 'best' to 'worst' has become a favourite national preoccupation. An end-of-century poll by BBC's Radio 4 in 1999 of twenty prominent historians, politicians, and commentators decided that Winston Churchill had been the 'best' prime minister over the previous hundred years, followed by Lloyd George and Clement Attlee. A different base was used for a 2004 survey by the University of Leeds and MORI, in which 139 academics specialising in twentieth-century British history and politics were asked to rank on a scale of one to ten how 'successful' or 'unsuccessful' they thought each twentieth-century prime minister had been in office. Attlee came first on this table with a mean score of 8.34, followed by Churchill, Lloyd George, and Thatcher, with the three Liberal prime ministers achieving a mean average of 6.18, Labour prime ministers 5.81, and the twelve Conservative prime ministers last with 4.81.[1]

The idea of ranking had taken hold, so much so that in the lead-up to the 2010 general election, *The Times* constructed a poll of *all* British prime ministers, with rankings given by correspondents at large, and by three specialists on the newspaper's in-house team, Ben Macintyre, Matthew Parris, and Peter Riddell. On this wider survey, Winston Churchill still came top, with Lloyd George second and Gladstone third, Pitt the Younger fourth, Thatcher fifth, and Peel sixth. John Major was one of the biggest risers, from close to the bottom of the twentieth-century tables to almost middle, twenty-eighth out of fifty-two, showing how perceptions of prime ministers can vary once they leave office.[2] A 2016 University of Leeds survey of eighty-two academics, focusing just on post-1945, saw the usual suspects in the top three berths, but another improved prime minister, Macmillan, climbing to the fourth slot.[3] Finally, Iain Dale, who edited a collected volume on prime ministers in late 2020, compiled a table with five of his authors of all prime ministers since 1721, the top six being Churchill, Gladstone, Pitt the Younger, Thatcher, Attlee, and Lloyd George with, at the other end, Compton, Devonshire, Canning, and Goderich, nudging Eden off his bottom slot in the earlier tables.[4]

Ranking of US Presidents, described by a believer in their value, Robert W Merry, as 'a substantial body of thought on presidential performance ... the closest we can come to history's judgment', has more value. Presidents serve fixed terms, fewer have served, and their records are more widely known. But the exercise is still flawed.[5]

Such lists are entertaining, but largely meaningless. Do not expect the pictures of the prime ministers that hang on the staircase in Number 10 to be reordered according to their rank any time soon. We cannot order prime ministers with anything like the same precision we rank the 'greatest' films or novels of all time. We can see the films and read the books today in the present, and can compare them, taking account of the different periods in which they were created. But we cannot go back and re-experience the premierships, any more than we can compare great stage actors like Sarah Bernhardt or Henry Irving with Maggie Smith or Ian McKellen, because their performances cannot be recreated. It is not even possible to rank sports people reliably over time, because even where, as with cricket, there is some comparable data, we cannot say W. G. Grace or Donald Bradman was 'better' than Viv Richards or Freddie Flintoff, because they were playing at such different times, where the frequency of matches, the equipment, and training were so different.

Comparative judgements on prime ministers are weakened further by our inadequate knowledge of all but the most recent incumbents, plus a sprinkling of others, Gladstone, Lloyd George, Churchill, and Attlee. Academics who know a great deal about the eighteenth century often lack the knowledge to make meaningful comparison with recent prime ministers. Subjective opinions are bound to weigh too, as is perhaps revealed in the Leeds polls.[6] But lists are rendered insubstantial most of all by the absence of agreed criteria on what constitutes 'success' for a prime minister. Many people know what a great novel or film looks like, but a great premiership? How can one rank those whose challenges differed over time? Besides, prime ministers do not begin on a level playing field. Much should be expected from those to whom much is given. Blair thus came to power in May 1997 with a considerable majority, a Labour Party and trade union movement united behind him, with a strong economy, and on a tide of popular and intellectual support. How can we rank him against his predecessor John Major, who came to office when the party had already been in power for over eleven years, was tired and deeply divided over Europe, with an economy in trouble, and a small majority steadily being chiselled away in by-elections?

In place of a numerical listing against vague criteria, we offer a series of designations, which describe what prime ministers actually did and achieved, eschewing ranking between and within each category.

AGENDA CHANGERS AND WHY THE OFFICE OF PM SURVIVIED. These prime ministers, as suggested in Chapters 3 and 4, are the figures who rose to the historic challenges of their period in power, won notable general elections, changed the course of the country, and with it, the way the job of prime minister operated. They either raised the standing of the country internationally, or bolstered the Union, key requirements for any prime minister, or both. Their influence was felt for many years after them, with successor prime ministers operating like them or deliberately choosing to be unlike them, but none escaping their shadows. They are: Robert Walpole, William Pitt the Younger, Robert Peel, Viscount Palmerston, William Gladstone, David Lloyd George, Clement Attlee, and Margaret Thatcher. Their premierships provide the answer to the question posed at the outset: how has the office survived? It endured principally because these prime ministers repeatedly reinvented the office for each new age. After the seventeenth century, there was no foreign invasion, nor revolution in mainland Britain, nor civil war sweeping the PM aside. The monarchy, equally, having learnt its lesson by the beginning of the eighteenth century, ceded power peacefully to the PM.

MAJOR CONTRIBUTORS. This next category sees eleven prime ministers who had a very decisive influence on the country, but were often sui generis, without the long-lasting mark on policy or the office that those in the agenda-changing class have. They are: William Pitt the Elder/Chatham, for his war leadership and being the first truly popular politician in the country; Lord Liverpool, who brought vast experience and stability to government, having held the posts of Foreign Secretary, Home Secretary, and War Secretary, oversaw the conclusion of the Napoleonic Wars and the unrest after it, and was one of the first prime ministers to see his job as coordinating other government departments; Earl Grey, passing the Great Reform Act and the Slavery Abolition Act in 1833, which went far further than the abolition of slavery itself in 1807 to root it out; Benjamin Disraeli, who passed social welfare legislation, was the first prime minister to attend a conference abroad, had an enduring impact on the Conservative Party, and shaped the role of the modern prime minister in the era of mass party politics.

Turning to the twentieth century: H. H. Asquith, who pushed the social policy agenda, above all with the 1911 National Insurance Act, and drove through the Parliament Act; Stanley Baldwin, who provided stability for the country in the volatile interwar years, helped induct Labour into parliamentary democracy, marginalising extremism on left and right, and saw the country through the abdication crisis; Winston Churchill was the supreme war leader of Britain at its greatest peril in the entire three hundred years, but he did not change the office, and lost two general elections (1945 and 1950) and just scraped home in his third (1951); Harold Macmillan, the first television prime minister, who drove decolonisation and the first attempt to join the European Community; Harold Wilson, who oversaw the liberalising policies under Roy Jenkins, and was the first prime minister since Lloyd George significantly to expand the size and reach of Number 10 but who, like Macmillan, did not successfully tackle Britain's chronic economic problems; Edward

Heath, for taking the country into the European Economic Community; and Tony Blair, for constitutional reforms, including devolution, an elected Mayor of London, and the Supreme Court, social and economic reforms including the minimum wage and being the first Labour prime minister to win three successive election victories, but who did not find an enduring solution to Britain's chronically troubled relationship with the EU, and became mired in the errors of Iraq.

POSITIVE STABILISERS. This third class of prime minister provided competent or better leadership which took the country forward, but were without the historic acts or changes of the 'major contributor' group. Henry Pelham was a brilliant manager of the House of the Commons and of the finances, who helped bring stability after the Jacobite uprising of 1745–6; the Duke of Newcastle financed war; Spencer Perceval, until cut short by his assassination, governed well in the face of economic depression and Luddite unrest, and successfully oversaw the conduct of the Peninsula War; the Duke of Wellington piloted through Catholic emancipation; Lord Salisbury provided stability at the end of the nineteenth century, incremental reform including county councils, steered the country successfully in Europe, and, more controversially, expanded the empire. Whilst undoubtably a success on his own terms, he was responsible for few fresh initiatives over his fourteen years, at a time of rapid change nationally and internationally.

In the twentieth century Arthur Balfour oversaw social reform, strengthened British defence, and negotiated the Entente Cordiale with France in 1904; Henry Campbell-Bannerman, while clearly overshadowed by Asquith and Grey, won a landslide in 1906 and introduced state pensions and free school meals, paving the way for later social reforms; Ramsay MacDonald brought Labour to power in its first two governments, showing the way for organised working-class and Labour support to play its role in Westminster politics, and oversaw steady reforms in the first four years of the National government after 1931; James Callaghan maintained stability for three years during turbulent years without a majority, and negotiated the IMF loan in 1976; John Major provided steady leadership after the pyrotechnics of the Thatcher decade, allowed the reforms to embed whilst taking them forward in his own direction, strengthened the economy, and found a temporary way for Britain to accommodate itself to the EU; Gordon Brown piloted Britain strongly through the Global Financial Crisis; and David Cameron strengthened the economy for six years during Britain's first peacetime coalition government since the 1930s, innovated with the National Security Council, military assistant and legal adviser at Number 10, while introducing some liberal reforms such as same-sex marriage.[7]

NOBLE FAILURES. A next class is 'noble failures', prime ministers who tried to do the right thing, were principled and dedicated, but became overwhelmed by the events they faced at the top. These five prime ministers come from each of the four centuries, with two in the nineteenth. Lord North provided strong financial leadership for his first five years in office, was a good House of Commons and elections manager, excelled at overseeing the finances to pay for the American war, and helped maintain political support in its early years till overwhelmed by its reversals; Lord John Russell was a passionate and effective reformer earlier in his career, and helped found the modern Liberal Party, but he failed as prime minister to deal with the Irish Famine, and mishandled the politics of reform, leaving the Conservatives to pass the 1867 Reform Act; Lord Derby, another figure who promised much and helped found the modern Conservative party, was unable to achieve all he wanted in his brief periods as prime minister, except the franchise reform not achieved by Russell; Neville Chamberlain, who had been such a vital reformer before he reached Number 10, was so desperate to avoid a war against strong adversaries in Germany, Japan and Italy, that he placed too much faith in his ability to secure an agreement; and Theresa May, who fought with almost superhuman energy and tenacity to achieve a Brexit on which her party could agree, but without the strategic clarity or interpersonal skills that prime ministers need if they are to succeed, and left with few of her ambitions for tackling burning injustices realised.

IGNOBLE FAILURES. Only seven prime ministers fall into this class, all of whom lacked a basic moral seriousness, or leadership ability, or both. George Grenville had little to show for his two years beyond extending the Stamp Act to the American Colonies, which inflamed them, and prosecuting radical protester John Wilkes; The Duke of Portland saw the biggest gap between periods in office for a prime minister (twenty-four years), but lacked the qualities to be a leader as either a young or an older one, providing competent cover for more dominant figures to do so; Henry Addington negotiated the unsuccessful Treaty of Amiens in 1802, but failed to command authority in either House of Parliament, leading to his fall; Lord Melbourne had little to show for his six years in power beyond inducting Victoria, while his louche style and involvement in scandals did nothing to add to the office; Lord Aberdeen; who was unable to provide effective leadership to the pungent politicians in his mixed ministry, failed to keep Britain out of the Crimean War, and to lead it successfully; Lord Rosebery lacked gravitas, failed to build on Gladstone's legacy, to give a clear direction, and led the Liberals into a defeat; and finally, Anthony Eden, a truly tragic case, principled and proud, but stubborn and naive, and who led the country into the disastrous Suez campaign. Never has a prime minister fallen so low from such a height.

LEFT ON THE STARTING LINE. A final category are those whose premierships were too short to judge their performance, which includes some who had much promise and earlier achievement to their name. They are: George Canning (120 days), Lord Goderich (145 days), Andrew Bonar Law (212 days), the Duke of Devonshire (226 days), Lord Shelburne (267 days), Lord Bute (318 days), Alec Douglas-Home (364 days), Lord Grenville (1 year, 43 days), the Duke of Grafton (1 year, 107 days), Lord Rockingham (1 year, 114 days), and Spencer Compton (1 year, 120 days).

SO WHAT MAKES FOR A SUCCESSFUL PREMIERSHIP?

No magic formula exists for a successful premiership, any more than for a high-achieving sports team, company, or work of art. But a four-point approach developed over my writing on PMs takes us perhaps closer to understanding some common ingredients that make success more likely, if not guaranteed: they are individuals, ideas, interests, and circumstances.[8]

'Individuals' start with the prime minister themselves. Our eight 'agenda changer' prime ministers shared some common attributes. They had *long apprenticeships*, in which they learnt about governing, made painful mistakes, and arrived at the top with a maturity and a wisdom, even if blended with impetuosity, which served them well. They had *clear ideas* about what they wanted to achieve in office which drove them forward, even if some of those ideas evolved or emerged only after they were in power, and these gave their premierships a coherence and force. They had a *moral seriousness* about their work, even if, as was the case with Walpole, Palmerston, and Lloyd George, they were far from moral in their personal conduct. Finally, they all possessed an *iron will*, bolstered by an intense work ethic and drive to get the job done. To these may be added possession of many of the skills discussed in Chapter 5, namely the ability to persuade colleagues in Cabinet and Parliament to get behind them, to communicate effectively near and far, abnormally high energy levels, robust health, genuine intellectual depth and agility, an equable temperament, and the ability to be utterly ruthless when required, sacking ministers, dumping policies, and changing direction.

Premierships are not solo acts: the prime minister is captain of the team, and to be successful, they need ministers who are experienced, skilful, determined, driven, loyal, and prepared to do the work for them. Few Cabinets from 1721 were more talented than Clement Attlee's from 1945–51, with the hugely experienced Bevin, Morrison, Dalton, and Cripps joined by Bevan and Gaitskell, and Asquith's peacetime government of 1908-14, featuring Lloyd George, Haldane, Grey, McKenna and Churchill. Even Cabinets with capable ministers, famously the Ministry of All the Talents (1806–7), are no guarantee of success. Gordon Brown tried to repeat the formula with his 'Government of All the Talents' (GOAT) by bringing five non-Labour experts into the government, albeit at a junior level, and not conspicuously successfully. So top Cabinet talent is sine quo non. Inside Number 10, they need just three or four outstandingly able operators, to lead the pack below them.

'Ideas' are equally essential to successful premierships. If a prime minister is fortunate to come to power on the crest of an intellectual wave, as Grey, Gladstone, Asquith/Lloyd George, Attlee, and Thatcher did, they have a head start. Lacklustre premiers scramble for ideas and go in for periodic 're-launches', which are never successful. Ideas mobilise, they enthuse, they bring divergent people together. The abolition of slavery was an idea, as was solving the Irish Question, imperial preference, the mixed economy, decolonisation, devolution, and privatisation.

Euroscepticism and Brexit were ideas, which proved insufficient for May to break through, but which helped Johnson win the general election in 2019. The question Conservative MPs were asking in 2021 is, beyond Brexit, and dealing with COVID-19, what were Johnson's ideas? Would his 'levelling up' have more traction than Major's 'citizen's charter' or Cameron's 'big society'? When Number 10 sends messages around departments asking for 'ideas', it is a sign that a premiership is in trouble. The portmanteau ideas tend to come in waves, every thirty or forty years, accounting in part for why the 'agenda changer' prime ministers crop up at roughly this frequency.

'Interests' need to run with a premiership rather than against it. Pitt the Younger was able to channel the financial interests and City, while Peel ran up against powerful landed interests that resisted his attempts to repeal the Corn Laws. Gladstone's premiership was boosted by his support from the press, grateful to him for his removal of paper duties. Asquith saw off the Lords, but was assaulted by challenges from the suffragettes, trade unions, and Irish nationalists, and Baldwin's premiership by hostility from the press, while Churchill was able, in masterly fashion, to align all the powerful interests in the nation behind the war effort from 1940–5. Trade unions helped bring about the ends of the premierships of Wilson in 1970, Heath in 1974, and Callaghan in 1979, while Thatcher was able to outflank them, ensuring that powerful business, financial, and media interests were supportive of her. The Civil Service is another interest: high-achieving prime ministers might adapt it to their taste, but fundamentally work with it. Declaring outright war on it, as Cummings found in 2019–20, is a dead end. Even the most powerful of prime ministers like Thatcher and Blair came across resistance from status quo elites, including judges and the professions. They are a fact of life in a pluralist democracy and need to be negotiated around. The art of the prime minister, as any leader, is the art of the possible.

'Circumstances' or 'events' finally help explain why some premierships succeed while others fail. Premierships can often be defined by their success at dealing with one 'big' event, if they have one. Wars are the most dramatic. Walpole's failures during the War of Jenkins' Ear helped bring about his own demise, while Pitt the Elder's leadership in the Seven Years' War made his name. The American War of Independence squashed North, while the French Revolutionary and Napoleonic Wars established Pitt the Younger's and Liverpool's reputations. The Crimean War finished off Aberdeen but elevated Palmerston. The First World War fatally damaged Asquith, as the Second World War did Chamberlain, while making Lloyd George and Churchill. Attlee's final demise in 1951 was hastened by paying for the Korean War, while Suez did for Eden, the Falklands boosted Thatcher, yet Blair never recovered from Iraq. Economic downturns, as we have also seen, can make or break prime ministers, as have existential crises, from the Irish Famine in the 1840s through to COVID-19 in the 2020s.

The length a prime minister serves is a critical circumstance: only twenty-five have been at the top longer than five years, and of the thirty who served less, it's hard to find many of consequence; Grey is a principal exception, the twenty-eighth longest-serving incumbent, who achieved much in his three years and nine months. Longevity is no guarantee of success though, the third and fourth longest-serving incumbents, Liverpool with fourteen years and ten months, and Salisbury on thirteen years and eight months, having less to show for it than might have been expected. Activism is not of course a necessary requirement for a success-ful premiership: Heath conspicuously did too much, with many of his policies not lasting. Sometimes, the nation needs a quiet premiership.

If a sweet-spot exists of perhaps five to eight years in office, sufficient time for the prime minister to make their mark, but not enough for them to grow stale or tired, the same notion of a golden mean applies to their age. Many were too old or ill when they became prime minster, with Canning, Campbell-Bannerman, Bonar Law and Chamberlain dying in or soon after leaving office. Many prime ministers were insufficiently well in office to perform at their best. They equally can be too young, including Devonshire (aged thirty-six on coming to office), Grafton (thirty-three), Rockingham (thirty-five), Rosebery (forty-six), and Blair and Cameron (forty-three), arguably lacking in experience for the highest office. Churchill would have been a disastrous prime minister earlier in his career: in May 1940, he was just right, as he himself recognised. Many of the more successful were aged between fifty and sixty-five, sufficiently experienced and blooded, but still with the energy and health to make the most of the opportunity. Pitt the Younger and Palmerston are the exceptions to this rule. Pitt (twenty-four) had wisdom and political skill beyond his years, while Palmerston had remarkable health and vitality for a seventy-year-old (though would likely have been a better PM still if younger).

Winning a parliamentary majority makes all the difference to whether a premiership is *successful*. So it's not surprising that all our eight 'agenda changer' prime ministers, and many in the second class as well, including Grey, Baldwin, Macmillan, and Blair, were able to benefit from significant majorities. With them, the prime minister can force through controversial policies; without them, they can spend their premierships fire-fighting. The strength of the economy is another circumstance that powerfully affects success. If robust, it provides the revenue for the prime minister to do what they want to do; while high unemployment and low tax yields, even if not the incumbent's fault, constrain them and reflect badly on them. The length of time a party has been in power can equally make or break a premiership: it is far harder to make a mark coming to office at the end of a long period of ascendancy or dominance, as Douglas-Home, Major, and Brown all found. Johnson may yet be an exception.

Prime ministers regularly sail into Downing Street thinking that they can buck these four trends. Ignorance is bliss, and ubiquitous. The history of the last three hundred years repeatedly shows that they do so only very rarely.

CAN THE VERDICT ON A PREMIERSHIP
BE IMPROVED AFTER IT IS OVER?

If a premiership ends in acrimony, as did Peel's in 1846, Balfour's in 1905 and May's in 2019, with the party split, the initial verdict may be more negative, as it can be when prime ministers suffer heavy electoral defeats, as Baldwin's in May 1929 or Major in May 1997. Initial verdicts on premierships though do not change much over time. Indeed, there can come a point mid-premiership, as Balfour found when Joseph Chamberlain resigned in 1903, or Major with 'Black Wednesday' in 1992, when it effectively begins to fall apart. The official documents might not be available for twenty or more years after a premiership ends in the National Archives at Kew, but it is already evident what it has achieved, or not, and the degree of confidence that the prime minister inspired in colleagues and in the country at large.

A series of edited books, beginning with *The Thatcher Effect* and concluding with *The Coalition Effect*, asked three main questions of each premiership:[9] what was the state of each of the major policy areas and institutions when the prime minister came to power, and what had changed at the time of their fall? To what extent was the prime minister themself responsible for initiating, driving, or supporting that change? Were the changes necessary, and successful? The last is the area that most needs the benefit of perspective, but in almost all cases, successful premierships were evident at the moment that they left office.

In the twentieth century, former prime ministers started to write their memoirs, hoping that by so doing, they would be able to 'set the record straight', as well as, to varying extents, settle old scores and make some money. But no prime ministerial memoir has ever significantly altered the perception of a premiership ('memoirs' technically are histories of a period, an autobiography just of the life, though the distinction has not always held). Asquith was the first prime minister to publish his memoirs last century, in two volumes in 1928, *Memories and Reflections, 1852–1927*,[10] followed by Balfour's *Retrospect: An Unfinished Autobiography* in 1930.[11] They set the pace at the very moment, ten years after the Great War, when the nation was ready to look back. Lloyd George, not to be outdone, followed up with his six volumes of war memoirs between 1933 and 1936.[12] No interwar prime minister succeeding him though published theirs – they were too ill or exhausted on quitting – and there was a gap until Churchill, who wrote his highly subjective account of the First World War in six volumes, *The World Crisis* (1923–31), then wrote his six-volume *The Second World War* (1948–53).[13] He confirmed the tradition that prime ministers could consult documents from their own period in government. Anthony Eden published three volumes, relying heavily on ghost writers, beginning with his self-justificatory *Full Circle* in 1960 on the years 1951–7 (in which he deliberately excluded mention of collusion with France and Israel over Suez), followed by two volumes in 1962 and 1965 on the prewar and war period.[14]

No peacetime prime minister has written at greater length than Harold Macmillan, six volumes between 1966 and 1973, although only the last three on his premiership.[15] Douglas-Home wrote a congenial and light autobiography, *The Way the Wind Blows*, in 1976, a genre others chose not to emulate, preferring doorstops.[16] Heath waited twenty-four years after leaving Number 10 before publishing *The Course of My Life* in 1998, which was less rancorous and more measured than had been anticipated.[17] No prime minister has been quicker off the mark than Harold Wilson, who published *The Labour Government 1964–1970: A Personal Record*, while he was still Leader of the

Opposition in 1971, and then *Final Term: The Labour Government 1974–1976* in 1979 on his last two years.[18] Since him, the convention has been firmly established: detailed volumes, drawing on the prime minister's and Cabinet official papers, and serialised in the newspapers, trumpeting 'revelations' (they seldom were). Six- or even seven-figure deals for the book and television rights have become almost a golden handshake entitlement of departed prime ministers. Thatcher thus produced her memoirs in 1993, Major in 1999, Blair in 2010, Brown in 2018, and Cameron in 2019, all impressive in their different ways. None has published diaries, and none since Macmillan seems to have kept one, but their aides and ministers, with more time on their hands, have done so. Cameron, perhaps a harbinger, was regularly interviewed, in quasi diary form, during his premiership by journalist Daniel Finkelstein, with the transcripts later informing Cameron's memoir *For the Record*. By the time a former prime minister has paid the team of researchers and drafters who help write the book, they often find there is less money left than they expected. Their memoirs are their last will and testament on the political scene. Interest in them dwindles rapidly thereafter.

Prime ministers entertain high hopes of their biographers, much as writers and artists do of theirs, and the selection of author, the content, and the degree of freedom that they enjoy, can be as equally contentious. 'Official histories', using government archives, originated with the Boer War, with the next series, on the First World War, extending to 109 volumes and concluded only in 1949.[19] Prime ministers, or their literary executors if they died early, emulated this tradition in appointing 'official' biographers, who have not usually had access to government papers, but are free to range over the prime minister's 'private' or personal papers. Their prime ministerial subject is dead by the time the book is published, but their families, friends and executors still breath down their necks as they write.

Official biographies had an unhappy early experience when Oxford historian G. M. Young was asked by Baldwin himself to write his biography. When published in 1952, after Baldwin's death in 1947, several insiders threatened to sue unless passages were removed, while historians and commentators considered the book too lightweight and insufficient to rehabilitate Baldwin after attacks, not least in the anonymous book *Guilty Men* (1940), on his role in appeasement.[20] In Martin Gilbert, Churchill's family found an assiduous historian, who took over the magnum opus from Churchill's son Randolph on his death in 1968, writing from volume three to volume eight.[21] None since has written at greater length, but few have written as elegantly as Charles Moore's three-volume official biography on Thatcher, published between 2013 and 2019. Alistair Horne wrote the two-volume official biography of Harold Macmillan[22] and Philip Ziegler single volumes on Wilson[23] and Heath,[24] but for all their undeniable merit, it's hard to see they have altered the perception of their subject any more than (despite the hopes of Eden's widow Clarissa) D. R. Thorpe would achieve in his biography, published in 2003. It did not rehabilitate Eden's reputation after Suez as the figure who bestrode Britain's foreign policy.[25] Ben Pimlott's 1992 biography of Harold Wilson came as close to enhancing his subject's stature as any.

The verdict on a premiership is created not after it is over, by memoirs, biographies, nor academic tomes, but by the actions of the incumbent when in office, albeit with scope for minor re-evaluation at the margins. However much prime ministers might want to change the perception of what they did, and however passionately they might believe that they were treated unfairly – by opponents, the media, colleagues – the truth is that they had their chance. If they spent more time standing back and reflecting on their task while they were in office, read more history, took more time for contemplation and honest evaluation of their place in history, they might have achieved more, rather than frittering time away, as too many have, on relaunches, reacting to news, personal animosities and vanity projects.

HAS THE JOB BECOME IMPOSSIBLE?

The prime minister operates under heavy constraints, which have increased in the last 50 years, and still more since 2000, as discussed in Chapter 6. The expectations for what prime ministers can achieve in office, encouraged not least by themselves, have placed almost impossible beliefs among the public of what they can accomplish. Their initial words on the doorstep of Downing Street, as we saw in Chapter 5, can reveal more about their naivety about the job than the practicalities of what lies ahead. Too many incomers are not well enough equipped or prepared to optimise their potential, with recent PMs in particular having little experience of running departments (a meagre three between the last five), or of the formative role of Leader of the Opposition (only two of the last six), which gives a unique window on the breadth of the job. Once inside the ill-configured Number 10, they fill it up with political appointees who know little about the way that government operates, but possess a belief, derived from dubious evidence, that they, unlike their predecessors, will make the system work: as failure after failure among recent political advisors to the prime minister have shown, they don't.

The average prime minister, since 1945, has been in power for four and a half years (compared to nearly nine years for the German Chancellor). This already short time is eaten up further when two or three years are spent learning about the job. Precious little time is left. The challenges and blows come in thick and furiously from day one. It makes holding to a steady course far harder for inexperienced prime ministers and political aides. The 24-hour news cycle since the 1990s and advent of social media from the 2010s have added further distractions on the prime minister, making some believe they have to respond quickly, thereby disconcerting Cabinet and Parliament who feel bypassed. Prime ministers have struggled to turn social media to their advantage, while devices like WhatsApp have added to the ability of dissident MPs to organise themselves out of the sight of whips.

Peter Ricketts, Britain's first National Security Advisor (2010–12) blames the pressures to react too quickly, and lack of reflection time, on mistakes over the Iraq war, the EU referendum, and the failure to prepare better for COVID-19.[26] Indeed, too often we have had a knee-jerk rather than a wise-head premiership. COVID-19 could and should have been better anticipated by No10. Jeremy Heywood told me near the end of his life that lack of strategic planning at the centre was its great weakness. In 2019, historian Peter Frankopan gave a seminar at No. 10: his final words still float through the air "my greatest worry for the future is a global pandemic". Throughout this book, I have tried to show that history matters, but has been too often ignored at the very heart of government.

But, in answer to one of the core questions in the book, and the title, the undoubted challenges have *not* made the job impossible. Agile incumbents throughout the three hundred years have negotiated their way round the difficulties du jour, turned them to their advantage, and come out on top. The job may have seemed at times to be impossible: but it is only because of the way incumbents have chosen to act in office; not because of any inherent unworkability of their office.

The British prime minister is in an enviable position alongside comparable roles abroad: to repeat, not being pinned down or defined by a written constitution, not having to operate alongside a directly elected head of state, not operating in a federal structure that sucks power away from London (albeit happening now with devolved administrations), and not having an electoral system as on the Continent and beyond which throws up coalition governments: the British electoral system, at least from 1945–2010, normally guaranteed a majority government. Not having the burden of a department to run means the prime minister can range more freely, while the refinements of the Cabinet Office and Number 10 plays to their advantage, but only if they understand how to make it work for them. Technological innovations during the last century have allowed the prime minister to talk directly to the nation, and with leaders abroad, at the push of a button. The real questions are: does the British system produce candidates for the top job of the highest calibre who can maximise the job's potential, and how can they be better prepared for what will greet them once in office?

HOW CAN THE JOB BE IMPROVED?

The prime minister is the most written about, but the most under-examined, part of the British constitution. More reporting and academic study has focussed on the incumbents than on any other figure in Britain. They are the subjects of intense scrutiny from daily news, historical and political science treatises, and curricula at universities and schools. But we have lacked serious enquiries into the operation of the *office* of prime minister, and how it might perform better. The one figure who could authorise such an official investigation is the very last person who would want to do so: the prime minister.

Here are five proposals which the book has been pointing towards, to allow the office to perform better, and the country to be led better, as the position goes into its fourth century. There has been only one agenda-changing prime minister in the last seventy years: Thatcher. These changes will pave the way for more.

FORMALISE THE POSITION OF DEPUTY PRIME MINISTER(S).
The job of prime minister has grown vastly in the first three centuries, as we have seen, but the number of hours in the day has not. Prime ministers have played with the idea of having deputies, and have often performed better when they have had one in either a formal or informal capacity. Our first proposal is that this irregular position should become formalised, to oversee *domestic* policy, chair the major Cabinet committees (with the exception of the National Security Council, chaired by the PM), and be responsible for much of the routine business of government. They should most definitely not have their own department to run, which some deputy prime ministers and First Secretaries of State have had (Whitelaw gave up his, the Home Office, in 1983). Recognition that the job of prime minister has simply become too much for any one person to manage without deputies needs to be accepted across the political spectrum.

The Foreign Secretary is equally part of the solution. The leaching out of their work with Britain's dwindling power abroad, and the prime minister taking over part of their duties, means they have more time at their disposal than the seniority of the office would suggest. They should thus take over much of the routine *external* responsibilities from the prime minister and, when the occasion merits it, host meetings and receptions in Number 10 (because of its superior status over the more capacious Foreign Office). The prime minister would in effect thus have two deputies, the senior one covering home and the other, foreign. The PM would have to feel secure enough to establish these two posts: it has been the lack of trust at the very top that has proved often corrosive of good governance. Where prime ministers have trusted their deputies, as Churchill did with Attlee in the war, or Major did Heseltine in 1995–7, the model works very successfully.

Formalising these two positions would clear up the question of succession in the event of an unexpected termination of a premiership, and would tidy up the messiness and ambiguity surrounding the positions of deputy prime minister, First Secretary of State, and Lord President. An additional bonus is they would give the PM extra support against the Chancellor of the Exchequer, which would now become the *fourth* most senior position in government (ranking order in Cabinet is another untidy area that would be improved by this change).

Prime ministers have for sixty and more years lacked thinking time, and for doing what they most need to do. It has changed since Macmillan (who was frequently overburdened, as he wrote in his memoirs) asked Attlee (who said 'I never felt under any sense of strain' as PM) to examine whether the burden had become excessive: no, he concluded then.[27] Use of the deputy prime minister and an enhanced role for the Foreign Secretary will allow the PM such time for what only *they* can do: ensuring that the principal policies and strategy of the government, on which it was elected, are being carried out; monitoring the performance properly (at last) of Secretaries of State running the departments; crisis management without crisis leadership; representing the country on the most important issues abroad; and better oversight of the nation's finances than the PM usually manages.

The prime minister will have more time too to meet a wider cross-section of people, engaging with them for more than just the current cursory conversations. More time for Parliament: their attendance has been in steady decline, oddly, since Britain became a full democracy. More time to consider longer term national issues that transcend narrow sectional interests and the next general election. More time to go to the theatre and cinema, to art galleries, to read books again, and to use Chequers more, as envisaged in its initial bequest: '[to] create and preserve a just sense of proportion'.[28] More time for their spouses, children, family, and friends which will ground and renew them. More time for exercise and their inner life. The nation needs measured, not fraught, prime ministers, nor the physically and mentally unhealthy incumbents who have often fretted through its rooms over the last 300 years. More time to travel to all parts of the four nations for far more than just the rushed flag-waving trips of today. It is many years since the prime minister had regular overnight stays in Northern Ireland, Scotland, and Wales. They are prime ministers of the whole United Kingdom: fancy new titles don't convince, but better engagement might. Time is the prime minister's most precious asset, and the current regimen is not allowing the incumbent to optimise it.

NUMBER 10 NEEDS TO BECOME MORE HIGH POWERED. Space, like time, needs to be much better used. Valuable room is taken up in Number 10 by a variety of people and functions that could be carried out as well elsewhere in Westminster or Whitehall, freeing up space for senior officials and aides to provide the prime minister with top quantitative analysis, without having to rely on Whitehall departments to do so. It would mean Number 10 can interrogate far more thoroughly material coming in from across Whitehall, not least from the Treasury. Rupert Harrison is one of many key aides who worked in Number 10 who realised how under-powered it was, often when it was too late to do anything.[29] Blair's sleek and targeted Delivery Unit from 2001 showed the way, but was abolished in 2010. Its first head, Michael Barber, later wrote that PMs should be be on top of detail, but selectively, while delegating prudently.[30] The National Security Council (2010) was another important centralisation. Cameron, who initiated it, said it allowed him to enhance his grip on the machine 'by having all the key foreign and security players at the same table'.[31] Number 10 needs to be more high-powered, less full of in-and-out political aides who, however talented at party matters and winning elections, know little of their boss's job of governing, and the environment in which he or she operates. Some of the arrivistes would not be found anywhere near the chief executive of a large organisation. Why in Downing Street? For far too much of its recent history, Number 10 has been chaotic, in a state of near constant flux, overseen by a prime minister who has little idea initially how to organise it, or by chiefs of staff who have little understanding of the intricacies of delivering for their PM in Whitehall and Westminster. Number 10 has been relaunched and reinvented more often in the last thirty years than Madonna: and it seldom works, because there is no institutional memory, or learning. This book shows repeatedly that prime ministers often performed best with a strategic, knowledgeable and orderly Number 10. The prime minister is the head of strategy: tactics, operations and delivery should be monitored and probed by Number 10 staff, freeing up the PM to range more widely.

RESET THE BALANCE BETWEEN THE PRIME MINISTER AND THE CHANCELLOR. Since the 1980s, the Chancellor has gained a destabilising amount of autonomous power, with no constitutional justification or legitimacy for doing so. It has not helped that so few prime ministers – even former Chancellors, such as Churchill or Callaghan – are economically literate. But even when they have been, as with Wilson or Brown, it is no guarantee of a smooth and productive relationship. The prime minister, not the Chancellor, however, is the nation's chief executive, and for the system to work, the Chancellor has to be subordinate to them: if they don't agree on fundamentals, the Chancellor has to go. Yet since Brown's Chancellorship (1997–2007), they have regularly thwarted the will of the prime minister, for no reason other than that the Treasury has the personnel and gall, and the Chancellor the raw political power and knowledge, to do so. We have seen repeatedly that *information* is one of the PM's greatest weapons: but here is one area they do not monopolise it.

How to reset the dial is the question. One option would be to reduce the influence of the Treasury. But the numerous attempts to do so have failed. Chopping its power or breaking it up would be too disruptive and might work no better. It may work abroad, but it is alien to the British tradition. Nor is putting a mini Treasury within the Number 10 complex. Endless fighting would result. Rather, a clear and widespread understanding is needed again that the job of Chancellor is to *support* the prime minister, and that it is the prime minister, not the Chancellor, who is senior at the Treasury. The prime minister's job, as it says, if not on the tin, then at least on the brass, i.e. the letterbox of Number 10, is to be the 'First Lord of the Treasury'. The nation's chief bean-counters, the Treasury, need to be reminded that first comes before second. Britain is governed significantly by convention. This particular convention has become clouded. It needs restoring in full. To do so, the Prime Minister needs to assert their rights as First Lord. Johnson's promotion of Treasury officials to the top of Number 10, and convening of joint Number 10-Treasury teams, are moves in the right direction. Establishing a new body, the Economic Security Council, chaired by the PM, to mirror the NSC, bringing together all the key economic ministers and officials, would help redress the imbalance. Cameron is a keen supporter: 'it is essential the PM is in a commanding position', he said.[32]

THE PRIME MINISTERSHIP AND NUMBER 10 NEED TO BECOME MUCH MORE DIVERSE. India and Australia have had only one female prime minister, Germany only one female Chancellor, Denmark two prime ministers, Finland and New Zealand three: under-representation of women in leadership is a global issue. Two female prime ministers out of fifty-five in Britain might not sound bad by comparison. But it is not enough, constituting less than 5 per cent of the last three hundred years, when Britain has been ruled by female monarchs for 45 per cent of that time, and women make up more than 50 per cent of the population. Britain has not had a BAME prime minister, in contrast to the United States with Barack Obama (2009–17). Amongst deputy prime ministers and First Secretaries of State, there have been no BAME candidates, to rival US Vice President Kamala Harris (2021–), and the only woman was more than fifty years ago: Barbara Castle (1968–70). Prime ministers have been drawn from an incredibly narrow social range. After a succession of prime ministers from 1964–97 from state schools, the public schoolboys have returned in force, holding the premiership for eighteen of the last twenty-four years, eight by two Old Etonians (Cameron and Johnson) and for ten years by Blair (Fettes College in Edinburgh). The conversation about Eton between Walpole and Johnson, which opened this book, should make us pause.

Staff in Number 10 come equally from a very narrow base, with women and BAME candidates largely absent until the twenty-first century, and with known LGBTQ candidates excluded on grounds of security until the last twenty years. Johnson's Number 10 is beginning to address gender at least, with Munira Mirza head of the Number 10 Policy Unit, Allegra Stratton Press Secretary, and Carrie Symonds, all highly influential voices. Officials, disproportionally from the Treasury and Foreign Office, have suffered from their own lack of diversity until very recently. Political appointees have similarly been narrow and self-reinforcing, with prime ministers promoting to their closest court people they know well, on whom they feel they can completely rely (understandably, given the commonality of betrayal in Westminster, but hardly optimal). Aides have come up through traditional party political routes, with hiring based, not on principles of equality, talent, and diversity, but on connections, loyalty, fit, and alignment to a particular agenda or court, deepening tribalism.

Number 10 throughout history would have been 'red flagged' by any equality and diversity code for recruiting staff in its own image and eschewing open applications, rather than actively seeking out those from different regional, social and ethnic backgrounds, and a diversity of viewpoints and ways of thinking. Homogeneous prime ministerial courts producing homogeneous thinking are inevitably the result. Guidelines and culture change are urgently needed. Number 10 should be a beacon, leading the country on ethical and dynamic employment practices. The message would be sent far and wide that diverse candidates are welcome in Number 10, and in its top job. Widening the pool of applicants for prime minister would be one of many gains.

PROFESSIONALISE UNDERSTANDING ABOUT THE PRIME MINISTER. The electorate might be shocked if they knew how little incoming prime ministers and their closest advisors know and understand about the history and operation of the office, its powers and constraints, and how the system works. Such ignorance would not be tolerated in an incoming leader of any other organisation, so why should we tolerate it in the British prime minister, the most important job in the land? Prime ministers and their aides regularly trash their predecessors, which, aside from bad manners, shows an unwillingness to learn. Handovers are often perfunctory. Incomers then try to rewrite the rules of the operation, as if they were Walpole in year zero. Senior civil servants, who carry institutional memory between successor administrations, are too often binned early for being tainted by the old regime, or are outnumbered by political appointees in Number 10. They rarely stay more than two years: too short. Lack of institutional memory causes avoidable errors. One of the more startling facts in the book is that the last five prime ministers, including the present incumbent, have served in only three Whitehall departments between them before becoming PM, in contrast to the five prime ministers before them, from Heath to Major, who collectively had twenty-three jobs in Whitehall beforehand, and the five prime ministers before them, from Attlee to Douglas-Home, who served in thirty-nine ministerial roles.

Ten years ago, Cabinet Secretary Jeremy Heywood set up the history group at Number 10 to try and instil more sense of collective understanding of past prime ministers, and how they and Number 10 have operated at their best. David Cameron was notably supportive. A parade of senior ex-Number 10 staff, biographers, and historians, like Frankopan, have given lunchtime talks in the Pillared State Room.

Prime ministers need to arrive with a much clearer understanding of what works, and what doesn't. The Institute for Government, set up in 2008, has done important work in spreading understanding about what ministers need to do to govern more effectively.[33] The separate functions in Number 10, Whitehall liaison, policy, communications, foreign, parliamentary, logistical, etc., need to be far more regularised, as they are in the offices of national leaders abroad, so that, when each new prime minister arrives, they have in place staff loyal to them, who show them how the particular area operates and how they can make it best work for them. Number 10 needs to move from being a chronically amateur into a professional and sleek outfit. Government needs to learn more from abroad too: 'it almost never looks to other countries to see what could be done better', laments former policy chief at Number 10, Camilla Cavendish.[34]

Britain does not need to have a written constitution. It does not need to have a new prime minister's department. It does not need electoral reform. It does need the apparatus that are already in place, historically time-honoured, to work better: to change and to modernise certainly – long overdue in the Civil Service – and then to settle down.

WAS IT ALL WORTH IT?

Prime ministers are human beings, who bleed and hurt and suffer. Behind closed doors, and occasionally in front of them, they cry. Throughout the book, we have accentuated the *human* nature of the job. Politics is a harsh game. MPs aspire to be ministers, ministers to be promoted to one of the top four posts, and most of those want to become prime minister. Very few manage it. No one makes them do it, but those who do scale to the top of what Disraeli described as the 'greasy pole' are often far from happy with the experience and their legacy.

The job should carry a health warning. Seven have died in office, and five dead within a year of leaving, with a further three within three years. Within ten years, half were dead. Given how young many were, it's not a great prospect. Remarkably few achieve what they hoped. Most leave involuntarily. In office, they are criticised, mocked, and undermined relentlessly. The deranged and terrorists constantly want to kill them and their loved ones. There is no peace. Many experienced pain earlier in their lives: one study suggests two thirds in office between 1812 and 1940 lost a parent in childhood, and asks whether their quest for power and prestige was motivated by protection against emptiness and insignificance.[35] This is dangerous territory, but there can be no doubting that only driven personalities want to become prime minister, and that the nervous strain of office on often outlier personalities is considerable.

If it is not that good for the prime minister, it is worse for their families. The experience of having a parent who is prime minister can put almost unbearable strain on children. The lack of normality in their lives, the difficulty being seen only for who their parents are rather than who they are, the burden of expectation that goes with that, and parental attention often sacrificed for the political career causing a degree of neglect, all take their toll. Inherited genes, which might have powered the parent to the top, can play out less well for their children. Yes, some have escaped the shadow and have had normal lives. But to take just one period of twenty years, three of Churchill's children died unhappily, Diana at the age of fifty-four, Randolph at the age of fifty-seven, and Sarah at the age of sixty-seven (Marigold had died at the age of three). Addiction or mental illness afflicted all three of them, and it was only Mary, the youngest, who had a long and stable life, marrying Christopher Soames, one-time British ambassador to Paris, and dying at the age of ninety-one. Eden's elder son Simon was killed in action at the end of the war in June 1945, while his younger, Nicholas, died aged fifty-four from complications from AIDS. Macmillan's marriage was fraught due to the prolonged affair between his wife Dorothy and the louche Conservative politician Bob Boothby. Their daughter Sarah died aged forty, suffering from alcoholism, an illness that also afflicted his son Maurice, who had a brief and not very successful political career under Heath.

Being a prime minister offers no protection from the agonies that can afflict all parents. Asquith's son Raymond was killed in action in 1916, in a war which saw five of Salisbury's ten grandsons dying, and two of Bonar Law's sons. 'Night seems to have descended on him ... he could only sit despondently gazing into vacancy ... obliterating light and happiness', wrote Bonar Law's biographer Blake of the losses.[36] Gordon and Sarah Brown's daughter Jennifer died in January 2002 soon after her birth, before he became PM. David and Samantha Cameron's son Ivan died aged six in February 2009. Rarely has a more moving House of Commons speech been made by a PM than by Brown when he offered the Camerons his condolences for 'an unbearable sorrow that no parent should have to endure'.[37]

Few spouses opted to be married to a prime minister, and while some managed to enjoy the experience, as many were unenthusiastic. Their own careers were dented, their lives put on hold, while living in the flat at the top of Downing Street offers no privacy or escape. Only in the last twenty-five years have they been paid by the state for what in effect has become 'a job'. Since 1945, all except the bachelor Heath took their spouses through the indignity of a very public departure: Attlee unceremoniously dumped in 1951 despite having won more votes than the Conservatives, Churchill finally eased out by his Cabinet, Eden in disgrace after Suez, Macmillan his government's focus lost and believing he was more unwell than he proved, and Douglas-Home ejected by the electorate. Wilson, cited as the exception who left at a moment of his own choosing, was a shadow of his former self in his final two years, suffering from alcohol and memory loss. Heath, Major, and Brown were all ousted in general elections, while Thatcher, Blair to some extent, and May had lost the confidence of their colleagues. Cameron resigned after the catastrophic policy reversal of defeat in the EU referendum which he had called. We might contrast the PM's first euphoric words with their final ones departing Number 10. The tears they shed do not always fade in the empty years ahead.

Prime ministers are often at a loss to know what to do after they resign. Portland, Addington, Wellington, and Russell all came back into government. In the twentieth century, Balfour and Douglas-Home returned as Foreign Secretaries, while Chamberlain continued as a minister in Churchill's wartime Cabinet as Lord President until too ill. Handling 'post-premierships' can be tricky when there is no equivalent status to that enjoyed by former US or French presidents: some money from the state for office staff, and lifelong police protection, are scant consolations. Finding a job in the private sector can be awkward, finding a role in government at home or abroad difficult, and a return to politics now ruled out. If their successors fail, they can feel frustrated; worse, if they succeed, they can feel inadequate, while all the time they watch on as their former colleagues and friends diminish what they tried to build. Heath retreated to his house, which he lavishly decorated with memorabilia, in the Cathedral Close in Salisbury, but remained deeply scarred by the way he believed he had been treated by Thatcher. Thatcher herself, angry at the way she was ousted, and by the direction in which Major took the party, had as melancholic a post-premiership as any since Eden.[38]

Major in contrast has had a sunny post-premiership, one he has certainly enjoyed more than his seven years in Number 10, with a status and respect as an elder statesman he never enjoyed inside. No former prime minister has tried harder to build an independent career than Tony Blair, setting up his own foundation, and working for progress in the Middle East and Africa, with climate change and inter-faith dialogue. But he has not had a sympathetic press, which never forgave him for the Iraq War, while he has learnt the bitter truth that world leaders are not very interested in *former* prime ministers. Brown, Cameron, and May have all chosen to make periodic political interventions, and all have many years ahead of them to do so. Indeed, there are now as many post-prime ministers alive, five, as at any point in history. The year 1842 saw four former prime ministers, Goderich, Grey, Wellington, and Melbourne, as again did 1964, briefly, until Churchill's death in 1965. It's a lot of talent for government, short of experience and wisdom, to squander.

In Cameron's final days in office, their children, for a treat, saw a one-off show by the Royal Shakespeare Company, performed in the walled garden at the back of Number 10. Extracts from the Bard's plays were acted out, selected before his rushed departure was known. None foresaw the poignancy of the Cameron family, huddled together in the front row, watching the murder scene from *Julius Caesar*, and Lady Macbeth plotting the death of Duncan. A few days later, they left Number 10 for good. That evening, daughter Florence turned at bedtime to her father and asked, 'Daddy, when are we going back home?'[39]

Was it all worth it, for the former prime ministers, their spouses, and children? They would of course say yes; but deep inside, they must wonder, as they have struggled to find a home, and reclaim their lives, after Downing Street.

Acknowledgments

Writing this book during a global pandemic, almost entirely remotely, away from libraries, archives, colleagues, and other resources has been a challenge, and not always a bad one. It would not have been possible without the aid of those listed below.

Firstly, I would like to thank senior researchers and co-authors Jonathan Meakin and Illias Thoms. I have known both of them for over ten years and we have worked on a number of books together. They are formidably bright, hard-working, and well-organised, and great company too – a vital ingredient. This was certainly one of the hardest books to write, but our daily early morning and afternoon phone meetings, imitating a daily pattern some PMs have adopted, helped refine the arguments in the book and it is stronger for their insights and hard work.

We were blessed with a team of exceptional researchers, led by Oliver Myers, who provided such outstanding support in the last few weeks of the project, above and beyond the call of duty, Lindsay Singh, Raymond Newell, Peter Gallagher, Samantha Cummings, Natasha Hornby and Ed Wyatt. They all contributed at different times immeasurably to the project. Previous researchers and co-authors from my other books on prime ministers and the Cabinet Office, Lewis Baston, Peter Snowdon, Daniel Collings, Guy Lodge, Jonathan Meakin and Raymond Newell, contributed equally as the culmination of forty years of study of the UK premiership.

We are indebted to archivists and librarians who proved particularly helpful when their institutions were closed in providing digital support: Oliver House at the Special Collections of the Bodleian Library in Oxford, Athena Demetriou and Rea Kavazi at Bodleian admissions,

Mark Dunton and Beth Brunton of the National Archives in Kew, Karen Robson of the Hartley Library in Southampton, and John Wells and Sian Collins from Cambridge archives.

Cambridge University Press have been exceptional publishers, with thanks to John Haslam and his team including Toby Ginsberg, Catherine Smith, Amy Watson, and Chris Burrows, and Damian Love our gritty copy-editor, up against a tough deadline, working remotely, and understanding of the exceptional difficulties of producing the book in lockdown. Thanks also to Aloysias Saint Thomas for his excellent typesetting.

Huge thanks to our agent Martin Redfern at Northbank, a first rank agent at a great agency.

Thanks to playwright and novelist Jonathan Smith who helped with the imagined conversations in Chapter 1.

I began writing this book while I was still Vice-Chancellor of the innovative and unique University of Buckingham, and I would like to thank my many colleagues there for their support, care, and kindness as always, including Deba Bardhan-Correia, Sandra Clarke, John Drew, Sue Edwards, Jo Harris, Joanna Leach, Barnaby Lenon, Alan Martin, Anthony O'Hear, Chris Payne, Nick Rees, Frances Robinson, Harin Sellahewa, Karol Sikora, Alan Smithers, Jane Tapsell, and James Tooley. From our London operation, I would like to thank in particular John Adamson, Saul David and Ed Smith. From my own office and environs, I would also like to thank the formidable team including Purnima Anhal, Diana Blamires, Julie Cakebread, Colleen Carter, Jenny Carter, Cherry Coombe, Sharon Horwood, Dean Jones, Bev Kelly, Sarah Rush, Raginee Scudamore, Heidi Stopps, Matt Thompson, and Betty Wicks. I would particularly like to thank Paul Graham, for his constant encouragement over my five years at the university, and for suggesting a steady stream of outstanding young researchers. My profound thanks also to Stephen Gray and Ingrid Jacoby, Chloe and Chris Woodhead, Charles and Frances Jackson, and Nick Hillman.

I would particularly like to thank all those who granted interviews for the book: Andrew Adonis, Richard Aldous, Stuart Ball, Margaret Beckett, John Bew, Jeremy Black, Andrew Blick, Vernon Bogdanor, Rodney Brazier, David Brown, Terence Burns, Robin Butler, John Campbell, John Clarke, Robert Crowcroft, David Dilks, Daniel Finkelstein, Catherine Haddon, William Hague, Brian Harrison, Rupert Harrison,

Angus Hawkins, William Anthony Hay, Robert Hazell, Simon Heffer, Kevin Hickson, Michael Jay, Dennis Kavanagh, John Kerr, Paul Lay, Dick Leonard, Nick Macpherson, Eliza Manningham-Buller, Kenneth Morgan, Philip Norton, Gus O'Donnell, Andrew O'Shaughnessy, David Owen, Rod Rhodes, Steve Richards, Peter Riddell, Keith Robbins, Andrew Roberts, Mark Sedwill, Caroline Slocock, Anne Somerset, Kevin Theakston, Andrew Turnbull, Hugo Vickers, Mark Vickers, Patrick Weller, Jane Wellesley, A. N. Wilson, Richard Wilson, and Edward Young.

I would particularly like to thank the exceptional cast of distinguished people who read sections of or the whole book, including Stuart Ball, Jeremy Black, Vernon Bogdanor, Rodney Brazier, Camilla Cavendish, David Dilks, Robert Hazell, Michael Jay, John Kerr, and Nick Macpherson. Especial thanks to the doyen of books about prime ministers, Dick Leonard. Anthony Goodenough and Daniel Finkelstein read the entire book in proofs, correcting errors and enriching the text.

A particular thanks must go to the history department at Exeter, above all to Jeremy Black, to whom I have spoken on this subject for many years, not least in a series of six podcasts earlier in 2020. He has inspired many historians with his unrivalled depth of historical understanding. Secondly, Bruce Coleman, who provided seventeen stunning submissions in the form of long memos on different aspects of this history, and then proceeded to comment meticulously on each chapter and section, and who has been the godfather of the book. We owe the greatest debt of gratitude to them both.

I began this book forty-five years ago when an undergraduate at Oxford, and would like to thank those who inspired me there, including David Butler, Vernon Bogdanor, Andrew Graham, Kenneth Morgan, 'Copper' Le May, Gillian Peele, and Dick Smethurst. At LSE, I was much inspired by my supervisor John Barnes, as well as the late George Jones and Patrick Dunleavy, and I began a lifelong friendship with my doctoral supervisor, David Dilks of Leeds, who provided many comments on this text drawing on his unrivaled knowledge of history.

At the Institute of Contemporary British History, which Peter Hennessy and I founded in 1987, I would like to thank several associated with it, including Brian Brivati, Kathleen Burk, Pippa Poppy Catterall, Richard Cockett, Peter Hennessy himself, Michael Kandiah, Stephanie Maggin, the late Dick Roberts, Virginia Preston, and Pat Thane. I met there two book collaborators, brilliant minds who became lifelong inspirations, Stuart Ball and Dennis Kavanagh.

At Eton College, thanks to Eleanor Hoare, Beck Price, and Paul Williams for the opening dialogue information, and to Dr John Taylor ex Tonbridge for Latin expletives.

On the Number 10 History Project, I would like to thank the many figures who have been such great colleagues there, including Andrew Blick, Jack Brown, Jon Davis, and David Heaton.

I put myself into my own full-throated lockdown for three months to write this book, which meant I let down colleagues in many organisation I am committed to, and my thanks for their understanding: Action for Happiness, IPEN, the RSC, Western Front Way-Via Sacra, and the National Archives Trust. On the other hand, it was my first book since my first when I haven't been working in or running organisations. Readers can decide if the extra time it gave me benefited the text.

Earlier versions of this book were tried out at many institutions and festivals, and I would like to thank David Runciman as well as the staff at Darwin College, Cambridge, Melvyn Bragg and the staff of Words by the Water Festival in the Lake District, John Adamson and the History Festival at the University of Buckingham, Jon Davis and Jack Brown at the Strand Group, at King's College, London, and David Tennant at Tonbridge School.

The book was written from October to December 2020 in Deal, Kent, in an AirBnB overlooking the sea c/o David Bennett. I would like to thank John and Louise James, Joe and Ginny Davies, and Flora and James Cockburn, as well as Vanessa Bellamy and Katie Garrod for their kind support and encouragement throughout. The manager of Copy Plus ensured that the text kept on flowing.

I finished this book on the fourth anniversary of my wife Joanna's death. Without her brilliance, inspiration, and support, none of the earlier books would have been written, and hence, neither would this book.

Finally, I would like to thank Sarah Sayer for her patience, love, and encouragement throughout the whole research and writing period, and my three children, Jessica, Susie, and Adam, without whom nothing would have been possible.

Notes

1 THE BOOKEND PRIME MINISTERS: WALPOLE AND JOHNSON

1. 'By Hercules!' (Latin).
2. Eleanor Hoare, Eton Archivist, Letter to the author, 16 October 2020; Beck Price, Archives Assistant, Letter to the author, 26 October 2020.
3. 'Wow!' (Latin).
4. 'I'm wasted' (Latin).
5. Jeremy Black, *Walpole in Power* (London: Sutton, 2001), p. 21.
6. John Carswell, *The South Sea Bubble* (London: Cresset Press, 1960), p. 243.
7. *Stamford Mercury*, 1 April 1721.
8. Black, *Walpole in Power*, p. 18.
9. Quoted in R. J. Minney, *No. 10 Downing Street: A House in History* (London: Cassell, 1963), pp. 44–7.
10. Count Hans Caspar von Bothmar was a Hanoverian minister who played an important part in the court of George I. Christopher Jones, *No. 10 Downing Street: The Story of a House* (London: BBC, 1985), p. 43.
11. *London Daily Post*, 23 September 1735.
12. *Guardian*, 24 July 2019.
13. *Metro*, 25 July 2019.
14. Nicholas Macpherson, 'The Origins of Treasury Control', speech, 16 January 2013, www.gov.uk/government/speeches/speech-by-the-permanent-secretary-to-the-treasury-sir-nicholas-macpherson-the-origins-of-treasury-control (accessed 24 November 2020).
15. Ragnhild Hatton, *George I* (New Haven, CT: Yale University Press, 2001), pp. 257–8.
16. Private information.
17. *The Times*, 4 September 2019.
18. Reed Browning, *The War of the Austrian Succession* (London: St Martin's Press, 1993), pp. 23–4.
19. Peter Jupp, *The Governing of Britain, 1688–1848: The Executive, Parliament and the People* (Abingdon: Routledge, 2006), pp. 18–21.
20. Jeremy Black, interview with Anthony Seldon, 14 February 2016.
21. Anne Somerset, *Queen Anne: The Politics of Passion* (London: HarperCollins, 2012), pp. 189–214.

22. David Scott, *Leviathan: The Rise of Britain as a World Power* (London: William Collins, 2013), p. 304.
23. J. H. Plumb, *The King's Minister* (London: Cresset, 1956), pp. 76–7.
24. Robert Tombs, *The English and Their History* (London: Allen Lane, 2014), p. 315.
25. Hatton, *George I*, pp. 128–31.
26. Tim Blanning, *George I* (London: Allen Lane, 2017), p. 60.
27. Paul Langford, *A Polite and Commercial People: England 1727–1783* (Oxford University Press, 1992), p. 38.
28. B. W. Hill, *Sir Robert Walpole* (London: Hamish Hamilton, 1989), *p*. 122.
29. Andrew Thompson, 'We're All Going on a Summer Holiday … to Hanover', *History of Government*, 27 August 2013, https://history.blog.gov.uk/2013/08/27/were-all-going-on-a-summer-holiday-to-hanover (accessed 17 November 2020).
30. Jeremy Black, interview with Anthony Seldon, 20 September 2020.
31. Andrew Thompson, *George II* (New Haven, CT: Yale University Press, 2011), *pp*. 69–70.
32. Ibid., *p*. 70.
33. Daniel Finkelstein, Baron Finkelstein, interview with Anthony Seldon, 30 March 2020.
34. Anthony Seldon, *10 Downing Street: The Illustrated History* (London: HarperCollins, 1999), p. 98.
35. Patrick Weller, interview with Anthony Seldon, 4 September 2020.
36. William Coxe, *Memoirs of the Life and Administration of Sir Robert Walpole, Earl of Orford*, vol. IV (London: Longman, Hurst, Rees, Orme and Brown, 1816), p. 258.
37. Peter Hennessy, 'The Role and Powers of the Prime Minister', *Parliament*, 15 March 2011, www.publications.parliament.uk/pa/cm201011/cmselect/cmpol con/writev/842/m2.htm (accessed 17 November 2020).
38. E 31/2/1/7778, fol. 49^r, National Archives, Kew; in C. Warren Hollister, 'The Origins of the English Treasury', *English Historical Review*, 93/367 (1978), pp. 262-75 (at 262).
39. Macpherson, 'Origins of Treasury Control'.
40. Andrew Blick and George Jones, *At Power's Elbow: Aides to the Prime Minister from Robert Walpole to David Cameron* (London: Biteback, 2013), pp. 38–9.
41. *The Times*, 5 October 2020.
42. H. T. Dickinson, *Walpole and the Whig Supremacy* (London: Hodder & Stoughton, 1973), p. 46.
43. Robin Lane-Fox, 'All in Good Taste', *Financial Times*, 16 August 2013.
44. Jeremy Black, interview with Anthony Seldon, 20 September 2020.
45. Andrew Blick and George Jones, *Premiership: The Development, Nature and Power of the Office of the British Prime Minister* (Exeter: Academic Imprint, 2010), p. 53.
46. William Coxe, who chronicled Walpole's government, thinks this sentence was taken greatly out of context, but confirms that Walpole said it. Coxe, *Memoirs of Walpole, Earl of Orford*, 3 vols. (London: Cadell, Jun & Davies, 1798), vol. III, pp. 349–50.
47. Dickinson, *Walpole and the Whig Supremacy*, p. 68.
48. Edward Pearce, *The Great Man: Sir Robert Walpole – Scoundrel, Genius and Britain's First Prime Minister* (London: Jonathan Cape, 2007), pp. 427–8.

49. Frank O'Gorman, *The Long Eighteenth Century: British Political and Social History 1688–1832* (London: Bloomsbury Academic, 1997), p. 94.

50. Blick and Jones, *At Power's Elbow*, p. 50; Coxe discussed the efforts to prosecute Walpole at length in Coxe, *Memoirs of Walpole*, vol. IV (1816 edn), pp. 284–321.

51. Blick and Jones, *At Power's Elbow*, p. 38.

52. Hennessy, 'Role and Powers of the Prime Minister'.

53. Hal Gladfelder, 'Introduction' in John Gay, *The Beggar's Opera and Polly*, ed. Hal Gladfelder (Oxford University Press, 2013), pp. xxi–xxii.

54. Jupp, *Governing of Britain, p.* 21.

55. Blick and Jones, *Premiership*, p. 53.

56. Scott, *Leviathan*, p. 295.

57. Rod Rhodes, interview with Anthony Seldon, 10 September 2020.

2 A COUNTRY TRANSFORMED, 1721–2021

1. Jeremy Black, interview with Anthony Seldon, 17 February 2016.

2. Mary Beggs-Humphreys, Hugh Gregor, and Darlow Humphreys, *The Industrial Revolution* (Abingdon: Routledge, 1959, repr. 2006), p. 48.

3. T. C. Barker and C. I. Savage, An *Economic History of Transport in Britain* (Abingdon: Routledge,1975, repr. 2011), p. 48.

4. Roy Porter, *London: A Social History* (London: Penguin, 1995), p. 106.

5. Charles Knight, *A History of England*, vol. VI: *1714–1783* (London: Bradbury and Evans, 1862), p. 263.

6. Johannes Kip, 'The Prospect of Whithall', Government Art Collection, 1724 www .artcollection.culture.gov.uk/artwork/1640 (accessed 15 November 2020).

7. William Hague, Baron Hague of Richmond, interview with Anthony Seldon, 20 March 2017.

8. William Anthony Hay, letter to the authors, 29 September 2020.

9. Ibid.

10. Elizabeth Longford, *Wellington: Pillar of State* (London: Harper & Row, 1970), p. 221.

11. David Cecil, *Lord M, or the Later Life of Lord Melbourne* (London: Constable, 1954), p. 280.

12. Sir Francis Grant, 'Queen Victoria Riding Out', RCIN 400749, Royal Collections Trust, Windsor.

13. P. J. Hugill, *World Trade Since 1431* (Baltimore, MD: Johns Hopkins University Press, 1993), p. 128.

14. Richard Gaunt, letter to the authors, 1 October 2020.

15. David Brown, interview with Anthony Seldon, 25 September 2020.

16. Robert Peel, '5 September 1842' in Charles Stuart Parker (ed.), *Sir Robert Peel: From His Private Papers*, 3 vols. (London: John Murray, 1899), vol. II, p. 585.

17. Stephen Roberts, 'The Companies Abroad', *Distant Writing,* 2012, www.distantwriting.co.uk /companiesandforeigntraffic.html (accessed 15 November 2020).

18. Angus Hawkins, interview with Anthony Seldon, 24 September 2020.

19. Angus Hawkins, interview with Anthony Seldon, 15 December 2017.

20. David Brown, interview with Anthony Seldon, 25 September 2020.

21. Angus Hawkins, interview with Anthony Seldon, 24 September 2020.

22. Douglas Hurd and Edward Young, *Disraeli or The Two Lives* (London: Weidenfeld & Nicolson, 2013), p. 229.

23. Edward Young, interview with Anthony Seldon, 25 September 2020.

24. 'Our Story', Royal Mail, 2020, www.royalmailgroup.com/en/about-us/our-story (accessed 24 November 2020).

25. Angus Hawkins, interview with Anthony Seldon, 15 December 2017.

26. J. L. Kieve, *The Telegraph: A Social and Economic History* (Newton Abbot: David & Charles, 1973), p. 176; Hugo Meyer, *The British State Telegraphs* (London: Macmillan, 1907), p. 78.

27. H. C. G. Matthew, *Gladstone 1809–1898* (Oxford: Clarendon Press, 1997), p. 147.

28. Elizabeth Bruton, '"The Cable Wars": Military and State Surveillance of the British Telegraph Cable Network during World War One' in Andreas Marklund and Rüdiger Morgens (eds.), *Historicizing Infrastructure* (Aalborg University Press, 2017).

29. P. M. Kennedy, 'Imperial Cable Communications and Strategy, 1870–1914', *English Historical Review*, 86/341 (1971), pp. 728–52 (at 751).

30. 'A History of Women in the UK Civil Service', p. 9, www.civilservant.org.uk/library/2 015_history_of_women_in_the_civil_service.pdf (accessed 4 December 2020).

31. Matthew, *Gladstone*, p. 316.

32. Angus Hawkins, interview with Anthony Seldon, 25 July 2019.

33. Andrew Roberts, interview with Anthony Seldon, 9 September 2020; R. J. Q. Adams, interview with Anthony Seldon, 30 September 2020.

34. R. J. Q. Adams, interview with Anthony Seldon, 30 September 2020.

35. Frances Lloyd George, *The Years that are Past* (London: Hutchinson, 1967), p. 91.

36. Ibid., p. 121.

37. Angus Hawkins, interview with Anthony Seldon, 24 September 2020.

38. Stuart Ball, letter to the authors, 6 October 2020.

39. David Dilks, letter to the authors, 2 October 2020.

40. Christopher H. Sterling, 'Churchill and Intelligence – Sigsaly: Beginning the Digital Revolution', *Finest Hour: The Journal of Winston Churchill*, 149 (2010), pp. 31–4.

41. 'Installation of telephone link between 10 Downing Street and the White House', PREM 11/3518, National Archives, Kew.

42. R. J. Q. Adams, letter to the authors, 30 September 2020.

43. '"Mr Balfour's Poodle"?', UK Parliament, 2020, www.parliament.uk/about/living-heritage/evolutionofparliament/houseoflords/parliamentacts/overview/balfour spoodle (accessed 15 October 2020).

44. Kenneth Morgan, interview with Anthony Seldon, 31 July 2017.

45. Geoffrey Dudley, *The Outer Cabinet: A History of the Government Car Service* (London: Government Car and Despatch Agency, 2008), p. 29.

46. Ibid.

47. 'Lloyd George Off to Paris: Bonar Law Makes the Trip, as Usually, by Airplane', *New York Times*, 12 January 1919.

48. Robert Self, *Neville Chamberlain: A Biography* (Aldershot: Ashgate, 2006), p. 212.

49. David Dilks, interview with Anthony Seldon, 2 October 2020.

50. Self, *Neville Chamberlain*, p. 312.

51. Peter Pigott, *Sailing Seven Seas: A History of the Canadian Pacific Line* (Toronto: Dundurn Press, 2010), p. 101.

52. Philip Williamson and Edward Baldwin (eds.), *Baldwin Papers: A Conservative Statesman, 1908–1947* (Cambridge University Press, 2004), p. 198.

53. Daniel Allen Butler, *Warrior Queens: The Queen Mary and Queen Elizabeth in World War II* (London: Pen & Sword, 2002), pp. 85, 92–5.

54. Charles Williams, *Harold Macmillan* (London: Weidenfeld & Nicolson, 2009) p. 314; 'Premier's Dramatic Peace Bid', *British Pathé*, 1958, www.britishpathe.com/video/prem iers-dramatic-peace-bid/query/Hard (accessed 10 November 2020).

55. Margaret Thatcher, 'Speech Presenting New Standard to No. 10 Squadron RAF', Margaret Thatcher Foundation, 30 September 1988, www.margaretthatcher.org/docu ment/107348 (accessed 15 November 2020).

56. 'Helicopter Arrangements for Camp David Conference', Eisenhower Presidential Library, 20 March 1959, www.eisenhowerlibrary.gov/sites/default/files/research/onl ine-documents/camp-david/macmillan.pdf (accessed 15 November 2020).

57. See 'Carlucci email to Colin Powell', 9 June 1987, Margaret Thatcher Foundation, for an early example of email correspondence at Number 10, www.margaretthatcher.org /document/110639 (accessed 15 November 2020).

58. 'Installations at Number 10 Timeline', www.gov.uk/government/history/10-downing-street (accessed 25 November 2020).

59. Harold Macmillan, 'Winds of Change' speech, delivered to the Parliament of South Africa, 3 February 1960.

60. 'United Kingdom', Soft Power 30, www.softpower30.com/country/united-kingdom (accessed 15 November 2020).

61. James Vernon, *Modern Britain: 1750 to the Present*, Cambridge History of Britain (Cambridge University Press, 2017), pp. 62–6; Callum G. Brown and W. Hamish Fraser, *Britain Since 1707* (London: Routledge, 2013), Kindle edition, location 5785.

62. K. Theodore Hoppen, *The Mid-Victorian Generation, 1846–1886* (Oxford University Press, 1998), pp. 129–30.

63. Robert Shepherd, *Westminster: A Biography: From Earliest Times to the Present* (London: Bloomsbury, 2012), pp. 309–10.

64. Vernon, *Modern Britain*, p. 13.

65. Ibid.

66. Charles Edward Trevelyan was permanent secretary to the Treasury, and Stafford Henry Northcote a future Chancellor of the Exchequer. Their report of 1854 had been commissioned by Gladstone when he was Chancellor.

67. Magnus Henrekson, 'The Peacock and Wiseman Displacement Effect: A Reappraisal and a New Test', *European Journal of Political Economy*, 6/3 (1990), pp. 245–60.

68. W. L. Stephen, *The Story of Number 10 Downing Street* (London: Stockwell, 1935), p. 9.

69. Robert Hazell, interview with Anthony Seldon, 22 October 2020.

70. B. R. Mitchell, *International Historical Statistics, 1750–2005: Europe* (London: Palgrave Macmillan, 2007).

71. 'Greater London, Inner London and Outer London, Population and Density History', *Demographia*, www.demographia.com/dm-lon31.htm (accessed 10 November 2020).

72. 'The Population of Cities in the United Kingdom 2020', *World Population Review*, 2020, www .worldpopulationreview.com/countries/cities/united-kingdom (accessed 7 November 2020).

73. Nathan Nunn and Nancy Qian, 'The Potato's Contribution to Population and Urbanization: Evidence from a Historical Experiment', *Quarterly Journal of Economics*, 126/2 (2001), pp. 593–650.

74. Rowland E. Prothero, *English Farming, Past and Present* (Cambridge University Press, 2013), p. 188.

75. Robert Blake, *Disraeli* (London: Methuen, 1966), p. 232.

76. Tombs, *The English*, p. 480.

77. Stephen Broadberry, Bruce M. S. Campbell, Alexander Klein, Mark Overton and Bas van Leeuwen, *British Economic Growth, 1270–1870* (Cambridge University Press, 2015), Table 5.6, p. 205.

78. Brown and Fraser, *Britain Since 1707*, Kindle edition, location 847.

79. S. J. D. Green, 'Review of Will Hay, "Lord Liverpool: A Political Life"', *Law and Liberty*, 13 May 2019, www.lawliberty.org/book-review/robert-jenkinson-second-earl-of-liverpool -guarantor-of-britains-stability-in-a-turbulent-time (accessed 15 November 2020).

80. Anthony Seldon and David Walsh, *The Public Schools and the Second World War* (London: Pen & Sword, 2020), pp. 245–50.

81. Jeremy Black, interview with Anthony Seldon, 14 February 2016.

82. Robert Blake, *The Office of Prime Minister* (Oxford University Press, 1975), p. 18.

83. Richard Adams and Xavier Greenwood, 'Oxford and Cambridge University Colleges Hold £21bn in Riches', *Guardian*, 28 May 2018.

84. Quoted in David Lammy, 'Review: "Who Runs This Place? The Anatomy of Britain in the 21st Century", Anthony Sampson', *Guardian*, 10 April 2004.

85. Linda Colley, *Britons: Forging the Nation 1707–1837* (New Haven, CT: Yale University Press, 2005).

86. Peter Catterall, 'The Party and Religion' in Anthony Seldon and Stuart Ball (eds.), *Conservative Century: The Conservative Party Since 1900* (Oxford University Press, 1994).

87. Popularised by preacher and suffragette Maude Royden-Shaw in a speech in London on 16 July 1917.

88. Eliza Filby, 'The Death of Tory Anglicanism', *Spectator*, 21 November 2013.

89. James A. Beckford, 'Politics and Religion in England and Wales', *Daedalus*, 120/3 (1991), pp. 179–201 (at 179).

90. 'Religion in England and Wales, 2011', Office for National Statistics (ONS), 11 December 2012, www.ons.gov.uk/peoplepopulationandcommunity/culturalidentity/ religion/articles/religioninenglandandwales2011/2012-12-11 (accessed 3 December 2020).

91. Elise Uberoi and Rebecca Lees, 'Ethnic Diversity in Politics and Public Life', House of Commons Library, 23 October 2020, https://commonslibrary.parliament.uk/research-briefings/sn01156 (accessed 31 December 2020).

92. 'Aliens Act', Jewish Virtual Library, 2008, www.jewishvirtuallibrary.org/aliens-act (accessed 25 November 2020).

93. 41,000 'from "Old Commonwealth" nations' and 123,000 'from the "New Commonwealth" nations', totalling 164,000, cited in: 'Record Immigration Levels to UK', *BBC News*, 20 October 2005, http://news.bbc.co.uk/2/hi/uk_news/4359756.stm (accessed 7 November 2020); 'Net Migration to UK Rises to 333,000 – Second Highest on Record', *BBC News*, 26 May 2016, www.bbc.co.uk/news/uk-politics-eu-referendum-36382199 (accessed 7 November 2020).

94. Net Migration to UK rises to 333,000.

95. Uberoi and Lees, 'Ethnic Diversity'.

96. Lady Williams (Jane Portal), lecture on Churchill at Number 10, November 2018.

97. See Caroline Slocock, *People Like Us: Margaret Thatcher and Me* (London: Biteback, 2018).

98. Caroline Slocock, interview with Anthony Seldon, 25 November 2020.

99. Rod Rhodes, interview with Anthony Seldon, 10 September 2020.

100. Tony Blair, *A Journey* (London: Arrow, 2010), p. 337.

101. Anthony Seldon with Lewis Baston, *Major: A Political Life* (London: Weidenfeld & Nicolson, 1997), p. 218.

102. Adrian Bingham, 'Monitoring the Popular Press: An Historical Perspective', History and Policy, 2 May 2005, www.historyandpolicy.org/policy-papers/papers/monitoring-the-popular-press-an-historical-perspective (accessed 20 October 2020).

103. Matthew, *Gladstone*, pp. 135–6.

104. Tom Clarke, *My Northcliffe Diary* (New York: Cosmopolitan; London: Victor Gollancz, 1931), p. 96.

105. Quoted in Byrum E. Carter, *The Office of the Prime Minister* (Princeton University Press, 1955), p. 91.

106. Raymond Newell and Anthony Seldon, 'Photography in British Political History' in R. A. W. Rhodes and Susan Hodgett (eds.), *What Political Science Can Learn from the Humanities* (London: Palgrave Macmillan, 2021).

107. 'History of Periodical Illustration', NC State University, 2020, https://ncna.dh.chass.ncsu.edu/imageanalytics/history.php (accessed 20 November 2020)

108. Bruce Colman, letter to the authors, 20 November 2020.

109. Nick Robinson, *Live from Downing Street: The Inside Story of Politics, Power and the Media* (London: Bantam, 2013), p. 68.

110. Peter Hennessy, *The Prime Minister: The Office and Its Holders since 1945* (London: Allen Lane, 2000), pp. 50–1.

111. Robinson, *Live from Downing Street*, p. 68.

112. Peter Mile and Malcolm Smith, *Cinema, Literature and Society: Elite and Mass Culture in Interwar Britain* (Breckenham: Croom Helm, 1987), p. 164.

113. 'About Newsreels and Cinemagazines', Learning on Screen: The British Universities and Colleges Films and Videos Council, 2020, www.learningonscreen.ac.uk/news reels/about (accessed 15 November 2020).

114. PRO T199-7, National Archives, Kew.

115. 'Neville Chamberlain's Declaration of War', *Observer*, 6 September 2009.

116. James Margach, *The Anatomy of Power: An Enquiry into the Personality of Leadership* (London: W. H. Allen, 1979), p. 137.

117. Quoted in Carter, *Office of the Prime Minister*, p. 106.

118. Jack Brown, *No. 10: The Geography of Power at Downing Street* (London: Haus, 2019), p. 97.

119. Harold Evans, *Downing Street Diary* (London: Hodder & Stoughton, 1981), p. 42.

120. Craig Oliver, *Unleashing Demons: The Inside Story of Brexit* (London: Hodder & Stoughton, 2016).

121. 'Mobile Internet Statistics', Finder, 10 November 2020, www.finder.com/uk/mobile-internet-statistics (accessed 15 November 2020).

3 THE LIMINAL PREMIERSHIP: FROM THE SAXONS TO 1806

1. Clive Bigham, *The Chief Ministers of England, 920–1720* (London: John Murray, 1923), pp. 2–5.

2. J. A. Giles (trans.) *The Anglo-Saxon Chronicle* (London: G. Bell & Sons, 1914), pp. 111–12.

3. David Bates, 'Odo, Earl of Kent (d. 1097)' in *Oxford Dictionary of National Biography* (Oxford University Press, 2004), www.doi.org/10.1093/ref:odnb/20543 (accessed 21 November 2020).

4. J. H. Baker, *An Introduction to English Legal History* (Oxford University Press, 2007), p. 15.

5. E. B. Fryde, D. E. Greenway, S. Porter, and I. Roy, *Handbook of British Chronology* (Cambridge University Press, 1996), pp. 70–2.

6. Ibid., pp. 70–2.

7. Bigham, *Chief Ministers*, p. 2.

8. A dilemma for the wealthy Tudor taxpayer: if he spent his money lavishly, then he clearly had enough to pay taxes to the king; if he saved his money frugally, he could easily dip into his savings to pay taxes to the king; 'Morton's Fork' in *The Oxford Dictionary of Phrase and Fable*, 16 October 2020, www.encyclopedia.com/humanities/dictionaries-thesauruses-pictures-and-press-releases/mortons-fork (accessed 21 November 2020).

9. Diarmaid MacCulloch, letter to the authors, 26 October 2020.

10. Diarmaid MacCulloch, 'Thomas Cromwell', talk at 10 Downing Street, 2019.

11. Tombs, *The English*, p. 165.

12. Paul Lay, interview with Anthony Seldon, 14 October 2020.

13. James I, quoted in Charles Howard McIlwain (ed.), *The Political Works of James I* (Cambridge, MA: Harvard University Press, 1918), p. 307.

14. Carter, *Office of the Prime Minister*, p. 15.

15. Mark A. Thomson, *A Constitutional History of England: 1642–1801* (London: Methuen, 1938), pp. 109–10.

16. Clarendon, quoted in Carter, *Office of the Prime Minister*, p. 16.

17. Mary Taylor Blauvelt, *The Development of Government in England* (New York: Macmillan, 1902), p. 35.

18. Carter, *Office of the Prime Minister*, p. 18.

19. Jupp, *Governing of Britain*, p. 19.

20. Queen Anne, 7 August 1710, quoted in 'A Review of the Life of John Duke of Marlborough' in John Benson Rose, *Historical Tracts* (London: William Clowes and Sons, 1869), p. 124.

21. Carter, *Office of the Prime Minister*, p. 19.

22. Shepherd, *Westminster*, p. 194.

23. Judith Lissauer Cromwell, *Good Queen Anne: Appraising the Life and Reign of the Last Stuart Monarch* (Jefferson, NC: McFarland, 2019), p. 126.

24. John Brewer, *The Sinews of Power: War and the English State, 1688–1783* (London: Unwin Hyman, 1989).

25. Paul Lay, interview with Anthony Seldon, 14 October 2020.

26. Carter, *Office of the Prime Minister*, p. 23.

27. Andrew Gimson, *Gimson's Prime Ministers* (London: Square Peg, 2018), p. 7.

28. Dick Leonard, *A History of British Prime Ministers* (London: Palgrave Macmillan, 2014), p. 33.

29. George II and Horace Walpole, quoted in Gimson, *Gimson's Prime Ministers*, p. 11.

30. Leonard, *History of British Prime Ministers*, p. 47.

31. Reed Browning, 'Thomas Pelham-Hobbes, duke of Newcastle (1693–1758)' in *Oxford Dictionary of National Biography* (Oxford University Press, 2004), www.oxforddnb.com/view/10.1093/ref:odnb/9780198614128.001.0001/odnb-9780198614128-e-21801 (accessed 26 November 2020).

32. H. T. Dickinson, quoted in Leonard, *History of British Prime Ministers*, p. 62.

33. P. J. Kulisheck, *The Duke of Newcastle, 1693–1768, and Henry Pelham, 1694–1754: A Bibliography* (London: Greenwood Press, 1997), p. xvii.

34. Richard Middleton, *The Bells of Victory: The Pitt–Newcastle Ministry and the Conduct of the Seven Years' War, 1757–1762* (Cambridge University Press, 1985), p. ix.

35. Andrew O'Shaughnessy, interview with Anthony Seldon, 18 October 2020.

36. E. N. Williams (ed.), *The Eighteenth-Century Constitution: Documents and Commentary* (Cambridge University Press, 1960), pp. 69, 85.

37. Edmund Burke, 'Thoughts on the Present Discontent' in *The Works* (Boston: Little, Brown, 1881), vol. I, p. 446.

38. Daniel Finkelstein, interview with Anthony Seldon, 20 March 2020.

39. Romney Sedgwick (ed.), *Letters from George III to Lord Bute, 1756–1766* (London: Macmillan, 1939), p. 196.

40. Philip Lawson, *George Grenville: A Political Life* (Oxford University Press, 1984), p. 202.

41. Ibid., p. 183.

42. Peter Whiteley, *Lord North: The Prime Minister Who Lost America* (London: Hambledon Press, 1996), pp. 135–6.

43. Leonard, *History of British Prime Ministers*, p. 91.

44. Lawson, *George Grenville*, p. 219.
45. Daniel Finkelstein, interview with Anthony Seldon, 20 March 2020.
46. Walter Bagehot, 'William Pitt, 1861' in Russell Barrington (ed.), *The Works and Life of Walter Bagehot*, vol. IV (London: Longmans, Green, 1915), p. 11.
47. Marie Peters, *Profiles in Power: The Elder Pitt* (Harlow: Addison, Wesley, Longmans, 1998), pp. 89, 98.
48. Middleton, *Bells of Victory*, p. 212.
49. Peters, *Profiles in Power*, p. 6.
50. Ibid., p. 175.
51. Ibid., pp. 181–4.
52. Leonard, *History of British Prime Ministers*, p. 129.
53. Ibid., p. 139.
54. Ibid., p. 141.
55. Andrew Roberts, interview with Anthony Seldon, 9 September 2020.
56. Davies, quoted in Carter, *Office of the Prime Minister*, p. 27.
57. Charles Fox, *Memoirs*, vol. I (London: R. Bentley, 1853), p. 203.
58. Andrew O'Shaughnessy, interview with Anthony Seldon, 18 October 2020.
59. Andrew O'Shaughnessy, *The Men who Lost America: British Command during the Revolutionary War and the Preservation of the Empire* (New Haven, CT: Yale University Press, 2013), p. 44.
60. Ibid., p. 76.
61. Whiteley, *Lord North*, pp. 227–8.
62. Lord North, quoted in Williams (ed.), *Eighteenth-Century Constitution*, p. 132.
63. Ibid., pp. 90–1.
64. O'Shaughnessy, *Men who Lost America*, p. 68.
65. Ibid.
66. Andrew O'Shaughnessy, interview with Anthony Seldon, 18 October 2020.
67. Blake, *Office of Prime Minister*, p. 27.
68. Lord Campbell, *The Lives of the Lord Chancellors*, vol. V (Philadelphia: Blanchard and Lea, 1851), p. 434.
69. William Hague, *William Pitt the Younger* (London: Harper Perennial, 2004), pp. 106–7.
70. Edmond Dziembowski, 'Lord Shelburne's Constitutional Views in 1782–3' in Nigel Aston and Clarissa Campbell (eds.), *An Enlightenment Statesman in Whig Britain: Lord Shelburne in Context, 1737–1805* (Woodbridge: Boydell Press, 2011), pp. 218–19.
71. Ibid., p. 219.
72. John Cannon, *The Fox–North Coalition* (Cambridge University Press, 1969), p. 59.
73. John Cannon, 'Lord Shelburne's Ministry, 1782–3: :A Very Good List"' in Aston and Campbell (eds.), *Enlightenment Statesman*, p. 174.
74. Andrew Roberts, interview with Anthony Seldon, 9 September 2020.
75. Letter from Lord Hardwicke to Duke of Newcastle, 3 January 1755, in Williams (ed.), *Eighteenth-Century Constitution*, pp. 130–1.
76. Jupp, *Governing of Britain*, p. 128.
77. Ibid.

78. Jeremy Black, interview with Anthony Seldon, 20 September 2020.

79. George III, quoted in Middleton, *Bells of Victory*, p. 19.

80. William Pitt, 4 April 1754, quoted in Williams (ed.), *Eighteenth-Century Constitution*, pp. 84–5.

81. J. H. Plumb, *The Growth of Political Stability in England, 1675–1725* (London: Macmillan, 1967), p. 105.

82. The specific laws repealed were 4 and 5 Anne (Regency Act), c. 20, cl. 27, 28 repealing 12 and 13 William III (Act of Settlement), 168–9, cc. 2, 3. The bill received the royal assent on 10 March 1706.

83. The Master of the Ordnance was the person in charge of artillery, fortifications, and military supplies. He was not in charge of army land forces and was an entirely separate position from the Commander in Chief. The artillery at this point was considered an entirely separate branch of the armed forces and wore different uniforms to the army; Williams (ed.), *Eighteenth-Century Constitution*, p. 111.

84. Duke of Argyll, 1 March 1739, in Williams (ed.), *Eighteenth-Century Constitution*, p. 116.

85. Anthony Seldon with Jonathan Meakin, *The Cabinet Office, 1916–2016* (London: Biteback, 2016), pp. 6–8; Historic Manuscripts Commission, *The Manuscripts of the Earl of Dartmouth* (London, 1887), pp. 372–3; see also Peter Thomas, *Tea Party to Independence: The Third Phase of the American Revolution, 1773–1776* (Oxford University Press, 1991), pp. 178–80.

86. Cabinet minutes, 18 August 1780, GEO/MAIN/3929, Royal Collection Trust, Windsor.

87. Jeremy Black, interview with Anthony Seldon, 14 February 2016.

88. 'Parliament' in *Encyclopaedia Britannica*, 5 May 2017, www.britannica.com/topic/Parliament (accessed 20 November 2020).

89. Jupp, *Governing of Britain*, p. 19.

90. James Waldegrave, *Memoirs, from 1754 to 1758* (London: John Murray, 1821), p. 117.

91. John Clarke, interview with Anthony Seldon, 20 October 2020.

92. Daniel Finkelstein, interview with Anthony Seldon, 20 March 2020.

93. Jupp, *Governing of Britain*, pp. 136–7.

94. Ibid., p. 33.

95. William Hague, interview with Anthony Seldon, 7 October 2020.

96. Bruce Coleman, email to the authors, 22 October 2020.

97. Waldegrave, *Memoirs*, p. 130.

98. Duke of Portland, quoted in David Wilkinson, *The Duke of Portland: Politics and Party in the Age of George III* (London: Palgrave Macmillan, 2003), p. ix.

99. Edmund Burke, 'A Letter to a Noble Lord' (1796), *Harvard Classics*, 24.4 (New York: P. F. Collier & Son, 1909–14), para 16, www.bartleby.com/24/4/1.html (accessed 20 November 2020).

100. Jeremy Black, interview with Anthony Seldon, 14 February 2016.

101. Michael Turner, *Pitt the Younger: A Life* (London: Hambledon, 2003), p. 94.

102. Leonard, *History of British Prime Ministers*, p. 201.

103. Hague, *William Pitt the Younger*, pp. 588–9.

104. William Pitt, *The Speech of the Right Honourable William Pitt, on a Motion for the Abolition of the Slave Trade*, House of Commons, 2 April 1792 (London: James Phillips, 1792).

105. John Bew, interview with Anthony Seldon, 27 September 2020.

106. Winston Churchill, 'Foreword' in *The War Speeches of William Pitt the Younger* (Oxford: Clarendon Press, 1940).

107. William Wilberforce, quoted in Asa Briggs, *The Making of Modern England, 1783–1867* (London: Harper & Row, 1959), pp. 148–9.

108. Andrew Roberts, interview with Anthony Seldon, 9 September 2020.

109. George Canning, 'Song for the Inauguration of the Pitt Club', 25 May 1802.

110. Hague, *William Pitt the Younger*, p. 565.

111. William Pitt the Younger, quoted in Gimson, *Gimson's Prime Ministers*, p. 54.

112. Tombs, *The English*, p. 430.

113. John Bew, interview with Anthony Seldon, 27 September 2020.

114. William Hague, letter to the authors, 8 October 2020.

115. Leonard, *History of British Prime Ministers*, pp. 210–11.

116. William Pitt the Younger, 16 May 1792, quoted in Hague, *William Pitt the Younger*, p. 316.

117. William Hague, letter to the authors, 8 October 2020.

118. Hague, *William Pitt the Younger*, pp. 584–5.

119. John Kerr, interview with Anthony Seldon, 19 September 2020.

120. Hennessy, *The Prime Minister*, p. 38; Blick and Jones, *Premiership*, p. 110.

121. Samuel Sandys, 1741, quoted in Williams (ed.), *Eighteenth-Century Constitution*, pp. 126–8.

122. Robert Walpole, quoted in Williams (ed.), *Eighteenth-Century Constitution*, p. 130.

123. Duke of Newcastle, quoted in Williams (ed.), *Eighteenth-Century Constitution*, p. 125.

124. Jupp, *Governing of Britain*, p. 18.

125. North, quoted in Carter, *Office of the Prime Minister*, p. 27.

126. Lewis Namier, *Crossroads of Power: Essays on Eighteenth-Century England* (London: Hamish Hamilton, 1962), p. 112.

127. H. Pellew, *Life of Viscount Sidmouth* (London: John Murray, 1847), p. 116.

128. *The Times*, 18 May 1805, and *The Times*, 8 July 1805, in Blick and Jones, *Premiership*, p. 112.

129. Hansard, House of Commons (HC) Debates, 29 April 1805, vol. 4, col. 495.

130. Ibid., col. 496.

131. Hansard, House of Lords (HL) Debates, 3 March 1806, vol. 6, cols. 277–8.

132. Blick and Jones, *Premiership*, p. 112.

133. Quoted ibid., p. 112.

134. Hansard, House of Commons (HC) Debate, 12 June 1846, vol. 87, col. 429.

135. Quoted in Vernon Bogdanor, 'Ministers Take the Biscuit', *Times Higher Education Supplement*, 3 October 1997.

136. Jupp, *Governing of Britain*, p. 18.

137. Blick and Jones, *Premiership*, p. 113. See Hansard, House of Lords (HL) Debate, 6 July 1895, vol. 35, col. 262; and Hansard, House of Lords (HL) Debate, 1 July 1895, vol. 35, col. 45.

138. Blick and Jones, *Premiership*, p. 113.

139. Ibid., p. 114

140. Ibid., pp. 114–15.

4 THE TRANSFORMATIONAL PRIME MINISTERS, 1806–2021

1. Norman Gash, *Lord Liverpool: The Life and Political Career of Robert Banks Jenkinson, Second Earl of Liverpool, 1770–1828* (Cambridge University Press, 1984), p. 1.

2. William Anthony Hay, interview with Anthony Seldon, 23 September 2020.

3. Bruce Coleman, letter to the authors, 26 November 2020.

4. David Brown, *Palmerston: A Biography* (New Haven, CT: Yale University Press, 2010), p. 241.

5. Robert Blake, *The Conservative Party from Peel to Churchill* (London: Eyre & Spottiswoode, 1970); subsequent volumes continued to 'Thatcher' and then finally to 'Major'.

6. Robert Crowcroft, interview with Anthony Seldon, 24 September 2020.

7. Jupp, *Governing of Britain*, p. 129.

8. Blick and Jones, *Premiership*, pp. 134–6.

9. Angus Hawkins, interview with Anthony Seldon, 24 September 2020.

10. Norman Gash, *Sir Robert Peel: The Life of Sir Robert Peel after 1830* (London: Longman, 1972), p. 286.

11. Jupp, *Governing of Britain*, p. 129.

12. Carter, *Office of the Prime Minister*, p. 33.

13. Robert Peel, in Parker (ed.), *From His Private Papers*, vol. ii, p. 575.

14. Ibid., vol. iii, p. 8.

15. Ibid., pp. 228–9.

16. Boyd Hilton, 'Peel: A Reappraisal', *Historical Journal*, 22/3 (1979), pp. 585–614 (at 587).

17. Gash, *Sir Robert Peel*, pp. 714–15.

18. Andrew Roberts, *Salisbury: Victorian Titan* (London: Weidenfeld & Nicolson, 1999), p. 13.

19. John Prest, 'Peel, Sir Robert' in *Oxford Dictionary of National Biography* (Oxford University Press, 2004), www.oxforddnb.com/view/10.1093/ref:odnb/978019861412 8.001.0001/odnb-9780198614128-e-21764 (accessed 23 December 2020).

20. John Morley, *The Life of William Ewart Gladstone* (London: Macmillan, 1903), p. 269.

21. Angus Hawkins, interview with Anthony Seldon, 24 September 2020.

22. Gladstone, in M. R. D. Foot and G. C. G. Matthew (eds.), *The Gladstone Diaries*, 14 vols. (Oxford University Press, 1968–94), vol. iii, p. 559 (13 July 1846); in Boyd Hilton, *A Mad, Bad, and Dangerous People? England, 1783–1846* (Oxford University Press, 2006), p. 506.

23. Bruce Coleman, letter to the authors, 26 November 2020.

24. Angus Hawkins, *The Forgotten Prime Minister: The 14th Earl of Derby*, vol. i: *Assent, 1799–1815* (Oxford University Press, 2007) and vol. ii: *Achievement, 1851–69* (Oxford University Press, 2008).

25. Angus Hawkins, interview with Anthony Seldon, 25 September 2020.

26. Gimson, *Gimson's Prime Ministers*, p. 110.

27. Jonathan Parry, 'Lord Derby', *History of Government*, 1 June 2016, https://history.blog.gov.uk/2016/06/01/lord-derby (accessed 25 November 2020).

28. Roy Hattersley 'Viscount Palmerston', in Iain Dale (ed.), *The Prime Ministers*, (London: Hodder & Stoughton, 2020), p. 214.

29. Ibid., p. 216.

30. Laurence Fenton, *Palmerston and The Times: Foreign Policy, the Press and Public Opinion in Mid-Victorian Britain* (London: I. B. Taurus, 2012), pp. 1–2.

31. Leonard, *History of British Prime Ministers*, p. 428.

32. David Brown, interview with Anthony Seldon, 25 September 2020.

33. E. D. Steele, *Palmerston and Liberalism, 1855–1865* (Cambridge University Press, 1991), p. 367.

34. Viscount Palmerston, memorandum dated 20 October 1861, Layard Papers, BL, Add Ms 38987, fol. 301.

35. Bruce Coleman, letter to the authors, 26 November 2020.

36. Richard Gaunt, 'From Country Party to Conservative Party: The Ultra-Tories and Foreign Policy' in Jeremy Black (ed.), *The Tory World: Deep History and the Tory Theme in British Foreign Policy, 1679–2014* (Farnham: Ashgate, 2015), p. 152.

37. Angus Hawkins, interview with Anthony Seldon, 24 September 2020.

38. John Campbell, *Pistols at Dawn: Two Hundred Years of Political Rivalry from Pitt and Fox to Blair and Brown* (London: Vintage, 2010), p. 90.

39. Bruce Coleman, letter to the authors, 17 November 2020.

40. Bruce Coleman, letter to the authors, 26 November 2020.

41. Bruce Coleman, letter to the authors, 17 November 2020.

42. Jeremy Black, interview with Anthony Seldon, 14 February 2016.

43. Nathaniel Rothschild, *'You have it, Madam'*: *The Purchase, in 1875, of Suez Canal Shares by Disraeli and Baron Lionel de Rothschild* (London: W. & J. Mackay, 1980), http://www.victorianweb.org/history/polspeech/suez.html (accessed 20 November 2020).

44. Bruce Coleman, interview with Anthony Seldon, 7 October 2020.

45. Blake, *Disraeli*, p. 764.

46. Ibid., p. 697.

47. Blake, *Office of Prime Minister*, p. 21.

48. Bruce Coleman, letter to the authors, 26 November 2020.

49. Richard Aldous, interview with Anthony Seldon, 17 September 2020.

50. Simon Heffer, 'William Gladstone' in Dale (ed.), *Prime Ministers*, p. 239.

51. Bruce Coleman, letter to the authors, 26 November 2020.

52. Stuart Ball (ed.), *The Advent of Democracy: The Impact of the 1918 Reform Act on British Politics* (Hoboken, NJ: Wiley-Blackwell, 2018), p. 2.

53. Matthew, *Gladstone*, p. 642.

54. Quoted in Peter John Jagger, *Gladstone* (London: Hambledon Press, 1998), p. xii.

55. Matthew, *Gladstone*, p. 253.

56. Ibid., p. 316.

57. Ibid., p. 236.

58. Algernon West in Horace G. Hutchinson (ed.), *Private Diaries of the Rt. Hon. Sir Algernon West* (New York: E. P. Dutton, 1922), p. 150.

59. Chris Wrigley, 'Gladstone and Labour' in Roland Quinault, Roger Swift, and Ruth Clayton Windscheffel (eds.), *William Gladstone: New Studies and Perspectives* (Abingdon: Routledge, 2012), p. 70.

60. Matthew, *Gladstone*, p. 173.

61. Ibid., p. 173.

62. Bruce Coleman, letter to the authors, 17 November 2020.

63. Matthew, *Gladstone*, pp. 641–2.

64. Eugenio Biagini, 'Gladstone's Legacy', in Quinault, Swift, and Windscheffel (eds.), *William Gladstone*, pp. 297–9.

65. Matthew, *Gladstone*, pp. 400–1.

66. David Marquand, *Ramsay MacDonald* (London: Richard Cohen, 1997), p. 330.

67. Blair, *A Journey*, p. 225.

68. John Bew, *Citizen Clem: A Biography of Attlee* (London: riverrun, 2017), p. 32.

69. Jeremy Black, History Interview Series with Anthony Seldon, Buckingham University, 8 May 2020.

70. Roberts, *Salisbury*.

71. Ibid., p. 328.

72. Paul Smith (ed.), *Lord Salisbury on Politics: A Selection of His Articles in Quarterly Review, 1860–1883* (Cambridge University Press, 1972); Paul Smith is quoted in Roberts, *Salisbury*, p. 837.

73. Seldon, *10 Downing Street*, p. 121.

74. John Grigg, *Lloyd George: from Peace to War 1912–16,* (London: Methuen, 1985) pp. 470–1.

75. David R. Woodward, *Lloyd George and the Generals* (Newark: University of Delaware Press, 1983), p. 199.

76. Damian Collins, 'David Lloyd George' in Dale (ed.), *Prime Ministers*, p. 301.

77. Seldon with Meakin, *Cabinet Office*, pp. 40–71.

78. Blick and Jones, *At Power's Elbow*, pp. 133–4.

79. John Turner, *Lloyd George's Secretariat* (Cambridge University Press, 1980), pp. 50–1, 116–20.

80. *Monthly Review of the U.S. Bureau of Labor Statistics*, 4 (January–June 1917), p. 770; *List of Board of Trade Records*, vol. IV (London: HMSO, 1978), p. 351.

81. A. J. McKenna, *100 Years of Government Communication* (London: OGL, 2018), pp. 23–4.

82. Woodward, *Lloyd George and the Generals*, p. 199.

83. Kenneth O. Morgan, 'David Lloyd George' in *Oxford Dictionary of National Biography*, repr. in Hugh Purcell, *Lloyd George* (London: Haus, 2006), p. 32.

84. Purcell, *Lloyd George*, pp. 141–2.

85. Kenneth O. Morgan, 'David Lloyd George' in Duncan Brack, Robert Ingham, and Tony Little (eds.) *British Liberal Leaders* (London: Biteback, 2015), p. 256.

86. Ibid.

87. John Campbell, interview with Anthony Seldon, 30 September 2020; see also John Campbell, *Lloyd George: The Goat in the Wilderness, 1922–1931* (London: Jonathan Cape, 1977).

88. Kenneth O. Morgan, Baron Morgan, interview with Anthony Seldon, 16 October 2020.

89. Quoted in Blick and Jones, *At Power's Elbow*, p. 145.

90. Philip Williamson, *Stanley Baldwin: Conservative Leadership and National Values* (Cambridge University Press, 1999).

91. Williamson and Baldwin (eds.), *Baldwin Papers*, pp. 3–4.

92. Stuart Ball, interview with Anthony Seldon, 29 September 2020.

93. Bruce Coleman, letter to the authors, 26 November 2020.

94. Kenneth O. Morgan, Baron Morgan, interview with Anthony Seldon, 16 October 2020.

95. Kevin Theakston and Mark Gill, 'Rating 20th-Century British Prime Ministers', *British Journal of Politics and International Relations*, 8/2 (2006), pp. 193–213.

96. Blick and Jones, *At Power's Elbow*, pp. 169–70.

97. Andrew Roberts, interview with Anthony Seldon, 9 September 2020.

98. Robert Crowcroft, interview with Anthony Seldon, 24 September 2020.

99. Lewis E. Lehrman, 'The Prime Minister and the General: Churchill and Eisenhower', *Finest Hour: The Journal of Winston Churchill*, 172 (2016), p. 15.

100. Anthony Seldon, 'Clement Attlee' in Dale (ed.), *Prime Ministers*, pp. 370–82.

101. Quoted in Patrick Diamond, 'Governing as a Permanent Form of Campaigning: Why the Civil Service is in Mortal Danger', *LSE BPP*, 13 August 2019, https://blogs.lse.ac.uk/po liticsandpolicy/why-the-civil-service-is-in-mortal-danger (accessed 9 December 2020).

102. Nicklaus Thomas-Symonds, *Attlee: A Life in Politics* (London: I. B Taurus, 2010), p. 271.

103. Vernon Bogdanor, interview with Anthony Seldon, January 2018.

104. John Bew, interview with Anthony Seldon, 27 September 2020.

105. Andrew Adonis, Baron Adonis, interview with Anthony Seldon, 29 September 2020.

106. Peter Hennessy, 'The Statecraft of Clement Attlee', The Thirteenth Annual Attlee Foundation Lecture, Queen Mary and Westfield College, University of London, 14 February 1995, p. 4.

107. Andrew Adonis, Baron Adonis, interview with Anthony Seldon, 29 September 2020.

108. Seldon, 'Clement Attlee', p. 373; Hansard, House of Commons (HC) Debates, 6 December 1945, vol. 416, cc. 2530–99.

109. Robert Hazell, 'Prime Ministers and the Constitution', *History of Government*, 24 April 2013, https://history.blog.gov.uk/2013/04/24/prime-ministers-and-the-constitution (accessed 19 November 2020).

110. John Ramsden, *The Making of Conservative Party Policy: The Conservative Research Department since 1929* (London: Longman, 1980), p. 265.

111. Philip Ziegler, *Edward Heath: The Authorised Biography* (London: HarperPress, 2010), p. xi.

112. George Hutchinson, *The Last Edwardian at No. 10: An Impression of Harold Macmillan* (London: Quartet, 1980).

113. Bruce Coleman, letter to the authors, 28 October 2020.

114. The title of a celebrated book by financial journalist Michael Shanks, *The Stagnant Society* (Harmondsworth: Penguin, 1961).

115. Alistair Horne, *Harold Macmillan`*, vol. II: *1957–1986* (London: Macmillan, 1989), pp. 556–65.

116. Roy Jenkins, 'Wilson, (James) Harold, Baron Wilson of Rievaulx (1916–1995)' in *Oxford Dictionary of National Biography* (Oxford University Press, 2004), www .oxforddnb.com/view/10.1093/ref:odnb/9780198614128.001.0001/odnb-978019 8614128-e-58000 (accessed 23 December 2020).

117. Hennessy, 'Statecraft of Clement Attlee', p. 4.

118. Graham Goodlad and Robert Pearce, *British Prime Ministers from Balfour to Brown* (Abingdon: Routledge, 2013), p. 170.

119. Northern Ireland border poll (1973), turnout 58.7 per cent.

120. Ben Pimlott, *Harold Wilson* (London: HarperCollins, 1992), pp. 617–18.

121. Andrew Thorpe, *A History of the British Labour Party* (London: Palgrave, 2001), pp. 145–65.

122. See Kevin Hickson and Jasper Miles (eds.), *James Callaghan: An Underrated Prime Minister?* (London: Biteback, 2020).

123. Vernon Bogdanor, 'Was "Sunny Jim" Really Such a Disastrous PM?', *Sunday Telegraph*, 22 November 2020.

124. Steve Richards, interview with Anthony Seldon, 14 September 2020.

125. See Richard Cockett, *Thinking the Unthinkable: Think-tanks and the Economic Counter-Revolution 1931–1983* (London: HarperCollins, 1994).

126. David Cannadine, *Margaret Thatcher: A Life and Legacy* (Oxford University Press, 2017), p. 120.

127. John Campbell, Martin Holmes, and G. W. Jones, 'Thatcherism', *Contemporary Record*, 1/3, (1987), pp. 2–24.

128. Charles Moore, *Margaret Thatcher: The Authorized Biography*, vol. III: *Herself Alone* (London: Allen Lane, 2019), p. 854.

129. Ibid., p. 853.

130. Dennis Kavanagh, interview with Anthony Seldon, 29 May 2020.

131. For one such comparison, see Cannadine, *Margaret Thatcher*, pp. 3, 82.

132. Moore, *Margaret Thatcher*, vol. III, pp. 53–5.

133. Cannadine, *Margaret Thatcher*, p. 121.

134. Seldon with Baston, *Major*, p. 152.

135. Chris Collins, letter to the authors, 20 November 2020.

136. Simon Jenkins, *Accountable to None: The Tory Nationalization of Britain* (London: Hamish Hamilton, 1995).

137. Robert Crowcroft, interview with Anthony Seldon, 24 September 2020.

138. Philip Norton, Baron Norton of Louth, interview with Anthony Seldon, 7 May 2020.

139. Anthony Seldon, 'The Cabinet Office and Coordination, 1979–87', in R. A. W. Rhodes and Patrick Dunleavy (eds.), *Prime Minister, Cabinet and Core Executive* (London: St Martin's Press, 1995), pp. 125–48.

140. See Anthony Seldon, 'Margaret Thatcher' in Anthony Seldon, *Blair* (London: Free Press, 2004), pp. 441–52.

141. Cannadine, *Margaret Thatcher*, p. 126.

142. Anthony Seldon and Guy Lodge, *Brown at 10* (London: Biteback, 2010), p. 41; *Guardian*, 13 September 2007.

143. Anthony Seldon and Peter Snowdon, *Cameron at 10: The Verdict* (London: William Collins, 2016), pp. 317–22.

144. Vernon Bogdanor, 'Thirty Years After She Quit, We Need a New Dose of Thatcherism', *Sunday Times*, 22 November 2020.

5 THE POWERS AND RESOURCES OF THE PRIME MINISTER, 1721–2021

1. Mark Sedwill, Baron Sedwill, interview with Anthony Seldon, 25 November 2020.

2. Gus O'Donnell, Baron O'Donnell, letter to the authors, 25 September 2020.

3. Andrew Turnbull, Lord Turnbull, interview with Anthony Seldon, 17 July 2020.

4. 'The Australian Constitution', p. 18, www.aph.gov.au/about_parliament/senate/pow ers_practice_n_procedures/constitution (accessed 30 November 2020).

5. 'Prime Minister: Roles, Powers and Restraints', *Australian Politics*, 2020, www .australianpolitics.com/executive/pm/prime-minister-roles-powers-restraints (accessed 26 November 2020).

6. 'Our Constitution', *New Zealand Now*, 22 June 2020, www.newzealandnow.govt.nz/liv ing-in-nz/history-government/our-constitution (accessed 26 November 2020).

7. Gavin McLean, 'Premiers and prime ministers' in *Te Ara – the Encyclopedia of New Zealand*, 1 December 2016, www.teara.govt.nz/en/premiers-and-prime-ministers (accessed 7 December 2020).

8. Gus O'Donnell, Baron O'Donnell, interview with Anthony Seldon, 18 September 2020.

9. See 'Elections in India', 2020, www.elections.in (accessed 26 November 2020).

10. Brendan O'Leary, 'An Taoiseach: The Irish Prime Minister', *West European Politics*, 14/2 (1991), pp. 133–62 (at 159).

11. 'Tasks of the Federal Chancellor', Chancellery, 2020, www.bundeskanzlerin.de/bkin-en/chancellery/tasks-of-the-chancellor (accessed 26 November 2020).

12. See John Kampfner, *Why the Germans Do It Better* (London: Atlantic, 2020).

13. 'The Function of the Prime Minister', Italian Government, www.governo.it/it/il-governo-funzioni-struttura-e-storia/la-funzione-del-presidente-del-consiglio/188 (accessed 26 November 2020).

14. Michael Calingaert, 'Italy's Choice: Reform or Stagnation', *Current History*, 107/707 (March 2008), pp. 105–11 (at 105–7), www.brookings.edu/wp-content/uploads/2016 /06/03_italy_calingaert.pdf.

15. Dennis Kavanagh, interview with Anthony Seldon, 29 May 2020.

16. Patrick Weller, interview with Anthony Seldon, 4 September 2020.

17. Ibid.

18. Public Administration Select Committee, *Taming the Prerogative: Strengthening Ministerial Accountability to Parliament* (HC 422, 2003–4) (London: Stationery Office), p. 5. See also Sebastian Payne, 'The Royal Prerogative' in S. Payne and M. Sunkin (eds.), *The Nature of the Crown: A Legal and Political Analysis* (Oxford University Press, 1999), pp. 77–110.

19. *The Cabinet Manual* (London: Cabinet Office, 2011), pp. 2–3, 8, 25.

20. A. V. Dicey, *Introduction to the Study of the Law of the Constitution*, 10th edn, (London: Macmillan: 1959), p. 424.
21. Walter Bagehot, *The English Constitution* (London: Chapman & Hall, 1867).
22. Kevin Theakston and Philip Connelly, *William Armstrong and British Policymaking* (London: Palgrave Macmillan, 2018), p. 64.
23. W. Armstrong, *Function of the Prime Minister and His Staff* (London: Cabinet Office Papers, 1947), p. 4, CAB 21/1638, National Archives, Kew.
24. Ibid., p. 5.
25. Ibid.
26. Ibid., pp. 8–9.
27. Gus O'Donnell, Baron O'Donnell, letter to the authors, 8 October 2020.
28. Andrew Blick, interview with Anthony Seldon, 1 September 2020.
29. *Cabinet Manual*, p. 21.
30. Ibid., pp. 3–4.
31. Catherine Haddon, interview with Anthony Seldon, 14 September 2020.
32. Gus O'Donnell, Baron O'Donnell, interview with Anthony Seldon, 18 September 2020.
33. *Ministerial Code* (London: Cabinet Office, August 2019), p. 10.
34. Gus O'Donnell, Baron O'Donnell, interview with Anthony Seldon, 18 September 2020.
35. Ibid.
36. Catherine Haddon, interview with Anthony Seldon, 14 September 2020.
37. Walter Bagehot, *The English Constitution: Second Edition* (London: Henry S. King, 1872), p. 49.
38. Seldon with Baston, *Major*; Seldon, *Blair*; Anthony Seldon with Peter Snowdon and Daniel Collings, *Blair Unbound* (London: Simon & Schuster, 2007); Seldon and Lodge, *Brown at 10*; Seldon and Snowdon, *Cameron at 10*; and Anthony Seldon with Raymond Newell, *May at 10* (London: Biteback, 2019) for numerous examples of this point in action.
39. See Seldon with Newell, *May at 10*.
40. Philip Norton, Baron Norton of Louth, interview with Anthony Seldon, 7 May 2020.
41. See Stuart Ball and Anthony Seldon (eds.), *The Heath Government 1970–1974: A Reappraisal* (Harlow: Longman, 1996).
42. Richard Wilson, interview with Anthony Seldon, 21 August 2020.
43. Richard Aldous, interview with Anthony Seldon, 19 September 2020.
44. Bruce Coleman, letter to the authors, 30 October 2020.
45. Anthony Seldon, 'The Cabinet System' in Vernon Bogdanor (ed.), *The British Constitution in the Twentieth Century* (Oxford University Press, 2003).
46. John Kerr, interview with Anthony Seldon, 19 September 2020.
47. Lewis Baston and Anthony Seldon, 'Number 10 under Edward Heath', in Ball and Seldon (eds.), *Heath Government*.
48. See Anthony Seldon, 'The Cabinet Office and Coordination, 1979–87', *Public Administration*, 68/1 (1990), pp. 103–21.
49. Margaret Beckett, interview with Anthony Seldon, 13 October 2020.
50. Seldon and Lodge, *Brown at 10*, p. 171.

51. Chris Mason, 'London 2012: What Exactly Is a Cobra Meeting?' *BBC News*, 23 July 2012, www.bbc.co.uk/news/uk-politics-18958032 (accessed 27 November 2020).

52. Seldon and Snowdon, *Cameron at 10*, pp. 38–9.

53. Seldon with Newell, *May at 10*, p. 377.

54. Gus O'Donnell, Baron O'Donnell, interview with Anthony Seldon, 18 September 2020.

55. Seldon with Newell, *May at 10*, p. 45.

56. Louise Dalingwater, 'Civil Service Reform and the Legacy of Thatcherism', *Observatoire de la Société Brittanique*, 17 (2015), pp. 61–78.

57. 'Great Offices of State', *The Cabinet Papers*, www.nationalarchives.gov.uk/cabinetpa pers/cabinet-gov/great-offices-of-state.htm (accessed 27 November 2020).

58. Bruce Coleman, letter to the authors, 12 November 2020.

59. Francis Beckett, *Clem Attlee: A Biography* (London: Richard Cohen, 1997), p. 285.

60. Andrew Adonis, Baron Adonis, interview with Anthony Seldon, 29 September 2020.

61. Jeremy Black, interview with Anthony Seldon, 14 September 2020.

62. Paul Langford, 'Prime Ministers and Parliaments: The Long View, Walpole to Blair', *Parliamentary History*, 25/3 (2006), pp. 382–94.

63. R. J. Q. Adams, letter to the authors, 21 September 2020.

64. Richard Wilson, Baron Wilson of Dinton, interview with Anthony Seldon, 21 September 2020.

65. Andrew Rawnsley, *Guardian*, 6 May 2001.

66. Interview with Paddy Ashdown quoted in Andrew Rawnsley, *The End of the Party: The Rise and Fall of New Labour* (London: Viking, 2010), pp. 150–1.

67. See Richard E. Neustadt, *Presidential Power and the Modern Presidents*, 3rd edn (New York: Free Press, 1990).

68. Philip Williamson, 'The Doctrinal Politics of Stanley Baldwin' in Michael Bentley (ed.), *Public and Private Doctrine: Essays in British History Presented to Maurice Cowling* (Cambridge University Press, 1993), p. 184.

69. Brian Jenner, letter to the authors, 30 November 2020.

70. Andrew Turnbull, interview with Anthony Seldon, 17 September 2020.

71. Kenneth Harris, '"A Prime Minister governs by curiosity ...": Harold Wilson Talks about His Job to Kenneth Harris', *Observer*, 24 October 1965, found in Hennessy, *The Prime Minister*, p. 54.

72. D. R. Thorpe, *Eden: The Life and Times of Anthony Eden, First Earl of Avon, 1897–1977* (London: Chatto & Windus, 2003), p. 46.

73. See Howard Gardner, *Multiple Intelligences* (New York: Basic Books, 1993).

74. Margaret Thatcher, *The Autobiography* (London: HarperPress, 2013), pp. 330–2.

75. Seldon with Newell, *May at 10*, pp. 76–8.

76. See Blick and Jones, *At Power's Elbow*; Dennis Kavanagh and Anthony Seldon, *The Powers Behind the Prime Minister: The Hidden Influence of Number Ten* (London: HarperCollins, 1999).

77. Richard Wilson, Baron Wilson of Dinton, interview with Anthony Seldon, 21 September 2020.

78. Vernon Bogdanor, interview with Anthony Seldon, 25 September 2020.

79. *The Cabinet Manual*, p. 22.

80. John Adams, letter to Abigail Adams, 19 December 1793, Smithsonian National Portrait Gallery.

81. Rodney Brazier, *Choosing a Prime Minister: The Transfer of Power in Britain* (Oxford University Press, 2020), p. 67.

82. David Guggenheim, 'Designated Survivor', ABC, 2016–19.

83. Anthony Seldon, 'Illness in Office is Nothing New for a Leader under Strain', *The Times*, 7 April 2020.

84. Hansard, 'Deputy Prime Minister', https://api.parliament.uk/historic-hansard/offi ces/deputy-prime-minister (accessed 27 November 2020).

85. Anthony Seldon, *Churchill's Indian Summer: The 1951–1955 Conservative Government* (London: Hodder & Stoughton, 1981), pp. 39–40.

86. Margaret Thatcher, *The Downing Street Years* (London: HarperCollins, 1993), p. 757; quoted in Brazier, *Choosing a Prime Minister*, p. 75.

87. Seldon with Baston, *Major*, p. 285.

88. Tony Newton deputised for Major at Prime Minister's Question Time on several occasions, including 10 December 1992: PMQT, www.johnmajorarchive.org.uk/ 1990–1997/pmqt-10-december-1992 (accessed 27 November 2020).

89. Michael Heseltine, *Life in the Jungle: My Autobiography* (London: Hodder & Stoughton, 2000), pp. 478–9.

90. Sarah Brown, *Behind the Black Door* (London: Ebury, 2011), p. 15.

91. Horace Walpole to Sir Horace Mann, 30 January 1757, in Mrs Paget Toynbee (ed.), *The Letters of Horace Walpole*, vol. IV: *1756–1760* (Oxford: Clarendon Press, 1903), p. 33.

92. Quoted in Kirsty McLeod, *The Wives of Downing Street* (London: Collins, 1976), p. 41.

93. Julia Peel to Sir Robert Peel, 21 August 1842, in George Peel (ed.), *The Private Letters of Sir Robert Peel* (London: John Murray, 1920), p. 204.

94. Mark Hichens, *Prime Ministers' Wives – and One Husband* (London: Peter Owen, 2004), Chapter 5, para. 1, loc. 983 (Kindle edn).

95. Brown, *Palmerston: A Biography*, p. 248.

96. Ibid., p. 247.

97. Gillian Gill, *We Two: Victoria and Albert: Rulers, Partners, Rivals* (London: Ballantine, 2009), p. 263.

98. K. D. Reynolds, 'Temple [*nee* Lamb], Emily Mary [Amelia], Viscountess Palmerston' in *Oxford Dictionary of National Biography* (Oxford University Press, 2004), www .oxforddnb.com/view/10.1093/ref:odnb/9780198614128.001.0001/odnb-97801986 14128-e-40959 (accessed 30 November 2020).

99. Henry Greville, Friday 20 October 1865, in Countess of Stafford (ed.), *Leaves from the Diary of Henry Greville*, vol. IV (London: Smith, Elder, 1905), p. 259.

100. Hichens, *Prime Ministers' Wives*, Chapter 6, para. 26, loc. 1334 (Kindle edn).

101. Matthew, *Gladstone*, p. 615.

102. Ibid., p. 535

103. Ibid., p. 310.

104. Quoted in Anne de Courcy, *Margot at War: Love and Betrayal in Downing Street, 1912–16* (London: Weidenfeld & Nicolson, 2014), p. 99.

105. Michael Brock and Eleanor Brock (eds.), *Margot Asquith's Great War Diary, 1914–1916: The View from Downing Street* (Oxford University Press, 2014), pp. 57–61.

106. Courcy, *Margot at War*, p. 266.

107. Ibid., p. 273.

108. Hichens, *Prime Minister's Wives*, Chapter 10, para. 26, loc. 2688 (Kindle edn),

109. Seldon, *10 Downing Street*, pp. 132–3.

110. *The Times*, 26 June 1945.

111. David Cameron, *For the Record* (London: William Collins, 2019), pp. 194–6.

112. Gaby Hinsliff, 'Under New Management: Is Carrie Symonds the Real Power at No 10?', *The Observer*, 29 November 2020.

113. Harold Macmillan, *Pointing the Way, 1959–1961* (London: Macmillan, 1972), p. 25.

114. John Campbell, *Margaret Thatcher: Grocer's Daughter to Iron Lady*, abridged edn (London: Vintage, 2009), pp. 129–30.

115. Seldon with Newell, *May at 10*, p. 59.

116. Blake, *Office of Prime Minister*, p. 51.

117. H. H. Asquith, *Fifty Years in Parliament*, vol. II, (London: Cassell, 1926), p. 185.

6 THE CONSTRAINTS ON THE PRIME MINISTER, 1721–2021

1. Robert Walpole, 1 February 1739, quoted in Dickinson, *Walpole and the Whig Supremacy* p. 89.

2. Langford, 'Prime Ministers and Parliaments', p. 394.

3. Ibid., p. 384.

4. Jeremy Black, interview with Anthony Seldon, 20 October 2020.

5. 'What Are the Biggest Government Defeats?', *BBC News*, 15 January 2019, www .bbc.co.uk/news/uk-46879887 (accessed 7 December 2020).

6. Vernon Bogdanor, interview with Anthony Seldon, January 2018.

7. Anthony Seldon and Pranay Sanklecha, 'United Kingdom: A Comparative Case Study of Conservative Prime Ministers Heath, Thatcher and Major', *Journal of Legislative Studies*, 10 (2004), pp. 53–65; and Philip Norton, 'Behavioural Changes: Backbench Independence in the 1980s', in P. Norton (ed.), *Parliament in the 1980s* (Oxford: Basil Blackwell, 1985), pp. 21–6.

8. Seldon with Newell, *May at 10*, pp. xv, 541–75.

9. Patrick Scott, 'With 28 Defeats and Resignations Galore was Theresa May the Weakest Prime Minister ever?', *Daily Telegraph*, 24 May 2019, www.telegraph.co.uk/politics/20 19/03/26/20-defeats-historic-loss-parliamentary-control-no-majority-theresa (accessed 7 December 2020).

10. Philip Cowley and Mark Stuart, *Revolts: Philip Cowley and Mark Stuart's Research on Parliament*, 2004, http://web.archive.org/web/2020*/Revolts.co.uk (accessed 14 November 2020).

11. Tim Bale, 'Will the New Tory Intake Help to Build a More Progressive Party? Don't Count on It', *Guardian*, 19 December 2019.

12. Gail Bartlett and Michael Everett, 'The Royal Prerogative', House of Commons Library, 17 August 2017, https://commonslibrary.parliament.uk/research-briefings/sn03861

(accessed 12 November 2020); for a full list of powers see Hennessy, 'Role and Powers of the Prime Minister'.

13. Public Administration Select Committee, *Taming the Prerogative*, p. 30.

14. Seldon and Snowdon, *Cameron at 10*, pp. 325–45.

15. Adam Cygan and Graham Cowie, 'The Prorogation Dispute of 2019: One Year On', House of Commons Library, 24 September 2020 (accessed at https://commonslibrary .parliament.uk/research-briefings/cbp-9006, 12 November 2020); see also Adam Cygan and Graham Cowie, 'Prorogation One Year On: A Case for Reform?', House of Commons Library, 24 September 2020, https://commonslibrary.parliament.uk/pro rogation-a-case-for-reform (accessed 12 November 2020).

16. Robert Hazell, interview with Anthony Seldon, 22 October 2020.

17. Ibid.

18. Robert Hazell, Turan Hursit, Harmish Mehta, and Peter Waller, 'Improving Parliamentary Scrutiny of Public Appointments', The Constitution Unit, July 2017, www.ucl.ac.uk/constitution-unit/sites/constitution-unit/files/pre-appt-scrutiny.pdf (accessed 12 November 2020).

19. Hannah White, 'The Liaison Committee: Function Matters More than Form', Institute for Government Blog, 21 April 2020, www.instituteforgovernment.org.uk/blog/liaiso n-committee-function-matters-more-form (accessed 1 December 2020).

20. Michael White, 'The History of PMQs', *Guardian*, 27 October 2011.

21. John Bercow, 'New Parliament, New Opportunity', speech to the Centre for Parliamentary Studies, 6 July 2010.

22. *Daily Telegraph*, 8 December 2005.

23. White, 'History of PMQs'.

24. Elise Uberoi and Richard Kelly, 'The Fixed-Term Parliaments Act', House of Commons Library, 14 January 2020, https://commonslibrary.parliament.uk/the-fixed-term- parliaments-act (accessed 12 November 2020).

25. Rodney Brazier, interview with Anthony Seldon, 20 October 2020.

26. Glen Dymond and Hugo Deadman, *The Salisbury Doctrine*, House of Lords Library Note, 30 June 2006, p. 1.

27. 'Government Defeats in the House of Lords', The Constitution Unit, 2020, www .ucl.ac.uk/constitution-unit/research/parliament/changing-role-house-lords/govern ment-defeats-house-lords (accessed 19 October 2020).

28. Robert Hazell, interview with Anthony Seldon, 22 October 2020.

29. Ibid.

30. Meg Russell, 'A More Legitimate and More Powerful Upper House? The Semi-Reformed House of Lords', ESRC Report, 2008, http://sp.ukdataservice.ac.uk/doc/6982/mrdoc/ pdf/6982_esrc_end-of-award_report.pdf (accessed 12 November 2020), p. 5.

31. 'Government Defeats in the House of Lords', UK Parliament, 2020, www.parliament.uk /about/faqs/house-of-lords-faqs/lords-govtdefeats (accessed 19 October 2020).

32. Russell, 'More Legitimate Upper House', p. 5.

33. Ibid.

34. M. Russell and P. Cowley, 'The Policy Power of the Westminster Parliament: The "Parliamentary State" and the Empirical Evidence' *Governance*, 29 (2016) 121–37, https://doi.org/10.1111/gove.12149 (accessed 12 November 2020).

35. Robin Butler, Baron Butler of Brockwell, interview with Anthony Seldon, 31 August 2020.

36. Pimlott, *Harold Wilson*, p. 619.

37. Seldon with Newell, *May at 10*, pp. 72–80.

38. Andrew Turnbull, Lord Turnbull, interview with Anthony Seldon, 17 September 2020.

39. Robin Butler, Baron Butler of Brockwell, interview with Anthony Seldon, 31 August 2020.

40. Ibid.

41. 'Ministerial Resignations Outside Reshuffles, by Prime Minister', Institute for Government, 2020, www.instituteforgovernment.org.uk/charts/ministerial-resignations-outside-reshuffles-prime-minister (accessed 1 December 2020).

42. Peter Hennessy and David Welsh, 'Lords of All They surveyed? Churchill's Ministerial "Overlords" 1951–1953', *Parliamentary Affairs*, 51/1 (1998), pp. 62–70.

43. *BBC News*, 7 July 1999.

44. Rupert Harrison, interview with Anthony Seldon, 30 November 2020.

45. J. A. G. Griffiths, *Politics of the Judiciary* (London: Fontana, 1977).

46. Philip Norton, Baron Norton of Louth, interview with Anthony Seldon, 7 May 2020.

47. David Allen Green, 'How the Myth of Judicial Activism Has Taken On a Life of Its Own', *Prospect*, 28 February 2020.

48. Seldon and Snowdon, *Cameron at 10*, p. 326.

49. Rodney Brazier, interview with Anthony Seldon, 20 October 2020.

50. Green, 'Myth of Judicial Activism'.

51. Priti Patel, Conservative Party Conference Speech, 4 October 2020; Boris Johnson, Conservative Party Conference Speech, 6 October 2020.

52. *Guardian*, 19 October 2020.

53. Robert Hazell, interview with Anthony Seldon, 22 October 2020.

54. 'Law For Lawmakers: A Justice Guide to the Law', University of Oxford Faculty of Law, 2015, www.law.ox.ac.uk/sites/files/oxlaw/justice_-_law_for_lawmakers.pdf, p. 25 (accessed 12 November 2020).

55. Robert Hazell, interview with Anthony Seldon, 22 October 2020.

56. Seldon and Lodge, *Brown at 10*, p. 390.

57. Tim Bale, 'How the Tory Party Can Solve Its Membership Crisis, in Three Easy Steps', *Guardian*, 3 October 2017; see also 'ESRC Party Members Project', www.esrcpartymembersproject.org (accessed 13 November 2020).

58. Stuart Ball, 'The 1922 Committee: The Formative Years 1922–45', *Parliamentary History*, 9/1 (1990), pp. 129–57(see p. 130).

59. Seth Thévoz, 'Inside the Elite Tory Fundraising Regime', *Open Democracy*, 9 December 2019, www.opendemocracy.net/en/dark-money-investigations/inside-elite-tory-fundraising-machine (accessed 1 December 2020).

60. 'More Powers for Scotland – What Happens Next?', GOV.UK, 22 January 2015, www.gov.uk/government/news/more-powers-for-scotland-what-happens-next (accessed 7 December 2020).

61. Hazell, 'Reinventing the Constitution: Can the State Survive?', CIPFA/Times Inaugural Lecture, 4 November 1998, www.ucl.ac.uk/constitution-unit/sites/constitution-unit/f iles/33.pdf (accessed 1 January 2021), p. 3.

62. Tony Travers, 'Local Government: Margaret Thatcher's Eleven Year War', *Guardian*, 9 April 2013.

63. Mark Sandford, 'Directly-Elected Mayors', House of Commons Library, 18 February 2019, https://commonslibrary.parliament.uk/research-briefings/sn05000 (accessed 13 November 2020).

64. Robert Hazell, interview with Anthony Seldon, 22 October 2020.

65. Margaret Thatcher, speech to Conservative Group for Europe, 16 April 1975.

66. Steve Richards, interview with Anthony Seldon, 14 September 2020.

67. Robert Hazell, interview with Anthony Seldon, 22 October 2020.

68. Joanna Dawson, Maria Lalic, and Sue Holland, 'Human Rights in the UK (Debate Pack)', House of Commons Library, 12 February 2020, https://commonslibrary .parliament.uk/research-briefings/cdp-2019-0031 (accessed 13 November 2020).

69. Matthew, *Gladstone*, p. 231.

70. Angus Hawkins, interview with Anthony Seldon, 24 September 2020.

71. Stanley Baldwin, speech at Queens Hall, 17 March 1931.

72. Leo McKinstry, *Attlee and Churchill* (London: Atlantic, 2019), pp. 591–2.

73. Nicholas Watt, 'Blair U-turn on EU Referendum', *Guardian*, 19 April 2004.

74. Steve Richards, interview with Anthony Seldon, 14 September 2020.

75. Ibid.

76. Robert Hazell, interview with Anthony Seldon, 22 October 2020.

77. *Guardian*, 12 June 2007.

78. Andrew Blick and George Jones, *At Power's Elbow*, pp. 32–4.

79. Bruce Coleman, letter to the authors, 5 December 2020.

80. Otto English, 'No Place for God in British Politics', *Politico Forum*, 23 December 2019.

81. *New York Times*, 9 October 1994.

82. *BBC News*, 19 October 2020.

83. *BBC News*, 25 November 2020.

84. Angus Hawkins, *The Forgotten Prime Minister: The 14th Earl of Derby*, vol. ii: *Achievement, 1851–1869* (Oxford University Press, 2008), p. 159.

85. Pimlott, *Harold Wilson*, p. 504.

86. *Daily Telegraph*, 3 January 1956.

87. *New Statesman*, 2 September 2020.

88. Cameron, *For the Record*, p. 430.

89. 'Past Prime Ministers', GOV.UK, 2020, www.gov.uk/government/history/past-prime-ministers (accessed 21 October 2020).

90. Robert Hazell, interview with Anthony Seldon, 22 October 2020.

91. The Prime Minister's African Tour, Cabinet C.60(66), 12 April 1960, p. 3, CAB 129/101/16, National Archives, Kew.

92. Ibid., pp. 2–3.

93. Rod Rhodes, interview with Anthony Seldon, 20 September 2020.

94. Elizabeth Knowles (ed.), *Oxford Dictionary of Modern Quotations* (Oxford University Press, 2007), p. 209.

95. John Campbell, interview with Anthony Seldon, 30 September 2020.

96. Alistair Horne, *Macmillan: The Official Biography* (London: Macmillan, 2008), pp. 495–7.

97. Extracts from a transcript of a telephone interview for the BBC Home Service with Harold Macmillan by Peter Hardiman Scott, 26 September 1963, DO 194/22, National Archives, Kew.

98. Bruce Coleman, letter to the authors, 21 October 2020.

99. John Fortescue (ed.), *The Correspondence of King George the Third, from 1760 to December 1783*, vol. ii (London: Cass, 1967), p. 54.

100. R. J. Q. Adams, letter to the authors, 21 September 2020.

101. David Dilks, letter to the authors, 14 October 2020.

102. David Owen, 'Diseased, Demented, Depressed: Serious Illness in Heads of State', *QJM: An International Journal of Medicine*, 96/5 (2003), pp. 325–66(at 329–30).

103. Ken Stowe, letter to the author for Kavanagh and Seldon, *Powers Behind the Prime Minister.* Robin Butler, Baron Butler of Brockwell, interview with Anthony Seldon, 8 February 2021.

104. The Electoral Commission, www.electoralcommission.org.uk (accessed 14 November 2020).

105. The House of Lords Appointments Commission, https://lordsappointments .independent.gov.uk/the-commission-2 (accessed 13 November 2020).

106.] Christopher Hope, 'Top Tory Donors Look Set to Lose Out on Peerages', *Daily Telegraph*, 19 July 2020; at the same time, three nominations (Tom Watson, Jon Bercow, and Karie Murphy) for the Lords by former Labour leader Jeremy Corbyn were also rejected: Peter Walker, 'Tom Watson Peerage Rejected by Lords Vetting Commission', *Guardian*, 1 June 2020.

107. The Commissioner for Public Appointments, https://publicappointmentscommis sioner.independent.gov.uk (accessed 13 November 2020).

108. The Judicial Appointments Commission, www.judicialappointments.gov.uk (accessed 13 November 2020).

109. Civil Service Commission, www.civilservicecommission.independent.gov.uk/about-the-commission (accessed 13 November 2020).

110. Robert Hazell, interview with Anthony Seldon, 22 October 2020.

111. Aubrey Allegretti, tweet, 25 May 2020, www.twitter.com/breeallegretti/status/12648 95719921631239 (accessed 13 November 2020); 'Code of Conduct for Special Advisors', Cabinet Office, December 2016, https://assets.publishing.service.gov.uk/ government/uploads/system/uploads/attachment_data/file/832599/201612_Cod e_of_Conduct_for_Special_Advisers.pdf (accessed 13 November 2020).

112. John Woodhouse, 'Freedom of Information Requests', House of Commons Library, 8 March 2019, https://commonslibrary.parliament.uk/research-briefings/sn02950 (accessed 13 November 2020).

113. Jeremy Heywood, Baron Heywood, interview with Anthony Seldon for *Cameron at 10* (2015).

114. Ben Worthy and Robert Hazell, 'Disruptive, Dynamic and Democratic? Ten Years of FOI in the UK', *Parliamentary Affairs*, 70/1 (2017), pp. 22–42.

115. Douglas Jay, *Change and Fortune: A Political Record* (London: Ebury, 1980), p. 131.

7 THE ECLIPSE OF THE MONARCHY, 1660–2021

1. John Bradshaw, Chief Justice, trial of King Charles I, 1 January 1649, quoted in 'A Charge against the King' in Samuel Rowson Gardiner (ed.), *The Constitutional Documents of the Puritan Revolution, 1625–1660* (Oxford University Press, 1906).

2. Henry Sydney, 'Invitation to the Prince of Orange, 30 June 1688' in Andrew Browning (ed.), *English Historical Documents, 1660–1714* (London: Eyre & Spottiswoode, 1953), pp. 120–2.

3. 'Bill of Rights', 1689, in Williams (ed.), *Eighteenth-Century Constitution*, pp. 26–33.

4. Tombs, *The English*, p. 305.

5. Cromwell, *Good Queen Anne*, p. 126.

6. Paul Kleber Monod, *Jacobitism and the English People, 1688–1788* (Cambridge University Press, 1993), pp. 173–8.

7. Williams (ed.), *Eighteenth-Century Constitution*, pp. 83–4.

8. Quoted in Jeremy Black, *George III: America's Last King* (New Haven, CT: Yale University Press, 2006), p. 44.

9. John Brooke, *King George III* (London: Constable, 1972), pp. 41–4.

10. Jeremy Black, *George III: Madness and Majesty*, Kindle edn (London: Allen Lane, 2020), p. 15.

11. George III to Sir Joseph Yorke, 9 January 1771, in Fortescue (ed.) *Correspondence of King George*, p. 204, quoted in Black, *George III: America's Last King*, p. 106.

12. John Clarke, interview with Anthony Seldon, 20 October 2020.

13. Quoted in Andrew O'Shaughnessy, '"If others will not be active, I must drive": George III and the American Revolution', *Early American Studies*, 2/1 (Spring 2004), pp. iii, 1–46.

14. Andrew Roberts, interview with Anthony Seldon, 9 September 2020.

15. Ibid.

16. Edmund Burke (ed.), *The Annual Register* (1791), p. 8.

17. John Clarke, letter to the authors, 6 November 2020.

18. Andrew Roberts, interview with Anthony Seldon, 9 September 2020.

19. Ibid.

20. O'Shaughnessy, *Men Who Lost America*, p. 30.

21. Ibid., pp. 30–41.

22. Letter from John Adams, Minister to Britain, to John Jay, Secretary of State, reporting on his audience with the king, 2 June 1785, National Archives, Records of the Continental and Confederation Congresses and the Constitutional Convention, www.archives.gov/exhibits/eyewitness/html.php?section=19 (accessed 9 December 2020).

23. Draft abdication letter of George III, 28 March 1783, Royal Collection Trust, GEO/MAIN/5367.

24. Black, *George III: America's Last King*, pp. 246–7.

25. John Clarke, interview with Anthony Seldon, 20 October 2020.

26. Bruce Coleman, letter to the authors, 7 October 2020.

27. Ibid.

28. Christopher Hibbert, *George III: A Personal History* (London: Penguin, 1999), p. 396.

29. Ibid., pp. 399–405.

30. See Arthur Aspinall (ed.), *The Correspondence of George, Prince of Wales, 1770–1812* (London: Cassell, 1964), pp. 4–5.

31. Lord Liverpool, Hansard, House of Lords (HL) Debates, 10 November 1820, vol. 3, col. 1746.

32. Terry Jenkins, 'The Queen Caroline Affair', *History of Parliament Online*, www .historyofparliamentonline.org/periods/hanoverians/queen-caroline-affair-1820 (accessed 2 December 2020); Leonard, *History of British Prime Ministers*, pp. 267–8.

33. E. A. Smith, *George IV* (New Haven, CT: Yale University Press, 1999), pp. 266–7.

34. A. N. Wilson, interview with Anthony Seldon, 9 October 2020.

35. Bruce Coleman, letter to the authors, 7 October 2020.

36. Philip Ziegler, *King William IV* (London: Collins, 1971), p. 289.

37. Jane Ridley, interview with Anthony Seldon, 9 September 2020.

38. Bruce Coleman, letter to the authors, 7 October 2020.

39. Bruce Coleman, letter to the authors, 12 November 2020.

40. Hugh Chisholm, 'Granville, Granville George Leveson-Gower, 2nd Earl', in Hugh Chisholm (ed.), *Encyclopaedia Britannica*, 11th edn, vol. xii (Cambridge University Press, 1911), p. 362.

41. Philip Norton, Lord Norton of Louth, interview with Anthony Seldon, 7 May 2020.

42. Simon Heffer, interview with Anthony Seldon, 12 September 2020.

43. H. C. G. Matthew and K. D. Reynolds, 'Victoria' in *Oxford Dictionary of National Biography* (Oxford University Press, 2004), www.oxforddnb.com/view/10.1093/ref:odnb/9780 198614128.001.0001/odnb-9780198614128-e-36652 (accessed 4 November 2020).

44. Anne Somerset, interview with Anthony Seldon, 20 November 2020.

45. Jane Ridley, interview with Anthony Seldon, 9 September 2020.

46. Ibid.

47. Anne Somerset, interview with Anthony Seldon, 20 November 2020.

48. 'State Opening of Parliament', UK Parliament, 2020, www.parliament.uk/about/how/ occasions/stateopening (accessed 12 November 2020).

49. Jane Ridley, *Bertie: A Life of Edward VII* (New York: Random House, 2012), p. 349.

50. Jane Ridley, interview with Anthony Seldon, 9 September 2020.

51. Roy Jenkins, *Asquith* (London: Collins, 1964), pp. 179–80.

52. Simon Heffer, interview with Anthony Seldon, 12 September 2020.

53. Philip Magnus, *King Edward the Seventh* (London: John Murray, 1964), pp. 301–5.

54. Rodney Brazier, 'The Monarchy' in Vernon Bogdanor (ed.), *The British Constitution in the Twentieth Century* (Oxford University Press, 2004), p. 72.

55. See Matthew Glencross, *The State Visits of Edward VII: Reinventing Royal Diplomacy for the Twentieth Century* (London: Palgrave Macmillan, 2016) for more on Edward's diplomatic efforts.

56. Simon Heffer, interview with Anthony Seldon, 12 September 2020.

57. Bruce Coleman, letter to the authors, 12 November 2020.

58. Janes Ridley, interview with Anthony Seldon, 9 September 2020.

59. Bruce Coleman, letter to the authors, 7 October 2020.

60. H. H. Asquith, quoted in Brazier, 'The Monarchy', pp. 72–3.

61. 'The House of Windsor', www.royal.uk/house-windsor (accessed 12 November 2020).

62. Quoted in Harold Nicolson, *George the Fifth: His Life and Reign* (London: Constable, 1970), p. 403.

63. Brazier, 'The Monarchy', p. 71.

64. Anne Sebba, *That Woman: The Life of Wallis Simpson, Duchess of Windsor* (London: Weidenfeld & Nicolson, 2011), p. 149.

65. Anne Sebba, letter to the authors, 11 November 2020.

66. Vernon Bogdanor, interview with Anthony Seldon, January 2018.

67. David Dilks, interview with Anthony Seldon, 2 October 2020.

68. Bruce Coleman, letter to the authors, 6 December 2020.

69. Bruce Coleman, letter to the authors, 7 October 2020.

70. Robert Rhodes James, *A Spirit Undaunted: The Political Role of George VI* (London: Little, Brown, 1998), p. 195.

71. Brazier, 'The Monarchy', p. 79.

72. Jane Ridley, interview with Anthony Seldon, 9 September 2020.

73. Brazier, 'The Monarchy', p. 80.

74. John Wheeler-Bennett, *King George VI: His Life and Reign* (London: Macmillan, 1958), p. 652.

75. 'Senex', Letter to the Editor, *The Times*, 2 May 1950.

76. Private interview.

77. Bagehot, *English Constitution*, p. 103.

78. Private interview.

79. 'A speech by The Queen to Parliament on her Silver Jubilee', www.royal.uk/silver-jubilee-address-parliament-4-may-1977 (accessed 12 November 2020).

80. Peter Hennessy, letter to the authors, 20 November 2020.

81. *Guardian*, 14 September 2014.

82. *BBC News*, 23 September 2014.

83. Vernon Bogdanor, interview with Anthony Seldon, 25 September 2020.

84. See Peter Morgan, *The Audience* (Gielgud Theatre), 13 February 2013; and Peter Morgan, *The Crown* (Netflix), 4 November 2016 to present.

85. Private interview.

86. Private interview.

87. See Frank Prochaska, *Royal Bounty: The Making of a Welfare Monarchy* (New Haven, CT: Yale University Press, 1995).

88. Private information.

89. Private interview.

90. Photographed almost every day of her life, with the first photograph taken of her by her father when she was a one-year-old princess in 1927. 'The Queen Is the Most Photographed Woman in the World – But She's Spent Plenty of Time Behind the Camera Too', *Radio Times*, 21 April 2016.

91. Sophie Campbell, 'Queen's Diamond Jubilee: Sixty Years of Royal Tours', *Daily Telegraph*, 11 May 2012.

92. Kim Hjelmgaard, 'Trump's UK Visit: What You Need to Know, from Royal Ceremony to Protests in London', *USA Today*, 3 June 2019, https://amp.usatoday.com/amp/1284 000001 (accessed 12 November 2020).

93. Charles Moore, interview with Anthony Seldon, 2 February 2021.

94. Private interview.

8 THE RISE AND FALL OF THE FOREIGN SECRETARY, 1782–2021

1. Jupp, *Governing of Britain*, p. 30.

2. Ibid., p. 29.

3. Tombs, *The English*, p. 304.

4. 'The Revolution of 1688' in *Encyclopaedia Britannica*, www.britannica.com/place/Unit ed-Kingdom/The-Revolution-of-1688#ref483187 (accessed 17 November 2020).

5. Act of Settlement 1701, in Williams (ed.), *Eighteenth-Century Constitution*, p. 59. Italics added for emphasis by the author.

6. Queen Anne to Archduke Charles, October 1704, quoted in James Falkner, *The War of the Spanish Succession, 1701–1714* (Barnsley: Pen & Sword, 2015), p. 87.

7. Quoted in Tombs, *The English*, p. 317.

8. Lord Carteret, quoted in Browning, *War of the Austrian Succession*, p. 100.

9. Pitt the Elder, quoted in Daniel Baugh, *The Global Seven Years' War, 1754–1763* (London: Pearson, 2011), pp. 26–7.

10. Middleton, *Bells of Victory*, p. 213.

11. Quoted in Douglas R. Cubbison, *All Canada in the Hands of the British: General Jeffrey Amherst and the 1760 Campaign to Conquer New France* (University of Oklahoma Press, 2014), p. 3.

12. Middleton, *Bells of Victory*, pp. 196–9.

13. O'Shaughnessy, *Men Who Lost America*, p. 25.

14. Ibid.

15. Ibid., p. 29.

16. Quoted ibid., p. 35.

17. Ibid., p. 186.

18. Patrick Salmon, letter to the authors, 27 November 2020.

19. Peter Hennessy, *Whitehall* (London: Free Press, 1989), p. 27.

20. C. R. Middleton, *The Administration of British Foreign Policy, 1782–1846* (Durham, NC: Duke University Press, 1977), p. 10.

21. Hennessy, *Whitehall*, pp. 27–8.

22. Algernon Cecil, *British Foreign Secretaries* (London: G. Bell and Sons, 1927), pp. v–vi.

23. Jupp, *Governing of Britain*, p. 121.

24. Hague, *William Pitt the Younger*, pp. 240–1.

25. Andrew O'Shaughnessy, interview with Anthony Seldon, 18 October 2020.

26. Jupp, *Governing of Britain*, p. 121.

27. William Hague, Baron Hague of Richmond, interview with Anthony Seldon, 7 October 2020.

28. John Kerr, Baron Kerr of Kinlochard, interview with Anthony Seldon, 19 September 2020.

29. Andrew Roberts, interview with Anthony Seldon, 9 September 2020.

30. William Anthony Hay, interview with Anthony Seldon, 24 September 2020.

31. John Bew, *Castlereagh: Enlightenment, War and Tyranny* (London: Quercus, 2011), p. 575.

32. Andrew Adonis, Baron Adonis, interview with Anthony Seldon, 29 September 2020.

33. Michael Hughes, *British Foreign Secretaries in an Uncertain World, 1919–1939* (London: Routledge, 2006), p. 1.

34. Cecil, *British Foreign Secretaries*, p. 5.

35. Hughes, *British Foreign Secretaries*, p. 1.

36. Anthony Seldon, *The Foreign Office* (London: HarperCollins, 2000), pp. 36–71.

37. Bruce Coleman, letter to the authors, 4 November 2020.

38. Andrew Thompson, *The Empire Strikes Back? The Impact of Imperialism on Britain from the Mid-Nineteenth Century* (Harlow: Pearson, 2005), p. 148.

39. Bruce Coleman, letter to the authors, 4 November 2020.

40. Bew, *Castlereagh*, p. xxviii.

41. Charles Esdaile, *Napoleon's Wars: An International History, 1803–1815* (London: Penguin, 2007), p. 500.

42. William Anthony Hay, interview with Anthony Seldon, 23 September 2020.

43. Bew, *Castlereagh*, p. 386.

44. William Anthony Hay, interview with Anthony Seldon, 23 September 2020.

45. Henry Kissinger, *Diplomacy* (London: Simon & Schuster, 1994), p. 90.

46. H. W. V. Temperley, 'The Later American Policy of George Canning', *American Historical Review*, 11/4 (July 1906), pp. 779–97 (at 781).

47. Viscount Palmerston, Hansard, House of Commons (HC) Debate, 1 March 1848, vol. 97, col. 122.

48. Brown, *Palmerston: A Biography*, pp. 289–91.

49. Carolly Erickson, *Her Little Majesty: The Life of Queen Victoria* (New York: Simon & Schuster, 1997), p. 121.

50. Douglas Hurd, *Choose Your Weapons: The British Foreign Secretary* (London: Weidenfeld & Nicolson, 2010), p. 98.

51. Paul Scherer, *Lord John Russell: A Biography* (London: Associated University Presses, 1999), p. 270.

52. Andrew Roberts, interview with Anthony Seldon, 9 September 2020.

53. David Brown, interview with Anthony Seldon, 25 September 2020.

54. Brown, *Palmerston: A Biography*, pp. 406–7.

55. David Brown, interview with Anthony Seldon, 25 September 2020.

56. Amanda Foreman, *A World Aflame: Britain's Crucial Role in the American Civil War* (London: Random House, 2012), pp. 324, 317–30.

57. Quoted ibid., p. 324.

58. Lord Salisbury, quoted in Roberts, *Salisbury*, p. 195.

59. Bodleian Library, Special Collections, Dept. Hughenden, 73/2.

60. Andrew Adonis, Baron Adonis, interview with Anthony Seldon, 29 September 2020.

61. A. L. Kennedy, *Lord Salisbury: Portrait of a Statesman* (London: John Murray, 1953), pp. 341–2.

62. Roberts, *Salisbury*, p. 841.

63. Ibid., pp. 749–51, 766–7.

64. Lord Newton, *Lord Lansdowne: A Biography* (London: Macmillan, 1929), p. 228.

65. Sean McMeekin, *July 1914: Countdown to War* (London: Icon, 2013), pp. 72–4.

66. Ibid., pp. 72–4.

67. Hurd, *Choose Your Weapons*, p. 228.

68. Asquith, quoted in V. Markham Lester, *HH Asquith: Last of the Romans* (London: Lexington, 2019), p. 196.

69. Ibid., p. 196.

70. Hughes, *British Foreign Secretaries*, p. 2.

71. McMeekin, *July 1914*, pp. 329–30, 302–403.

72. Hurd, *Choose Your Weapons*, p. 231.

73. Edward Grey, *Twenty-Five Years, 1892–1916* (New York: Frederick A. Stokes, 1925), pp. 20, 61.

74. Hughes, *British Foreign Secretaries*, p. 2.

75. Arthur Aspinall (ed.), *The Letters of King George IV* (Cambridge University Press, 1938), p. lxxi.

76. Russell to Palmerston, 1 October 1848, Palmerston Papers (Broadlands Papers), University of Southampton Library, GC/RU/225.

77. Quoted in David Brown, *Palmerston and the Politics of Foreign Policy, 1846–55* (Manchester University Press, 2002), p. 112.

78. Bruce Coleman, letter to the authors, 12 November 2020.

79. Simon Heffer, interview with Anthony Seldon, 12 September 2020.

80. Ziegler, *Edward Heath*, p. 388.

81. Hughes, *British Foreign Secretaries*, p. 40.

82. Cecil, *British Foreign Secretaries*, p. 4.

83. Bruce Coleman, letter to the authors, 12 November 2020.

84. Ian Johnston and Rob McAuley, *The Battleships* (London: Macmillan, 2000), pp. 113–16.

85. Hughes, *British Foreign Secretaries*, pp. 30–1.

86. Seldon with Meakin, *Cabinet Office*, pp. 41–9.

87. Hughes, *British Foreign Secretaries*, p. 22.

88. Earl of Ronaldshay, *The Life of Lord Curzon*, vol. III (London: Ernest Benn, 1928), p. 316; quoted in Alan J. Sharp, 'The Foreign Office in Eclipse, 1919–22', *History*, 61/202 (1976), pp. 198–218 (at 198).

89. Purcell, *Lloyd George*, p. 92.

90. Kenneth O. Morgan, Baron Morgan, interview with Anthony Seldon, 16 October 2020.

91. Allen Packwood, *How Churchill Waged War: The Most Challenging Decisions of the Second World War* (Barnsley: Pen & Sword, 2018), p. 26.

92. Andrew Roberts, *Churchill: Walking with Destiny* (London: Allen Lane, 2018), p. 970. Peter Ricketts, *Hard Choices: What Britain Does Next* (London: Atlantic Books, 2021), p. 19.

93. Hurd, *Choose Your Weapons*, p. 360.

94. Michael Jay, Baron Jay of Ewelme, interview with Anthony Seldon, 22 September 2020.

95. Winston Churchill, Hansard, House of Commons (HC) Debates, 11 May 1953, vol. 515, cols. 883–98; McKinstry, *Attlee and Churchill*, pp. 589–90.

96. Robert Rhodes James, *Anthony Eden* (London: Weidenfeld & Nicolson, 1987), p. 417.

97. John Kerr, Baron Kerr of Kinlochard, letter to the authors, 6 December 2020.

98. Robin Butler, Baron Butler of Brockwell, interview with Anthony Seldon, 31 August 2020.

99. Ibid.

100. Richard J. Aldrich and Rory Cormac, *The Black Door: Spies, Secret Intelligence and British Prime Ministers* (London: William Collins, 2016), p. 26.

101. Ibid., p. 132.

102. Hennessy, *The Prime Minister*, p. 83.

103. Anthony Seldon, 'When, How and Why the FCO Lost Out to Downing Street and the Prospects for Power Returning to the FCO', talk at the FCO, 6 February 2020.

104. Michael Jay, Baron Jay of Ewelme, interview with Anthony Seldon, 22 September 2020.

105. Gordon Brown, *My Life, Our Times* (London: Random House, 2017) pp. 241–2.

106. Seldon and Lodge, *Brown at 10*, pp. 14, 181.

107. Anthony Seldon, 'Conclusion: The Prime Minister's Office from John Martin to Chris Martin' in Andrew Holt and Warren Dockter (eds.), *Private Secretaries to the Prime Minister* (Abingdon: Routledge, 2017).

108. John Kerr, Baron Kerr of Kinlochard, interview with Anthony Seldon, 19 September 2020.

109. Cameron, *For the Record*, p. 142.

110. William Hague, Baron Hague of Richmond, interview with Anthony Seldon, 7 October 2020.

111. Peter Hennessy interview with Robert Armstrong, Downing Street, 6 November 2012, www .cabinetsecretaries.com/_lib/pdf/Former%20Cabinet%20Secretary%20Lord%20Armst rong%20Interview%20with%20Lord%20Hennessy.pdf (accessed 20 November 2020).

112. Charles Moore, *Margaret Thatcher: The Authorized Biography*, vol. i: *Not For Turning* (London: Allen Lane, 2013), pp. 710–16.

113. Peter Riddell, interview with Anthony Seldon, 10 November 2020.

114. Robert Saunders, 'Britain at the End of History', *New Statesman*, 7 October 2020.

115. Thatcher, *Autobiography*, p. 418.

116. Robin Cook, *The Point of Departure* (London: Pocket Books, 2003), p. 7.

117. Seldon with Newell, *May at 10*, pp. 73–4.

118. William Hague, Baron Hague of Richmond, Interview with Anthony Seldon, 7 October 2020.

9 THE RISE, AND RISE, OF THE CHANCELLOR OF THE EXCHEQUER, 1660–2021

1. J. M. Keynes quoted in G. C. Peden, *The Treasury and British Public Policy, 1906–1959* (Oxford University Press, 2000), p. 19.

2. Macpherson, 'Origins of Treasury control'.

3. Ibid.

4. 'Treasurers and Commissioners of the Treasury 1660–1870' in J. C. Sainty (ed.), *Office-Holders in Modern Britain*: vol. I, *Treasury Officials 1660–1870* (University of London, 1972), pp. 16–28.

5. 'History, Origin and Traditions of the Budget', *interbudget.co.uk*, http://web.archive.org/web/20131224110937/http://www.interbudget.co.uk/history-budget.html (accessed 24 November 2020).

6. Lewis Namier, 'GRENVILLE, George (1712–70), of Wotton, Bucks.', in L. Namier and J. Brooke (eds.), *The History of Parliament: The House of Commons 1754–1790* (London: HMSO, 1964), www.historyofparliamentonline.org/volume/1754–1790/member/grenville-george-1712–70#footnote53_hsk8at4 (accessed 25 November 2020).

7. Henry Roseveare, quoted in Macpherson, 'Origins of Treasury Control'.

8. J. H. Plumb, *Sir Robert Walpole: The Making of a Statesman* (London: Cresset Press, 1956), pp. 76–7.

9. Quoted in Macpherson, 'Origins of Treasury Control'.

10. Patrick O'Brien, 'Political Biography and Pitt the Younger as Chancellor of the Exchequer', *History*, 83/270 (1998), pp. 225–33.

11. 'Deal, Kent: From Smuggler's Haunt to Tourist Town', Official Deal Tourist Information, www.aboutdeal.co.uk/smuggling (accessed 23 November 2020).

12. Macpherson, 'Origins of Treasury Control'.

13. Richard Cooper , 'William Pitt, Taxation, and the Needs of War', *Journal of British Studies*, 22/1 (1982), pp. 94–103.

14. Bruce Coleman, letter to the authors, 8 December 2020.

15. Ibid.

16. Angus Hawkins, interview with Anthony Seldon, 24 September 2020.

17. Matthew, *Gladstone*, p. 110.

18. Simon Read, *Independent*, 20 March 2013.

19. William Gladstone, *Political Speeches in Scotland, November and December 1879* (Edinburgh: Andrew Elliot, 1879), p. 148.

20. Quoted in Richard Toye, 'Prime Ministers and Their Chancellors', *History of Government Blog*, 1 August 2012, https://history.blog.gov.uk/2012/08/01/prime-ministers-and-their-chancellors (accessed 24 November 2020).

21. Quoted in Olive Anderson, 'Loans versus Taxes: British Financial Policy in the Crimean War', *Economic History Review*, 16/2 (December 1963), pp. 314–27 (at 314).

22. Nicholas Macpherson, Baron Macpherson of Earl's Court, interview with Anthony Seldon, 2 October 2020.

23. Lord Milton, Hansard, House of Commons (HC) Debate, 1 June 1827, vol. 17, col. 1124.

24. Toye, 'Prime Ministers and Their Chancellors'.

25. Matthew, *Gladstone*, p. 114.

26. Peden, *The Treasury*, p. 6.

27. Quoted in Macpherson, 'Origins of Treasury Control'.

28. Peden, *The Treasury*, p. 16.

29. Bruce Coleman, letter to the authors, 8 December 2020.

30. Lord Salisbury, Hansard, House of Lords (HL) Debates, 1 February 1900, vol. 78, col. 237.

31. Peden, *The Treasury*, p. 8.

32. Ibid.

33. Morgan, 'David Lloyd George', p. 248.

34. Roy Jenkins, *The Chancellors* (London: Macmillan, 1998), p. 172.

35. Quoted in Roy Jenkins, *Mr Balfour's Poodle* (London: Collins, 1968), p. 76.

36. Toye, 'Prime Ministers and Their Chancellors'.

37. David Lloyd George, speech at Mansion House, 21 July 1911; reported in *The Times*, 22 July 1911.

38. Grey, *Twenty-Five Years*, p. 228.

39. Roy Jenkins, *Asquith*, rev. edn (London: Collins, 1978), p. 329.

40. Jenkins, *The Chancellors*, pp. 174–5.

41. Peden, *The Treasury*, p. 12.

42. Nicholas Macpherson, Baron Macpherson of Earl's Court, letter to the authors, 6 December 2020.

43. Peden, *The Treasury*, p. 4.

44. Toye, 'Prime Ministers and Their Chancellors'.

45. Bruce Coleman, letter to the authors, 9 December 2020.

46. J. Grigg, according to Robert Boothby, *Recollections of a Rebel* (London: Hutchinson, 1978), p. 46, cited in Peden, *The Treasury*, p. 17.

47. Seldon with Meakin, *Cabinet Office*, pp. 54–6.

48. Peden, *The Treasury*, pp. 15–16.

49. Ibid., p. 25.

50. Ibid., p. 18.

51. Ibid., p. 24.

52. Edmund Dell, *The Chancellors: A History of the Chancellors of the Exchequer, 1945–90* (London: HarperCollins, 1996), p. 19.

53. Nicholas Macpherson, Baron Macpherson of Earl's Court, interview with Anthony Seldon, 2 October 2020.

54. Bew, *Citizen Clem*, p. 457.

55. Peden, *The Treasury*, p. 13.

56. Ibid., pp. 11–12.

57. E. H. H. Green, 'The Treasury Resignations of 1958: A Reconsideration', *Twentieth Century British History*, 11/4 (2000), pp. 409–30.

58. Nigel Birch, *The Times*, 14 July 1962, quoted in D. R. Thorpe, *Selwyn Lloyd* (London: Jonathan Cape, 1989), p. 345.

59. Douglas Allen, Baron Croham, interview with Anthony Seldon, British Oral Archive of Political and Administrative History, LSE, 20 September 1980.

60. John Campbell, *Roy Jenkins: A Biography* (London: Weidenfeld & Nicolson, 1983), p. 126.

61. Philip Ziegler, 'How the Last Tory–Liberal Deal Fell Apart', *Sunday Times*, 9 May 2010.

62. Macpherson, 'Origins of Treasury Control'.

63. John Kerr, Baron Kerr of Kinlochard, interview with Anthony Seldon, 19 September 2020.

64. John Major, *The Autobiography* (London: HarperCollins, 1999), p. 206; Seldon with Baston, *Major*, p. 210.

65. Dell, *The Chancellors*, pp. 434–6.

66. Private information.

67. Jim Callaghan, *Time and Chance* (London: Collins, 1987), p. 435.

68. Denis Healey, *The Time of My Life* (London: Michael Joseph, 1989), pp. 430–1.

69. John Kerr, Baron Kerr of Kinlochard, interview with Anthony Seldon, 19 September 2020.

70. Andrew Turnbull, Baron Turnbull, interview with Anthony Seldon, 17 September 2020.

71. Nigel Lawson, *The View from No. 11: Memoirs of a Tory Radical* (London: Bantam Press, 1992), p. 463.

72. Ibid., p. 492.

73. Dell, *The Chancellors*, p. 511.

74. Gus O'Donnell, Baron O'Donnell, interview with Anthony Seldon, 25 September 2020.

75. Quoted in Dell, *The Chancellors*, p. 515.

76. Ibid., p. 521; Lawson, *View from No. 11*, p. 583.

77. Raymond Newell, letter to the authors, 5 December 2020.

78. Norman Lamont, 'Out of the Ashes' in Howard Davies (ed.), *The Chancellors' Tales: Managing the British Economy* (London: Polity, 2006), p. 147.

79. Lionel Barber, 'The Treasury Today: A Devalued Currency?', *Prospect*, 30 November 2020.

80. Norman Lamont, Hansard, House of Commons (HC) Debates, 9 June 1993, Series 6, vol. 226, col. 285.

81. Major, *Autobiography*, p. 680.

82. Gus O'Donnell, Baron O'Donnell, interview with Anthony Seldon, 25 September 2020.

83. Ibid.

84. Ken Clarke, *Kind of Blue: A Political Memoir* (London: Pan Macmillan, 2016), Kindle edn, loc. 5101–10.

85. Private information.

86. Macpherson, 'Origins of Treasury Control'.

87. Ed Balls, speech at King's College London, 20 November 2020.

88. Richard Wilson, Baron Wilson of Dinton, interview with Anthony Seldon, 21 September 2020.

89. 'Mandelson' chapter, in Seldon, *Blair*.

90. Seldon with Snowdon and Collings, *Blair Unbound*, pp. 210–11.

91. John Kerr, Baron Kerr of Kinlochard, interview with Anthony Seldon, 19 September 2020.

92. Seldon with Snowdon and Collings, *Blair Unbound*, pp. 346–7.

93. Gus O'Donnell, Baron O'Donnell, interview with Anthony Seldon, 18 September 2020.

94. Barber, 'Treasury Today'.

95. *Guardian*, 31 August 2008.

96. Seldon and Lodge, *Brown at 10*, pp. 133–4.

97. Cameron, *For the Record*, pp. 179–80.

98. Rupert Harrison, interview with Anthony Seldon, 30 November 2020.

99. Gus O'Donnell, Baron O'Donnell, interview with Anthony Seldon, 18 September 2020.

100. Seldon with Newell, *May at 10*, p. 169.
101. Ibid., p. 171.
102. Philip Hammond, interview with Anthony Seldon, 4 June 2020.
103. Seldon with Newell, *May at 10*, p. 646.
104. Private information.
105. Rupert Harrison, interview with Anthony Seldon, 30 November 2020.
106. Rupert Harrison, interview with Anthony Seldon, 30 November 2020.
107. Barber, 'Treasury Today'.
108. Alex Thomas, 'The Reshuffle Demonstrates the PM's Power – But Does Not Mean the End of the Treasury', Institute for Government, 13 February 2020, www .instituteforgovernment.org.uk/blog/reshuffle-prime-minister-power-does-not-mean-end-treasury (accessed 14 December 2020).

10 THE IMPOSSIBLE OFFICE?

1. 'Rating British Prime Ministers', University of Leeds and MORI survey, 29 November 2004, www.ipsos.com/ipsos-mori/en-uk/rating-british-prime-ministers (accessed 6 December 2020).
2. *The Times*, 5 May 2010.
3. 'Rating British Prime Ministers', Leeds and MORI survey; Kevin Theakston, 'Academics Rate David Cameron among Worst Post-War Prime Ministers', *The Conversation*, 13 October 2016, www.theconversation.com/academics-rate-david-cameron-among-wors t-post-war-prime-ministers-66780 (accessed 6 December 2020).
4. Iain Dale, 'Ranking our 55 Prime Ministers – An Impossible Task, But a Fascinating One', 12 November 2020, www.iaindale.com/articles/ranking-our-55-prime-ministers-an-impossible-task-but-a-fascinating-one (accessed 6 December 2020).
5. Robert W. Merry, 'His wild swing missed but Donald Trump has beaten America into his image', *The Sunday Times*, 8 November 2020. See also Robert W. Merry, *Where They Stand: The American Presidents in the Eyes of Voters and Historians* (New York: Simon & Schuster, 2012).
6. 'Rating British Prime Ministers', Leeds and MORI survey; Theakston, 'Academics Rate David Cameron'.
7. David Cameron, interview with Anthony Seldon, 3 February 2021.
8. Anthony Seldon, 'Ideas Are Not Enough' in David Marquand and Anthony Seldon (eds.), *The Ideas that Shaped Post-War Britain* (London: Fontana, 1996), pp. 257–89.
9. Dennis Kavanagh and Anthony Seldon (eds.), *The Thatcher Effect* (Oxford: Clarendon Press, 1989); Anthony Seldon and Mike Finn (eds.), *The Coalition Effect, 2010–2015* (Cambridge University Press, 2015).
10. H. H. Asquith, Earl of Oxford, *Memories and Reflections, 1852–1927*, 2 vols. (London: Little, Brown, 1928).
11. Arthur Balfour, *Retrospect: An Unfinished Autobiography, 1848–1886* (London: Houghton Mifflin, 1930).
12. David Lloyd George, *War Memoirs of David Lloyd George*, 6 vols. (London: Little, Brown, 1936).

13. Winston Churchill, *The Second World War*, 6 vols. (London: Houghton Mifflin, 1948–53).

14. Anthony Eden, *Full Circle: The Memoirs of Sir Anthony Eden* (London: Cassell, 1960); Anthony Eden, *Facing the Dictators* (London: Cassell, 1962); Anthony Eden, *The Reckoning* (London: Cassell, 1965).

15. Harold Macmillan, *Riding the Storm, 1956–1959* (London: Macmillan, 1971); *Pointing the Way, 1959–1961* (London: Macmillan, 1972); *At the End of the Day, 1961–1963* (London: Macmillan, 1973).

16. Alec Douglas-Home, *The Way the Wind Blows: An Autobiography of Lord Home* (London: HarperCollins, 1976).

17. Edward Heath, *The Course of My Life: The Autobiography of Edward Heath* (London: Hodder & Stoughton, 1998).

18. Harold Wilson, *The Labour Government, 1964–1970: A Personal Record* (London: Weidenfeld & Nicolson, 1971); Harold Wilson, *Final Term: The Labour Government, 1974–1976* (London: Weidenfeld & Nicolson, 1979).

19. Seldon with Meakin, *Cabinet Office*, pp. 62–3.

20. G. M. Young, *Stanley Baldwin* (London: Hart-Davis, 1952); Cato, *Guilty Men* (London: Victor Gollancz, 1940). 'Cato' was a pseudonym; the book was written by Michael Foot, Frank Owen, and Peter Howard.

21. Martin Gilbert, *Winston S. Churchill, Three: The Challenge of War: 1914–1916* (London: Heinemann, 1971–88).

22. Horne, *Harold Macmillan*, vol. i: *1894–1956*, and vol. ii: *1957–86* (London: Macmillan, 1989).

23. Philip Ziegler, *Wilson: The Authorised Life* (London: Weidenfeld & Nicolson, 1993).

24. Philip Ziegler, *Edward Heath : The Authorised Biography* (London: HarperPress, 2010).

25. D. R. Thorpe, *Eden: The Life and Times of Anthony Eden, First Earl of Avon, 1897–1977* (London: Chatto & Windus, 2003).

26. Ricketts, *Hard Choices*, p. 9.

27. Clement Attlee, Denis Pitts, *Clem Attlee: The Granada Historical Records Interview* (London: Panther Books, 1967), p. 47. Harold Macmillan, *Pointing the Way, 1959–1961* (London: Macmillan, 1972), p. 374. I am indebted to David Dilks for these references.

28. Norma Major, *Chequers: The Prime Minister's Country House and Its History* (London: HarperCollins, 1996), p. 13.

29. Rupert Harrison, letter to the authors, 2 December 2020.

30. Michael Barber, *How to Run a Government* (London: Penguin, 2016), pp. 105–6.

31. David Cameron, interview with Anthony Seldon, 3 February 2021.

32. David Cameron, interview with Anthony Seldon, 3 February 2021.

33. For example, see 'Political Economy of Growth and Institutional Reform in theUK', Institute for Government,March 2018, www.instituteforgovernment.org.uk/our-work/policy-making/political-economy-growth-and-institutional-reform-uk (accessed 11 December 2020).

34. Camilla Cavendish, Letter to Anthony Seldon, 29 December 2020.

35. Lucille Iremonger, *The Fiery Chariot: A Study of British Prime Ministers and the Search for Love'* (London: Seeker and Warburg, 1970), See Hugh Berrington, 'Review Article: The Fiery Chariot: British Prime Ministers and the Search for Love', *British Journal of Political Science*, 4:3 (1974), pp. 345–69.

36. Quoted in Seldon and Walsh, *Public Schools*, p. 246.

37. *Guardian*, 25 February 2009.

38. See Moore, *Margaret Thatcher*, vol. III.

39. Cameron, *For the Record*, p. 694.

Bibliography

PRIMARY SOURCES

ARCHIVAL SOURCES

Royal Archives, Windsor

By permission of Her Majesty Queen Elizabeth II
GEO/MAIN/3929
GEO/MAIN/3929
GEO/MAIN/5367
RCIN 400749

The National Archives

CAB 21/1638
CAB 129/101/16
DO 194/22
E 31/2/1/7778
T199/7
PREM 11/3518

Hansard

Hansard, House of Commons (HC) Debates, 29 April 1805, vol. 4, cols. 495–6
Hansard, House of Lords (HL) Debates, 3 March 1806, vol. 6, col. 277–8
Hansard, House of Lords (HL) Debates, 10 November 1820, vol. 3, col. 1746
Hansard, House of Commons (HC) Debate, 1 June 1827, vol. 17, col. 1124
Hansard, House of Commons (HC) Debate, 12 June 1846, vol. 87, col. 429
Hansard, House of Commons (HC) Debate, 1 March 1848, vol. 97, col. 122
Hansard, House of Lords (HL) Debate, 1 July 1895, vol. 35, col. 45
Hansard, House of Lords (HL) Debate, 6 July 1895, vol. 35, col. 262
Hansard, House of Commons (HC) Debates, 6 December 1945, vol. 416, cols. 2530–99

Hansard, House of Commons (HC) Debates, 11 May 1953, vol. 515, cols. 883–98
Hansard, House of Commons (HC) Debates, 9 June 1993, Series 6, vol. 226, col. 285
Hansard, 'Deputy Prime Minister', https://api.parliament.uk/historic-hansard /offices/deputy-prime-minister (accessed 27 November 2020)

Other Archival

Adams, John, letter to Abigail Adams, 19 December 1793, Smithsonian National Portrait Gallery
Adams, John, Minister to Britain, letter to John Jay, Secretary of State, reporting on his audience with the king, 2 June 1785, National Archives, Records of the Continental and Confederation Congresses and the Constitutional Convention, www.archives.gov/exhibits/eyewitness/html.php?section=19 (accessed 9 December 2020)
Allen, Douglas, Baron Croham, interview with Anthony Seldon, British Oral Archive of Political and Administrative History, LSE, 20 September 1980
Bodleian Library, Special Collections, Dept. Hughenden, 73/2
'Carlucci email to Colin Powell', 9 June 1987, Margaret Thatcher Foundation, www .margaretthatcher.org/document/110639 (accessed 15 November 2020)
'Helicopter Arrangements for Camp David Conference', Eisenhower Presidential Library, 20 March 1959, www.eisenhowerlibrary.gov/sites/defa ult/files/research/online-documents/camp-david/macmillan.pdf (accessed 15 November 2020)
Kip, Johannes, 'The Prospect of Whitehall', Government Art Collection, 1724, www .artcollection.culture.gov.uk/artwork/1640 (accessed 15 November 2020)
Palmerston, Viscount, memorandum dated 20 October 1861, Layard Papers, British Library, Add Ms 38987, fol. 301
'Premier's Dramatic Peace Bid', *British Pathé*, 1958, www.britishpathe.com/vide o/premiers-dramatic-peace-bid/query/Hard (accessed 10 November 2020)
Russell, John, Lord Russell, to Palmerston, 1 October 1848, Palmerston Papers (Broadlands Papers), University of Southampton Library, GC/RU/225

NEWSPAPERS AND MAGAZINES

Adams, Richard, and Greenwood, Xavier, 'Oxford and Cambridge University Colleges Hold £21bn in Riches', *Guardian*, 28 May 2018
Bale, Tim, 'How the Tory Party Can Solve Its Membership Crisis, in Three Easy Steps', *Guardian*, 3 October 2017
    'Will the New Tory Intake Help to Build a More Progressive Party? Don't Count on It', *Guardian*, 19 December 2019
Barber, Lionel, 'The Treasury Today: A Devalued Currency?', *Prospect*, 30 November 2020
Bogdanor, Vernon, 'Ministers Take the Biscuit', *Times Higher Education Supplement*, 3 October 1997
    'Thirty Years After She Quit, We Need a New Dose of Thatcherism', *Sunday Times*, 22 November 2020

'Was "Sunny Jim" Really Such a Disastrous PM?', *Sunday Telegraph*, 22 November 2020

Campbell, Sophie, 'Queen's Diamond Jubilee: Sixty Years of Royal Tours', *Daily Telegraph*, 11 May 2012.

English, Otto, 'No Place for God in British Politics', *Politico Forum*, 23 December 2019.

Filby, Eliza, 'The Death of Tory Anglicanism', *Spectator*, 21 November 2013

Green, David Allen, 'How the Myth of Judicial Activism Has Taken on a Life of Its Own', *Prospect*, 28 February 2020

Green, S. J. D., 'Review of Will Hay, "Lord Liverpool: A Political Life"', *Law and Liberty*, 13 May 2019, www.lawliberty.org/book-review/robert-jenkinson-second-earl-of-liverpool-guarantor-of-britains-stability-in-a-turbulent-time (accessed 15 November 2020)

Harris, Kenneth, '"A Prime Minister governs by curiosity ... ": Harold Wilson Talks about His Job to Kenneth Harris', *Observer*, 24 October 1965

Hinsliff, Gaby, 'Under New Management: Is Carrie Symonds the Real Power at No 10?', *Observer*, 29 November 2020

Hjelmgaard, Kim, 'Trump's UK Visit: What You Need to Know, from Royal Ceremony to Protests in London', *USA Today*, 3 June 2019, https://amp.usatoday.com/amp/1284000001 (accessed 8 December 2020).

Hope, Christopher, 'Top Tory Donors Look Set to Lose Out on Peerages', *Daily Telegraph*, 19 July 2020

Lammy, David, 'Review: "Who Runs This Place? The Anatomy of Britain in the 21st Century", Anthony Sampson', *Guardian*, 10 April 2004

Lane-Fox, Robin, 'All in Good Taste', *Financial Times*, 16 August 2013

'Lloyd George Off to Paris: Bonar Law Makes the Trip, as Usually, by Airplane', *New York Times*, 12 January 1919

Mason, Chris, 'London 2012: What Exactly Is a Cobra Meeting?' *BBC News*, 23 July 2012, www.bbc.co.uk/news/uk-politics-18958032 (accessed 27 November 2020)

Merry, Robert W., 'His wild swing missed but Donald Trump has beaten America into his image', *The Sunday Times*, 8 November 2020

'Neville Chamberlain's Declaration of War', *Observer*, 6 September 2009

'The Queen Is the Most Photographed Woman in the World – But She's Spent Plenty of Time Behind the Camera Too', *Radio Times*, 21 April 2016

Saunders, Robert, 'Britain at the End of History', *New Statesman*, 7 October 2020.

Scott, Patrick, 'With 28 Defeats and Resignations Galore Was Theresa May the Weakest Prime Minister Ever?', *Daily Telegraph*, 24 May 2019, www.telegraph.co.uk/politics/2019/03/26/20-defeats-historic-loss-parliamentary-control-no-majority-theresa (accessed 7 December 2020)

Seldon, Anthony, 'Illness in Office is Nothing New for a Leader under Strain', *The Times*, 7 April 2020

'Senex ', Letter to the Editor, *The Times*, 2 May 1950

Theakston, Kevin, 'Academics Rate David Cameron among Worst Post-War Prime Ministers', *The Conversation*, 13 October 2016, www.theconversation.com/aca

demics-rate-david-cameron-among-worst-post-war-prime-ministers-66780 (accessed 6 December 2020)

Thévoz, Seth, 'Inside the Elite Tory Fundraising Regime', *Open Democracy*, 9 December 2019, www.opendemocracy.net/en/dark-money-investigations /inside-elite-tory-fundraising-machine (accessed 1 December 2020)

Travers, Tony, 'Local Government: Margaret Thatcher's Eleven Year War', *Guardian*, 9 April 2013

Walker, Peter, 'Tom Watson Peerage Rejected by Lords Vetting Commission', *Guardian*, 1 June 2020

Watt, Nicholas, 'Blair U-turn on EU Referendum', *Guardian*, 19 April 2004

White, Michael, 'The History of PMQs', *Guardian*, 27 October 2011

Ziegler, Philip, 'How the Last Tory–Liberal Deal Fell Apart', *Sunday Times*, 9 May 2010

BBC News, 7 July 1999

BBC News, 23 September 2014

BBC News, 19 October 2020

BBC News, 13 November 2020

BBC News, 25 November 2020

Daily Telegraph, 3 January 1956

Daily Telegraph, 8 December 2005

Guardian, 6 May 2001

Guardian, 12 June 2007

Guardian, 13 September 2007

Guardian, 31 August 2008

Guardian, 25 February 2009

Guardian, 14 September 2014

Guardian, 24 July 2019

Guardian, 19 October 2020

Independent, 20 March 2013

London Daily Post, 23 September 1735

Metro, 25 July 2019

New Statesman, 2 September 2020

New York Times, 9 October 1994

Stamford Mercury, 1 April 1721

The Times, 26 June 1945

The Times, 5 May 2010

The Times, 4 September 2019

The Times, 5 October 2020

SPEECHES AND LECTURES

Baldwin, Stanley, speech at Queens Hall, 17 March 1931

Balls, Ed, speech at King's College, London, 20 November 2020

Bercow, John, 'New Parliament, New Opportunity', speech to the Centre for Parliamentary Studies, 6 July 2010

Canning,George, 'Song for the Inauguration of the Pitt Club', 25 May 1802

Gladstone, William, *Political Speeches in Scotland, November and December 1879* (Edinburgh:Andrew Elliot, 1879)

Hennessy, Peter, 'The Statecraft of Clement Attlee', The Thirteenth Annual Attlee Foundation Lecture, Queen Mary and Westfield College, University of London, 14 February 1995

Johnson, Boris, Conservative Party Conference Speech, 6 October 2020

Lloyd George, David, speech at Mansion House, 21 July 1911; reported in *The Times*, 22 July 1911

Macmillan, Harold, 'Winds of Change' speech, delivered to the Parliament of South Africa, 3 February 1960

Macpherson, Nicholas, 'The Origins of Treasury Control', speech, 16 January 2013, www.gov.uk/government/speeches/speech-by-the-permanent-secretary-to-the-treasury-sir-nicholas-macpherson-the-origins-of-treasury-control (accessed 24 November 2020)

Patel, Priti, Conservative Party Conference Speech, 4 October 2020

Pitt, William, *The Speech of the Right Honourable William Pitt, on a Motion for the Abolition of the Slave Trade*, House of Commons, 2 April 1792 (London:James Phillips, 1792)

Seldon, Anthony, 'When, How and Why the FCO Lost Out to Downing Street and the Prospects for Power Returning to the FCO', talk at the FCO, 6 February 2020

Thatcher, Margaret, speech to Conservative Group for Europe, 16 April 1975
'Speech Presenting New Standard to No. 10 Squadron RAF', *Margaret Thatcher Foundation*, 30 September 1988, www.margaretthatcher.org/document/10 7348 (accessed 15 November 2020)

Williams, Lady (Jane Portal), lecture on Churchill at Number 10, November 2018

MEMOIRS AND DIARIES

Asquith, H. H. *Fifty Years in Parliament*, vol. II, (London: Cassell, 1926)
Memories and Reflections, 2 vols. (London: Little, Brown, 1928)

Balfour, Arthur, *Retrospect: An Unfinished Autobiography, 1848–1886* (London: Houghton Mifflin, 1930)

Brock, Michael, and Eleanor Brock (eds.), *Margot Asquith's Great War Diary, 1914–1916: The View from Downing Street* (Oxford University Press, 2014)

Brown, Gordon, *My Life, Our Times* (London: Random House, 2017)

Brown, Sarah, *Behind the Black Door* (London: Ebury, 2011)

Callaghan, Jim, *Time and Chance* (London: Collins, 1987)

Cameron, David, *For the Record* (London: William Collins, 2019)

Churchill, Winston, *The Second World War*, 6 vols. (London: Houghton Mifflin, 1948–53)

Clarke, Ken, *Kind of Blue: A Political Memoir* (London: Pan Macmillan, 2016)

Cook, Robin, *The Point of Departure* (London: Pocket Books, 2003)

Douglas-Home, Alec, *The Way the Wind Blows: An Autobiography of Lord Home* (London: HarperCollins, 1976)

Eden, Anthony, *Facing the Dictators* (London: Cassell, 1962)

Full Circle: The Memoirs of Sir Anthony Eden (London: Cassell, 1960)

Anthony, *The Reckoning* (London: Cassell, 1965)

Foot, M. R. D., and G. C. G. Matthew (eds.), *The Gladstone Diaries*, 14 vols. (Oxford University Press, 1968–94)

Fox, Charles, *Memoirs*, vol. I (London: R. Bentley, 1853)

Greville, Henry, Friday 20 October 1865, in Countess of Stafford (ed.), *Leaves from the Diary of Henry Greville*, vol. IV (London: Smith, Elder, 1905)

Grey, Edward, *Twenty-Five Years, 1892–1916* (New York: Frederick A. Stokes, 1925)

Healey, Denis, *The Time of My Life* (London: Michael Joseph, 1989)

Heath, Edward, *The Course of My Life: The Autobiography of Edward Heath* (London: Hodder & Stoughton, 1998)

Heseltine, Michael, *Life in the Jungle: My Autobiography* (London: Hodder & Stoughton, 2000)

Hutchinson, Horace G. (ed.), *Private Diaries of the Rt. Hon. Sir Algernon West* (New York: E. P. Dutton, 1922)

Lawson, Nigel, *The View from No. 11: Memoirs of a Tory Radical* (London: Bantam Press, 1992)

Lloyd George, David, *War Memoirs of David Lloyd George*, 6 vols. (London: Little, Brown, 1936)

Lloyd George, Frances, *The Years that are Past* (London: Hutchinson, 1967)

Macmillan, Harold, *At the End of the Day, 1961–1963* (London: Macmillan, 1973)

Pointing the Way, 1959–1961 (London: Macmillan, 1972)

Riding the Storm, 1956–1959 (London: Macmillan, 1971)

Major, John, *The Autobiography* (London: HarperCollins, 1999)

Thatcher, Margaret, *The Autobiography*, (London: HarperPress, 2013)

The Downing Street Years (London: HarperCollins, 1993)

Waldegrave, James, *Memoirs, from 1754 to 1758* (London: John Murray, 1821)

Wilson, Harold, *Final Term: The Labour Government, 1974–1976* (London: Weidenfeld & Nicolson, 1979)

The Labour Government, 1964–1970: A Personal Record (London: Weidenfeld & Nicolson, 1971)

PRINTED PRIMARY SOURCES

Aspinall A. (ed.), *The Correspondence of George, Prince of Wales, 1770–1812* (London: Cassell, 1964)

(ed.), *The Letters of King George IV* (Cambridge University Press, 1938)

Attlee, Clement and Pitts, Denis, *Clem Attlee: The Granada Historical Records Interview* (London: Panther Books, 1967)

Browning, Andrew (ed.), *English Historical Documents, 1660–1714* (London: Eyre & Spottiswoode, 1953)

Burke, Edmund, 'A Letter to a Noble Lord' (1796), *Harvard Classics*, 24.4 (New York: P.F. Collier & Son, 1909–14), para 16, www.bartleby.com/24/4/1.html (accessed 20 November 2020)

'Thoughts on the Present Discontent' in *The Works* (Boston: Little, Brown, 1881)

Clarke, Tom, *My Northcliffe Diary* (New York: Cosmopolitan; London: Victor Gollancz, 1931)

Fortescue, John (ed.), *The Correspondence of King George the Third, from 1760 to December 1783*, vol. ii (London: Cass, 1967)

Gardiner, Samuel Rowson (ed.), *The Constitutional Documents of the Puritan Revolution, 1625–1660* (Oxford University Press, 1906)

Giles, J. A. (trans.), *The Anglo-Saxon Chronicle* (London: G. Bell & Sons, 1914)

Historic Manuscripts Commission, *The Manuscripts of the Earl of Dartmouth* (London, 1887)

McIlwain, Charles Howard (ed.), *The Political Works of James I* (Cambridge, MA.: Harvard University Press, 1918)

Parker, Charles Stuart (ed.), *Sir Robert Peel: From His Private Papers*, 3 vols. (London: John Murray, 1899)

Paget Toynbee, Mrs (ed.), *The Letters of Horace Walpole*, vol. iv: *1756–1760* (Oxford: Clarendon Press, 1903)

Peel, George (ed.), *The Private Letters of Sir Robert Peel* (London: John Murray, 1920)

Quarterly Review, 1860–1883 (Cambridge University Press, 1972)

'A Review of the Life of John Duke of Marlborough' in John Benson Rose, *Historical Tracts* (London: William Clowes and Sons, 1869)

Williams, E. N. (ed.), *The Eighteenth-Century Constitution: Documents and Commentary* (Cambridge University Press, 1960)

OFFICIAL SOURCES

The Cabinet Manual (London: Cabinet Office, 2011)

Civil Service Commission, www.civilservicecommission.independent.gov.uk/about-the-commission (accessed 13 November 2020)

'Code of Conduct for Special Advisors', Cabinet Office, December 2016, https://assets.publishing.service.gov.uk/government/uploads/system/uploads/attachment_data/file/832599/201612_Code_of_Conduct_for_Special_Advisers.pdf (accessed 13 November 2020)

The Commissioner for Public Appointments, https://publicappointmentscommissioner.independent.gov.uk (accessed 13 November 2020)

Cygan, Adam, and Cowie, Graham, 'The Prorogation Dispute of 2019: One Year On', House of Commons Library, 24 September 2020, https://commonslibrary.parliament.uk/research-briefings/cbp-9006 (accessed 12 November 2020)

'Prorogation One Year On: A Case for Reform?', House of Commons Library, 24 September 2020, https://commonslibrary.parliament.uk/prorogation-a-case-for-reform (accessed 12 November 2020)

Dawson, Joanna, Lalic, Maria, and Holland, Sue, 'Human Rights in the UK (Debate Pack)', House of Commons Library, 12 February 2020, https://commonslibrary.parliament.uk/research-briefings/cdp-2019–0031 (accessed 13 November 2020)

Dymond, Glen, and Deadman, Hugo, *The Salisbury Doctrine*, House of Lords Library Note, 30 June 2006

Electoral Commission, www.electoralcommission.org.uk (accessed 14 November 2020)

'Government Defeats in the House of Lords', The Constitution Unit, 2020, www
.ucl.ac.uk/constitution-unit/research/parliament/changing-role-house-lords
/government-defeats-house-lords (accessed 19 October 2020)

'Government Defeats in the House of Lords', UK Parliament, 2020, www
.parliament.uk/about/faqs/house-of-lords-faqs/lords-govtdefeats
(accessed 19 October 2020)

Hazell, Robert, Hursit, Turan, Mehta, Hamish, and Peter Waller, 'Improving
Parliamentary Scrutiny of Public Appointments', The Constitution Unit,
July 2017, www.ucl.ac.uk/constitution-unit/sites/constitution-unit/files/pr
e-appt-scrutiny.pdf (accessed 12 November 2020)

House of Lords Appointments Commission, https://lordsappointments
.independent.gov.uk/the-commission-2 (accessed 13 November 2020)

Judicial Appointments Commission, www.judicialappointments.gov.uk (accessed
13 November 2020)

List of Board of Trade Records, vol. IV (London: HMSO, 1978)

Ministerial Code (London: Cabinet Office, August 2019)

'Ministerial Resignations Outside Reshuffles, by Prime Minister', Institute for
Government, 2020, www.instituteforgovernment.org.uk/charts/ministerial-
resignations-outside-reshuffles-prime-minister (accessed 1 December 2020)

Monthly Review of the U.S. Bureau of Labor Statistics, 4 (January–June 1917)

'More Powers for Scotland – What Happens Next?', GOV.UK, 22 January 2015,
www.gov.uk/government/news/more-powers-for-scotland-what-happens-
next (accessed 7 December 2020)

'Past Prime Ministers', GOV.UK, 2020, www.gov.uk/government/history/past-
prime-ministers (accessed 21 October 2020)

'Peter Hennessy interview with Robert Armstrong', Mile End Group, 6 November
2012, www.cabinetsecretaries.com/_lib/pdf/Former%20Cabinet%20Secreta
ry%20Lord%20Armstrong%20Interview%20with%20Lord%20Hennessy.pdf
(accessed 20 November 2020)

Public Administration Select Committee, *Taming the Prerogative: Strengthening
Ministerial Accountability to Parliament* (HC 422, 2003–4) (London: Stationery
Office)

Russell, Meg, 'A More Legitimate and More Powerful Upper House? The Semi-
Reformed House of Lords', ESRC Report, 2008, http://sp.ukdataservice.ac.uk/
doc/6982/mrdoc/pdf/6982_esrc_end-of-award_report.pdf (accessed 12
November 2020)

Sandford, Mark, 'Directly-Elected Mayors', House of Commons Library,
18 February 2019, https://commonslibrary.parliament.uk/research-
briefings/sn05000 (accessed 13 November 2020)

Uberoi, Elise, and Kelly, Richard 'The Fixed-Term Parliaments Act', House of
Commons Library, 14 January 2020, commonslibrary.parliament.uk/the-
fixed-term-parliaments-act (accessed 12 November 2020)

Uberoi, Elise, and Lees, Rebecca, 'Ethnic Diversity in Politics and Public Life',
House of Commons Library, 23 October 2020, https://commonslibrary
.parliament.uk/research-briefings/sn01156 (accessed 31 December 2020)

White, Hannah, 'The Liaison Committee: Function Matters More than Form',
Institute for Government Blog, 21 April 2020, www.instituteforgovernment

.org.uk/blog/liaison-committee-function-matters-more-form (accessed 1 December 2020)

Woodhouse, John, 'Freedom of Information Requests', House of Commons Library, 8 March 2019, https://commonslibrary.parliament.uk/research-briefings/sn02950 (accessed 13 November 2020)

SECONDARY SOURCES

JOURNAL ARTICLES

Anderson, Olive, 'Loans versus Taxes: British Financial Policy in the Crimean War', *Economic History Review*, 16/2 (December 1963), pp. 314–27

Ball, Stuart, 'The 1922 Committee: The Formative Years 1922–45', *Parliamentary History*, 9/1 (1990), pp. 129–57

Beckford, James A., 'Politics and Religion in England and Wales', *Daedulus*, 120/3 (1991), pp. 179–201

Calingaert, Michael, 'Italy's Choice: Reform or Stagnation', *Current History*, 107/707 (March 2008), pp. 105–111, www.brookings.edu/wp-content/uploads/2016/06/03_italy_calingaert.pdf (accessed 26 November 2020)

Campbell, John, Holmes, Martin, and Jones, G. W., 'Thatcherism', *Contemporary Record*, 1/3, (1987), pp. 2–24

Cooper, Richard, 'William Pitt, Taxation, and the Needs of War', *Journal of British Studies*, 22/1 (1982), pp. 94–103

Dalingwater, Louise, 'Civil Service Reform and the Legacy of Thatcherism', *Observatoire de la Société Brittanique*, 17 (2015), pp. 61–78

Green, E. H. H., 'The Treasury Resignations of 1958: A Reconsideration', *Twentieth Century British History*, 11/4, (2000), pp. 409–30.

Hennessy, Peter, and Welsh, David, 'Lords of All They Surveyed? Churchill's Ministerial "Overlords" 1951–1953', *Parliamentary Affairs*, 51/1 (1998), pp. 62–70

Henrekson, Magnus, 'The Peacock and Wiseman Displacement Effect: A Reappraisal and a New Test', *European Journal of Political Economy*, 6/3 (1990), pp. 245–60

Hilton, Boyd, 'Peel: A Reappraisal', *Historical Journal*, 22/3 (1979), pp. 585–614

Hollister, C. Warren, 'The Origins of the English Treasury', *English Historical Review*, 93/367 (1978), pp. 262–75

Kennedy, P. M., 'Imperial Cable Communications and Strategy, 1870–1914', *English Historical Review*, 86/341 (1971), pp. 728–52

Langford, Paul, 'Prime Ministers and Parliaments: The Long View, Walpole to Blair', *Parliamentary History*, 25/3 (2006), pp. 382–94

Lehrman, Lewis E., 'The Prime Minister and the General: Churchill and Eisenhower', *Finest Hour: The Journal of Winston Churchill*, 172 (2016), p. 15

Nunn, Nathan, and Qian, Nancy, 'The Potato's Contribution to Population and Urbanization: Evidence from a Historical Experiment', *Quarterly Journal of Economics*, 126/2 (2001), pp. 593–650

O'Brien, Patrick, 'Political Biography and Pitt the Younger as Chancellor of the Exchequer', *History*, 83/270 (April 1998), pp. 225–33

O'Leary, Brendan, 'An Taoiseach: The Irish Prime Minister', *West European Politics*, 14/2 (1991), pp. 133–62

O'Shaughnessy, Andrew, '"If others will not be active, I must drive": George III and the American Revolution', *Early American Studies*, 2/1 (Spring 2004), pp. iii, 1–46

Owen, David, 'Diseased, Demented, Depressed: Serious Illness in Heads of State', *QJM: An International Journal of Medicine*, 96/5 (2003), pp. 325–66

Russell, M., and Cowley, P., 'The Policy Power of the Westminster Parliament: The "Parliamentary State" and the Empirical Evidence' *Governance*, 29 (2016), pp. 121–137, https://doi.org/10.1111/gove.12149 (accessed 12 November 2020)

Seldon, Anthony, 'The Cabinet Office and Coordination, 1979–87', *Public Administration*, 68/1 (1990), pp. 103–21

Seldon, Anthony, and Sanklecha, Pranay, 'United Kingdom: A Comparative Case Study of Conservative Prime Ministers Heath, Thatcher and Major', *Journal of Legislative Studies*, 10 (2004), pp. 53–65

Sharp, Alan J., 'The Foreign Office in Eclipse, 1919–22', *History*, 61/202 (1976), pp. 198–218

Sterling, Christopher H., 'Churchill and Intelligence – Sigsaly: Beginning the Digital Revolution', *Finest Hour: The Journal of Winston Churchill*, 149 (2010), pp. 31–4

Temperley, H. W. V., 'The Later American Policy of George Canning', *American Historical Review*, 11/4 (July 1906), pp. 779–97

Theakston, Kevin, and Gill, Mark, 'Rating 20th-Century British Prime Ministers', *British Journal of Politics and International Relations*, 8/2 (2006), pp. 193–213

Worthy, Ben, and Hazell, Robert, 'Disruptive, Dynamic and Democratic? Ten Years of FOI in the UK', *Parliamentary Affairs*, 70/1 (2017), pp. 22–42

CHAPTERS IN BOOKS

Baston, Lewis, and Seldon, Anthony, 'Number 10 under Edward Heath' in S. Ball and A. Seldon (eds.), *The Heath Government 1970–1974* (Harlow: Longman, 1996)

Biagini, Eugenio, 'Gladstone's Legacy' in Roland Quinault, Roger Swift, and Ruth Clayton Windscheffel (eds.), *William Gladstone: New Studies and Perspectives* (Abingdon: Routledge, 2012)

Brazier, Rodney, 'The Monarchy' in Vernon Bogdanor (ed.), *The British Constitution in the Twentieth Century* (Oxford University Press, 2004)

Bruton, Elizabeth, '"The Cable Wars": Military and State Surveillance of the British Telegraph Cable Network during World War One' in Andreas Marklund and Rüdiger Morgens (eds.), *Historicizing Infrastructure* (Aalborg University Press, 2017)

Cannon, John, 'Lord Shelburne's Ministry, 1782–3: "A Very Good List"' in Nigel Aston and Clarissa Campbell (eds.), *An Enlightenment Statesman in Whig Britain: Lord Shelburne in Context, 1737–1805* (Woodbridge: Boydell Press, 2011)

Catterall, Peter, 'The Party and Religion' in Anthony Seldon and Stuart Ball (eds.), *Conservative Century: The Conservative Party Since 1900* (Oxford University Press, 1994)

Chisholm, Hugh, 'Granville, Granville George Leveson-Gower, 2nd Earl' in HughChisholm (ed.), *Encyclopaedia Britannica*, 11th edn, vol. XII (Cambridge University Press, 1911)

Churchill, Winston, 'Foreword' in *The War Speeches of William Pitt the Younger* (Oxford: Clarendon Press, 1940)

Collins, Damian, 'David Lloyd George' in Iain Dale (ed.), *The Prime Ministers* (London: Hodder & Stoughton, 2020)

Dziembowski, Edmond, 'Lord Shelburne's Constitutional Views in 1782–3' in Nigel Aston and Clarissa Campbell (eds.), *An Enlightenment Statesman in Whig Britain: Lord Shelburne in Context, 1737–1805* (Woodbridge: Boydell Press, 2011)

Gaunt, Richard, 'From Country Party to Conservative Party: The Ultra-Tories and Foreign Policy' in Jeremy Black (ed.), *The Tory World: Deep History and the Tory Theme in British Foreign Policy, 1679–2014* (Farnham: Ashgate, 2015)

Gladfelder, Hal, 'Introduction' in John Gay, *The Beggar's Opera and Polly*, ed. Hal Gladfelder (Oxford University Press, 2013)

Hattersley, Roy, 'Viscount Palmerston' in Iain Dale (ed.), *The Prime Ministers* (London: Hodder & Stoughton, 2020)

Heffer, Simon, 'William Gladstone' in Iain Dale (ed.), *The Prime Ministers* (London: Hodder & Stoughton, 2020)

Kavanagh, Dennis, and Seldon, Anthony (eds.), *The Thatcher Effect* (Oxford: Clarendon Press, 1989)

Lamont, Norman, 'Out of the Ashes' in Howard Davies (ed.), *The Chancellors' Tales: Managing the British Economy* (London: Polity, 2006)

Morgan, Kenneth O. , 'David Lloyd George' in Duncan Brack, Robert Ingham, and Tony Little (eds.), *British Liberal Leaders* (London: Biteback, 2015)

Newell, Raymond, and Seldon, Anthony, 'Photography in British Political History' in R. A. W. Rhodes and Susan Hodgett (eds.), *What Political Science Can Learn from the Humanities* (London: Palgrave Macmillan, 2021)

Norton, Philip, 'Behavioural Changes: Backbench Independence in the 1980s' in P. Norton (ed.), *Parliament in the 1980s* (Oxford: Basil Blackwell, 1985)

Payne, Sebastian, 'The Royal Prerogative' in Sebastian Payne and Maurice Sunkin (eds.), *The Nature of the Crown: A Legal and Political Analysis* (Oxford University Press, 1999)

Seldon, Anthony, 'The Cabinet Office and Coordination, 1979–87' in R. A. W. Rhodes and Patrick Dunleavy (eds.), *Prime Minister, Cabinet and Core Executive* (London: St Martin's Press, 1995)

'The Cabinet System' in Vernon Bogdanor (ed.), *The British Constitution in the Twentieth Century* (Oxford University Press, 2003)

'Clement Attlee' in Iain Dale (ed.), *The Prime Ministers* (London: Hodder & Stoughton, 2020)

'Conclusion: The Prime Minister's Office from John Martin to Chris Martin' in Andrew Holt and Warren Dockter (eds.), *Private Secretaries to the Prime Minister* (Abingdon: Routledge, 2017)

'Ideas are Not Enough' in David Marquand and Anthony Seldon (eds.), *The Ideas that Shaped Post-War Britain* (London: Fontana, 1996)

Williamson, Philip, 'The Doctrinal Politics of Stanley Baldwin' in Michael Bentley (ed.), *Public and Private Doctrine: Essays in British History Presented to Maurice Cowling* (Cambridge University Press, 1993)

Wrigley, Chris, 'Gladstone and Labour' in Roland Quinault, Roger Swift, and Ruth Clayton Windscheffel (eds.), *William Gladstone: New Studies and Perspectives* (Abingdon: Routledge, 2012)

BOOKS

Aldrich, Richard J., and Cormac, Rory, *The Black Door: Spies, Secret Intelligence and British Prime Ministers* (London: William Collins, 2016)

Allen Butler, Daniel, *Warrior Queens: The Queen Mary and Queen Elizabeth in World War II* (London: Pen & Sword, 2002)

Bagehot, Walter, *The English Constitution* (London: Chapman & Hall, 1867)

The English Constitution, 2nd edn (London: Henry S. King, 1872)

'William Pitt, 1861' in Russell Barrington (ed.), *The Works and Life of Walter Bagehot*, vol. IV (London: Longmans, Green, 1915)

Baird, Julia, *Victoria: The Queen* (London: Random House, 2016)

Baker, J. H., *An Introduction to English Legal History* (Oxford University Press, 2007)

Ball, Stuart (ed.), *The Advent of Democracy: The Impact of the 1918 Reform Act on British Politics* (Hoboken, NJ: Wiley-Blackwell, 2018)

Ball, Stuart, and Seldon, Anthony (eds.), *The Heath Government 1970–1974: A Reappraisal* (Harlow: Longman, 1996)

Barber, Michael, *How to Run a Government,* (London: Penguin, 2016)

Barker, T. C. and Savage, C. I., *An Economic History of Transport in Britain* (Abingdon: Routledge,1975, repr. 2011)

Baugh, Daniel, *The Global Seven Years' War, 1754–1763* (London: Pearson, 2011)

Beckett, Francis, *Clem Attlee: A Biography* (London: Richard Cohen, 1997)

Beggs-Humphreys, Mary, Gregor, Hugh, and Humphreys, Darlow, *The Industrial Revolution* (Abingdon: Routledge, 1959, repr. 2006)

Bentley, Michael, *Politics Without Democracy: 1815–1914*, 2nd edn (Oxford: Blackwell, 1996)

Bew, John, *Castlereagh: Enlightenment, War and Tyranny* (London: Quercus, 2011)

Citizen Clem: A Biography of Attlee (London: riverrun, 2017)

Bigham, Clive, *The Chief Ministers of England, 920–1720* (London: John Murray, 1923)

Black, Jeremy, *George III: America's Last King* (New Haven, CT: Yale University Press, 2006)

George III: Madness and Majesty, Kindle edn (London: Allen Lane, 2020)

Walpole in Power (London: Sutton, 2001)

Blair, Tony, *A Journey* (London: Arrow, 2010)

Blake, Robert, *The Conservative Party from Peel to Churchill* (London: Eyre & Spottiswoode, 1970)

Disraeli (London: Methuen, 1966)

The Office of Prime Minister (Oxford University Press, 1975)

Blanning, Tim, *George I* (London: Allen Lane, 2017)

Blauvelt, Mary Taylor, *The Development of Government in England* (New York: Macmillan, 1902)

Blick, Andrew, and Jones, George, *At Power's Elbow: Aides to the Prime Minister from Robert Walpole to David Cameron* (London: Biteback, 2013)

Premiership: The Development, Nature and Power of the Office of the British Prime Minister (Exeter: Imprint Academic, 2010)

Boothby, Robert, *Recollections of a Rebel* (London: Hutchinson, 1978)

Brack, Duncan, Ingham, Robert, and Little, Tony (eds.) *British Liberal Leaders* (London: Biteback, 2015)

Brazier, Rodney, *Choosing a Prime Minister: The Transfer of Power in Britain* (Oxford University Press, 2020)

Brewer, John, *The Sinews of Power: War and the English State, 1688–1783* (London: Unwin Hyman, 1989)

Briggs, Asa, *The Making of Modern England, 1783–1867* (London: Harper & Row, 1959)

Broadberry, Stephen, Campbell, M. S., Bruce, Alexander Klein, Overton, Mark, and van Leeuwen, Bas, *British Economic Growth, 1270–1870* (Cambridge University Press, 2015)

Brooke, John, *King George III* (London: Constable, 1972)

Brown, Callum G., and Fraser, W. Hamish, *Britain Since 1707* (London: Routledge, 2013)

Brown, David, *Palmerston: A Biography* (New Haven and London: Yale University Press, 2010)

Palmerston and the Politics of Foreign Policy, 1846–55 (Manchester University Press, 2002)

Brown, Jack, *No. 10: The Geography of Power at Downing Street,* (London: Haus, 2019)

Browning, Reed, *The War of the Austrian Succession* (London: St Martin's Press, 1993)

Burke, Edmund (ed.), *The Annual Register* (London: J. Dodsley, 1791)

Campbell, John, *Lloyd George: The Goat in the Wilderness, 1922–1931* (London: Jonathan Cape, 1977)

Margaret Thatcher: Grocer's Daughter to Iron Lady, abridged edn (London: Vintage, 2009)

Pistols at Dawn: Two Hundred Years of Political Rivalry from Pitt and Fox to Blair and Brown (London: Vintage, 2010)

Roy Jenkins: A Biography (London: Weidenfeld & Nicolson, 1983)

Campbell, Lord, *The Lives of the Lord Chancellors*, vol. v (Philadelphia: Blanchard and Lea, 1851)

Cannadine, David, *Margaret Thatcher: A Life and Legacy* (Oxford University Press, 2017)

Cannon, John, *The Fox–North Coalition* (Cambridge University Press, 1969)

Carswell, John, *The South Sea Bubble* (London: Cresset Press, 1960)

Carter, Byrum E., *The Office of the Prime Minister* (Princeton University Press, 1955)

Cato, *Guilty Men* (London: Victor Gollancz, 1940)

Cecil, Algernon, *British Foreign Secretaries* (London: G. Bell and Sons, 1927)

Cecil, David, *Lord M, or the Later Life of Lord Melbourne* (London: Constable, 1954)

Clarke, Charles, James, Toby S., Bale, Tim, and Diamond, Patrick (eds.), *British Conservative Leaders* (London: Biteback, 2015)

Clarke, Charles, and James, Toby S. (eds.), *British Labour Leaders* (London: Biteback, 2015)

Cockett, Richard, *Thinking the Unthinkable: Think-tanks and the Economic Counter-Revolution 1931–1983* (London: HarperCollins, 1994)

Colley, Linda, *Britons: Forging the Nation 1707–1837* (New Haven, CT: Yale University Press, 2005)

Courcy, Anne de, *Margot at War: Love and Betrayal in Downing Street, 1912–16* (London: Weidenfeld & Nicolson, 2014)

Coxe, William, *Memoirs of the Life and Administration of Sir Robert Walpole, Earl of Orford*, 3 vols. (London: Cadell, Jun and Davies, 1798)

Memoirs of the Life and Administration of Sir Robert Walpole, Earl of Orford, vol. IV (London: Longman, Hurst, Rees, Orme and Brown, 1816)

Crines, Andrew S., and Hickson, Kevin (eds.), *Harold Wilson: The Unprincipled Prime Minister? Reappraising Harold Wilson* (London: Biteback, 2016)

Cromwell, Judith Lissauer, *Good Queen Anne: Appraising the Life and Reign of the Last Stuart Monarch* (Jefferson, NC: McFarland, 2019)

Cubbison, Douglas R., *All Canada in the Hands of the British: General Jeffrey Amherst and the 1760 Campaign to Conquer New France* (University of Oklahoma Press, 2014)

Dell, Edmund, *The Chancellors: A History of the Chancellors of the Exchequer, 1945–90* (London: HarperCollins, 1996)

Dicey, A. V., *Introduction to the Study of the Law of the Constitution*, 10th edn, (London: Macmillan, 1959)

Dickinson, H. T., *Walpole and the Whig Supremacy* (London: Hodder & Stoughton, 1973)

Donoughue, Bernard, *Downing Street Diary: With Harold Wilson in No. 10* (London: Jonathan Cape, 2005)

Dudley, Geoffrey, *The Outer Cabinet: A History of the Government Car Service* (London: Government Car and Despatch Agency, 2008)

Erickson, Carolly, *Her Little Majesty: The Life of Queen Victoria* (New York: Simon & Schuster, 1997)

Esdaile, Charles, *Napoleon's Wars: An International History, 1803–1815* (London: Penguin, 2007)

Evans, Harold, *Downing Street Diary* (London: Hodder & Stoughton, 1981)

Falkner, James, *The War of the Spanish Succession, 1701–1714* (Barnsley: Pen & Sword, 2015)

Fenton, Laurence, *Palmerston and The Times: Foreign Policy, the Press and Public Opinion in Mid-Victorian Britain* (London: I. B. Taurus, 2012)

Foreman, Amanda, *A World Aflame: Britain's Crucial Role in the American Civil War* (London: Random House, 2012)

Fryde, E. B., Greenway, D. E., Porter S., and Roy, I., *Handbook of British Chronology* (Cambridge University Press, 1996)

Gardner, Howard, *Multiple Intelligences* (New York: Basic Books, 1993)

Gash, Norman, *Lord Liverpool: The Life and Political Career of Robert Banks Jenkinson, Second Earl of Liverpool, 1770–1828* (Cambridge University Press, 1984)
  Sir Robert Peel: The Life of Sir Robert Peel after 1830 (London: Longman, 1972)
Gilbert, Martin, *Winston S. Churchill*, vols. III–VIII (London: Heinemann, 1971–88)
Gill, Gillian, *We Two: Victoria and Albert: Rulers, Partners, Rivals* (London: Ballantine, 2009)
Gimson, Andrew, *Gimson's Prime Ministers* (London: Square Peg, 2018)
Glencross, Matthew, *The State Visits of Edward VII: Reinventing Royal Diplomacy for the Twentieth Century* (London: Palgrave Macmillan, 2016)
Goodlad, Graham, and Pearce, Robert, *British Prime Ministers from Balfour to Brown* (Abingdon: Routledge, 2013)
Griffiths, J. A. G., *Politics of the Judiciary* (London: Fontana, 1977)
Grigg, John, *Lloyd George: from Peace to War 1912–16*, (London: Methuen, 1985).
Hague, William, *William Pitt the Younger* (London: Harper Perennial, 2004)
Hatton, Ragnhild, *George I* (New Haven, CT: Yale University Press, 2001)
Hawkins, Angus, *The Forgotten Prime Minister: The 14th Earl of Derby*, vol. I: *Assent, 1799–1815* (Oxford University Press, 2007)
  The Forgotten Prime Minister: The 14th Earl of Derby, vol. II: *Achievement, 1851–1869* (Oxford University Press, 2008)
Heffer, Simon, *The Age of Decadence: Britain 1880 to 1914* (London: Random House, 2017)
Hennessy, Peter, *The Prime Minister: The Office and Its Holders since 1945* (London: Allen Lane, 2000)
  Whitehall, (London: Free Press, 1989)
Hibbert, Christopher, *George III: A Personal History* (London: Penguin, 1999)
Hichens, Mark, *Prime Ministers' Wives – and One Husband* (London: Peter Owen, 2004)
Hickson, Kevin, and Miles, Jasper (eds.), *James Callaghan: An Underrated Prime Minister?* (London: Biteback, 2020)
Hill, B. W., *Sir Robert Walpole* (London: Hamish Hamilton, 1989)
Hilton, Boyd, *A Mad, Bad, and Dangerous People? England, 1783–1846* (Oxford University Press, 2006)
Hoppen, K. Theodore, *The Mid-Victorian Generation, 1846–1886* (Oxford University Press, 1998)
Horne, Alistair, *Harold Macmillan*, vol. I: *1894–1956* (London: Macmillan, 1989)
  Harold Macmillan, vol. II: *1957–86* (London: Macmillan, 1989).
  Macmillan: The Official Biography (London: Macmillan, 2008)
Hughes, Michael, *British Foreign Secretaries in an Uncertain World, 1919–1939* (London: Routledge, 2006)
Hugill, P. J., *World Trade Since 1431* (Baltimore, MD: Johns Hopkins University Press, 1993)
Hurd, Douglas, *Choose Your Weapons: The British Foreign Secretary* (London: Weidenfeld & Nicolson, 2010)
Hurd, Douglas, and Young, Edward, *Disraeli or The Two Lives* (London: Weidenfeld & Nicolson, 2013)
Hutchinson, George, *The Last Edwardian at No. 10: An Impression of Harold Macmillan* (London: Quartet, 1980)

Iremonger, Lucille, *The Fiery Chariot: A Study of British Prime Ministers and the Search for Love* (London: Secker & Warburg, 1970)

James, Robert Rhodes, *Anthony Eden* (London: Weidenfeld & Nicolson, 1987)

   A Spirit Undaunted: The Political Role of George VI (London: Little, Brown, 1998)

Jay, Douglas, *Change and Fortune: A Political Record* (London: Ebury, 1980)

Jenkins, Roy, *Asquith* (London: Collins, 1964; rev. edn 1978)

   The Chancellors (London: Macmillan, 1998)

   Mr Balfour's Poodle (London: Collins, 1968)

Jenkins, Simon, *Accountable to None: The Tory Nationalization of Britain* (London: Hamish Hamilton, 1995)

John Jagger, Peter, *Gladstone* (London: Hambledon Press, 1998)

Johnston, Ian, and McAuley, Rob, *The Battleships* (London: Macmillan, 2000)

Jones, Christopher, *No. 10 Downing Street: The Story of a House* (London: BBC, 1985)

Jones, Clyve (ed.), *Britain in the First Age of Party: 1680–1750* (London: Hambledon Press, 1987)

Jupp, Peter, *The Governing of Britain, 1688–1848: The Executive, Parliament and the People* (Abingdon: Routledge, 2006)

Kampfner, John, *Why the Germans Do It Better* (London: Atlantic, 2020)

Kavanagh, Dennis, and Seldon, Anthony, *The Powers Behind the Prime Minister: The Hidden Influence of Number Ten* (London: HarperCollins, 1999).

Kennedy, A. L., *Lord Salisbury: Portrait of a Statesman* (London: John Murray, 1953)

Kieve, J. L., *The Telegraph: A Social and Economic History* (Newton Abbot: David & Charles, 1973)

Kissinger, Henry, *Diplomacy* (London: Simon & Schuster, 1994)

Knight, Charles, *A History of England*, vol. VI: *1714–1783* (London: Bradbury and Evans, 1862)

Knowles, Elizabeth (ed.), *Oxford Dictionary of Modern Quotations* (Oxford University Press, 2007)

Kulisheck, P. J., *The Duke of Newcastle, 1693–1768, and Henry Pelham, 1694–1754: A Bibliography* (London: Greenwood Press, 1997)

Langford, Paul, *A Polite and Commercial People: England 1727–1783* (Oxford University Press, 1992)

Lawson, Philip, *George Grenville: A Political Life* (Oxford University Press, 1984)

Leonard, Dick, *A History of British Prime Ministers* (London: Palgrave Macmillan, 2014)

Lester, V. Markham, *HH Asquith: Last of the Romans* (London: Lexington, 2019)

Longford, Elizabeth, *Wellington: Pillar of State* (London: Harper & Row, 1970)

Magnus, Philip, *King Edward the Seventh* (London: John Murray, 1964)

Major, Norma, *Chequers: The Prime Minister's Country House and Its History* (London: HarperCollins, 1996)

Margach, James, *The Anatomy of Power: An Enquiry into the Personality of Leadership* (London: W. H. Allen, 1979)

Marquand, David, *Ramsay MacDonald* (London: Richard Cohen, 1997)

Marr, Andrew, *The Making of Modern Britain: From Queen Victoria to V.E. Day* (London: Macmillan, 2009)

Matthew, H. C. G., *Gladstone 1809–1898* (Oxford: Clarendon Press, 1997)

McKenna, A. J., *100 Years of Government Communication* (London: OGL, 2018)

McKinstry, Leo, *Attlee and Churchill* (London: Atlantic, 2019)

McLeod, Kirsty, *The Wives of Downing Street* (London: Collins, 1976)

McMeekin, Sean, *July 1914: Countdown to War* (London: Icon, 2013)

Merry, Robert W., *Where They Stand: The American Presidents in the Eyes of Voters and Historians* (New York: Simon & Schuster, 2012).

Meyer, Hugo, *The British State Telegraphs* (London: Macmillan, 1907)

Middleton, C. R., *The Administration of British Foreign Policy, 1782–1846* (Durham, NC: Duke University Press, 1977)

Middleton, Richard, *The Bells of Victory: The Pitt–Newcastle Ministry and the Conduct of the Seven Years' War, 1757–1762* (Cambridge University Press, 1985)

Mile, Peter, and Smith, Malcolm, *Cinema, Literature and Society: Elite and Mass Culture in Interwar Britain* (Breckenham: Croom Helm, 1987)

Minney, R. J., *No. 10 Downing Street: A House in History* (London: Cassell, 1963)

Mitchell, B. R., *International Historical Statistics, 1750–2005: Europe* (London: Palgrave Macmillan, 2007)

Mitchell, L. G., *Lord Melbourne: 1779–1848* (Oxford University Press, 1997)

Monod, Paul Kleber, *Jacobitism and the English People, 1688–1788* (Cambridge University Press, 1993)

Moore, Charles, *Margaret Thatcher: The Authorized Biography*, vol. i: *Not For Turning* (London: Allen Lane, 2013)

   Margaret Thatcher: The Authorized Biography, vol. iii: *Herself Alone* (London: Allen Lane, 2019)

Morley, John, *The Life of William Ewart Gladstone* (London: Macmillan, 1903)

Namier, Lewis, *Crossroads of Power: Essays on Eighteenth-Century England* (London: Hamish Hamilton, 1962)

Neustadt, Richard E., *Presidential Power and the Modern Presidents*, 3rd edn (New York: Free Press, 1990)

Newton, Lord, *Lord Lansdowne: A Biography* (London: Macmillan, 1929)

Nicolson, Harold, *George the Fifth: His Life and Reign* (London: Constable, 1970)

O'Gorman, Frank, *The Long Eighteenth Century: British Political and Social History 1688–1832* (London: Bloomsbury Academic, 1997)

Oliver, Craig, *Unleashing Demons: The Inside Story of Brexit* (London: Hodder & Stoughton, 2016)

O'Shaughnessy, Andrew, *The Men Who Lost America: British Command during the Revolutionary War and the Preservation of the Empire* (New Haven, CT: Yale University Press, 2013)

Packwood, Allen, *How Churchill Waged War: The Most Challenging Decisions of the Second World War* (Barnsley: Pen & Sword, 2018)

Pares, Richard, *King George III and the Politicians* (Oxford: Clarendon Press, 1953)

Pearce, Edward, *The Great Man: Sir Robert Walpole – Scoundrel, Genius and Britain's First Prime Minister* (London: Jonathan Cape, 2007)

Peden, G. C., *The Treasury and British Public Policy, 1906–1959* (Oxford University Press, 2000)

Pellew, H., *Life of Viscount Sidmouth* (London: John Murray, 1847)

Peters, Marie, *Profiles in Power: The Elder Pitt* (Harlow: Addison, Wesley, Longmans, 1998)

Pigott, Peter, *Sailing Seven Seas: A History of the Canadian Pacific Line* (Toronto: Dundurn Press, 2010)

Pimlott, Ben, *Harold Wilson* (London: HarperCollins, 1992)

The Queen: Elizabeth II and the Monarchy, Diamond Jubilee edn (London: HarperPress, 2012)

Plumb, J. H., *The Growth of Political Stability in England, 1675–1725* (London: Macmillan, 1967)

The King's Minister (London: Cresset, 1956)

Sir Robert Walpole: The Making of a Statesman (London: Cresset Press, 1956)

Porter, Roy, *London: A Social History* (London: Penguin, 1995)

Prochaska, Frank, *Royal Bounty: The Making of a Welfare Monarchy* (New Haven, CT: Yale University Press, 1995)

Prothero, Rowland E., *English Farming, Past and Present* (Cambridge University Press, 2013)

Pugh, Martin, *The Making of Modern British Politics: 1867–1945*, 3rd edn (Oxford: Blackwell, 2002)

Purcell, Hugh, *Lloyd George* (London: Haus, 2006)

Ramsden, John, *The Making of Conservative Party Policy: The Conservative Research Department since 1929* (London: Longman, 1980)

Rawnsley, Andrew, *The End of the Party: The Rise and Fall of New Labour* (London: Viking, 2010)

Richards, Steve, *The Prime Ministers: Reflections on Leadership from Wilson to Johnson* (London: Atlantic, 2020)

Ricketts, Peter, *Hard Choices: What Britain Does Next* (London: Atlantic Books, 2021).

Ridley, Jane, *Bertie: A Life of Edward VII* (New York: Random House, 2012)

Roberts, Andrew, *Churchill: Walking With Destiny* (London: Allen Lane, 2018)

Salisbury: Victorian Titan (London: Weidenfeld & Nicolson, 1999)

Robinson, Nick, *Live from Downing Street: The Inside Story of Politics, Power and the Media* (London: Bantam, 2013)

Ronaldshay, Earl of, *The Life of Lord Curzon*, vol. III (London: Ernest Benn, 1928)

Sainty, J. C. (ed.), *Office-Holders in Modern Britain*, vol. I: *Treasury Officials 1660–1870* (University of London, 1972)

Scherer, Paul, *Lord John Russell: A Biography* (London: Associated University Presses, 1999)

Scott, David, *Leviathan: The Rise of Britain as a World Power* (London: William Collins, 2013)

Sebba, Anne, *That Woman: The Life of Wallis Simpson, Duchess of Windsor* (London: Weidenfeld & Nicolson, 2011)

Sedgwick, Romney (ed.), *Letters from George III to Lord Bute, 1756–1766* (London: Macmillan, 1939)

Seldon, Anthony, *10 Downing Street: The Illustrated History* (London: HarperCollins, 1999)

Blair (London: Free Press, 2004)

Churchill's Indian Summer: The 1951–1955 Conservative Government (London: Hodder & Stoughton, 1981)

The Foreign Office (London: HarperCollins, 2000)

Seldon, Anthony, with Baston, Lewis, *Major: A Political Life* (London: Weidenfeld & Nicolson, 1997)

Seldon, Anthony, and Lodge, Guy, *Brown at 10* (London: Biteback, 2010)

Seldon, Anthony, with Meakin, Jonathan, *The Cabinet Office, 1916–2016* (London: Biteback, 2016)

Seldon, Anthony, with Newell, Raymond, *May at 10* (London: Biteback, 2019)

Seldon, Anthony, and Snowdon, Peter, *Cameron at 10: The Verdict* (London: William Collins, 2016)

Seldon, Anthony, with Snowdon, Peter, and Collings, Daniel, *Blair Unbound* (London: Simon & Schuster, 2007)

Seldon, Anthony, and Walsh, David, *The Public Schools and the Second World War* (London: Pen & Sword, 2020)

Seldon, Anthony, and Finn, Mike (eds.), *The Coalition Effect, 2010–2015* (Cambridge University Press, 2015)

Self, Robert, *Neville Chamberlain: A Biography* (Aldershot: Ashgate, 2006)

Shakespeare, Nicholas, *Six Minutes in May: How Churchill Unexpectedly Became Prime Minister* (London: Harvill Secker, 2017)

Shanks, Michael, *The Stagnant Society* (Harmondsworth: Penguin, 1961)

Shepherd, Robert, *Westminster: A Biography: From Earliest Times to the Present* (London: Bloomsbury, 2012)

Slocock, Caroline, *People Like Us: Margaret Thatcher and Me* (London: Biteback, 2018)

Smith, E. A., *George IV* (New Haven, CT: Yale University Press, 1999)

Somerset, Anne, *Queen Anne: The Politics of Passion* (London: HarperCollins, 2012)

Steele, E. D., *Palmerston and Liberalism, 1855–1865* (Cambridge University Press, 1991)

Stephen, W. L., *The Story of Number 10 Downing Street* (London: Stockwell, 1935)

Theakston, Kevin, and Connelly, Philip, *William Armstrong and British Policymaking* (London: Palgrave Macmillan, 2018)

Thomas, Peter, *Tea Party to Independence: The Third Phase of the American Revolution, 1773–1776* (Oxford University Press, 1991)

Thomas-Symonds, Nicklaus, *Attlee: A Life in Politics* (London: I. B Taurus, 2010)

Thompson, Andrew, *The Empire Strikes Back? The Impact of Imperialism on Britain from the Mid-Nineteenth Century* (Harlow: Pearson, 2005)

George II (New Haven, CT: Yale University Press, 2011)

Thomson, Mark A., *A Constitutional History of England: 1642–1801* (London: Methuen, 1938)

Thorpe, Andrew, *A History of the British Labour Party* (London: Palgrave, 2001)

Thorpe, D. R., *Eden: The Life and Times of Anthony Eden, First Earl of Avon, 1897–1977* (London: Chatto & Windus, 2003)

Selwyn Lloyd (London: Jonathan Cape, 1989)

Tombs, Robert, *The English and Their History* (London: Allen Lane, 2014)

Turner, John, *Lloyd George's Secretariat* (Cambridge University Press, 1980)

Turner, Michael, *Pitt the Younger: A Life* (London: Hambledon, 2003)

Vernon, James, *Modern Britain: 1750 to the Present*, Cambridge History of Britain (Cambridge University Press, 2017)

Wheeler-Bennett, John, *King George VI: His Life and Reign* (London: Macmillan, 1958)

Whiteley, Peter, *Lord North: The Prime Minister Who Lost America* (London: Hambledon, 1996)

Wilkinson, David, *The Duke of Portland: Politics and Party in the Age of George III* (London: Palgrave Macmillan, 2003)

Williams, Charles, *Harold Macmillan* (London: Weidenfeld & Nicolson, 2009)

Williamson, Philip, *Stanley Baldwin: Conservative Leadership and National Values* (Cambridge University Press, 1999)

Williamson, Philip, and Baldwin, Edward (eds.), *Baldwin Papers: A Conservative Statesman, 1908–1947* (Cambridge University Press, 2004)

Woodward, David R., *Lloyd George and the Generals* (Newark: University of Delaware Press, 1983)

Young, G. M., *Stanley Baldwin* (London: Hart-Davis, 1952)

Ziegler, Philip, *Edward Heath: The Authorised Biography* (London: HarperPress, 2010)

King William IV (London: Collins, 1971)

Wilson: The Authorised Life (London: Weidenfeld & Nicolson, 1993)

WEB SOURCES

'About Newsreels and Cinemagazines', Learning on Screen: The British Universities and Colleges Films and Videos Council, 2020, learningonscreen .ac.uk/newsreels/about (accessed 15 November 2020)

'Aliens Act', Jewish Virtual Library, 2008, www.jewishvirtuallibrary.org/aliens-act (accessed 25 November 2020)

'The Australian Constitution', p. 18, www.aph.gov.au/about_parliament/senate/ powers_practice_n_procedures/constitution (accessed 30 November 2020)

Bartlett, Gail, and Everett, Michael, 'The Royal Prerogative', House of Commons Library, 17 August 2017, https://commonslibrary.parliament.uk/research-briefings/sn03861 (accessed 12 November 2020)

Bates, David, 'Odo, Earl of Kent (d. 1097)' in *Oxford Dictionary of National Biography* (Oxford University Press, 2004), www.doi.org/10.1093/ref:odn b/20543 on 21 November 2020)

Bingham, Adrian, 'Monitoring the Popular Press: An Historical Perspective', History and Policy, 2 May 2005, www.historyandpolicy.org/policy-papers/p apers/monitoring-the-popular-press-an-historical-perspective (accessed 20 October 2020)

Browning, Reed, 'Thomas Pelham-Hobbes, Duke of Newcastle (1693–1758)' in *Oxford Dictionary of National Biography* (Oxford University Press, 2004), www .oxforddnb.com/view/10.1093/ref:odnb/9780198614128.001.0001/odnb-9780198614128-e-21801 (accessed 26 November 2020)

Cowley, Philip, and Stuart, Mark, *Revolts: Philip Cowley and Mark Stuart's Research on Parliament*, 2004, revolts.co.uk/?page_id=2 (accessed 14 November 2020)

Dale, Iain, 'Ranking our 55 Prime Ministers – An Impossible Task, But a Fascinating One', 12 November 2020, www.iaindale.com/articles/ranking-our-55-prime-ministers-an-impossible-task-but-a-fascinating-one (accessed 6 December 2020)

'Deal, Kent: From Smuggler's Haunt To Tourist Town', Official Deal Tourist Information, www.aboutdeal.co.uk/smuggling (accessed 23 November 2020)

Diamond, Patrick, 'Governing is a Permanent Form of Campaigning: Why the Civil Service is in Mortal Danger', *LSE BPP*, 13 August 2019, http://blogs

.lse.ac.uk/politicsandpolicy/why-the-civil-service-is-in-mortal-danger (accessed 9 December 2020)

'Elections in India', 2020, elections.in (accessed 26 November 2020)

'ESRC Party Members Project', www.esrcpartymembersproject.org (accessed 13 November 2020)

'The Function of the Prime Minister', Italian Government, www.governo.it/it/il-governo-funzioni-struttura-e-storia/la-funzione-del-presidente-del-consiglio /188 (accessed 26 November 2020)

'Greater London, Inner London and Outer London, Population and Density History', *Demographia*, www.demographia.com/dm-lon31.htm (accessed 10 November 2020)

'Great Offices of State', *The Cabinet Papers*, nationalarchives.gov.uk/cabinetpa pers/cabinet-gov/great-offices-of-state.htm (accessed 27 November 2020)

Hazell, Robert, 'Prime Ministers and the Constitution', *History of Government*, 24 April 2013, https://history.blog.gov.uk/2013/04/24/prime-ministers-and-the-constitution (accessed 19 November 2020)

Hennessy, Peter, 'The Role and Powers of the Prime Minister', 15 March 2011, www.publications.parliament.uk/pa/cm201011/cmselect/cmpolcon/wri tev/842/m2.htm (accessed 17 November 2020)

'Henry Campbell-Bannerman', *Number10*, 25 August 2008, web.archive.org/ web/20080825211340/http://www.number10.gov.uk/history-and-tour /prime-ministers-in-history/henry-campbell-bannerman (accessed 24 November 2020)

'History, Origin and Traditions of the Budget', *interbudget.co.uk* (accessed at web. archive.org/web/20120117205111/http://www.interbudget.co.uk/history-budget.html on 24 November 2020).

'History of Periodical Illustration', NC State University, 2020, https://ncna .dh.chass.ncsu.edu/imageanalytics/history.php (accessed 20 November 2020)

'A History of Women in the UK Civil Service', p. 9, www.civilservant.org.uk/library/ 2015_history_of_women_in_the_civil_service.pdf (accessed 4 December 2020)

'The House of Windsor', www.royal.uk/house-windsor (accessed 8 December 2020)

'Installations at Number 10 Timeline', www.gov.uk/government/history/10-downing-street (accessed 25 November 2020)

Jenkins, Roy, 'Wilson, (James) Harold, Baron Wilson of Rievaulx (1916–1995)' in *Oxford Dictionary of National Biography* (Oxford University Press, 2004), www .oxforddnb.com/view/10.1093/ref:odnb/9780198614128.001.0001/odnb-9780198614128-e-58000 (accessed 23 December 2020)

Jenkins, Terry, 'The Queen Caroline Affair', *History of Parliament Online*, www .historyofparliamentonline.org/periods/hanoverians/queen-caroline-affair-1820 (accessed 2 December 2020)

'Law For Lawmakers: A Justice Guide to the Law', University of Oxford Faculty of Law, 2015, www.law.ox.ac.uk/sites/files/oxlaw/justice_-_law_for_lawmak ers.pdf, p. 25 (accessed 12 November 2020)

Matthew, H. C. G., and Reynolds, K. D., 'Victoria' in *Oxford Dictionary of National Biography* (Oxford University Press, 2004), www.oxforddnb.com/view/10 .1093/ref:odnb/9780198614128.001.0001/odnb-9780198614128-e-36652 (accessed 4 November 2020)

McLean, Gavin, 'Premiers and Prime Ministers' in *Te Ara – the Encyclopedia of New Zealand*, 1 December 2016, www.TeAra.govt.nz/en/premiers-and-prime-ministers (accessed 7 December 2020)

'Mobile Internet Statistics', Finder, 10 November 2020, www.finder.com/uk/mobile-internet-statistics (accessed 15 November 2020)

'Morton's Fork' in *The Oxford Dictionary of Phrase and Fable*, 16 October 2020, www.encyclopedia.com/humanities/dictionaries-thesauruses-pictures-and-press-releases/mortons-fork (accessed 21 November 2020)

'"Mr Balfour's Poodle"?', UK Parliament, 2020, www.parliament.uk/about/living-heritage/evolutionofparliament/houseoflords/parliamentacts/overview/balfourspoodle (accessed 15 October 2020)

Namier, Lewis, 'GRENVILLE, George (1712–70), of Wotton, Bucks' in L. Namier and J. Brooke (eds.), *The History of Parliament: The House of Commons 1754–1790* (London: HMSO, 1964), www.historyofparliamentonline.org/volume/1754–1790/member/grenville-george-1712–70#footnote53_hsk8at4 (accessed 25 November 2020)

'Net Migration to UK Rises to 333,000 – Second Highest on Record' *BBC News*, 26 May 2016, www.bbc.co.uk/news/uk-politics-eu-referendum-36382199 (accessed 7 November 2020)

'Our Constitution', *New Zealand Now*, 22 June 2020, newzealandnow.govt.nz/living-in-nz/history-government/our-constitution (accessed 26 November 2020)

Our Story', Royal Mail, 2020, www.royalmailgroup.com/en/about-us/our-story (accessed 24 November 2020)

'Parliament' in *Encyclopaedia Britannica*, 5 May 2017, www.britannica.com/topic/Parliament (accessed 20 November 2020)

Parry, Jonathan, 'Lord Derby', *History of Government*, 1 June 2016, https://history.blog.gov.uk/2016/06/01/lord-derby (accessed 25 November 2020)

PMQT – 10 December 1992, www.johnmajorarchive.org.uk/1990–1997/pmqt-10-december-1992 (accessed 27 November 2020)

'Political Economy of Growth and Institutional Reform in the UK', Institute for Government, March 2018, www.instituteforgovernment.org.uk/our-work/policy-making/political-economy-growth-and-institutional-reform-uk (accessed 11 December 2020)

'The Population of Cities in the United Kingdom 2020', *World Population Review*, 2020, www.worldpopulationreview.com/countries/cities/united-kingdom (accessed 7 November 2020)

Prest, John, 'Peel, Sir Robert' in *Oxford Dictionary of National Biography* (Oxford University Press, 2004), www.oxforddnb.com/view/10.1093/ref:odnb/9780198614128.001.0001/odnb-9780198614128-e-21764 (accessed 9 December 2020)

'Prime Minister: Roles, Powers and Restraints', *Australian Politics*, 2020, www.australianpolitics.com/executive/pm/prime-minister-roles-powers-restraints (accessed 26 November 2020)

'Rating British Prime Ministers', University of Leeds and MORI survey, 29 November 2004, www.ipsos.com/ipsos-mori/en-uk/rating-british-prime-ministers (accessed 6 December 2020)

'Record Immigration Levels to UK', *BBC News*, 20 October 2005, http://news.bbc.co.uk/2/hi/uk_news/4359756.stm (accessed 7 November 2020)

'Religion in England and Wales, 2011', Office for National Statistics (ONS), 11 December 2012, www.ons.gov.uk/peoplepopulationandcommunity/culturalidentity/religion/articles/religioninenglandandwales2011/2012–12-11 (accessed 3 December 2020)

'The Revolution of 1688' in *Encyclopaedia Britannica*, www.britannica.com/place/United-Kingdom/The-Revolution-of-1688#ref483187 (accessed 17 November 2020)

Reynolds, K. D., 'Temple [*nee* Lamb], Emily Mary [Amelia], Viscountess Palmerston' in *Oxford Dictionary of National Biography* (Oxford University Press, 2004), www.oxforddnb.com/view/10.1093/ref:odnb/9780198614128.001.0001/odnb-9780198614128-e-40959 (accessed 30 November 2020)

Roberts, Stephen, 'The Companies Abroad', *Distant Writing*, 2012, www.distantwriting.co.uk/companiesandforeigntraffic.html (accessed 15 November 2020)

Rothschild, Nathaniel, *'You have it, Madam': The Purchase, in 1875, of Suez Canal Shares by Disraeli and Baron Lionel de Rothschild* (London: W & J Mackay, 1980), www.victorianweb.org/history/polspeech/suez.html (accessed 20 November 2020)

'A Speech by the Queen to Parliament on her Silver Jubilee', www.royal.uk/silver-jubilee-address-parliament-4-may-1977 (accessed 12 November 2020)

'State Opening of Parliament', UK Parliament, 2020, www.parliament.uk/about/how/occasions/stateopening (accessed 12 November 2020)

'Tasks of the Federal Chancellor', Chancellery, 2020, www.bundeskanzlerin.de/bkin-en/chancellery/tasks-of-the-chancellor (accessed 26 November 2020)

Thomas, Alex, 'The Reshuffle Demonstrates the PM's Power – But Does Not Mean the End of the Treasury', Institute for Government, 13 February 2020, www.instituteforgovernment.org.uk/blog/reshuffle-prime-minister-power-does-not-mean-end-treasury (accessed 14 December 2020)

Thompson, Andrew, 'We're All Going on a Summer Holiday … to Hanover', *History of Government*, 27 August 2013, https://history.blog.gov.uk/2013/08/27/were-all-going-on-a-summer-holiday-to-hanover (accessed 17 November 2020)

Toye, Richard, 'Prime Ministers and Their Chancellors', *History of Government*, 1 August 2012, https://history.blog.gov.uk/2012/08/01/prime-ministers-and-their-chancellors (accessed 24 November 2020)

'United Kingdom', Soft Power 30, www.softpower30.com/country/united-kingdom (accessed 15 November 2020)

'What Are the Biggest Government Defeats?', *BBC News*, 15 January 2019, www.bbc.co.uk/news/uk-46879887 (accessed 7 December 2020)

TELEVISION AND THEATRE

Guggenheim, David, *Designated Survivor*, ABC, 2016–19

Morgan, Peter, *The Audience* (Gielgud Theatre), 13 February 2013

The Crown (Netflix), 4 November 2016 to present

Index